IDLENESS, WATER, AND A CANOE

In the spring of 1940, subscribers to *Queen's Quarterly* read that the 'ingredients of a holiday in Canada are idleness, water, and a canoe.' This statement bears witness to the enduring importance of the canoe, generations after the decline of the North American fur trade. Jamie Benidickson explains that the canoe's merit lies not strictly in its function as a transportation vehicle, but in its promise of unrestricted mobility, leisure, and independence. *Idleness, Water, and a Canoe* is a study of the place of the canoe in Canadian life, with comparative references to the United States and Britain. A blend of history, economic analysis, technical information, and social commentary, it examines the rise of the canoe's popularity and its influence on leisure activity, economics and tourism, and literature and advertising in this country.

Drawing on books, newspaper articles, original records, unusual ephemera, and interviews with paddlers, the author describes the evolution and cultural significance of two centuries of recreational paddling. He explores why canoeists have constantly sought new summer waterways, how they have practised their craft, and how much influence paddling for pleasure has had on them and on the societies in which they live. The many facets of recreational paddling are illustrated and described in a series of reflections on subjects ranging from the paddler's quest for physical and spiritual renewal to what the future holds for voyageurs and their pastime. Benidickson also discusses the evolution of canoe design and manufacturing, the formation of canoe clubs and organizations, the economics of recreational travel, and the paddler's role in environmental protection.

Not only will this book appeal to those interested in history, sociology, aesthetics, geography, and sports and leisure studies, but its broad scope and accessible style will recommend it to the many outdoor enthusiasts who plan yearly canoeing trips.

JAMIE BENIDICKSON is an associate professor in the Faculty of Law at the University of Ottawa, and co-author of *The Temagami Experience*.

JAMIE BENIDICKSON

Idleness, Water, and a Canoe: Reflections on Paddling for Pleasure

UNIVERSITY OF TORONTO PRESS

Toronto Buffalo London

© University of Toronto Press Incorporated 1997
Toronto Buffalo London
Printed in Canada

ISBN 0–8020–0945–X (cloth)
ISBN 0–8020–7910–5 (paper)

Printed on acid-free paper

Canadian Cataloguing in Publication Data

Benidickson, Jamie
  Idleness, water, and a canoe

  Includes index.
  ISBN 0-8020-0945-X (bound)
  ISBN 0-8020-7910-5 (pbk.)

  1. Canoes and canoeing – Canada.   2. Canoes and
  canoeing – Social aspects – Canada.   3. Canoes
  and canoeing – United States.   4. Canoes and
  canoeing – Great Britain.   I. Title.

  GV776.15.A2B46 1997   797.1′22′0971   C96-932271-2

University of Toronto Press acknowledges the financial assistance to its
publishing program of the Canada Council and the Ontario Arts Council.

Contents

Illustrations follow pages 16 and 156

Preface

'The ingredients of a holiday in Canada,' Howe Martyn instructed readers of the *Queen's Quarterly* in the spring of 1940, 'are idleness, water and a canoe.' The statement reflects the continuing significance of this traditional small watercraft long after the decline of the North American fur trade. Paddling for pleasure had somehow become a subject worthy of reflection, and idleness had not yet completed its descent into apparent indolence.

The history of recreational paddling may well be one of those 'why didn't I think of that?' sorts of topics. The story might have been written long ago. And it might yet be written, for you will not find it here – at least not as history with a beginning, a middle, and an end attached to one another with what pass for causal connections. I may have contemplated such a narrative at an earlier point in an undertaking which has lasted – part time – for too long and kept me off the water for far too many spring weekends.

There is certainly history here, but I do not offer it to tell the intriguing, often fascinating, and possibly continuing tale of who paddled where first or fastest. Instead, I have written a book with several broad themes. First, the book is about why apparently normal people have paddled canoes and kayaks for pleasure and continue to do so. Second, the book is about how canoeists have practised their craft, built their boats, camped in comfort, and coped more or less successfully with insects and other perils. Most generally, the book is about the experience of canoeing, a subject linked to why and how, although that is merely the start of the relationship.

There are many answers to explain paddlers' attraction to their pastime. They are about the love of landscape, about being closer to God, about doing something our ancestors did, about getting away from it all (whatever 'it' may be), and about finding and healing ourselves. It is characteristic of many recreational pursuits that their appeal may differ from one participant to another. Satisfaction comes to some canoeists from adventure; others relish the refining of skills and competition; still others enjoy the sense of fellowship to be found in canoeing, or, conversely, the exquisite solitude. The diverse attractions of recreational canoeing also have much to do with how paddlers spend their land-based lives and with the societies in which those lives unfold.

Today, paddlers come from all over the globe, but for present purposes I deal largely with Canada, making reference here and there to Great Britain and the United States. In Canadian historical writing, canoeing is most often associated with the exploits of voyageurs or the traditional Indian way of life. The canoe is recognized as the vehicle of the colourful fur traders and their aboriginal suppliers, and perhaps even as an essential means of travel for later prospectors and geological surveyors who approached the landscape with their own sense of its possibilities. Although the magazine *Outdoor Canada* informed its readers in 1908 that 'in Canada canoeing has been for many years the foremost aquatic sport,' the status of the canoe as a focus for recreation failed to attract much subsequent attention. The craft was too commonplace to be remarkable for those who summered inattentively around the waterways, or it was used most expertly in settings too remote to be observed.

In Britain, despite very high estimates of the number of Canadian-style open canoes headquartered along the Thames River and other waterways at the turn of the century, the suggestion that paddling enjoyed a measure of prominence comparable to its status in Canada would have been implausible. Nevertheless, the exotic nature of these small vessels aroused curiosity, and the canoeing exploits of John 'Rob Roy' MacGregor were still widely remembered by those who considered him the leading popularizer (perhaps even the originator) of modern canoe travel.

Recreational canoe travel also had an active following in many parts of the United States. Watercraft manufactured by J. Henry Rushton and his competitors were highly prized, and readers of Dillon Wallace's *The Lure of the Labrador Wild* shared the author's vision of wilderness adventure, although they hoped to avoid the tragic fate of Wallace's companion, Leonidas Hubbard, Jr, who had perished in the northland only a few years earlier.

Paddlers from Canada, Britain, and the United States now participate on coastal and inland waters in a variety of sub-specialities of canoeing and kayaking ranging from flatwater racing through wilderness travel, each combining some measure of tradition with new sources of appeal. Along-side the traditional open canoe – still sixteen feet long, and completely impervious to metrification – the watercraft themselves have become highly refined. This is especially true, perhaps, for those engaged in coastal touring or passionately devoted to whitewater weekends. Whatever their shape, these vessels have in common the characteristic that their motive power is supplied by the occupants.

The continuing attraction of manual propulsion requires some ex-planation in an age when future-oriented holiday-makers are already booking seats on spacecraft or preparing for virtual enjoyment in care-free cyberspace. Participants often cite the well-known challenge and inspiration behind the mountaineer's attempt on a peak – 'because it's there.' But as the pressures of human population on a finite environment become more overwhelming, the traditional stimulus is increasingly com-bined with a modern variant – 'because it won't be there for long.'

Skill and technique on the water and around the campsite remain matters of pride and satisfaction for most paddlers who go back a second time, and to a point I have recorded information on how things were done. Yet this book is not a manual; the nineteenth-century mosquito repellents described here are not recommended. And while I may also discuss where canoeists have travelled, sometimes in detail, this is not a guidebook. It is not about geography, and it is certainly not intended to get you anywhere, even though the question of routes and destinations frequently dominates the fireside conversation of paddlers.

Reminiscing about past journeys and anticipating a planned expedition are absorbing off-season preoccupations. These activities, however, tell us as much about the paddlers themselves as about itineraries and campsites. That is because, as many have noted, the canoeist's journey is more often than not a voyage of self-discovery, with 'understanding' being the desti-nation of successful travellers.

The influence of canoeing on the lives of individual participants seems often to have been profound. Some paddlers claim to have been trans-formed; others are merely wistful, perhaps regretting the elusiveness of a transformation that never quite took place. Yet beyond the realm of individual experiences lies the still more general or collective experience of canoeing – the cultural legacy this once employment, sometime sport, and occasional pastime has created as the paddler's society has undergone significant changes in composition and demeanour. One recent royal commissioner even spoke of Canada as a canoe, possibly suggesting that public officials should more regularly be outfitted with paddles if they are to be dispatched on missions likely to lead them up the proverbial creek or into the treacherous metaphorical environment of 'whitewater' politics, where even U.S. presidents may find the going a bit rough.

The suggestion – a long-standing one in some aboriginal mythologies – that the canoe carries communities rather than individual paddlers points to another important dimension of the story. If canoe journeys create personal challenges that permit self-understanding, do they also foster an appreciation of the canoeist's companions, whether contemporary travellers, predecessors, or those who may later travel the same waterways?

Acknowledgments

I have had the benefit of assistance and advice from many people in the course of exploring these themes and questions. Richard St Louis, Marika Farrell, Allison Russell, and Sue Meyer provided research assistance. As well as undertaking research, Cynthia Ramsay helped me greatly by imposing order on an otherwise unmanageable accumulation of notes and documents.

Alan Wilson, Bruce Hodgins, Shelagh Grant, John Wadland, Gwyneth Hoyle, Kate Ramsay, Oliver Cock, Roger MacGregor, Becky Mason, and Larry Turner patiently read rougher versions of the manuscript or its parts and offered much-appreciated suggestions and encouragement. Once again, Gerry Hallowell of the University of Toronto Press provided valuable editorial guidance. As manuscript editor, Theresa Griffin significantly improved the clarity of the text.

For permission to quote from or to reproduce copyright material, I am grateful to all those who so willingly agreed to have their work appear in these pages. Specific acknowledgment of permissions to quote from copyright material is made here to McClelland & Stewart, Inc., The Canadian Publishers, for *Wilderness Tips* by Margaret Atwood, for *Paddle to the Amazon* by Don Starkell, for *Weathering It* by Douglas LePan, for *Tom Thomson: The Silence and the Storm* by Harold Town and David J. Silcox, and for *Post Script to Adventure* by J. King Gordon; to Alfred A. Knopf for *Blues* by John Hersey, for *The White Man's Indian* by Robert Berkhofer, and for *Listening Point* by Sigurd F. Olson; to Doubleday Canada Limited for *White Eskimo* by Harold Horwood; to Douglas and McIntyre for *The Black Canoe: Bill Reid and the Spirit of Haida Gwaii* by Robert Bringhurst; to Cambridge University Press for *Beauty, Health, and Permanence: Environmental Politics in the United States, 1955–1985* by Samuel P. Hays; and to Houghton Mifflin Co.

for *Deliverance* by James Dickey. Care has been taken to trace the owner-ship of copyright material. In case of errors or omissions, information enabling me to rectify any reference or credit in subsequent editions would be welcome.

Quite a number of people whose specific contributions are acknowl-edged in the notes willingly agreed to interviews. I am grateful for their insights and the stimulating conversations we enjoyed.

IDLENESS, WATER, AND A CANOE

1

Idleness, Water, and a Canoe: Popular Images and Personal Experiences

Even in the modern world, where effective mobility seemingly depends on high-performance automobiles, supersonic jets, or generously powered speedboats, people paddle for pleasure and images of the canoe abound. The images are readily found in advertising, in art, on public buildings, on coinage, and on the highly denominated postage of the late twentieth century. Such visual reminders and symbolic echoes invite consideration of what the canoe continues to represent. Does it linger in our consciousness merely as a nostalgic relic, and only because the moulders of contemporary sensibilities have not yet succeeded in transferring popular perceptual allegiances to some modern digital icon? Or is the canoe genuinely evocative of sentiments and experiences that remain widely entrenched and are constantly being adapted through renewal?

To answer such questions – if indeed they can be answered at all – one certainly needs to consider the experiences of those who have actually dipped their blades into the water. In addition, the many images of the craft that have appeared in visual and in literary form merit attention. Both the personal experiences of canoeists and public perception or symbolic associations help to illuminate the significance of paddling for pleasure. On the assumption that most readers will bring personal experience to page one, these reflections begin in the public or cultural realm.

The canoe remains a surprisingly common and important feature of the urban landscape. No visitor to Canada could fail to see it depicted somewhere, for in recent years the canoe has appeared prominently in commercial advertising campaigns promoting milk, cigarettes, alcohol, credit cards, real estate, and at least one provincial lottery. Had it not been for an unexplained scandal involving the loss of dies and samples, the canoe would have been on every dollar coin in Canada. Whether a visitor would encounter a canoe on the water is an entirely different matter.

Why images of a traditional, non-mechanized watercraft that is most likely to be used in solitude and the outdoors should persist in an overwhelmingly urban society can best be appreciated by considering what the canoe symbolizes. Not long ago an organization representing dairy farmers, in one of its advertisements, depicted a youthful pair of healthy and vigorous canoeists paddling over a sea of frothing milk (see the illustrations at the end of this chapter). If this image promoted the dietary health and physical well-being of the general population, who would object? Paddlers, indeed, might take some pride in their association with this beneficial endeavour. The canoe is just as likely, however, to appear in advertising on behalf of the beer, liquor, and tobacco industries (illustrated). Are we then to associate the product with the sport, or the sport with the product? And with what result? Do these substances threaten the purity and integrity of the fit and active outdoor enthusiast, who is fully familiar with the widely publicized hazards to health posed by the abuse of alcohol and tobacco? But the image of the canoe – an accommodating little watercraft – might evoke the passions of those rugged and hardy souls who may be equally willing to run a little risk with white water or white smoke. For some, a relaxing drink is a legitimate reward in the aftermath of strenuous physical exertion. The same might be said of a restful cigarette, an indulgence that in the circumstances may even evoke the memory of the voyageurs whose labours were regularly interrupted for a pipe on the shoreline.

The same facility for accommodating a rather broad range of values is illustrated by the way in which the canoe served a major bank by symbolizing the advantages of a credit-card lifestyle while simultaneously being associated with the more conventional or homespun image projected by the promoters of a provincial lottery. The most unpretentious citizens of cornerstore Ontario, including a folksy and engaging character known as 'Miss Penelope' who promoted Lottario, can venture forth into the woods, however modest their winnings from the televised weekly draw. While the 'just plain folks' who splash around from time to time in the family canoe might aspire to the jackpot, those whose financial future already seems more secure could also look forward to a leisurely paddle. To put the matter another way, some might win enough money to put the old canoe aside even as others might have sufficient income to enjoy the pleasures of paddling whenever they felt so inclined.

In the spring of 1996, buses promoting B.C. Hydro's energy conservation program could be found on the streets of downtown Vancouver. The provincial utility encouraged many of its customers to turn out the lights with a wilderness scene accompanied by the simple message 'Canoeists, you save more than power.' How much reinforcement of the utility's pricing mechanism can be provided by the city dweller's thoughts of a summer on the water remains, of course, to be determined.

Images of the canoe, as an element of popular culture, conjure up a range of personal and collective values with ample potential to stimulate a variety of reactions. How the canoe acquired so many ambiguous and occasionally even contradictory associations and how they subsequently evolved is worth some attention. Reference to a few notable cultural landmarks may be illuminating.

In the first half of the twentieth century, the flourishing interest in Canadian landscape painting associated with Tom Thomson and artists in the Group of Seven enhanced the significance of the canoe as an important symbol and image of Canadian life.[1] Direct representations of the canoe, such as in J.E.H. MacDonald's painting *The Beaver Dam* or *The Red Canoe*, were infrequent, but the canoe's role in the evolution of the new 'Canadian' style of landscape art was widely understood. If the paintings reflected the artists' attempts to record their experience of a remote but accessible landscape, that experience often involved canoeing, a means of travel that afforded a distinctive perspective and encouraged an unusual form of contemplation. Of course, theirs was not the first generation of artists to travel by canoe, but they were distinctive in their preference for a non-mechanized form of travel when more 'convenient' alternatives were already becoming widely available.

Tom Thomson's life – and his death in Canoe Lake in July 1917 – were central (see illustration). 'Tom Thomson and Algonquin Park are virtually synonymous from 1913 until Thomson's untimely death in 1917,' wrote the art historian J. Russell Harper,[2] and this impression is confirmed by other writings on the artist's life and work which appeared shortly after his death and continued into the 1930s and 1940s. Even the titles of these volumes often emphasized the connection of the artist to the landscape and the importance of the canoe in Thomson's life. Blodwen Davies, for example, produced *Paddle and Palette: The Story of Tom Thomson* (1930); and in *A Study of Tom Thomson: The Story of a Man Who Looked for Beauty and Truth in the Wilderness* the artist was 'celebrated as a canoeman, although to be a competent canoeman is no distinction in Canada where a canoe constitutes the only means of transportation over such large areas.'[3] The cairn in Thomson's memory at Canoe Lake serves as a continuing reminder of the links between the artist, the landscape, and the canoe, although later biographers have reminded us of Thomson's farm background and of the fact that as an early twentieth-century painter with a passion for Algonquin Park he was 'not such an exception.'[4]

For A.Y. Jackson, too, the canoe provided access to the landscapes depicted in so many well-known paintings and sketches. Jackson remarked in his autobiography, *A Painter's Country*, that 'camping and canoeing have been my favourite pastimes and though I never was an expert like Thomson or MacIver, I managed to get around.'[5] Many of Jackson's sketching trips among the Georgian Bay islands were solo expeditions, but he canoed as well with Dr James M. MacCallum, 'patron saint to the Group of Seven,' and with MacCallum's sons. Jackson often paddled in the Georgian Bay and Muskoka district; his 1922 expedition down the Mississagi River route from Biscotasing on the Canadian Pacific Railway line resulted from MacCallum's wish to follow Tom Thomson's earlier travels.

While the paintings of Thomson, the Group of Seven, and other artists provided visual reminders of the canoe, literary figures also contributed in their own way. Having mastered some fundamental woodcraft skills, the Englishman Archie Belaney worked in around 1912 as a ranger for the Ontario Department of Lands and Forests in the Mississagi Forest Reserve, gradually transforming himself into Grey Owl.[6] There he met the characters who were later to appear as 'rivermen' in *Tales of an Empty Cabin*. These men, who earned their living on the water, were professional rather than recreational canoeists – some of the twentieth-century descendants of the voyageurs:

How I loved them, with their trousers baggy at the knees from long hours, and days, and months of kneeling – no, not in prayer, but in a canoe ... How I loved them for their sharp, barbed, gritty humour, their unparalleled skill in profanity, their easy-going generosity. For these were no kitchen-garden woodsmen or carpet knights, but hard-bitten bush-wackers, nurtured in hardship, who lived precariously by first principles, and who at no time called a shovel an agricultural implement ... White man, red-skin and half-breed, they belonged to that fraternity of freemen of the earth whose creed it is that all men are born equal, and that it is up to a man to stay that way. For in this society, the manner of a man's speech, where he comes from, his religion or even his name are matters of small moment and are nobody's business but his own.[7]

Grey Owl's career as an author and lecturer in Canada, the United States, and the United Kingdom during the 1930s greatly contributed to popular awareness of the historic and continuing importance of the canoe as an integral feature of the central Canadian landscape. In *Men of the Last Frontier*, for example, photographs of rivermen in the rapids or on the portage both reinforced the narrative emphasis on paddling as the skill that made the wilderness accessible and helped to illustrate the celebrated virtues of the hardy and generous characters involved.[8] Not necessarily models on which urban recreational paddlers would aspire to pattern themselves, 'the rivermen' nevertheless played a role in sustaining a canoeing tradition in Canadian life, and in infusing that legacy with feelings of self-reliance not unrelated to the same nationalist sentiment within the country that has sometimes been associated with twentieth-century artists.[9] Indeed, by the time Grey Owl's popularity as a writer and speaker peaked in the 1930s, the self-reliant canoeist was a well-established icon.

In New York City, where recreational canoeing achieved an enormous popularity in the 1870s and 1880s, civic politicians representing various factions in the community were portrayed in a range of self-propelled watercraft including a Herald and a sectional canoe. An unidentified advocate of the 'citizens' movement' was left to flounder about in a tub (illustrated). Readers of *Life*, where this cartoon appeared in 1883, were evidently expected to know many of the basic refinements in canoe design.

As industrialized states, Canada among them, periodically face the challenge of responding to economic hardship and dislocation, certain basic policy options appear to be available. Interventionist strategies for government action exist alongside a competing preference for relying more heavily on individual effort and personal initiatives. 'Johnny Canuck,' a paddler of the independent persuasion, clearly leaned towards the latter alternative, as political cartoons reveal. In one early twentieth-century cartoon, 'Johnny' displays characteristic self-reliance as he guides the imperilled vessel *Canadian Industry* through the hazardous turbulence of 'Hard Times Rapids' to reach 'Prosperity Bay' (see illustration). Johnny Canuck's pointed views on other fundamental questions of national policy, including Canada's economic relations with the United States, were also demonstrated using the imagery of the canoe. Thus, in late 1910, on the eve of a watershed Canadian federal election, Johnny declined Uncle Sam's offer to use the reciprocity paddle to help Canada through the treacherous waters of international trade (illustrated). Johnny had put on a little weight when the *Financial Post* magazine examined the country's economic prospects for 1986, but the lone paddler could still be found in the midst of the latest free trade controversy.[10]

Senior politicians have also found themselves in the company of canoes deftly manoeuvred by sharp-pencilled editorial cartoonists. A well-known image by political cartoonist Frank Edwards captured the independence and flair of one former Canadian prime minister on the portage trail; Pierre Elliott Trudeau would require no introduction to experienced North American paddlers of his generation (illustrated).

Royal visitors have found themselves in treacherous canoe waters over the years. Prince Andrew and Sarah Ferguson, before their separation, were among the latest in the tradition. They suffered somewhat at the hands of the newspapers in the early part of a visit to Canada in 1987, when above the caption 'New Voyageurs' the *Globe and Mail* illustrated the Duchess of York and her lady-in-waiting paddling around Old Fort William at Thunder Bay on Lake Superior wearing white gloves. Then, Frank Edwards, who confesses that a lifelong association with the canoe makes it a natural – perhaps unconscious – element of his perspective on events of the day, portrayed the couple on the water with Sarah at the stern and the family butler pouring tea from centre thwart.[11] The *Star*, however, sought to correct these misrepresentations with a cover photo and feature story on the 'two-week love trek into the wilds.' 'She's gone canoeing into the wilderness with Andy while the outside world waits for news of the stork,' wrote Walter Baran, who also reported the opinion of a source close to the expedition that 'it's a hellhole of a second honeymoon for the duchess.' For those readers keeping track, the scholarly reference here is to the *Star* of 11 August 1987, which appeared in grocery stores not far from the *National Enquirer.*

At issue in many of these images linking public figures to an innocent-looking watercraft is the significance of paddling your own canoe. Pierre Trudeau was renowned for paddling his own canoe, while members of the royal family were somewhat unfairly lampooned for not paddling theirs. The virtues of paddling one's own canoe, an expression which the *Oxford Dictionary of English Proverbs* (3d edition) explains as 'to make one's way by one's own exertions,' are deeply rooted, but were never more fully elaborated than in the following mid-nineteenth-century Irish ballad:

> I've travelled about a bit in my time,
> And of troubles I've seen a few,
> But found it better in ev'ry clime
> To paddle my own canoe;
> My wants are small I care not at all,
> If my debts are paied when due,

I drive away strife, in the ocean of life
While I paddle my own canoe.

I have no wife to bother my life,
No lover to prove untrue,
But the whole day long, with a laugh and a song
I paddle my own canoe
I rise with the lark, and from daylight till dark
I do what I have to do
I'm careless of wealth, if I've only the health
To paddle my own canoe.

It's all very well to depend on a friend,
That is, if you've proved him true,
But you'll find it better by far in the end
To paddle your own canoe,
To borrow is dearer by far than to buy
A maxim tho old still true
You never will sigh, if you only will try
To paddle your own canoe.

If a hurricane rise in the mid'day sky
And the sun is lost to view
Move steadily by, with a steadfast eye
And paddle your own canoe.
Fields the daisies that grew in bright green
Are blooming so sweet for you
So never sit down, with a tear or a frown
But paddle your own canoe.

The chorus exhorted listeners to 'love your neighbour as yourself' and
'never sit down with a tear or a frown, but paddle your own canoe.'[12]

The tradition of self-reliance, exhibited in the time-honoured practice
of figuratively paddling your own canoe, might not always offer appropriate guidance. Indeed, even the mid-nineteenth-century English contemporaries of the Irish balladeer noted limitations on what people could be
expected to do for themselves. Thus, in the aftermath of a series of
disasters occasioned by bursting dams and reservoirs, the *Times* of London
argued that those threatened with the possibility of similar misfortune
could not be expected to assume personal responsibility for their own

interests; public inspections and other forms of control or support were required. 'We insure against fire; we have fire engines and fire escapes,' the paper observed, 'but we do not keep cork floats and canoes in our bedrooms.'[13]

Signs of the proverb's adaptation to new realities have been plentiful in recent years. For example, David Kilgour, a disaffected Conservative member of Canada's House of Commons who strongly criticized his own government's performance in the western region of the country, presented the following image of Confederation: 'We're all inhabitants of this fragile canoe and we must help each other.'[14] Then, Keith Spicer, the chair of a consultation program on Canadian constitutional reform, added the thought that 'there is clearly enough room for all of us in the mythical canoe called Canada, providing we open our minds and respect each other's dignity in our diversity.'[15] Provincial politicians have also associated themselves with multicultural voyages. Thus, in proclaiming the Alexander Mackenzie Voyageur Route across Ontario, Natural Resources Minister Bud Wildman argued that Mackenzie's explorations in the company of his French-speaking and aboriginal companions helped to connect Canada from coast to coast, and showed 'what Canadians can achieve together by working toward a common goal.'[16]

At the same time that images of canoe travel were being used in the interests of political cohesion, the limitations of team-paddling were dramatically revealed in a prominent sportswear manufacturer's catalogue. A photograph of kayakers outfitted in Patagonia gear and engaged in intense discussion with whitewater surging all around them bore the caption 'Kayak instructors, Brit Rob Gaffney and Frog Benoît Gauthier discuss the Quebec question on the Ottawa River.' An astute commentator summed up his understanding of the image concisely: 'Two paddlers, one common vessel and internal strife distracting the navigation of the treacherous waters around them.'[17]

Not long after these impressions of political paddling entered circulation, Ovide Mercredi, the national chief of the Assembly of First Nations, joined the campaign for team-paddling with a book of essays, *In the Rapids: Navigating the Future of First Nations*, on the political aspirations of aboriginal Canadians. His co-author, Mary Ellen Turpel, having expressed her personal fear that relations between aboriginal peoples and Canadians generally might deteriorate further, reformulated her concern in metaphorical terms. 'In other words,' she wrote, 'the great rapids we are collectively facing will tip our canoes, and drown our hopes.'[18] This image is reminiscent of a long-standing aboriginal description of the relations between Native and non-Native societies in North America, as explained by members of the Haudenosaunee Confederacy. Treaties between the Haudenosaunee and European nations were recorded in the 'Two Row Wampum,' in which two purple rows, symbolizing Native and European peoples, are separated by three beads of wampum, which represent peace, friendship, and respect. As explained to members of a special parliamentary committee on aboriginal self-government, the two purple rows 'will symbolize two paths or two vessels, travelling down the same river together. One, a birch bark canoe, will be for the Indian people, their laws, their customs and their ways. The other, a ship, will be for the white people and their laws, their customs and their ways. We shall each travel the river together, side by side, but in our own boat. Neither of us will try to steer the other's vessel.'[19]

Bill Reid, a renowned Haida craftsman whose dramatic sculptures fascinate an international audience with their blending of traditional themes and modern messages, provided his own paddler's metaphor of the canoe as lifeboat or Noah's ark. *The Black Canoe*, installed in 1991 in the new Canadian chancery building in Washington, D.C., offers its passengers some shelter from ecological apocalypse and some possible future in a sea of uncertainty. Robert Bringhurst, author of *The Black Canoe: Bill Reid and the Spirit of Haida Gwaii*, describes the scene:

A black canoe sits motionless in the water. Like a lifeboat, it is filled to overflowing. Some of its passengers are incongruously serene, others intent, still others jumpy or distraught. A man in formal dress stands imperturbably amid-ships. But this vessel's living cargo consists of more than human beings. There are birds, bears, a frog and other animals, some on watch and the others urgently paddling. A raven the size of a grizzly is steering. The beaver is gritting his buck teeth; the eagle is biting the bear's paw; the wolf has his fangs in the eagle's wing. Yet for all their activity, these figures are now as motionless as the canoe: caught in mid-stroke by the black bronze, while the water – so long as the pumps work – skirls beneath them.

Few stories are older or more widespread than that of the great flood. And the ecological metaphor of a lifeboat crowded with mammals, birds and amphibians is difficult to miss, like the realization that there is nowhere to escape to.[20]

Whether the issue is federalism, relations between aboriginal and non-aboriginal peoples in North America, or ecological imperatives, the image of the self-reliant canoeist is transformed: the craft of the individualist re-emerges as a vehicle of community, compelling cooperation and collective action. This is another side of the canoe in public life. The common interests of groups and communities have displaced more personal struggles as sources of meaning for this apparently very malleable symbol.

The canoe will no doubt continue to serve as a symbol for the independent-minded, but the coming of age of cooperative canoeing can now be confirmed. The most persuasive illustrations again derive from the economic sphere, where the canoe has accommodated new thinking in relation to the reorganization of the workplace to meet international competition. Surprisingly, the canoe has played a role in the adaptation to Canada of team-based and collaborative approaches to improving industrial efficiency, ostensibly inspired by developments in Japan, Germany, and Sweden. As a *Financial Post* columnist explained, Outward Bound, the international outdoor education concern, is now 'sharpening its appeal to the business community.'[21] A promotional brochure explains that 'the qualities necessary in today's business world cannot be mastered solely through traditional professional development training methods.' Accordingly, using its own program of canoeing and rock climbing, Outward Bound provides courses which stress 'team-building, leadership, risk taking and problem-solving' in an atmosphere in which cooperation, leadership, and trust can be 'cultivated and refined.' Participants – 'individually and as a team' – will gain new perspectives.[22] As one commentator explained, 'the courses are designed to build team spirit, confidence, trust and other virtues among groups more at home in the cut and thrust of office politics and endless meetings.'[23]

The relationship between the structured outdoor endeavours of the training program and certain generic business challenges has been spelled out for promotional purposes: 'When a Campbell manager is paddling over open water or negotiating her way up an 80 ft. rock face, it's a clear lesson that success depends upon gaining the cooperation and trust of a teammate. This is not so different from everyday business situations.'[24] Survivors' accounts have not yet been linked to rising stock prices, but positive reaction in various forms has been reported. These offerings are typical: 'If something doesn't work, try it again'; 'There is a lack of competition among us here in the woods. You don't see that in the world we come from'; 'Patience ... You learn the value of patience.'[25]

One of the more intriguing examples of collaborative canoe management must centre on the author Pierre Berton's proposition that a Canadian is someone who knows how to make love in a canoe (not illustrated).[26] The hypothesis is difficult to substantiate on the basis of conventional research methodology. According to survey results from the late 1980s, only 18 per cent of the population indicated that they had engaged in sex in a moving vehicle 'such as a car, boat, train, plane or bus.'[27] Nor have other forms of inquiry produced supportive results. A review of instructional canoeing programs, even modern variants of the experiential type, provides no indication that the relevant techniques and positions are the subject of formal educational initiatives. Similarly, a review of the promotional literature emanating from canoe manufacturing companies over the years fails to suggest that factors other than weight and manoeuvrability are essential to an assessment of this type of watercraft. This situation is somewhat surprising in light of the challenge with which Thomas Chandler Haliburton's well-known fictional character Sam Slick presented mid-nineteenth-century builders: 'If I was a gal,' Slick observed of the bark canoe, 'I'd always be courted in one, for you can't romp there, or you'd be upset. It's the safest place I know of.'[28] With the disappearance of the classic Sponson, whose full-gunwale air chambers made it virtually untippable, the search for improved canoe stability has seemingly been abandoned, although creative canoeists might imagine the popular Sportspal as a modern equivalent.

Biographical and autobiographical references supporting Berton's proposition have not been located, and the suggestion therefore remains without even anecdotal support.[29] Indeed, what little evidence does exist on the subject of the canoe as a suitable location (now better known as a venue) for sex comes from the realm of fiction, and much of this evidence is essentially negative in its implications. The youthful campers who populate the short fiction of Margaret Atwood never quite get around to aquatic amorousness. Some protagonists actually resist the opportunities available, although puddles in the bottom of the boat might have contributed to the dampening of George's passions in 'Wilderness Tips':

In the afternoon, Prue took him for a paddle in one of the leaking canvas-covered canoes from the boathouse. He sat in the front, jabbing ineptly at the water with his paddle, thinking about how he would get Portia to marry him. Prue landed him on a rocky point, led him up among the trees. She wanted him to make his usual rakish, violent, outlandish brand of love to her on the reindeer moss and pine needles; she wanted to break some family taboo. Sacrilege was what she had in mind: that was as clear to him as if he'd read it. But George already had his plan of attack worked out, so he put her off. He didn't want to desecrate Wacousta Lodge: he wanted to marry it.[30]

Michael Ondaatje's novel *In the Skin of a Lion* features a canoeing encounter, as the wounded thief Caravaggio, having made his way to a cottage not far from Bobcaygeon, Ontario, explores the surrounding shoreline. A woman in another canoe hails him and paddles over.

Red hair. The clear creamy skin of a witch. She wore a hat tied with a scarf and she waved to him in absolute confidence that if he was in a canoe on this lake he was acceptable and safe, even though every piece of clothing he wore was stolen from the blue bureau in the cottage. The lavender shirt, the white ducks, the tennis shoes. Performing intricate strokes she pulled up alongside him.[31]

Anxious for company after several spring weeks alone on the quiet lake, the woman, Anne, launches conversation with a man in a familiar canoe – again stolen. Nothing, however, ensues from the encounter, as Caravaggio (in greater need of refuge than companionship) withdraws from her confident approach.

Only the potential hazards of love on the water are experienced in Mark Schreiber's novel *Princes in Exile*, when two young cancer patients at summer camp attempt some romantic preliminaries in a canoe. When Ryan moves closer to Holly in order to share a kiss, she makes no effort to deter him or to turn her head away. 'But I forget that we are in a canoe,' he recalls, and the vessel capsizes with the shift in weight: 'I kiss the water instead of Holly and get a mouthful up my nose. I struggle, which is unnecessary since I am wearing a life jacket, but the shock of being thrown into the lake and my inability to see through the dark water or touch bottom frightens me. When I surface I gasp for air and look for Holly.' The immediate aftermath of this immersion produces feelings of warmth and closeness between the two, amounting even to a feeling that 'in this moment it seems that we have always been together, that we go back many centuries and have many centuries to go.' But again, the damp reunion remains unconsummated.[32]

We ought not to dismiss entirely a proposition so closely connected with Canadian national identity and the popular imagination. It may well be that the canoe has played a significant role at least as a facilitator of intimate assignations. Sandra Gwyn suggests as much – frequently – in her prize-winning work *The Private Capital: Ambition and Love in the Age of Laurier*.[33] Gwyn quotes her source, 'Amaryllis,' at length on one of Governor-General Lord Minto's notable canoeing expeditions with Lola Powell in the years around the turn of the century:

His Excellency has a fine little canoe and is as expert with a paddle as any Canadian. He enjoys it immensely too. While the flotilla of canoes was drifting down the river, some rain fell but 'when you're in the shade with a very pretty maid, it doesn't much matter what the weather may do' and it is much the same in a canoe ... A steamer hove in sight and canoes and canoeists were taken aboard.[34]

Gwyn, acknowledging that 'we cannot know for certain,' satisfied herself that 'it is impossible to believe they were not lovers.' She next faces a 'puzzling question' of some consequence: 'Exactly when and where did they manage to be lovers?' Among possible solutions to this rather funda- mental question, Gwyn favours the suggestion that summer outings in a canoe might provide the answer. 'Long private excursions' ten or twelve miles up the Gatineau would have provided suitable opportunities for 'a ramble into the woods,' assuming the absence of 'pesky lumbermen.'[35] The Governor-General's prowess is attested to by comparison, by being read against Gwyn's assessment of another pair of Ottawa paddlers, the youthful poets and public servants Archibald Lampman and Duncan Campbell Scott. Gwyn refers to 'quite an ambitious adventure for a couple of novice canoeists to squeeze into a single afternoon: a round trip of about seven miles, with another couple of miles of portaging.'[36] More evidence surely is required to fit Lord Minto into Pierre Berton's Cana- dian mould.

Evidence is overwhelming, however, in support of the less robust – or less rigorous – hypothesis that the canoe has had a considerable influence on the nature of romance in Canada. The craft has been widely associated with courtship or simply with romantic afternoon and evening outings on the small lakes and waterways in and around so many urban centres. A quiet evening in a canoe could provide the opportunity for extended conversation. The canoe setting, intimate in itself and not as easily subject to disruption and distraction as the soda shop, the front porch, or a park bench, permitted acquaintanceships to deepen without interruption. Pro- posals of marriage, generally made from the stern to the bow, were certainly not unknown. Not only were romantic experiences in a canoe common in the personal lives of many, they were also memorably de- picted in popular culture, most notably in the several versions of the film *Rose Marie*.[37]

The images of the canoe resulting from its historical associations, its metaphorical applications, and its continuing use by generations of rec- reational paddlers are many and varied. For some the canoe symbolizes adventure, challenge, or competition either in the company of peers or with the potentially inhospitable elements. For others, solitude, romance, and the aquatic equivalent of pastoralism come more readily to mind. Through the personal experience of generations of participants and the commentary of observers, canoeing has become embedded in the popular imagination, as these reflections seek to demonstrate and explain by examining the attractions of recreational canoe use, the practice of wilderness travel, and the contemporary cultural legacy of paddling for pleasure.

Irreplaceable Milk.

The canoe appears regularly in commercial advertising for a wide range of products and services, as illustrated in this and the three following advertisements. In addition to the advertisements shown here for milk, beer, and cigarettes, promotional images featuring paddlers and their craft have recently been used by banks, hotels, airlines, and communications companies, among others. *Above*: 'Irreplaceable Milk' (Courtesy of Dairy Farmers of Ontario)

Upper Canada Lager label (Courtesy of The Upper Canada Brewing Company)

Trapper Beer label (Courtesy of the Niagara Falls Brewery)

WARNING: Health and Welfare Canada advises that danger to health increases with amount smoked — avoid inhaling. Average per Cigarette — Export "A" Extra Light Regular "tar" 8.0 mg., nicotine 0.7 mg. King Size "tar" 9.0 mg., nicotine 0.8 mg.

Export 'A' advertisement (Courtesy of RJR-Macdonald, Inc.)

Tom Thomson and Arthur Lismer, shown here fishing on Canoe Lake, Algonquin Park, in 1914, were among the many Canadian artists whose canoeing
experience influenced their perception of the landscapes they painted. (Courtesy
of the McMichael Canadian Art Collection Archives)

This cartoon from an 1883 issue of *Life* illustrates the turbulent nature of New York politics during the Tammany Hall era. The presence of various types of canoes, including a Herald from the Peterborough district and a sectional model, suggests the prominence of recreational paddling as a contemporary pastime.

Can Paddle His Own Canoe.

Uncle Sam: "Can I help you Johnnie?"
Jack Canuck (who has safely run the rapids): "Not with that weapon, uncle."

These two political cartoons from the magazine *Industrial Canada* (early 1900s) reflect the tradition of self-reliance often associated with wilderness travellers.

Through the Rapids in Safety.

Jack Canuck: "Well! we're past the bad spot and there's no damage to the canoe."

Canoes appear frequently in the political cartoons of Frank Edwards, whether
or not the characters in them have had much personal experience of paddling.
In this 1980 cartoon Prime Minister Pierre Trudeau heads off down the portage
trail to reflect about his future. A summer camper and a wilderness traveller,
Trudeau in fact had a long-standing relationship with the canoe. (Courtesy of
Frank Edwards)

In 1953 Glenn Lewis, a high school student from Kelowna, British Columbia, was working as a dishwasher and salad chef at a Banff hotel when the opportunity arose to put his second-hand camera to work. Lewis shot a memorable roll of film of Marilyn Monroe trying her hand at paddling under the watchful eye of a member of the Royal Canadian Mounted Police. She was in the vicinity to film *River of No Return*. (Courtesy of Glenn Lewis)

2

A Useful Vessel: A Trout, a Moose, and a Canoe

Well known to Indian fur trappers, professional woodsmen, and others whose lives or livelihoods depended on the land, the utilitarian canoe has also served the recreational interests of anglers and hunters for a very long time. Much of the early North American sportsman's outdoor activity involved – and often required – the canoe, and a well handled one at that. For this reason the watercraft itself and the arts associated with its use were closely observed by people better known to us for their accomplishments in business, the professions, trades, military affairs, or the arts. Officers of the major fur trading companies, for example, enjoyed opportunities for hunting and fishing by canoe in the early nineteenth century.[1] Yet while fishing and hunting were certainly associated with the canoe, for the outdoor enthusiasts of the nineteenth century the canoe played an essentially functional and supporting role; it was basically a means to an end.

In providing a means of entry not otherwise obtainable to fish and game country, the canoe's contribution might be far from inconsequential, and an arduous canoe trip could provide its own rewards in the form of opportunities for sport. Thus, a report on 'the trout of the Menjamagossippi' (now better known as the Lady Evelyn) emphasized that the trip, with 'six portages of the hardest kind' to be endured, was 'no cinch.' 'Imagine,' readers were urged, 'carrying a canoe or a heavy pack up a rock slope of forty-five degrees, more or less, or jumping from boulder to boulder without falling in a grand jumble of pack, canoe, curses and smiles.' Opportunities commensurate with the ordeal awaited the intrepid anglers, for 'scarcely had the first fly fallen gently on the water, when there was a swirl of a great tail, a glorious strike, a singing of the reel.' Eventually, following the customary 'battle royal,' the angler/

portager was rewarded with 'a two-pound beauty, with shining sides and a belly as red as flame,' flopping against the ribs of the canoe.[2]

Catching fish was clearly the animating attraction of the piscatorial pastime. A woman on the Nipigon, one of the most renowned of northern Ontario's fishing rivers at the turn of the century, recalled her first encounter with a trout in its natural element. 'Shall I ever forget it?' Bergathora rhetorically inquired. 'The boat dancing in the rapids; my crude cast – when whirr! away went my line, miles and miles, I thought. I can still feel that circulation of blood; but I did not quite lose my head.' As her husband and two guides looked on, Bergathora's struggle lasted thirteen minutes. Although she 'trembled like a leaf; not a hairpin was left,' her husband declined to intervene. 'You must kill your first trout,' he insisted. And she did – 'a beauty of three pounds.' Looking back on her accomplishment, Bergathora reflected with satisfaction that those thirteen minutes alone justified the experience.[3] Without the triumph and the trophy, the canoe trip could not easily have been explained.

In the ranks of the outdoor enthusiasts of Bergathora's generation, women were comparatively rare, a fact partially explained by the broader function of sport in a society increasingly preoccupied with industrial and commercial activity from which women were still largely excluded. In the words of a short-lived nineteenth-century periodical, sport consists 'in the relief of man from business confinement, that recreation may be obtained with rod and gun, in the woods, on the lakes or along the river banks.' Yet lest readers misconceive the particular contribution and significance of such pursuits as hunting and fishing, the magazine carefully explained that 'casting for trout, or playing the noble salmon, afford opportunities for the display of more manly qualities than a novice is apt to suspect.' The specific moral lesson was to be found in the relationship between performance in a pleasurable pastime on the water and performance in the context of the 'business confinement' from which fishing or hunting offered relief: 'Patience and judgment, as well as a certain degree of skill, are requisite to success, and who will say that these are not equally essential in other pursuits in life?'[4] Indeed, American commentators expressed the relationship still more firmly, describing a very paragon: 'A genuine sportsman must possess a combination of virtues which will fill him so full that no room can be left for sin to squeeze in.' The inventory of virtues began with an inclination to rise early, although the true outdoorsman would also be 'ambitious, temperate, prudent, patient of toil, fatigue, and disappointment; courageous, watchful, intent upon his business; always ready, confident, cool; kind to his dog, civil to the girls, and courteous to his brother sportsmen.'[5]

Although sport fishing and hunting once took place in close proximity to settlements and nascent urban centres, development gradually forced participants to seek out more secluded if not remote woodlands and waterways, often using the canoe. Though the outings themselves might be seen as pleasurable and rewarding, the fireside reminiscences of fishermen/canoeists and their reflections about formative experiences on whatever lakes and rivers were at hand often reveal intricate linkages between recreational diversion and the fundamental preoccupations of daily life. Through constant interplay, happenings on and off the water influence and illuminate each other in myriad subtle though important ways. This was certainly true of the quest for fish and game in a canoe, and may well be true of the relationship between other recreational pursuits and the ordinary lives of their practitioners.

As William Hume Blake, a Toronto lawyer and author, explained, 'The science of fishing can be had from books, the art is learned by the catching and losing of fish.' 'Some knowledge of the science adds immeasurably to the pleasure of the sport,' Blake added, 'but the practitioner is the man to back for score.' To emphasize his claim that 'the widest discrepancy' separated the skilled and the unskilled fisherman, Blake offered the story of two rafts, 'each with two rods aboard, that fished the same waters for an equal period of time.' Of these, 'one returned with six trout, the other with eighteen dozen! Therefore in forming an opinion of a water from description, the rating of the observer is not the least important thing to have in mind.'[6] It was quite common for outdoorsmen to attribute a successful performance to qualities and characteristics that were themselves sources of moral satisfaction and affirmed the self-worth and self-awareness of the participant.

The character of the fisherman's tale has changed somewhat over the centuries since Izaak Walton penned a consoling account of the rural English countryside for his dispossessed Royalist contemporaries in the mid-seventeenth century.[7] Yet something more than coincidence accounts for the recurrent linkage between the most thoughtful fishermen's tales and the pressing concerns of their societies; hence, the central preoccupation of a classic twentieth-century account of the sport with very much broader themes. 'Try to remember that we are going after food,' admonishes the Fisherman-Philosopher in John Hersey's reflections on the quest for bluefish off the Atlantic coast, 'that we are, in a way, exploring our place in the systems of life in the universe.' Hersey concedes on behalf of fellow enthusiasts 'that our place, when we think we've found it, isn't always comfortable.' 'Sometimes it's awful,' he acknowledges, 'but often it's also awesome and very beautiful. It's what we have and must live with, at any rate.'[8] As the angler's place in the scheme of things has changed, so canoeists have experienced the influence of shifting concerns in the societies around them.

Sidney Kendall, a twenty-five-year-old student of divinity, writing after an unsatisfactory attempt to extract dinner from the depths of one of Quebec's Laurentian lakes, carefully scrutinized the technique of his guide, Xavier: 'I had been lying in the stern of the canoe taking in every movement and making a mental inventory of every part of the process, and I now began to see the philosophy of it all.' Lacking the close supervision of his guide, Kendall's performance had been sadly deficient. 'If so much caution and stealth were required, and such deep-laid schemes were needed, no wonder we had caught nothing.' Under Xavier's influence, 'there was no ringing laughter to alarm the fish, no shadow of the canoe sweeping along, no splashing of the paddle.' Xavier, 'making his strokes so carefully and cautiously that not a sound was heard,' also substituted a small green paddle for the new white paddle Kendall had employed.[9]

Many others acknowledged that the canoe, especially under the control of an experienced Native guide paddling with 'noiseless stroke,' offered a unique means of access to promising pools.[10] The acclaimed American canoe-builder J.H. Rushton of Canton, New York, gave fishermen the benefit of his advice on paddling techniques. The double-bladed paddle was easier to learn to use, Rushton admitted, but for hunting, the single-bladed paddle 'will be much preferred by most canoeists.' Again, quiet access was the issue, for 'it would be next to impossible to approach game with a paddle flourishing in the air, and though you could unjoint the double-bladed one, you would find the regular single one much better for ordinary cruising.'[11]

There may well have been an element of enjoyment in the early sportsman's relationship with the canoe, that is, an appreciation surpassing the recognition of its utility. The author Susanna Moodie's enchantment with 'the gentle craft' certainly suggests as much. She recalled of her Upper Canadian pioneering experience during the 1830s, 'My husband had purchased a very light cedar canoe, to which he attached a keel and sail; and most of our leisure hours, directly the snows melted, were spent upon the water.' This canoe, at least, was already a leisure craft, even in the service of the ongoing quest for fish and game, for as Moodie further explained:

These fishing and shooting excursions were delightful. The pure beauty of the Canadian water, the sombre but august grandeur of the vast forest that hemmed us in on every side and shut us out from the rest of the world, soon cast a magic spell upon our spirits, and we began to feel charmed with the freedom and solitude around us. Every object was new to us. We felt as if we were the discoverers of every beautiful flower and stately tree that attracted our attention, and we gave names to fantastic rocks and fairy isles, and raised imaginary houses and bridges on every picturesque spot which we floated past during our aquatic excursions. I learned the use of the paddle, and became quite proficient in the gentle craft.[12]

Despite the force of such sentiments, for some time, enjoyment clearly remained subordinate to utility as the canoe's raison d'être. In mid-century, however, the balance began to shift.

John MacGregor, a barrister of the Inner Temple and a keen amateur student of marine propulsion, visited North America in 1859. The future exploits of the well-publicized traveller who was later heralded as 'Rob Roy' MacGregor, the father of modern recreational canoeing, were influenced by his introduction to the canoe's role in sport along Canada's east coast. MacGregor was led to believe by one of his fellow transatlantic passengers that game abounded along the internal bays, a preserve he was permitted to enjoy on condition that its existence not be reported back in England, where others might find the prospect sufficiently attractive to draw them to an otherwise unknown and secluded retreat. The canoe was just the means for undertaking 'a sporting tour on a river thickly wooded, and the favourite resort of reindeer and moose.' Logistical arrangements were unappealing, for the sportsman would 'live in his boat, or in a rude hut of bark, and half his time will be employed in wading, as he pushes the canoe over shallows, while the other half will be spent in cutting a way through the tangled jungle of tree-branches that block up the stream.' MacGregor later sought significantly higher levels of comfort on canoe journeys through Europe and the Middle East. These expeditions laid the foundations for his prominence as a paddler and as author of *A Thousand Miles in the Rob Roy Canoe on Twenty Rivers and Lakes of Europe*, among other enormously popular volumes.[13]

Arthur P. Silver, touring Atlantic Canada as a sportsman some decades after MacGregor, was more appreciative of the traditional birch-bark canoe, celebrating it as the 'very soul and poetry of motion.'[14] It rests serenely, he continued, 'upon the distracted waters, calm as the iris that broods over the raging cataract,' and he marvelled to observe the craft 'traverse the placid lake, as silently as the silver moonbeam that steals across its surface.' But Silver's memories, recorded as 'A Birch-Bark Canoe Trip,' are more concerned with his exploits and adventures with rod and gun along New Brunswick's Nepisiguit River than with paddling, an activity he largely experienced at second hand. The paddling on this 'birch-bark canoe trip' was done by the 'muscular arms of my two Indians.' Silver, having obtained a fishing permit, 'willingly rested them at the principal salmon pools.' At other times, 'gun in hand,' he reclined 'as comfortably as circumstances admit of on the motley baggage.' Or, with Joe and Peter poling the heavy-laden craft upstream, the author reflected upon one 'very pretty spectacle' or another. 'Looking over the brow of the cliff, below in diminished perspective, the Indians, with every nerve and muscle at full tension, were to be seen, forcing the canoe through the seething water, sometimes scarcely gaining a foot in five minutes. The picture was framed by the walls of dark rocks on both sides of them.' The salmon pools, and Silver's memorable successes in them, are the true subject of his tale, along with other conquests and triumphs over a bear, a bull moose, and a wide variety of unfortunate game birds and waterfowl.

Silver's canoe trip illustrates in an extreme fashion the phenomenon that while the canoe was essential to certain forms of late nineteenth-century recreational activity, actual paddling by the sportsman or sportswoman was often merely incidental to the experience. Indeed, exertion might even have been detrimental to the pleasures of the chase, and a good many recreational canoe travellers of this era did little if any paddling themselves. When asked to imagine a challenging portage, they did just that – imagined the actual labour of the portage being carried out by able and experienced guides. Thus, a group of Chicago authors visiting the Temagami district of northeastern Ontario frankly admitted that portages were not all that difficult when guides were on hand to carry canoes and baggage: 'A canoe weighs seventy-five pounds but an Ojibway guide will pick it up, put it on his shoulders and pace as happily and steadily over a portage as an ordinary man would carry his spring overcoat.'[15]

Along some of the better-travelled recreational canoe routes in districts favoured by anglers, a minor ground transport industry actually seems to have arisen. Near Nipigon village, for example, an Indian with team and wagon was generally available to haul canoes, provisions, and camp outfit over a two and a half mile trail. The 1917 tariff, as reported by E.E.

Millard, was four dollars, a significant cost at that time, but – upon reflection – a sum he was prepared to pay in the circumstances: 'The service is really worth it, and more; for saving valuable time he practically prolongs your vacation nearly a day.'[16] Observations of this nature convey the impression that canoe travel, in particular the portage, was not an end in itself from the perspective of those who were primarily concerned with the quest for fish or wildlife.

Reginald Drayton, a young man with time on his hands early one fall in the 1870s, found the portages of Ontario's Buckhorn district, where he had chosen to go hunting without the services of a sturdy guide, 'an unspeakable bore.' He was also sceptical that the canoe would prove a suitable vessel from which to hunt:

I had been saying to John that it was very difficult to shoot with the rifle out of a canoe owing to the motion as an eighth of an inch deflection at the muzzle wd. make a difference of many inches at 100 yards, just then I saw a lune [*sic*] and must needs illustrate my idea when as is often the case when one makes an assertion matters turned out totally wrong for I hit the poor beggar in the stern.[17]

At the end of the nineteenth century, Perry D. Frazer addressed the seemingly widespread impression that it was dangerous to use a shotgun in a canoe. Not so, he protested, urging readers of a Forest and Stream publication to believe that 'with reasonable care it is perfectly safe.' Moreover, a little camouflage in the form of 'bunches of leaves or grass' might serve to conceal the canoe from one's intended targets. For good measure, Frazer reviewed further advantages offered by the canoe to anyone in search of game:

The lover of stillhunting finds in the noiseless paddling canoe with single blade a sure method of finding game, for all animals – from the tiny squirrel to the lordly moose – frequent the shores of rivers and lakes of the country they inhabit. Not only do they come to the water's edge to slake their thirst, but, like man, they have great appreciation of the cool, shaded banks, and the sound of the murmuring waves, and are loath to leave places at all times beautiful and inviting.[18]

Frazer may have succeeded in articulating the attractions of the canoe for those hunters who were prepared to abandon the craft on account of the perceived risks, assuming, of course, that a more suitable vessel was available. But it has been hard to dispel the notion that the canoe threatens the safety of sportsmen. Anglers and hunters, however, may well be responsible for some of their own misfortunes, as Harold Town and David P. Silcox have suggested in reporting – in a manner my grandmother might have called indelicate – that 'the large majority of drowned canoe fishermen are found with their flies open.'[19]

The young English poet Rupert Brooke, perhaps an improbable adventurer, arrived in Winnipeg on 30 July 1913. He then embarked in the company of his host, Howard Falk, for a hunting lodge near Lake George, some seventy miles from the city. In a letter of 3 August Brooke stated, 'I never expected to pass my twenty-sixth birthday with a gun and fishing tackle, without any clothes on, by a lake, in a wood infested by bears, in a country where there aren't ten people within five miles and half of those are Indians.'

A couple of days earlier he had recorded his active (if possibly reluctant) participation in the aftermath of a successful deer hunt. As the canoe approached his campsite, Brooke was struck by the sight of a deer, immense in his estimation, 'the size of a small pony.' With the water lapping close to the gunwales, the hunters had transported the carcass some six miles around the lakeshore, finally depositing the body in the muddy shallows not far from a campfire which had been lit to illuminate the proceedings:

For two hours we pulled and hauled at this creature, tugging at a rope over the branch of a birch. Then the trapper got an axe and hacked the beast's head off: with the great antlers it weighs some hundred pounds. At length we got the carcass hanging up and supported it with sticks. I got cut and scratched and smeared with the creature's insides. It was a queer sight, lit up by the leaping flames of the fire, which the woman fed – the black water of the lake, muddy with trampling at the edge, and streaked with blood, the trapper in the tree, this great carcass hanging at one end of the rope, my friend and an Indian and I pulling our arms out at the other, the head gazing reproachfully at us from the ground, everybody using the most frightful language, and the rather ironical and very dispassionate stars above.[20]

Readers of the published account of Brooke's canoeing experience in the Manitoba wilderness were treated to a less gruesome vision of the state of nature. Mindful of the sensibilities of a broader readership, Brooke described 'a far and solitary beach of dark, golden sand, close by a deserted Indian camp,' with wildlife in abundance. Stealing quietly around the lakeshore by canoe, the visitor might encounter a bear lumbering by, or even a caribou. In a passage far removed from description of the slaughter he had witnessed, Brooke remembered 'a little red deer coming down to the water to drink, treading the wild edge of lake and forest with a light, secret, and melancholy grace.'[21]

As Brooke's experience and the earlier comments of John MacGregor indicate, people were willing to travel considerable distances in pursuit of sport. Certainly, the economic potential of recreational fishing and hunting was not lost on observers. Robert Barnwell Roosevelt, uncle of a future U.S. president and the man whose opinion on the relationship between virtuous character and successful sportsmanship was quoted earlier, served from 1868 to 1888 as head of the New York State Fish Commission.[22] Programs to restock the state's lakes began in New York's popular Adirondack region in the 1880s, and the state of Maine pioneered both fish and game conservation measures, partly for the purpose of attracting visitors to the outdoors. Ten years into the twentieth century, Kelly Evans found it curious that with statistics available on agriculture, mining, and timber harvesting, the nearby jurisdiction of Ontario still had virtually no information on tourism, and particularly little regarding the role of fish and game. Noting the financial success of Maine's fish and game conservation measures, including a licensing scheme, Evans urged provincial legislators to contemplate similar initiatives: 'Now, if the Province of Ontario received twenty-five million dollars of money in that way, without giving up a stick of timber or a pound of mineral, it would mean really the great resources of other States and other countries turned into gold and brought and left here, for which we only give after all, as it were, an amusement.'[23] Others, including F.G. Aflalo, an energetic chronicler of English sport, concurred. He considered Canada's waterways to be 'precious as playgrounds, the summer haunts of thousands of anglers, and seemingly inexhaustible for all who camp a little distance from the more frequented holiday resorts.'[24]

Semi-official promotional endorsements such as the 1925 pamphlet *Canoeing in Canada* eventually proclaimed the attractions awaiting the angler/canoeist: 'One travels far to find the treasures of the north, and not without reward. If the canoeist comes in search of fish, his quest will not be in vain, for the Canadian lakes and streams are famous for their fish. Whatever particular variety of angling one prefers, there is no lack of opportunity.'[25] Brook trout, lake trout, black bass, pickerel, pike, dore, ouananiche, rainbow trout, and other species were to be had in abundance. Indeed, sport fish were so plentiful that 'the skilful angler need never go hungry, and what more appetizing dish can be had than fried trout with a strip of bacon, eaten by the camp fire beneath the shade of a pine tree, while the merry-hearted song-sparrows provide the music.'[26]

Experienced outdoor vacationers, as the brochure's author knew well, had a particular enthusiasm for actual consumption. Occasionally they recorded the nature of their pleasure and enjoyment:

Trout we ate, and always more trout. Big fellows broiled with strips of bacon craftily sewn in and out of the pink flesh; medium fellows cut into steaks; little fellows fried crisp in corn-meal; big, medium, and little fellows mingled in component of the famous north country bouillon, whose other ingredients are partridges, and tomatoes, and potatoes, and onions, and salt pork, and flour in combination delicious beyond belief.[27]

Here, again, the appeal of the canoe was to be found in its utility as a means of reaching trout, trout, and more trout. And residents and visitors sojourning in Canada in search of an outdoor encounter with fish and game soon discovered, in an era when automobiles were few, highways limited, and ATVs still mercifully unknown, that railway travel was an almost indispensable element of any extended vacation. The railways knew this too.

The Canadian National Railways responded annually to hundreds of requests for information on accessible canoe routes. The task seemed entirely consistent with the CNR's claim to have deliberately constructed 'pioneer lines, purposely located with a view to opening up the natural resources and to introduce population and capital to what would otherwise remain primitive and stagnant.' The railway, then, considered itself 'the natural avenue of all who seek the newer hunting and fishing resources and particularly those vacationists who crave for experiences more novel and exciting.' This particular sector of the market was encouraged by an extensive series of brochures and guidebooks offering opportunities for adventurous twentieth-century vacationers to 'do deeds that whip up the physical sinews that most of the year lie dormant.' A five-hundred-mile canoe outing from Prince George, British Columbia, to Peace River Crossing would be free of 'picnic parties,' although government surveyors, northbound outfits of the Hudson's Bay Company, or even 'a party of famous explorers' might appear along the route. The lines of the CNR were at the disposal of any canoeist hoping to 'reach out when opportunity offers to play our part in any exploit by field and river and re-enact even for a little time and in our own small way the stirring annals of our pioneer fathers.'[28] But with the ties to pioneering ancestors gradually beginning to weaken, the wilderness travellers of the 1920s to whom the CNR first made its appeal would eventually be encouraged to devote less effort to fishing and hunting, and to consider instead the forms of recreation referred to in the title of one of the leading pamphlets, *Canoe Trips and Nature Photography.*

Of course there have always been elements of necessity in the canoeist's relationship to fish and wildlife, as *Canoeing in Canada* subtly hinted in its observation that 'the skilful angler need never go hungry.' Arthur Silver, too, had noted the stirring feelings associated with a bright morning in October when 'the prow of the yellow canoe cuts the gently resisting current, rifles all aboard, together with a few days' frugal rations.'[29] The need to supplement frugal rations inspired wilderness travellers to cast a very purposeful lure or to scan the shoreline constantly for a source of fresh meat.

Early recreational paddlers often depended on the land to a greater or lesser degree. If successful, they might indeed feast on nature's bounty; if unsuccessful, they would enjoy a less nourishing diet or perhaps suffer a worse fate. Leonidas Hubbard, an ambitious young journalist with the American magazine *Outing,* paid the ultimate price of those whose need for nourishment from the land exceeded their ability to gather its resources. Hubbard's death in a fateful Labrador exploration of the early 1900s was the subject of intense inquiry and concern at the time. Subsequent generations of wilderness travellers have also had occasion to reflect on the fate of this zealous adventurer. Hubbard's outfit included fishing tackle, but through miscalculation the party failed to obtain suitable gill netting. Commentators have often wondered whether better equipment might have altered the outcome.[30]

Survival has continued to be part of the linkage between canoeists and consumable resources, and reminders of some ultimate level of human dependence on the natural world still often penetrate the paddler's consciousness. In the summer of 1988, fish and blueberries sustained a party of four canoeists who were swamped by cross-currents and high water in the Thelon River, some five hundred kilometres east of Yellowknife in Canada's Northwest Territories. Black flies took their toll while the paddlers awaited rescue in the form of a Canadian Armed Forces Twin Otter.[31] Such episodes are far from uncommon, but the adventure of fishing from a canoe has not been reserved for sportsmen or those struggling to survive a perilous mishap.

The young Eric Sevareid – about to embark on a journalistic career with the *Minneapolis Journal,* and not yet an internationally acclaimed war correspondent and broadcaster – and his companion Walter Port may have been partially attracted by the prospects for fishing when they set out in 1930 on an expedition from Minneapolis to York Factory on Hudson Bay. Certainly, they demonstrated a keen interest in fishing possibilities along the course of their route. Following momentary paralysis at the sight of a six-foot sturgeon, which they initially mistook for a log, the two young paddlers 'began circling and casting our line madly, although we knew that a net was the only instrument with which sturgeon could be caught.' They recognized, as well, their good fortune in losing the sturgeon, for 'even if we had hooked the fish, it probably would have pulled us under water.'[32] Carp, however, were among the early victims, when the boys came upon hundreds of the fish 'leaping up and down in the muddy, shallow water of a little lagoon.' As Sevareid later reported in his time-honoured tale *Canoeing with the Cree*: 'The temptation was too much. Up went our trouser legs and in we waded with the paddles. We killed five big ones, one weighing about twelve pounds. We saved the best for ourselves and gave the others to a farmer for his chickens, in return for some cold bottles of pop.'[33] This unorthodox technique proved effective nonetheless. Not much farther along the waterway, sympathetic fishermen 'were so astounded at finding we were going to eat carp that they gave us a pickerel.'[34] Such impressions of a bountiful North American environment were characteristic of the recreational traveller's perception of the wilderness landscape as a playground, and an unlimited one at that.

European canoeists, encountering their fellow citizens at somewhat closer quarters, have experienced and expressed rather different reactions in the presence of fishermen. In the course of the journey described in *An Inland Voyage*, a Continental canoe trip originating in Antwerp, Belgium, in 1876, Robert Louis Stevenson and Sir Walter Simpson encountered a great many fishermen, generally 'stupefied with contentment' and manifesting 'a strange diversity of opinion ... as to the kind of fish for which they set their lures.' Stevenson, only just called to the Scottish bar and not yet clear as to his vocation, expressed his own attitude towards anglers:

I do not affect fishes unless when cooked in sauce; whereas an angler is an important piece of the scenery, and hence deserves some recognition among canoeists. He can always tell you where you are, after a mild fashion; and his quiet presence serves to accentuate the solitude and stillness, and remind you of the glittering citizens below your boat.[35]

This observation, apart from its literary interest as an early offering from one who would become the immensely popular author of *Treasure Island*, is also notable for the clear distinction drawn between the canoeist and the angler.

The generally amicable relations between canoeists and anglers suggested by Stevenson's account have not been universal. Canoeists often found themselves unwelcome on many of Britain's salmon rivers, where anglers, having bought or rented exclusive fishing rights, deeply resented any intrusion upon or disturbance to their enjoyment. The columns of *The Field*, a British sporting journal, often contained attempts to explain and mediate friction between fishermen and the canoe cruisers who could be found with increasing frequency after the 1890s on 'out-of-the-way salmon rivers and quiet country trout streams.' Legal action against the intrusive impact of recreational paddlers was not unknown, for as the British angler might express the point: 'Let the canoeist rent his water at the same rate as that paid by the trout angler, and he will put himself in court. One canoeist passing along a stretch of trout water would infallibly spoil the sport of every angler on it for some time.'[36] Decades later, the situation remained virtually unchanged: Nigel Nicolson had an unfortunate encounter with fishermen in the course of his second canoe trip, along the Great Stour between Ashford and Canterbury. Riparian fishermen, claiming that the fingerling trout were upset by the passing canoes, remained impervious to Nicolson's protests that canoes surely 'appeared to them [the fingerlings] simply larger trout sliding peacefully over their nursery shoals.' Having lost the argument, Nicolson and two friends were 'obliged to portage the canoes half a mile or so to another person's stretch of the river, from which we hoped he was absent, poaching another owner's trout.'[37] Operating at close quarters as they do on many rivers, British canoeists and anglers have struggled repeatedly to achieve some formal accommodation of interests.[38]

Recreational canoe travel has seldom provoked the degree of antagonism exhibited by fishermen along the banks of quiet British waterways when their patience and purposeful concentration were frustrated by those paddling for pleasure. It is nevertheless worthwhile to remember that this seemingly innocent and apparently pleasurable activity has not been free from controversy; nor has it been the subject of universal admiration. Although the canoe once contributed greatly to the enjoyment of anglers and hunters in North America by providing access to fish and game (often, indeed, furthering their well-being if not their actual survival), the sportsmen who adopted the canoe for its utility were not long in abandoning it, as ostensibly more convenient modes of transport became available in the form of bass boats, float planes, and sturdy vehicles with four-wheel drive. Nor, with the passage of time, did the canoe's role remain merely supportive.

The disengagement of recreational canoeing from the quest for fish and game was intermittent and gradual. For some paddlers the separation began in the nineteenth century, while for others the presumption long persisted that if you were going paddling you were naturally going hunting, or were at the very least setting off in search of serious fish. Raoul Clouthier, who spent two weeks paddling through Quebec from Maniwaki to Angliers by way of Barrière and Grand Lake Victoria in 1928, was sufficiently concerned with this presumption that he provided an extensive rebuttal at the conclusion of a report on his vacation travel.

Expecting questions about the object of the journey, Clouthier forthrightly disavowed various forms of the traditional rationale and other plausible justifications:

We did not start with the intention of hunting as it was closed season. As far as fishing was concerned, none of us were keen anglers and, besides, it was not necessary to go in as far as that to look for trout and bass, two varieties of fish not to be found in the waters of the Upper Ottawa River. And we were not out prospecting, nor were we hoping to locate the lost plane of any transatlantic flyers.

After denying any explanation linked to practicality, Clouthier confronted the challenge of formulating a positive rationale. Observers, he recognized, would be curious to know what might prompt otherwise responsible adults 'to undertake that journey, with its hardships and dangers, its long days spent in a canoe, under a scorching sun, its harassing portages and its cool nights, with nothing but a thin silk sheet over our heads.' Alternative holidays were available in the form of a fashionable beach resort, and more comfortable – even luxurious – means of transportation could certainly be found. Clouthier's best effort at explanation was simple and eloquent:

It was nothing but the call of Nature, the love of the great open air, the lure of the wild and deserted forest which seem dormant in the heart of every man and to which every real sportsman is so responsive!

No man can define the attraction and the disadvantages of heat, thirst, flies, long hours bent on a paddle, under rain or sunshine, hard carries over rough portages, all things inherent to such a trip made through unfrequented territories. What then urges one to go, knowing well what is in store for him? Perhaps the charm lies in magnificent sunrise and sunset scenes, or in contending with the forces of Nature by one's own physical power. Or is it the soothing calm of the forest, the restful horizons of silvery lakes, the alluring noise of rapids and water-falls? The question is hard to answer! One goes in spite of all, accepting in advance whatever may happen. He goes and returns satisfied, even if he only brings back memories of the beautiful panoramas he has had the privilege of admiring, memories of pleasant evenings spent around the camp fire, listening to the myste-rious voices of the wild, memories of the freedom he has enjoyed, far from the tentacles of civilization.[39]

Raoul Clouthier's explanation touches on many themes commonly found in other accounts of the pleasures of recreational paddling: the appeal of the landscape, freedom from the constraining influence of urban life, the therapeutic benefits of outdoor activity, and exposure to the healing influence of the northern pines.

3

The Healing Pines

James Dickson, a land surveyor, encouraged late nineteenth-century readers of *Camping in the Muskoka Region*, his account of a canoe trip, to visit the wilderness with the thought that 'at the close of our holiday we return to our labours among our fellow-men, invigorated and strengthened, both in mind and body.'[1] Among Dickson's contemporaries, a certain number of women also regarded outdoor camping as a highly beneficial experience. 'If a man can do this,' Ella Walton reflected at the close of the century, 'why, under modified conditions, cannot a woman?' She concluded that camping, 'properly undertaken,' offered ideal conditions for 'weary mothers, energetic housekeepers, brain-workers, and fagged-out society women' to enjoy a brief respite from their daily cares and 'a surcease from mental worry.'[2]

The canoe trip became a widely recognized form of rehabilitation through exertion, although the range of ailments subject to the remedy and the precise operational principle of the cure have not been clinically confirmed. The benefits derived from the exercise of paddling, the contemplation of landscape, and the breathing in of fresh air have all been ventured as explanations why so many have turned to canoeing over the years for a measure of relief from illness, injury, or the stresses of daily living.

In fact, no less a figure than 'Rob Roy' MacGregor, who had achieved international renown on the basis of his canoe travel during the 1860s, had offered his own reflections on the purposes of paddling:

It cannot be concealed that continuous physical enjoyment ... is dangerous luxury if it be not properly used. When I thought of the hospitals in London, of the herds of squalid poor in fetid alleys, of the palefaced ragged boys, and the vice, sadness, pain, and poverty we are sent to do battle with, if we be true Christian soldiers, I could not help asking, 'Am I right in thus enjoying such comfort, such scenery, and such health?'

MacGregor's answer to the moral perils of physical health and pleasure reflected the Victorian ideals of philanthropic commitment to which his later life was increasingly devoted. His happiness would not be right unless put to some higher purpose; or as he expressed it, the enjoyment of canoeing was 'to get vigour of thought and hand, and renewed energy of mind, and larger thankfulness, and wider love, and so, with all the powers recruited, to enter the field again more eager and able to be useful.'[3]

Many charitable causes benefited from MacGregor's personal efforts and financial contributions. His series of canoe trips along the waterways of France, Germany, and Switzerland and in still more exotic canoe country around the Jordan River provided the subject matter for such publications as *A Thousand Miles in the Rob Roy Canoe on Twenty Rivers and Lakes of Europe*, *Rob Roy on the Jordan*, and *Voyage of the Yawl Rob Roy*. These celebrated writings produced significant earnings, which he directed to philanthropic causes along with the proceeds of dozens of speaking engagements throughout Britain.

Many less altruistic canoeists explained the virtues of recreational paddling with reference to feelings of mental or physical well-being that resulted from the experience of the outdoors and the natural environment: 'For the man who leads a sedentary life, there could be no better prescription than a trip of this kind, where he will have nothing worse to worry him than how to satisfy a voracious appetite; and will return bright of eye and with a wealth of memories that will not end with the summer vacation.'[4] Such sentiments about the curative effect of seasonal holidays on the water have been expressed by succeeding generations, each responding to its own sense of the wear and tear of daily work or of professional and business life. They have typically been associated with the contrast between the burdensome pressures of urban existence and a more relaxed, less hurried regime found in the outdoors.

The therapeutic attraction of recreational canoeing has perhaps increased in periods in which the pressure of industrial change or the constraints of urbanization have seemed most acute. It is by no means surprising, therefore, that such sentiments were common around the turn of the century, when the Canadian economy was undergoing a marked and rapid transformation, or that in the United States, recreational canoeing initially flourished in the period of economic expansion following the Civil War. That the restoration rationale coincided with the growing availability of leisure time must have been particularly convenient – at least for some; in so far as mental and physical renewal were directed towards strengthening the canoeist for a return to the insistent demands of the workplace, employment, and professional life, the holiday was sufficiently purposeful – and laborious – to escape censure.

The appeal of recreational canoeing was often recognized in conjunction with the attractions of camping, which was growing in popularity during the 1880s. 'It is becoming more and more the endeavour of all classes in the city to be in the country for a while at least, if not possible for the whole summer,' remarked one observer, adding in explanation that 'the confining influences the year round, and the impure atmosphere in the hot season, necessitate the change apart from the natural predisposition which exists more or less developed in every being.'[5] The suggestion of universality misrepresented the circumstances of a large segment of the population, but the apparent continuation of the summering trend had established outings in the countryside as something of a North American middle-class ritual by the turn of the century. Campers and canoeists enjoyed a very wide selection of suitable locations, although many preferred forest reserves, parks, and other designated campgrounds.

Inspired by the tireless campaigning of Verplanck Colvin, a man who devoted his life to the Adirondack wilderness, a series of legislative measures culminated in 1894 with constitutional reform to ensure that New York's state-owned forest preserve 'shall be forever kept as wild forest lands.' With its basic character secured, the Adirondacks region attracted two hundred thousand visitors in the summer of 1900.[6] For its part, Algonquin Park, established as a forest reserve in Ontario one year before New York's forever-wild designation, had not achieved the Adirondack's visitorship levels. Yet Algonquin, too, attracted increasing numbers of wilderness-seeking vacationers. With the passing of spring into summer, the thoughts of city residents turned towards vacationing, for 'the prospect and anticipation of an outing in the country does much to make bearable the lot of a city man.'[7]

Young Sidney Kendall and his colleagues were very much a part of this tradition as they set out for the Laurentians, 'on peaceable thoughts intent, anxious for nothing more than a few weeks ruralizing among the lakes and hills.' Members of the party simply expected to gather enough strength and renew their spirits sufficiently to survive the next college term.[8] The Presbyterian minister Charles Gordon, better known to generations of readers of Canadian fiction as Ralph Connor, was another whose summer outings on the water became a vital part of what we might now describe as a fitness regime. 'It is one of the supreme joys of life to be thoroughly fit,' the Reverend Gordon sermonized. 'Joy is really well-being,' he opined in sharing the origins of this 'great discovery,' made after five gruelling weeks of canoe travel:

It was worth all the agony of knees, ankles and toes, all the hotbox of the shoulder blade, all the staggering backbreak of the portage, all the long weariness of the unending swing of the paddle, worth all just to be fit. Ready to meet with a spring everything and anything the hour may bring you. To wake and be willing to spring from your spruce bed ready for your morning dive, ready for sowbelly and blackstrap and flapjack with a fish, if you are lucky, ten minutes from the hook to the pan, ready for the swift smooth technique of camp-breaking and canoe-packing ... I say life is one gay song for the man fit for his day. And a man gets fit by observing the inexorable laws of life, work, food and rest in proper proportion and environment.

For Gordon, 'fit and bubbling with life,' the satisfactions were elemental, if decidedly male:

I can carry my load across the portage at the Indian trot. I can pack my canoe, too, over the portage, if the carry isn't too long, for I am no giant. I can paddle a day of twelve hours and come in fresh enough to cook supper or make our beds or get wood for our night fire. And, best of all, I have learned something about a canoe.

Continuing in this didactic spirit, Gordon pressed home the lesson of fitness. It is 'being right with yourself and your world ... being as God meant you to be.'[9] This appreciation of the outdoors, this taking pleasure in it – particularly in the cause of self-improvement – represented something of a transformation in outlook, for earlier generations had often regarded the forest as an obstacle to settlement and to their vision of progress, comfort, and civilization. Indeed, Anna Jameson, one of Ralph Connor's literary forerunners, had once remarked that 'a Canadian settler hates a tree.'[10]

Charles Gordon was certainly not alone in suggesting that canoeing, along with such other active outdoor experiences as hiking and camping, were more valuable than a resort or cottage holiday. Tent-dwellers were 'of higher caste in the society of the red god's worshippers, because they live closer to nature and their love for the open is more sincere.'[11] Another unidentified camping enthusiast discussed in Rod and Gun the 'rest cure' in a canoe: 'The thoughts of the crowding multitude of things which in the city present their insistent claims were beginning to melt away and become as a dim memory of unessentials ... The chief impression left on the mind is of a bigness, a freedom, that in the city or even in the trim countryside, is altogether lacking.'[12] Apart from Gordon's physical regime, the benefits of canoeing for those with leisure and the opportunity to participate in the activity were often linked to mental health or psychological well-being.

Dillon Wallace, who survived the ill-fated Labrador expedition that ended the life of his journalist colleague Leonidas Hubbard in 1903, had undertaken the trip at least in part as a means of recovering from the premature loss of his young wife from consumption, or tuberculosis. As Wallace's experience suggests, the healing influence of nature was largely directed towards the relief of anxiety and stress. Other examples abound, including Robert Louis Stevenson's memorable account of the European voyage of the *Arethusa* and the *Cigarette*, in which the young author strongly suggested that the physical demands on a paddler, however repetitive, were far from stressful. The brain, he explained, 'had a whole holiday and went to sleep.' The occasional church spire and the odd leaping fish might catch the canoeist's attention, but these hardly disturbed the restfulness of the journey:

The central bureau of nerves, what in some moods we call Ourselves, enjoyed its holiday without disturbance, like a Government Office. The great wheels of intelligence turn idly in the head, like fly-wheels, grinding no grist. I have gone on for half an hour at a time, counting my strokes and forgetting the hundreds. I flatter myself the beasts that perish could not underbid that, as a low form of consciousness.[13]

There is at least a suggestion in the future author's account that the very act of paddling contributes directly to the beneficial results experienced by the canoeist. Not only does he seem to be absorbed in the repetitive action of the stroke, but as this little outing took place along the canals and populated interior waterways of Europe, the influence of outdoor camping – let alone the bracing air of the North American wilderness – has been removed from the equation. The overwhelming tendency, however, has been to view the natural environment as a healing influence as much as any physical activity.

A notable landmark in the history of therapeutic recreation was the publication in 1869 of the Reverend William H.H. Murray's *Adventures in the Wilderness, or Camp-life in the Adirondacks.* The proclamations of the minister of Boston's Park Street Church concerning the health-giving advantages of the Adirondack region, and especially the virtues of exposure to the aromatic forest air, contributed to a dramatic flow of cure-seeking visitors. Not all the cure-seekers benefited from their encounter with the outdoors, and at least three of the hopefuls died in the course of their exertions.[14]

Murray's promotion of the Adirondacks helped to launch more than a few careers. In 1874, J. Henry Rushton, a young New Yorker who had worked the lumber mills and supported himself briefly as a clerk in a shoe store, anxiously sought relief from a dry hacking cough. With a view to testing the benefits of the Adirondack treatment Rushton crafted his first boat, probably a skiff rather than the canoes for which he would soon be famous as a builder.[15] The physician Edward Livingston Trudeau, having experienced some relief from tuberculosis during an Adirondack summer in 1875, stayed on and within a few years had established a sanatorium at Saranac Lake. Emphasizing rest rather than a more vigorous therapy, Dr Trudeau's initiative nonetheless further popularized the Adirondack wilderness cure.[16]

Healing places hardly originated with canoeing, as the ancient history of European spas confirms. However, North American pinelands were popularized on the basis of the distinctive restorative contributions claimed by their promoters. In the early years of the twentieth century, promoters shamelessly touted the Ontario village of Gravenhurst as a 'natural health resort' with an international reputation 'for the cures effected in cases of lung trouble, pulmonary diseases, hay fever, malaria,' and an ostensibly significant list of further ills temptingly identified as 'etc.' Some of the town's permanent residents were said to be visitors who had come back to the community after a cure in order to 'banish forever any recurrence of their deep-seated maladies.'[17] Municipal officials in Gravenhurst may have been fortunate to escape the fate of the unfortunate promoters of 'Nature's Creation,' a treatment for those conditions leading up to various forms of tuberculosis, weak lungs–bronchitis–asthma–coughs, and general debility. The formula's backers ran afoul of federal legislation on the advertising of patent medicines and were successfully prosecuted in colourful proceedings pitting the testimonials of 'cured' users against the expert evidence of physicians and other specialists who were unable to identify any practical effect whatsoever associated with the drugs.[18]

Several years later – in the 1920s – the appeal of the Ontario summer was remarkably undiminished as provincial advertising brochures continued to champion the health-giving attributes of the northern lakes and forests. Algoma, for example, offered not only 'the most enchanting scenes that the human mind can conceive,' but an atmosphere well suited to the 'restful recuperation of the convalescent.' Hay fever was allegedly unknown in Algonquin Park, the 'health and recreation resort' whose canoeable waterways and virgin forests of pine, spruce, and balsam were, provincial officials added modestly, 'unexcelled in this part of the continent.'[19] Throughout Ontario, 'all the restful, re-invigorating, health-giving influences offered by Mother Nature in her primeval splendor are available to those who have the will to partake of her bounty, at small expense and without discomfort.'[20]

For sheer audacity, however, the promotional endeavours of the Temiskaming and Northern Ontario Railway on behalf of the Temagami district are unsurpassed:

To those living in limestone regions where the water is hard, the lakes and rivers filled with muddy silt, and therefore urinary and malarial troubles prevalent, a month or more each year in Temagami must add to the span of life and probably prevent years of excruciating agony. Can you afford to be so busy that you cannot give yourself this opportunity for increased health and happiness?[21]

As expressed by John Boyle O'Reilly, an American journalist and athlete of Irish origin, anyone whose eyes, shoulders, or lungs were suffering from the confines of the workplace would find that 'the sun and the wind and the delicious splash of the river on face and breast and arms' could effect a cure. And for such people, a two-week canoe trip was a godsend, offering more health and rejuvenation than they could obtain from 'a lazy, expensive and seasick voyage to Europe, or three months' dawdle at a fashionable watering place.'[22]

North American entrepreneurs did not fail to notice the commercial potential of the canoe and the wilderness in the quest for health and fitness. Spas and alpine resorts were established to take advantage of several natural phenomena, as had occurred in Europe. But hot springs were by no means essential ingredients of the potion of the outdoors. No less an institution than the Canadian National Railways made available to its passengers a guide to campcraft and wood lore premised on the conviction that the out-of-doors 'appeals to every normal, healthy individual.' 'Whatever the cause,' readers were assured, 'we revel in the bigness, the freshness and the wholesomeness of it all.' The physiological foundations of the appeal of the outdoors were graphically linked to the canoe: 'The lungs expand to inhale the pure clean air. The muscles harden under the unwonted exercise of paddle and portage.'[23]

Despite twentieth-century modernization, the inclination to seek a cure for one's ailments on the waterways and portage trails has not disappeared, even if the proverbial association with snake oil remedies is much less pronounced. Eric Morse, the leader of a distinguished group of mid-twentieth-century voyageurs-vacationers, described a virtually instantaneous process of revitalization: 'Although we had been on our way for less than 48 hours, the complete isolation and the absorption with wind and waves had put us in another world, another existence.'[24] Omond Solandt, one of Eric Morse's canoeing associates, referred to his mother's description of the canoeing and camping experience as having 'days that iron the wrinkles out of your soul.'[25]

Other devoted followers of the rest cure have illustrated the basis of their convictions. Jack Hambleton, a popular outdoor columnist, thought that one of the attractions of a fishing trip into the north country was that 'when you get up along some quiet little stream and you are away from the crowds ... Nature just heals a lot of your inborn and out-of-sight wounds.' He claimed to have observed the process at work on the veteran Liberal politician Harry Nixon, who served briefly as premier of Ontario in the 1940s. Though initially 'looking white, sick and worried,' Nixon became a different person 'as soon as he got up on Lake Opeongo and changed into some old clothes.'[26]

Don Starkell's extraordinary 'paddle to the Amazon,' a canoe trip from Winnipeg, Manitoba, to South America in the years 1980–2, had its origins in the collapse of his marriage. Born in 1932, Starkell spent much of his early life at the Children's Home on Winnipeg's Academy Road or in the care of foster parents, one of whom introduced him to canoeing on a small creek in North Kildonan. Paddling became Starkell's 'antidote' for childhood feelings of insecurity and alienation: 'I felt free, independent, self-sufficient. When I was paddling that canoe, I was in control.' Competitive canoeing – both amateur and professional – provided a continuing focus for his rehabilitation and personal development, so in the aftermath of his painful marriage break-up it was natural that he would return to the waterways. Starkell's marital therapy took the form of 'a monumental canoe trip,' a two-year expedition of some twelve thousand miles.[27]

But claims about the restorative influence and health-giving effects of nature and canoeing have not been confined to the relief of spiritual anxiety and mental stress. Douglas LePan, a scholar, public servant, and diplomat who is perhaps best known to canoeists for his poetry, referred explicitly in verse to the curative powers of the canoe trip in a physical as well as psychological sense:

> ... here are crooked nerves made straight,
> The fracture cured no doctor could correct.
> The hand and mind, reknit, stand whole for work.[28]

LePan's imagery forms part of the high-water mark for white pine therapy.

It is somewhat more problematic to test propositions about the therapeutic influence of camping and canoe travel than merely to document the claims that have appeared regularly for over a century. There is no shortage of testimonials. L.O. Armstrong, chief colonization officer for the Canadian Pacific Railway in the early 1900s, offered his views on the virtues of a rigorous summer outing. He insisted that his eyesight had improved as a result of 'holidays in the woods.' At fifty-two, after wearing glasses for a decade, Armstrong reported that two or three days' paddling and portaging produced such relief to 'overstrained nerves' that 'for ordinary reading and letter writing the use of the glasses can be dispensed with in a way that would be quite impossible while in the city and at ordinary avocations.'[29] Armstrong's association with a railway active in the business of delivering reasonably prosperous passengers to its chain of wilderness lodges and rural hotels might cause us to discount his evidence on this issue, but this report is by no means an isolated one. Dana Starkell, who accompanied his father to the shores of South America, not only established the basis for a career as a musician during the journey, but also put asthma behind him.

Recently, more systematic efforts have been made to assess the contribution of canoeing to physical well-being apart from general fitness, notably in relation to cystic fibrosis and cancer. In a study commissioned by the Toronto Rotary Club, Bernadette Ferry of the Department of Social Work at the Hospital for Sick Children examined the beneficial effects of summer camping for young victims of cystic fibrosis. The CF child, in the words of the study, 'brings with him a serious health problem, a regimented, time consuming set of daily treatments, a tarnished self-image, a strong sense of social isolation and all too often a fatalistic and rebellious attitude to life.' Whether the experience of summer camp could help to alleviate some or all of these features of the child's condition was the subject of the inquiry. In particular, the research was intended to determine whether improvements in physical health could be detected; whether children's understanding and management of their medical condition would increase; whether greater self-confidence would result, accompanied by some moderation in the CF child's feelings of isolation; and whether, more generally, a maturing would take place that would help the CF victim to 're-evaluate his potential for personal growth and development.'

In 1973 and again in 1974, arrangements were made for patients to spend a month at Camp Couchiching, a site made available to the staff of the Cystic Fibrosis Clinic of the Hospital for Sick Children by the Anglican Diocese of Toronto. Fifty-eight children from communities across southern Ontario participated in a camp program with emphasis on water sports, including swimming, sailing, water-skiing, and canoeing. In the second summer of the program, ten campers selected from the participant group embarked upon the pioneering experience of a five-day canoe trip in Algonquin Park. Medical treatments continued 'bi-daily' at designated sites, where the camp truck arrived with generators, compressors, and other necessary equipment.

The boys who participated – and no doubt a few of the staff and organizers – were initially apprehensive about the physical demands of the outing. Upon successful completion of the trip and with no ill effects to report, observers noted that the young canoeists' 'awareness of newly discovered potential coupled with the joy of having shared plain good fun resulted in 10 very enthusiastic and exuberant "out-trippers."' To realize that their physical limitations were not as severe as they had previously assumed was 'a very definite benefit' for the participants. Overall, the study's conclusions were positive, finding that the greatest gains related to improvement in the physical health of the children and their understanding of the disease itself, to the provision of temporary relief for their parents, and to the enjoyment of a pleasant vacation by the participants. Significant, though less marked, gains were found in the children's ability to manage their disease, their emotional acceptance of it, and their increased maturity.

On the basis of this data it would seem that a month long summer camp for children with cystic fibrosis is a very worthwhile program. For the child who so often feels 'alone' in his dilemma, the exposure to a peer group dealing with similar problems and the opportunity for relaxed, informal discussions with professionals sensitive to his needs is not only a beneficial experience, but in many cases, it would seem, a necessary experience if the child is to develop his full potential.[30]

In association with the Canadian Cancer Society, the Canadian Outward Bound Wilderness School designed and introduced a pilot project in the fall of 1989 for people who have experienced cancer and the stress associated with the disease. After a successful initial program, the organizers offered two further courses in 1990, explaining that their goal was 'to enhance the wellness process and to help the participants view their experience of cancer as a challenge, not a limitation.' Underlying the initiative was a desire to understand more fully the nature of a possible 'connection between wellness and personal will.'[31] And although that connection may be strengthened with program support such as that offered by Outward Bound, as a number of individuals have recorded, simply taking action on one's own can be a positive experience, one in which canoeing can figure prominently.

Sue Sherrod, a Dallas physician specializing in anaesthesiology, recognized the long canoe trip as one means by which she might regain perspective and reassert control over a life driven by the desperate regime of treatments that followed her diagnosis as a cancer sufferer. 'What else can I do?' she asked herself, focusing on the mental and emotional aspects of cancer. 'If I can get these areas of life in better order won't I be more able to fend off this dread disease?' She was already a canoeist when a friend's remark about a Yukon River trip sparked an insight that transformed her outlook:

In a flash I recognize this as a perfect opportunity to end a year of total immersion in the battle against cancer. I could step off the train, at the end of twelve long months of hurtling along, racing to treatments, to work, to group meetings, to therapy sessions, and to doctor's appointments. I could finally rest. On the river, which has always represented peace for me, I could stop thinking about cancer. I immediately say to Beth, 'I want to go.'[32]

Other recent initiatives have sought to deliver therapeutic benefits to canoeists with disabilities. For example, Wild Wise, a Winnipeg-based non-profit corporation associated with the Society for Manitobans with Disabilities, since the late 1980s has organized canoeing tours for participants, who are accepted regardless of age or disability. Founded by Paul Lewis, a registered nurse who went on to study medicine at McMaster University in Hamilton, Wild Wise developed under the guidance of its executive director Allan Bayne and its trip leader Paul Nelham. Participants have claimed benefits and personal satisfaction the nature and origins of which Bayne aptly describes as 'elusive.' Solitude and isolation from conventional surroundings are no doubt contributing factors, but, as Nelham explains the program's approach, personal relations must also play a role:

When I and my staff take people out with a disability they don't get treated any differently than anybody else on the trip; their needs are met just like anybody else's, and if the need isn't valid, it doesn't get met. They don't get catered to in the sense that we bow and grovel every time they say 'boo,' but in the same sense we also make sure that they are comfortable, just like anybody else ... They are just people out there having a good time, working together to accomplish a goal and whatever it takes they all do. One of the things that is important to our philosophy is that we 'job share' and we break down a job into segments. You allow people to do what they can do.

Thus it is not uncommon to find a wheelchair at a Wild Wise campsite, with its occupant possibly tending the fire, assembling tent poles, or otherwise contributing to the general welfare of the group.[33]

The potential contributions of this and comparable programs are suggested by *A Resource Manual on Canoeing for Disabled People*, a guide prepared by Michael Arthur and Stacy Ackroyd-Stolarz. Their review outlines a range of therapeutic purposes that might be served by canoeing: 'Canoeing [helps] to develop upper body strength in a rehabilitation program; canoe camping is an excellent vehicle to begin the development of social skills through the cooperative activity a trip requires; canoeing may be a significant contribution to mental health as it provides a restorative retreat from the stresses and strains of a modern day world.'[34] The British Canoe Union's *Guide to Canoeing with Disabled Persons* offers similar observations alongside detailed commentary on possible responses to the particular challenges involved when amputees or the victims of a number of disabling diseases such as multiple sclerosis, muscular dystrophy, and polio participate in canoe outings.[35]

The healing potential of wilderness travel and the outdoors has also been directed at those – both young and old – whose emotional and psychological suffering can be traced to a variety of social causes. Patti Thom, a director of Camp Tanamakoon, explained that '[a] lot of kids [come] to camp from broken homes because of drug or alcohol abuse,' and that it is an objective of the camp 'to make children stronger, more independent, more able to deal with problems.'[36] More than a few camps, often relying on the canoe trip as a central element of their program, have been dedicated to some form of social rehabilitation. Camp Outlook, founded in 1969, established a wilderness canoe-tripping program staffed largely by students of Queen's University in Kingston, Ontario. Outlook's campers, described as underprivileged and delinquent children aged thirteen to seventeen, the majority of whom are referred from social service agencies, would rarely have experienced wilderness travel. Canoe trips of six to ten days' duration in Algonquin Park provide the setting for intensive contact that can make for 'an individual and group experience of lasting value.' While campers gain in self-confidence, staff too develop a broadened understanding.[37] One female counsellor argued that the canoe trip experience with Camp Outlook would also provide participants with an opportunity to appreciate women as something other than passive creatures or sex objects, for women are fully involved in planning the trip, running the camp, and sterning the canoes.[38]

Boundless Adventures, an organization whose first trip took place in June 1983, evolved into a unique year-round education facility, operating in partnership with several dozen social service agencies dedicated to the needs of inner city youth, the mentally handicapped, adult psychiatric patients, seniors, and women's groups.[39] The 'curriculum' for each Boundless program – generally a five-day outing – is designed on a cooperative basis with agency staff, who ordinarily participate themselves, accompanying their 'clients' into the winter woods or along wilderness waterways. Well over three hundred participants in the Boundless summer program are involved in canoeing.

Steven Gottlieb, the executive director, presents the program's therapeutic contribution in modest terms, insisting that Boundless operates only as an adjunct to treatment:

We're not health professionals. We don't purport to have any long-term impact on our clients. What we purport to do is bring groups closer together, to help people discover their inner strengths by testing their personal limits. We like to see ourselves as providing an opportunity for agencies to learn more about their clients in a different environment and we want to provide our clients with a good ol' fun time.[40]

Jim Risk, a former staff member with Boundless, is another observer whose experience as a guide and leader with both publicly supported and commercial canoe-tripping programs has given him an interesting perspective on their strengths and limitations as a means of transforming behaviour. Speaking of Boundless, Risk explains how wilderness represented a new environment for urban residents, who would learn from the challenges they experienced in various situations along the route. Leaders expected river travel – including whitewater stretches – to present a level of excitement that would remain within the bounds of safety for the participants. Fear on the part of participants occasionally produced 'runners,' or 'kids who took off,' just before a set of rapids, yet Jim Risk's impression is overwhelmingly that most enjoyed the experience and recorded a sense of accomplishment they could not get in the city. The transformative effects were hard to assess. On the one hand, 'a kid by day four would be much different towards us than day one. I think they'd be a lot more genuine. They'd pitch in.' Some would come to appreciate the outdoors, and most would see collaboration within the group in a positive light. On the other hand, said Risk, demonstrating a sense of realism about the practicalities, 'there's not a lot you can do in five days ... I don't know whether I can claim any long-term therapeutic effect at all.'[41]

There are studies, however, to suggest that certain positive – and lasting – benefits are derived from canoeing and wilderness challenge programs. The Women of Courage initiative at Outward Bound, introduced in 1988, was specifically intended to contribute to the well-being and rehabilitation of women who had experienced violence and abuse.[42] Groups of nine women, typically accompanied by a counsellor from the referral agency where they had previously undergone traditional therapy, participate in week-long programs under the supervision of female Outward Bound staff.

In view of the explicitly therapeutic objective of the program, Outward Bound arranged for an evaluative study to be undertaken with particular attention given to the issues of self-esteem and self-confidence. On the basis of questionnaires administered before the course, immediately following completion, and some six months afterwards, Philip Blackford, Outward Bound's executive director, reported findings that were encouraging. Following the course, there were improvements in the immediate or short-term state of the participants' confidence and self-image. That, of course, is much as one would expect, especially in relation to a population whose outlook was significantly depressed in comparison with overall norms in the community. More striking, however, was evidence of a positive shift in the participants' sense of overall self-worth and potential. As Blackford interprets the results:

Having left Outward Bound with a renewed sense of confidence and self-esteem, these women were going back into their day-to-day lives more willing to take risks, more willing to try something that they may not have tried in the past, and by doing that they experienced at least some new level of success which allowed them to try again the next time. And so as time went on, their overall world view of themselves over the whole period of life actually continues to improve.[43]

Whereas in voluntary programs the choice of participating in a canoe trip either on one's own or in association with a referring agency is left to the individual, in certain courses of treatment the canoe trip has occasionally been incorporated as a formal requirement.

Homeward Bound in Massachusetts and Project DARE (Development through Adventure, Responsibility, and Education) in Ontario were among the earlier and more elaborate examples of outdoor adventure programming for delinquent youth. Project DARE began in 1971 as an initiative of the provincial Ministry of Correctional Services, the objective of which was to offer 'a unique experience for the multiple recidivist who had failed in the regular training school system.' The program's goal was behaviour modification, with the wilderness experience and training in outdoor skills clearly relegated to the status of means only.

DARE staff were understandably cautious, insisting that the adventure program ought not to be regarded as a panacea. Nonetheless, a senior DARE official argued, on the basis of several years' experience with the project, that the operational theory was essentially sound and supported certain conclusions. A change in attitude and in personal outlook is often demanded by the transition from familiar urban surroundings to the natural environment. Properly managed, this willingness to adjust may serve as a catalyst for ongoing growth and change. Exhilarating activities such as canoeing offer both challenge and excitement, accompanied by the rewards of immediate accomplishment and satisfaction. Such activities, it is argued, 'speak deeply to the needs of students to feel competent.' The small-group structure of the camping and canoeing party enhances progress on the social front by encouraging collaborative teamwork, which 'helps to build trust in human relations.' In addition, trips are structured to take advantage of any dramatic experiences that may offer opportunities for greater self-understanding. Assuming the possibility of building on such insights at the end of the program, once again a process of transformation may be encouraged. DARE, accordingly, overcomes some of the limitations of the promising (but often unfulfilled) potential of a new experience by insisting that the canoe trip be 'viewed in the total context of a young person's life.' Overall, the learning climate offered by the canoe trip helps to establish supportive personal relationships, relationships that are 'warm, intimate and equal, where people may interact with respect, dignity and humanity.'[44]

These observations on the working assumptions of the overtly interventionist Project DARE may offer some insights into the rehabilative potential of canoeing through what I have chosen to call healing pines. The DARE program relies heavily on separation from well-established patterns of behaviour and from the familiar surroundings that reinforce these. The change of environment, the novelty of the outdoor experience, and the intensity of the personal relationships that may develop in a round-the-clock community produce nothing more than an opportunity for change.

Whether or not the potential for restoring one's health in the outdoors or for reorienting a participant's values is realized clearly depends on much that is external to the canoe trip. Yet in either case, advocates assign a great transformative potential to the experience of wilderness canoeing. Comparable possibilities for spiritual enlightenment and renewal or for personal development and character-building are also often associated with wilderness canoe travel.

4

God's Country

In periods of general intellectual uncertainty or in moments of personal anxiety, many people have turned to the natural environment, hoping to renew spiritual values or to reaffirm some lost or threatened sense of order. For others, wilderness and the outdoors may actually have initiated feelings of awe and wonder that later culminated in reverence for the being, force, or power that called these spaces into existence. Such feelings might arise from several forms of experience in the outdoors. Alpine climbers, for example, have always claimed a special connection between their pastime and a spiritual appreciation of nature. Thus, speaking on the subject of Canada's mountain heritage, Arthur Wheeler told members of the Canadian Club shortly before the First World War that 'the one spot above all others where there is no place for an atheist is on the summit of a mountain peak.'[1] For his part, Bill Mason, an artist and the celebrated maker of such film classics as *Paddle to the Sea*, *The Rise and Fall of the Great Lakes*, and *Waterwalker*, has asserted the pre-eminent place of the canoe in the natural order. 'When you look at the face of Canada and study the geography carefully,' Mason once wrote, 'you come away with the feeling that God could have designed the canoe first and then set about to conceive a land in which it could flourish.'[2]

Born in Winnipeg in 1929, Mason acquired a deep appreciation of canoeing from Chuck Tipp, who directed Manitoba Pioneer Camp when the young Bill Mason first attended as a camper in 1945. Operated by Inter-Varsity Christian Fellowship, Manitoba Pioneer had a dedicated staff and nascent but expanding wilderness travel program that provided a very supportive environment for Mason's Christian commitment and his evolving appreciation of nature and the Canadian landscape.[3] Like many youngsters, Mason readily made the transition from camper to junior staff member at Manitoba Pioneer. Unlike most, after completing his studies in fine arts at the University of Manitoba, he was able to transform his devotion to God's wilderness into an artistic career that led to professional recognition in the form of numerous film industry awards, including two Oscar nominations, as well as the enduring affection and respect of thousands of canoeists, to whom he offered inspiration and instruction.[4] 'So who's laughing now?' he would eventually ask about his years of sketching and filming in the outdoors. 'I spent most of my life roaming around out here and getting paid for it.'[5]

Wilderness Treasure, which marked Mason's professional début as a filmmaker, was produced for Inter-Varsity Christian Fellowship in 1959 and later distributed by the National Film Board of Canada. The canoe trip which is the subject of *Wilderness Treasure* provides a vehicle for the celebration of nature as a manifestation of God's work. 'Kum Ba Ya' and 'How Great Thou Art' share the musical honours with traditional voyageur tunes, as the narrative explores connections between wilderness travel and the canoeist's relationship with the Creator: 'There are many treasures in the wilderness for those who learn to look and listen, but the deeper treasures need an understanding that only the Creator himself can give. We've turned from the book of Nature to the book of the written word of God and then back again with an ever deeper appreciation of the one who wrote them both.' The canoe trip experiences recorded in *Wilderness Treasure* and other Manitoba Pioneer ventures were deliberate expeditions into God's world. 'He made it and He placed us in it so that we might delight in it with Him, master it through the wisdom He gave us, use it to His glory and learn from it something of His greatness so that we might bow before Him.'

Thirty years after filming *Wilderness Treasure*, Mason offered the same spiritual lesson in instructional publications designed to convey advice on the art and practice of canoeing to growing numbers of participants: 'A journey by canoe along ancient waterways is a good way to rediscover our lost relationship with the natural world and the Creator who put it all together so long ago.'[6] Mason's enthusiasm for canoeing was unbounded, remarkable even to Eric Morse and his wife, Pamela, whose own devotion to northern waterways is legendary. As Pamela later recalled their conversations, Bill Mason was frequently inclined to talk about his early encounters with the White Dog River, before dams flooded the watershed. 'There's a stretch of water,' Mason would gleefully call to mind, 'and, man, you just bomb it!'[7] In watching Mason skilfully at play in the rapids one suspects a sentiment very much akin to that attributed to the 1924 British Olympic champion Eric Liddell in the film *Chariots of Fire*: 'When I run I feel His pleasure.'

When he died of cancer in 1988, Mason's reputation was international. He was a figure of inspiration for canoeists and the best-known modern exponent of the Christian camping tradition.[8] But he was not its originator. Certainly he was not alone, for the Canadian landscape has provided many generations of wilderness paddlers with opportunities for what one thoughtful observer has described as 'spiritual reassurance.'[9]

The wilderness landscape offered spiritual sanctuary and opportunities for renewal to many nineteenth-century outdoorsmen. 'Happy is the man whose soul is so in harmony with nature,' wrote Sidney Kendall, 'that he finds his chief delight in forest and mountain, flood and field, and draws an unusual pleasure from the contemplation of not only the mightiest but the humblest works of God; such a man can never be really unhappy.' Kendall was aware that the sentiments he expressed were not universal, that for some 'the virgin wilderness represents just so much lumber, or a cover for game: nothing more.'[10]

The poet Rupert Brooke was one visitor to the wilds of North America who gave little indication that what many saw as natural splendour might serve to inspire, at least not without the work of a gifted wordsmith. The young Englishman recorded that it was the 'feeling of fresh loneliness that impresses itself before any detail of the wild.' He seemed unwilling to acknowledge a spiritual potential in the landscape, even though its emptiness afforded his soul 'indefinite room to expand.' On its own, the environment was hardly uplifting: 'There is no one else within reach, there never has been anyone; no one else is thinking of the lakes and hills you see before you.' Dismissing the natural features around him as 'only pools of water and lumps of earth,' lacking both names and tradition, Brooke saw them as 'dumbly waiting their Wordsworth or their Acropolis to give them their individuality, and a soul.'[11]

Kendall, however, was confident in his response to opinions such as those later expressed by Brooke. Another person, he argued, when moving 'among the stately pines' will experience 'feelings akin to those that are experienced when he treads the aisles of some venerable cathedral; the silent forest is to him a temple not made with hands.'[12] In the course of his own sporting adventures in Atlantic Canada, Arthur Silver echoed the sentiment when he proclaimed that 'the glorious sun is touching all things with heavenly alchemy.'[13]

Canoeists who felt compelled to defend their recreational pastime from charges that it amounted to a mere waste of time also invoked the basic wholesomeness and morality of the sport. 'It does not lead to any kind of frivolity, vice, or intemperance,' defenders argued, 'but is rather opposed to all these.' Paddling encouraged 'strength and activity, both of mind and body'; but most significantly, wilderness travel by canoe promoted reverence on the part of its practitioners: 'The canoeist, brought to face the beauties and terrors of nature in silence and alone, is ... more likely to turn his mind to grave and worthy thoughts concerning these things, and the Ruler of them, than he who is hurried along in the distractions of a crowd in trains, coaches, and hotels.'[14]

Although we now readily assume that the canoeist is most likely to experience spiritual enrichment in the wilderness of North America, the most celebrated spiritual canoe trip of the nineteenth century was 'Rob Roy' MacGregor's journey to the headwaters of the Jordan River. Having set out from Alexandria, where the latest version of his trademark 'Rob Roy' canoe – modelled originally on kayaks he had seen in Canada – arrived in October 1868, MacGregor spent the remainder of the year navigating ancient waterways, confident in his belief that 'as no voyager has been mentioned in history to have floated on them thus, it may well be supposed that their full beauties and all their dangers have never been seen before.'[15] An account of the expedition soon appeared, its elaborate title invoking biblical geography – *The Rob Roy on the Jordan, Nile, Red Sea, and Gennesareth, etc.: A Canoe Cruise in Palestine and Egypt, and the Waters of Damascus*. The Jordan, of course, figured centrally in his narrative because 'the springs of this stream so renowned are precisely what the *Rob Roy* came so far to see.' MacGregor's tale combined personal adventure and history with the unravelling of geographical puzzles, yet it was beyond question the story of a modern pilgrimage: 'Already we have lingered where Christ had visited a high mountain, and the Law and the Prophets had met the Gospel each by its noblest representative, to discourse on the great event which is the centre of God's dealings with mankind, the offering of His Son. But now we are looking to where He lived most among men.'[16]

Throughout 1870, the residents of dozens of British towns and cities enjoyed MacGregor's illustrated public lectures on the Jordan expedition, bought his new book with enthusiasm, and benefited from its author's willingness to donate the proceeds of publication and the speaking engagements to any number of local causes and charities. Reviewers were generally favourable, welcoming another account of the lone canoeist's exploits in foreign lands and celebrating the accomplishments of this curious Victorian adventurer. To some observers the author and lecturer showed 'a genial, kindly spirit, and a desire to do good.' MacGregor, a writer 'specially fitted for his task by his intimate acquaintance with the history and geography of the Old Testament,' had produced 'one of the most amusing as well as practical works we have seen on the subject of the Holy Land,' remarked one reviewer. Certain commentators were nevertheless offended by the author's tendency to preach and moralize.[17]

Already well known from his earlier adventures, MacGregor found his stature further enhanced by the Jordan tour. Although he soon became much less active on the water, his association with the Holy Land was entirely in keeping with the legacy of charitable works and public service for which MacGregor was remembered at the time of his death in 1892:

His influence with young men of all classes was remarkable. His ready sympathy with their difficulties attracted them, and his own manly character and pursuits won their admiration. His aim seemed ever to be to show them that Christianity is meant to encourage and elevate the best feelings of our nature, by setting its stamp on every innocent and helpful recreation, with the ultimate view to their own best good and the glory of God. His canoe and other expeditions were the outcome more of a strong and aspiring nature than, as has mistakenly been suggested, of a restless disposition; they gave him a large acquaintance with life and manners, increasing thereby his usefulness in intercourse with others.[18]

But however prominent a role he had played in the emergence of recreational canoeing, MacGregor's exploits linking the canoe with the heavily populated landscape of biblical history never made that setting a ritual destination for religious experiences in canoeing. Instead, the apparent absence of documented human experience from the North American landscape made its wilderness seem to provide opportunities for spiritual insight and reflection.

In any number of testimonials, contact with nature and concomitant isolation from conventional social distractions were the essential conditions of spiritual enlightment. 'It is only a canoe,' Leslie Peabody assured the readers of *Outing* in 1901, 'that can give you these noiseless intimate hours when you listen to the breathing of the world and become a part of the vibrating mystery.'[19] For the readers of *Cosmopolitan*, Isobel Knowles, too, insisted a few years later that

the wild abandon of nature nowhere is so impressive as from the level of its lakes and rivers, and the canoeist riding over its expanses centaur-like – for the canoe and the paddler are as one – feels a part of the great outdoors. The unutterable soul of the waters, and of the trees and the grasses beyond, speak, in the strange sweet voices of nature, and I hear and understand. The friendly branches reach out and caress me, the rippling wavelets patter a musical babble, lapping my hands as I dip the paddle over the side, and no voice of discord mars the sweet harmony.[20]

Eric Sevareid suggested that the cleanliness, expanse, and manifest strength of the north cast a spell on those who travelled there. The result was a 'purifying realization that one is living close to the fundamental elements of life.'[21] While vacationing on Lac la Croix in Quetico country during the 1930s, Florence Jaques may not have felt closer to creation, but the landscape evoked in her a depth of association that seemed to have eluded Rupert Brooke: 'It is so savagely sweet here; a pagan loveliness – Grecian paganism, untouched and pure. With all its wildness you would never be afraid.'[22]

Some regard the separation of spiritual and secular activity as vital to the appreciation of wild nature. Wilderness, argues cultural historian Jonathan Bordo, is

a natural or physical domain which has been deliberately exempted from human use. It is sacred precinct on the analogy to the temple or cathedral whose site and grounds, exempted both temporally and spatially from ordinary human use, have to be large enough 'to ensure physical and psychological separation from the human dominated environment.' It has to be removed from ordinary human occupation in the same way, following the sacred precinct analogy, that the religious experience is removed from ordinary human doings.[23]

It has been suggested, however, that for other cultures, occupation of the land and direct dependence on it for food, fuel, and other material supplies is no obstacle to spiritual appreciation. Chipewyan residents of the Thelon River valley, for example, have referred to the remote terrain that is their homeland as 'God's country' or a 'Garden of Eden' in the sense that the area is a place of life and renewal for the caribou, musk-ox, fox, geese, and other species with which the Natives' lives are so closely intertwined. James Raffan, who has paddled extensively through this challenging canoe country and studied the impressions of its indigenous residents and non-aboriginal visitors, explains what he describes as a 'spiritual respect' for the land:

In the Chipewyan view, the Thelon is much more than a functional place, or a good place to hunt, or a good place to live because there is wood for heat and shelter; the Thelon is connected, as birthplace in an overall cyclical scheme of life on their lands ... The land is connection to the Creator. The Creator is understanding. The land, therefore, is the people's connection to understanding.[24]

Christianity has not always been associated with the landscape with anything like the degree of intimacy implied by the Chipewyan example. Moreover, powerful arguments have represented it as hostile to the natural environment. In an influential paper on the historical roots of the ecological crisis, Lynn White, Jr, in particular has argued that 'to a Christian a tree can be no more than a physical fact. The whole concept of the sacred grove is alien to Christianity and to the ethos of the West.'[25] Despite the force of White's assessment, many paddlers have not hesitated to draw upon the experience of landscape in their personal lives for spiritual enrichment and a sense of affirmation.

The general nature of the Christian camping experience is reflected clearly in the canoe trip logs of a group of businessmen who, during the early decades of the twentieth century, regularly paddled as the 'Tillicum Crews.' The 1923 expedition, lasting from 4 to 18 August, took sixteen men from almost as many small business ventures through the Temagami district of northeastern Ontario. The expedition's diarist, recalling highlights of the holiday in the log's introduction, opened with reflections on the first Sunday evening campfire service. The ceremony, he felt, 'will remain bright in the mind's picture gallery of all the men there.' 'It is ever a great inspiration,' he continued, 'to sit in the company of earnest men, especially there in the great amphitheatre of the Heavenly Majesty so gloriously displayed ... The calm radiance of the stars mirrored in the waters almost at our feet, was as the Balm of Gilead after the hustle and noise of the city and bade us turn our thoughts to the Author of it all.' The Scriptures read around the campfire proved 'so suitable to the grandeur of the night which, with the silent sentinel pines, hemmed us in like the folds of some vast cloak.'[26] Annual canoeing expeditions along these lines provided the Tillicum Crews with cherished opportunities to reaffirm their spiritual orientation and commitment.

Although the spiritual influence of nature was essentially personal, God's wilderness – occasionally now secularized as 'Sunset Country' – was never without commercial potential and institutional appeal. Thus, in an era much less sensitive than our own to the occasional awkwardnesses of formal associations between church and state, provincial officials were willing to find evidence of God's hand in the order – and disorder – of the local geography. The wilderness as a manifestation of God's creative force was a common theme even in the promotional literature of the early twentieth century. The Algoma district, for example, offered 'the most enchanting scenes that the human mind can conceive or Divine Providence provide for the diversion of the harassed business man or woman,' while to the west in Quetico country and the Kenora and Rainy River regions the summer visitor 'is brought more intimately into relation with the dignity, simplicity and the tenderness of nature – the outward expression of the Divinity.'[27] Manitoba Pioneer Camp's Shoal Lake site in northwestern Ontario was in a district with a long history of Christian camping. The Winnipeg YMCA's Camp Stevens – originally a Bible institute on the nearby Lake of the Woods – could trace its origins to the early 1890s. Not long into the twentieth century, visitors to Camp Stevens – depending on their choice of routes – might well have noticed the extensive operation of an Anglican summer camp along the shore.

Other parts of the Northern Shield have provided settings for worship and Christian fellowship. In 1917, Taylor Statten – already a prominent figure in organized camping circles, the YMCA, and other youth movements of the early twentieth century – sponsored a gathering of specialists in 'Boys' Work.' About twenty people from across Canada gathered at Canoe Lake in Algonquin Park for a two-week program under the direction of Philip Fagans, the executive director of the Woodcraft League of America.[28]

In 1918, soon after the first Canoe Lake workshop, the *Manual* for Tuxis boys aged fifteen to seventeen appeared, with an extensive discussion of campcraft and canoeing for both training and program purposes. Operating under the auspices of the YMCA, the Tuxis movement in Canada, which corresponded to the Comrades organization in the United States, 'exemplified dynamic and athletic liberal Christian training' and was 'the main youth wing of the social gospel,'[29] a Protestant reform movement of the early twentieth century whose adherents sought to address the challenges of an emerging collective society on the basis of Christian values.[30] Formally a project of the National Council of the YMCA's Committee on Canadian Standard Efficiency Training, the Tuxis manual was appropriately endorsed by various agencies of the Methodist, Anglican, Presbyterian, Congregational, and Baptist Convention churches. Comparable American initiatives were pursued under the umbrella of Christian Citizenship Training.[31]

Taylor Statten's 'highly idealistic plans for the future of Canadian boyhood' involved an initiative in leadership that was intended to foster a nationwide network. Writing in his capacity as National Boys' Work secretary of the YMCA, Statten invited 'a few boy enthusiasts' to a ten-day camp to live 'with God, with Nature and with each other.' The hundred and forty participants at the Tuxis training camp in August 1920 – at another Canoe Lake site – included boys' leaders from each of the provinces. The participation of young men from England, New Zealand, the United States, India, China, and Japan gave the event an international character. University faculty members and a significant number of Protestant ministers served as instructors in a program that combined physical activity, informal talks, and demonstrations. As Taylor Statten's biographer has explained, the purpose of the camp was to assist these workers 'to understand and interpret Nature in her grandest and least spoiled form, and through Nature to learn more of Nature's God.' The ten-day session in Algonquin Park was designed to strengthen the participants' ability to discharge 'their responsibilities as leaders and moulders of Canada's coming manhood.' The basic formula was successfully repeated in 1921, by which time many of the participating religious organizations had established their own boys' camps. For his part, Taylor Statten was becoming increasingly absorbed with a private camp for boys, Camp Ahmek.[32]

Algonquin Park, having been established in 1893 for the purposes of watershed conservation and wildlife protection, also began to attract a wide range of recreational activity.[33] Camp Minnesing on Burnt Island Lake in Algonquin Park was one of several wilderness hotels constructed by the Grand Trunk Railway between 1903 and 1913. Following a consolidation of railway lines, in the 1920s Minnesing became one of the Canadian National Railways' three Algonquin Park lodges. It then passed into the hands of a group who modernized the facilities for use as a summer Bible study site. A Bible study method developed by Dr Henry Burton Sharman became central to the new Minnesing program.

Sharman, the author or compiler of *Records of the Life of Jesus Christ*[34] and other volumes that formed the basis of an approach to Bible study focusing on a comparative reading of the Gospels, profoundly influenced the Student Christian Movement through the Algonquin Park program.[35] Canoeing was among the abundant 'opportunities for physical upbuilding,' but the aim of the summer seminar was clear: 'To discover the figure of Jesus Christ from a study of the earliest available records of his activities, and to recover the content of his teaching for its bearing upon the personal understanding, direction, and motivation of life.'[36] The Minnesing formula, as described in the testimonials of alumni, was effective indeed. One student camper, recalling a few of the thoughts that came to mind 'in study group, canoe or by the evening fire,' reported that one of his compatriots felt herself 'coming together' at Minnesing, where the environment could produce an 'integrated personality' and teach, among other things, 'the habit of living in the present.' 'When the present is so attractive that the mind can imagine no more happy state, then we are not tempted to look forward.'

In 1946, after more than two decades of operation under Sharman's direction, the Minnesing property was acquired by the Sessions family of Fredonia, New York. Manley M. Sessions had been a camper in the district for some years before the sale of his New York business forced him to seek a new occupation, a quest that led to the acquisition of Minnesing. The Reverend Dr Sharman, then of Carmel, California, at one point found a 'trifling offer' from Sessions to be 'wholly unacceptable.'

Sharman eventually agreed to sell, in part perhaps as a consequence of the determined campaign orchestrated by Sessions to provide assurances as to the worthiness of his intentions for the Burnt Island Lake camp. Taylor Statten of Camp Ahmek, having first determined that the site could not be operated economically in conjunction with his own existing interests, provided a letter of reference, emphasizing to the California minister that Sessions intended a camp 'of the recreational type' which 'no doubt ... will be well conducted.' Richard Firth, Sessions's minister at the First Presbyterian Church in Fredonia, indicated that the prospective purchaser was not only a long-time member of the church, but 'a leader and teacher in our department of religious education' who intended to use the property for 'purposes which are closely related to those which motivated your program in Canada.' From New York the executive secretary of the Chautauqua County YMCA added his voice to the chorus with the observation that the Sessions family 'have been active in religious and character-building work in the community.' This fact, the writer thought, 'would give an assurance that this would not be just another resort without constructive aim.'

On his own behalf, Sessions explained that he and his family proposed to operate Minnesing as a resort for 'eastern college outing clubs and possible nature-study clubs.' The plan was to take groups of about forty young people for two-week periods. But when Minnesing opened for business under the new ownership, it was described as an 'out of the ordinary cedar log resort in the heart of the canoe country.' In so far as groups of any kind were still expected to enjoy the accommodation, 'no expense was spared to make the lodges comfortable, spacious and permanent.' The equipment included 'the best of everything.'[37]

If adolescents such as those who summered with Sharman at Minnesing had enjoyed the luxury of 'coming together' more or less at their own pace and with their own personal objectives firmly in view, some children's camps have been charged with using high-pressure tactics to promote religious conversion. It was not uncommon, argues the historian David MacLeod, for agency camps associated with the YMCA and Tuxis tradition to combine a 'calculated balance of boyish activism by day and serious evangelism at the evening campfire.' A description of the operation at Brooklyn's Camp Tuxis in 1904 suggests how the drama was expected to unfold:

The boys ... are unusually thoughtful and tender. The stars twinkling overhead [and] the sighing of the breeze in the tree tops ... tend towards turning the mind of the boy towards the God of nature ... A few of the older and more manly boys give their personal testimony and now and then a tear falls unheeded down some cheek. It is the critical hour that settles a boy's destiny.

MacLeod has assumed a certain amount of backsliding on the part of campers upon returning home, on the ground that 'camp directors had encouraged confusion between the wind in the trees and the Holy Spirit'; but he has also noted a reluctance among camp leaders to abandon a formula that may have contributed significantly to spiritual reflection and has often grounded genuine lifelong commitment.[38]

Parents and campers doubtless had varied reactions to the inclusion of Bible study and religious services in the framework of an intense summer camp experience. Dorothy Sangster, writing in mid-century on the annual question, Should you send your child to camp? remarked frankly that one man's meat may be another's poison: 'One father I talked with was irritated because his children came home from a small sectarian church camp singing endless hymns and playing Bible Baseball – a table game with moves based on Biblical characters. Another father might have been delighted.'[39] Bible baseball may have been one of the more transitory pastimes, spawned, perhaps, as a regrettable afterthought in the broad tradition sometimes labelled 'muscular Christianity.' But enough has been said to indicate the wide scope of the tendency to associate camping, especially canoe camping, with opportunities for spiritual awakening, growth, or renewal.

'The paddler,' the young Pierre Elliott Trudeau affirmed in the 1940s, 'will have returned a more ardent believer from a time when religion, like everything else, became simple. The impossibility of scandal creates a new morality, and prayer becomes a friendly chiding of the divinity, who has again become part of our everyday affairs.' To illustrate the point, the future Canadian prime minister recounted the comments of his companion Guy Viau: 'We got along very well with God, who is a damn good sport. Only once did we threaten to break off diplomatic relations if he continued to rain on us. But we were joking. We would never have done so, and well he knew it. So he continued to rain on us.'[40]

Camp leaders elsewhere regularly combined outdoor living generally and canoeing in particular with a devotional summer experience. The 1950s brochures of Manitoba Pioneer Camp, where Bill Mason had summered not many years earlier, explained the increasingly intertwined emphases of its mission. Describing itself as a Christian recreational camp, Manitoba Pioneer clearly articulated the two central aims of its program: 'the development of skills which make for the utmost enjoyment of an outdoor holiday, and the fostering of a vital relationship with the Creator.' The daily program was designed with the pursuit of those two objectives in mind. On the skills side, swimming, rowing, canoeing, sailing, aquaplaning, and water-skiing for more senior campers were offered, along with handicrafts, archery, riflery, volleyball, and other land sports. Those who had achieved a certain level of proficiency enjoyed overnight trips away from the main camp, canoe trips, and regattas. At the same time, Christian education was incorporated into the daily camp schedule by means of morning devotions at the breakfast table and a more extended late-afternoon Bible study period.[41]

The relationship of Christian community and the outdoors has been an important theme in the work and teaching of Gordon Stewart, a long-time staff member of the Inter-Varsity Christian Fellowship who served for many years as director of Manitoba Pioneer. With a camping background that included instructional work at Ontario's Bark Lake leadership centre and staff time at Camp Kandalore in Haliburton, Ontario, Stewart was well suited to preside over the further evolution of his organization's wilderness program. Although the staff almost invariably shared a common underlying faith, Stewart concluded that 'most of them lacked any theology ... that really adequately dealt with the environment.' The challenge, accordingly, was to encourage staff – and ultimately campers – to formulate a broader perspective on their understanding. 'It wasn't enough to simply have a mentality that we travelled through the natural environment, but that we recognized it as a sacred trust.'

Most urbanites found this notion hard to understand, Stewart observes, the more so when confronted with the associated contradictions:

If you enter what is a 'wilderness,' by your very entrance into it, it is no longer a wilderness. But you live with the complexities of that kind of reality by saying, we travel through it in such a way that we respect what we find and we leave it as little marked by our presence as we can. The interdependence of humans and other animals and vegetable life and the water that we find and so on, was something that more and more we became both conscious of and sought to teach respect for.

But lest anyone imagine that the new theology was nothing more than the ecology of a warm July, Stewart returns to the camp's second enduring dimension, arguing that two aspects of the relationship to the creation and the creator remain central: 'We're understanding the kind of symbiosis that exists between the natural order and ourselves; and we're understanding our relationship to one another as a community in the midst of that situation.'

The canoe trip was vital, both as the quintessential expression of interdependence in community and as an experience to promote appreciation of the natural environment and understanding of the idea of human stewardship of God's wilderness: 'It has certain basic elements in it; we need one another; we need one another's skills; and we learn together to respect, not only one another in the community but also the environment in which we travel. We can destroy what we find if we're not careful.' A similar understanding informs a work such as *The Black Canoe* by the Haida artist Bill Reid.

As Stewart explains the educational process, we see again the transformative potential so often associated with the canoe trip:

If children, for instance, who are growing into a sense of adulthood, have that kind of focused community experience through a vehicle like a canoe trip, they have made some tremendous strides in their perceptions. How transferable that is into ordinary life is another matter. But even to have the vision of the possibilities, seems to me part of what it is to be a human ... Part of that too surely has to do with our understanding of the gift of the natural order to us; the gift which stresses our stewardship of it as opposed to our simply managing it, or expropriating it for our own uses. And to take that gift and to honour it for what it is, and to be able in a sense to pass it on to the next generation is I think a precious privilege.[42]

But while there can be no doubt that Pioneer Camp remained firmly in the Christian tradition that inspired Bill Mason in the 1940s and led directly to *Wilderness Treasure* in 1959, it is equally apparent that the evolving concern for God's country involved an intense awareness of a physical and natural environment under a growing threat. *The Rise and Fall of the Great Lakes* (1966) and *Death of a Legend* (1968), among Mason's more environmentally critical films, were not far removed from the pathway being followed by others in the Christian tradition as the twentieth century unfolded. Mason's appreciation of the splendour and vulnerability of the natural environment, including its wildlife, was enriched by his extensive experience as a canoeist. Similarly, his understanding of human responsibilities and obligations to nature was underpinned by his sense of the relationship between nature and the God in whom he so firmly believed. An understanding of the reinforcing relationship between Mason's religious values and his sense of wonder and enthusiasm for the outdoors helps to resolve the dilemma he sometimes expressed of being too much of a Christian for his paddling friends and too much of a canoeist for those who shared his profound spiritual commitment.

The concern for community, and the importance of relationships within a small group – for which the canoe trip was so well suited – can be seen in contexts outside the organized camping movement. The Reverend Lois Wilson, a former moderator of the United Church of Canada, an author, a teacher, and a good many other things besides, has never spent much time away from water. 'I cannot conceive of not being on a lake in the summer ... I associate it with renewal, with refreshment, with being in a different space to get ready for the winter.' This lifelong pattern of seasonal renewal on the lakeshores of the Canadian Shield began for Lois at the age of three months, when, as the youngest of five children of a United Church minister, she vacationed in a tikinagan (a cradle board) in the bottom of a canoe. The family tradition of tenting and canoeing holidays dates at least from the time of her parents' canoeing honeymoon, and became a virtually unalterable pattern that lasted through the 1930s on the lakes around Port Arthur, including Superior itself and Lake Nipigon. Then, for many years, the islands of the Lake of the Woods served as the family's summer home. Lois and her husband, Roy, honeymooned there in 1950, entirely successfully it would appear, although she later confessed: 'I didn't marry a canoeist. I forgot to check that out.'

For most of the 1960s, Lois Wilson was back at the Lakehead, where both she and Roy served as United Church ministers. Here she managed to combine her love of canoeing with her responsibilities for the Christian education of young women from the congregation. For most of a decade, Wilson organized canoe trips of a week or ten days' duration for the older girls. The inspiration was straightforward enough: 'It occurred to me that since I loved canoeing maybe they would too.'

Each summer she led groups of about sixteen girls on canoe outings in the Quetico district west of Thunder Bay. Initially, the participants – girls around fifteen years of age – came from the congregation, but in time the group included friends and other applicants from farther afield. Prior canoeing experience was certainly not a prerequisite; indeed, much of the learning was simply about the acquisition of basic camping and canoeing skills, as the young women met and mastered whatever challenges the route and the environment placed in their path. The usefulness of spruce gum to repair torn canvas was among the little survival tricks Lois was once happy to remember learning from her father, and more than pleased to pass on to the victims of a set of rapids on one of her summer expeditions. But the learning, as Wilson later reflected, was not all practical or oriented towards skills. The summer outings were, at heart, 'a venture in Christian education to learn how to live together and to really put us in a context where we could explore some of the biblical insights about what life's about.' With varying degrees of explicitness, this basic impulse animated any number of canoe trips and camp programs during the middle decades of the century.

Wilson is clear that her own Christian faith has come through an understanding of Jesus rather than through nature. Nature 'enhances and fulfils that, but the key to me is the person.' This enhancement, however, can be significant, and Wilson is firmly convinced of the contribution the wilderness can make to an appreciation of the spiritual dimensions of human existence:

The wilderness experience itself is an experience in spirituality ... I mean there is no way you can be in the wilderness without being aware of the creation. I mean, think of the Native people. And also think of being aware of the fundamental things like rock and water and fire and, you know, the elements of things ... So if you get yourself into the wilderness, then I think it talks to you if you shut up long enough, and let it come in on you.

As a source of insights into spirituality, nature has much to offer, with the weather playing a significant role as tutor. According to reflections reminiscent of Pierre Trudeau's acceptance of his limited authority over the incidence of rainfall, Wilson, too, accepted and learned from her inability to control the weather:

Certainly when I was a kid ... I knew ... I could never control the weather. You have to learn to go with it ... And in the city you don't pay any attention to the weather. You feel you're in control, or you try to be. Whereas out in the bush the wind can hold you or rain can hold you or thunder and lightning, all sorts of things ... Who do you think you are anyway? You're just a little person. I mean that's a wonderful thing to be reinforced. There is a sense in which you are part of it. You know, you're not over and above it. You're dependent on it; I mean there is interdependence for sure.

The canoe is an element of the vulnerability that produces real exposure to the elements, thereby reinforcing the lessons of humility.

All the canoe trips Wilson led involved morning worship and a daily Bible study session. Apart from that, participants would do whatever they chose to do – travel, camp, meditate, frolic (within reason) – while the outdoor setting itself provided a backdrop to enrich the understandings acquired. The leisure context allowed participants to relax and to know they were 'not sitting with a blackboard in some church basement getting some stuff crammed into you.' The pedagogical principle at work was simply that 'you can't go camping like that and not know each other.' In consequence, Wilson learned things about the girls on paddling trips that she might never otherwise have discovered, and they learned things about her. Each canoe trip, she estimates, was worth 'three years of ordinary living.' Beyond this deeper appreciation of one another, a further dimension of the experience, over and above learning how to paddle and studying the Bible, revolved around what it means to live in community. Some of the lessons, she recalled, came at a price: 'One girl steps in the spaghetti and ruins the supper and there's no more. You learn about community.' The young women also benefited from being on their own, 'because then we could skinny dip at night and not have the boys around. That was very nice. There was a freedom in that. And during the day too. Wear what we like and do what we like and nobody was trying to impress anybody.'[43]

The recreational canoe trip as described here allowed spiritually oriented campers to reaffirm and to renew their faith in natural settings far removed from the conventions of urban life. The solitude permitted prolonged reflection, while the scale of nature, ranging from the intimate to the majestic, invited further contemplation and reinforced a sense of order and integrity that the constant random motion of the city often undermines. Some particular virtues, with humility a notable example, were also encouraged by the isolation and vulnerability to the elements that form part of canoe travellers' experience. At the same time, the typically communal nature of the canoe trip frequently nurtured a sense of fellowship among participants. How many actually were transformed in some way, spiritually inspired for the first time or in an enriched way, by wilderness canoe travel is more problematic. In other settings, notably the organized youth camps, which became increasingly common over the course of the twentieth century, quite deliberate efforts were sometimes made to promote a metamorphosis of the participants.

5

The Canadian Summer Boy

If exposure to the healing pines afforded restorative possibilities to the 'brain-fagged, weary denizens' of crowded cities, and the majestic wilderness of God's country promised spiritual inspiration or renewal, then a wilderness experience might provide younger canoeists, boys certainly, with practical opportunities for self-development and for testing themselves. A summer experience outdoors, and the canoe trip in particular, often furnished the setting for a formative encounter between youthful campers and a challenging environment. Such experiences were expected to stand them in good stead through the years ahead, for the challenges to be faced and overcome in the rugged outdoors were thought to foster and encourage the development of talents and characteristics such as resourcefulness, ingenuity, and generosity that would equip their possessors to succeed in a variety of later callings and careers.

Canoeing was said to be ideally suited to the development of a boy's character, for the life of the canoeist was seen to be simple, elemental, and primitive.[1] 'Those who seek the pleasures afforded by the canoe and its infinite waterways,' argued the author of an early canoeing guidebook, 'have a great reward in the exercise of ingenuity, the overcoming of obstacles, in developing a creative instinct.'[2] Youthful participants, especially, might benefit from canoe travel, for as the brochure of a leading children's camp explained, 'nothing is so fascinating to the adventurous spirit of a boy as a trip of this nature.'

Cochrane's Camp, originally founded in 1903, and perhaps better known in later years as Camp Temagami, ran trips ranging in length from a few days to several weeks. These canoe expeditions offered (or imposed) experience in portaging, tent pitching, and outdoor cookery, in which each boy would 'take turn at similar duties for his own instruction and the general good of the party.'[3] Either with an organized youth camp or in the company of their fathers, boys would benefit from improved physical health and the proper formation of character: 'And what lessons of manliness, cheery stoicism and self-reliance the primitive life in tents must teach them.'[4] Nearby Camp Keewaydin provided essentially the same package of benefits to boys drawn largely from the United States. Keewaydin campers were soon regularly involved in northern canoe travel to the shores of James Bay via the Rupert, the Harricanaw, the Albany, and other major rivers.

As explained by Bruce W. Hodgins, a historian and camp director, young people were unlikely to be the motivating force behind their own formation. 'In a sense, all children who went tripping were first "sent"; if they enjoyed the experience, they gradually took on the cause and insisted on repeating it annually.'[5] The rationale for the sending took many forms, even including a child's own request inspired by a friend's positive report. Yet as a laudatory review of the Keewaydin Canoe Camp sought to emphasize, highly functional considerations might influence parental decisions about summer camping: 'The parents of the youngsters and students who have spent a vacation in Temagami have not failed to be impressed with the improved conditions physically and mentally of their sons and heirs. Many would find the cost of a holiday in Temagami for their youngsters a valuable investment.'[6] Somewhat more subtly, the *Chicago Inter-Ocean* delivered the same message: 'The American boy takes kindly to the wilderness, and in return the mother of all men gives him strength, physical, mental, moral. And the young fellow who has learned to take care of himself in the wilderness has a better chance to succeed in any walk of life to which his lot may call him.'[7]

Landscape was central to the transformation. This was the crucible in which character could develop, far removed from the less savoury influences and distractions that were presumed to be found in crowded urban centres. Boys dispatched to the blue lakes and rocky shores of the Northern Shield country were not pioneers who went to the wild lands to extract natural riches. Rather, they went there to have something instilled in them. The product of these influences, in which the canoe trip played such a significant role, might eventually emerge as an individual possessing or appreciating such qualities as independence, perseverance, and leadership. In the words of one scribe, 'Self reliance, resource, and independence are brought out as much as possible so that the boy may become a true white Indian.'[8]

The encounter with the primitive and with the ordeals of the outdoors was thought to be valuable from the perspective of individual character formation, but as F.F. Appleton suggested in the immediate aftermath of the First World War, outdoor life might also be regarded as a 'national asset' on the strength of its contribution to the formation of 'clear-thinking, manly-men, men with the strength and staying qualities that the world needs today.'[9] Nor were such sentiments confined to North America. Tanneguy de Wogan travelled extensively in a paper canoe, the *Qui-vive*. In championing a life on the water, however, de Wogan pressed his French countrymen to consider the practical advantages that would accrue to the nation from a serious canoeing regimen. As recently as 1870, the Germans had proved themselves more adept than the local inhabitants at moving through the French countryside. To remedy his countrymen's vulnerability, de Wogan advocated paddling and invoked for inspiration the spirit of the hardy Canadian pioneers. De Wogan found canoeing 'un des sports les plus propres à douer nos enfants de cette aptitude à supporter les fatigues, de cette endurance, comme disent les Anglais, que nous ne possédons pas encore complètement.' Driving the point home, he insisted, 'Oui, c'est le canotage que sont fait des jarrets et les biceps, les bons jarrets et les bons biceps, tels que, par example, en ont, de père en fils, les pionniers canadiens.'[10]

Such assertions about the contribution of outdoor life to physical and character development, to one's professional and commercial prospects, and even to national security have prompted more critical assessments from later commentators, who have targeted the so-called cult of manliness for serious reconsideration. One critic has remarked, for example, that in certain respects, camping around the turn of the century represented 'a nostalgic longing for the apparent simplicity of a masculine past as educators envisaged a complex industrial present.' In the context of organized primitiveness, the argument runs, canoe camping endeavoured 'not to foster rebellion against an enervating culture but to increasingly redirect male anxieties, to reassert a traditional masculinity within the bounds of an extended complacency and obedience to the emerging industrial order.'[11] In part because of the watercraft's association with the explorers and commercial adventurers of a comparatively recent past, canoeing was readily linked in the early years of the twentieth century to 'traditional routes to manhood which had marked an earlier time.'[12] In so far as a new generation of urban North American males was apprehensive about the less wholesome and less desirable influences of the city, 'the isolation of a boys' camp in the wilderness provided the training ground needed for a transition from boyhood to manhood which was free from city vices.'[13] Precisely how a wilderness experience might prepare young men for their future urban lives requires further consideration.

Given the wide range of talents that young canoeists might have to call upon, even in the context of supervised adventure, opportunities would arise for campers to observe and perhaps to emulate much-admired qualities of character. In the more leisurely environment of the turn of the century, when the foundations of youth camping were established, it took a good many summers to produce a 'Canadian summer boy,' whatever his nationality or ultimate purpose might be.

Mastery of the canoeist's art – among other skills – was not achieved without a significant apprenticeship necessitating a considerable dedication of time and effort. As Henry Chadwick explained in *Sports and Pastimes of American Boys*, the knowledge of paddling and sailing was merely the foundation of the canoeist's essential learning. In anticipation of the need to make extensive repairs, the canoeist must also 'learn to be a boat-builder.' The skills of the sailmaker were needed too, 'for he will always be trying to make improvements in the rig of his canoe.' Cooking was naturally part of the repertoire, and included an ability to deal with 'the problems of building a fire with wet wood and of finding provisions in a wilderness.' Moreover, the paddler 'must learn geography with a minuteness with which only the man can learn who personally explores streams on which no boat, except a canoe, has ever floated.' That was not all, for Chadwick also informed his readers that young men 'must learn the art of running rapids and detecting at a glance where the channel through them lies – an art which, more than any other art or known science, develops decision of character.' Discomfort was to be stoically disregarded or, preferably, even welcomed, for boys 'must learn that wet and cold and heat and damp are of no consequence, and can even be made sources of delight.' Above all, boys would have to learn to 'bear with the infirmities of the canoeist who cruises in company with him, and never to shirk his rightful turn of duty in connection with scouring the frying pan.'[14]

Such an inventory of the ordinary demands of a holiday on the waterways clearly carried the suggestion that many of life's challenges – both real and imagined – might have to be confronted in the wilderness environment into which youngsters were transported by canoe. Overcoming the obstacles encountered in some sense constituted a rite of passage and presaged future performance in a variety of situations.

The appeal of the canoe trip as a promising setting for personal development has endured, with succeeding generations adjusting the expectations to accommodate changing values while preserving essential elements of the traditional formula. The experience has been aptly likened to a quest involving the three-part structure of separation or departure from the familiar, an encounter with unknown forces leading to some form of enlightenment or accomplishment, and the return of the seeker – subtly or perhaps quite dramatically transformed – to the point of origin.[15]

Eric Sevareid's experience demonstrates that one didn't need summer camp training to launch a youthful paddling career with transformative implications. In *Canoeing with the Cree*, Sevareid, the future journalist and broadcaster, recounted the story of a 2250-mile expedition from Minneapolis to York Factory on Hudson Bay in which he took part at the age of seventeen with his nineteen-year-old friend Walter Port. 'It was not so much a test of the body,' Sevareid made clear, for 'the body takes care of itself at that age.' Instead, it was 'a test of will and imagination, and they too, at seventeen, have a power and potency which rarely again return to a man in like measure.' Sevareid later recalled of their last big jump into the wilderness from Norway House, in northern Manitoba, 'I knew instinctively that if I gave up now, no matter what the justification, it would become easier forever afterwards to justify compromise with any achievement.'[16] The outdoors performed its assigned task as teacher, for when Eric and Walter returned in October 1934 to their old school in Minneapolis, they saw high school boys and girls from a new perspective: 'We realized that we were looking at them through different eyes. We realized that our shoulders were not tired under the weight of our packs. It was as though we had suddenly become men and were boys no longer.'[17] Although his interest in recreational paddling subsequently diminished, Sevareid relished the challenge he had set himself and delighted in his accomplishments. But introductory voyages have not always been successful.

Nothing, short of the experience itself, could lead one through the anguish and emotional perils of transferring a too-hearty enthusiasm for canoeing to the next generation as well as does 'The Canoe Trip,' a short story by the Nova Scotia author Budge Wilson. Charles, struggling to overcome the oppressively rugged demands his own father imposed at the time of Charles's first father-son expedition, and desperate to instil in eight-year-old Luke the love of canoeing he eventually learned himself, falls victim to a set of aspirations far exceeding the boy's physical capabilities. Parental expectations for the inaugural outing are high, as Charles imagines 'himself and Luke, year after year, setting out in companionable peace and mute understanding, to explore the river systems, to ski the woods, to hike through miles of wilderness.' They will be, in Charles's insistent vision of the future, 'two men doing man things, bringing home tales, fish, wild flowers and adventures, to entertain and nourish his wife and three daughters.'

But Luke, a decade short of the eighteen-year-old outdoorsman Charles has cast in the bow paddler's role, performs according to chronology and not to his father's script. Luke doesn't pack the matches, so lunch is cold; he doesn't see obstacles beneath the water's surface, so the canoe hits a rock; and his youthful awkwardness in an unstable watercraft is a continuing irritant. When Charles finally explodes with, 'Turn around you little fool! And see if just for once you can do it carefully. Try, just try, not to be so fucking clumsy,' he realizes that in under a minute he has totally undermined 'eight years of trying to be a perfect father.'[18]

The overall effectiveness of early camping and canoeing programs in achieving the various character-oriented objectives attributed to them by their original promoters and later critics will never be subject to systematic assessment. However, the proposition that camping and canoeing have the power to influence the course of young lives can be considered from several perspectives. We have testimonials; we have analyses of how a canoe trip offers valuable insights into decision-making and leadership; and, thanks to some enterprising pioneer researchers, we have the results of a limited survey of the views of a group of boys who were – take your choice – either carefree summer campers or the targeted subjects of a program calculated to improve their personal attributes and career prospects.

In a personal account of the enduring influence of the Ontario landscape on their careers, Michael Budman and Don Green, the co-creators of the Roots footwear and clothing chain, explained, 'Wherever we go we carry the lifestyle of Algonquin Park with us.' Having been introduced to canoe trips as summer campers, Budman and Green continued to paddle. 'There is not,' they argued, 'a better experience for building character. It's very rigorous and demanding with everyone working and pulling together and it's an invaluable experience in life.'[19] Another young Canadian, charged with the administration of a six-million-dollar famine relief budget, found himself responsible for guiding a convoy of trucks through the Sudanese desert to destinations that external aid workers had not visited in months. Peter Dalglish attributed his success in this formidable undertaking to his canoeing experience in Canada, which had nourished resourcefulness and a sense of adventure. Exercising 'huge amounts of responsibility' as a teenaged canoe trip leader, he had had opportunities to develop some of the skills and qualities that later allowed him to cross the Sahara with not much more than a set of 1928 British expeditionary maps and an old camp compass.[20] But such convictions – and others that could readily be accumulated – attest only to the belief of a few individuals that their paddling experience was the source of personal benefits or insights which have later proved to be of value. Although the opposite view tends not to be recorded, the ranks of former paddlers may be full of people who are more inclined to say, 'I didn't get much out of canoeing; it's no big deal.' To understand how the learning process might work, a more elaborate analysis is required of the ways in which formative insights and lifetime benefits can be derived from what many observers would be inclined to see as not much more than a holiday.

In the reflective essay 'On Canoes and Constitutions,' Roderick A. Macdonald, who at the time of writing was dean of law at McGill University in Montreal, has tackled a question often found perplexing: How can leadership be taught, or, viewed from another perspective, how can leadership be learned? Macdonald explores leadership in the context of a canoe trip, providing an analysis of the paradox that being in charge will not necessarily allow a leader to command. The point of departure is simply the assumption that those embarking on a canoe trip share an underlying commitment to an enjoyable experience. More or less by corollary – presuming that participants have signed on voluntarily – 'a degree of responsiveness to the needs and wishes of those being led' constitutes a constraint on those in charge. Trip leaders exercise their authority against this backdrop, and, to the extent that the basic expectations are pursued and satisfied, 'members of the expedition either explicitly or tacitly confer upon trip leaders, each in their own domain, a wide margin of discretion to take major decisions.'

As an activity extending over several days or weeks, rather than a contest or event of short duration, the canoe trip continually creates new sets of circumstances in which decisions must be taken and authority exercised. That, as Macdonald explains, has implications for relationships between leaders and for the allocation of responsibilities. For example, although the cook and the guide may have more or less equal authority at the start of a trip based on the contribution that the work of each makes to the well-being of participants, any number of factors – from weather, through route, to 'pure hazard' – may alter their status. In addition, where responsibilities for such functions as navigation, campsite selection, and the preparation of meals have been allocated to several individuals, the boundaries that seemingly divide these functions may shift under constant pressure from changing circumstances:

Should the camp site manager prove ineffectual, the guide may well end up making the real decisions about choice of camp site (ostensibly determined, of course, by the exigencies of tomorrow's paddling schedule), and the cook may effectively take control over camp site layout, including placement of tents and allocation of on-site tasks (ostensibly determined, of course, by the complexity of the meal to be cooked, or the need to finish dinner before an impending storm, or whatever).

Not only does the canoe trip offer a dynamic setting for the exercise and observation of leadership, it also imposes a remarkably responsive feedback mechanism: the leader who affirms the possibility of crossing the next stretch of open water ahead of the coming storm will be publicly accountable for the soundness of such a judgment in reasonably short order.

Macdonald explains the further implications of feedback learning in the canoe trip setting:

Disorganization in one sector has a spill-over effect. If tent site choice is to the swiftest, inappropriate tactical manoeuvering on the water (including in rapids) to gain an advantage may result. The guide's judgement then becomes open to evaluation not only as to its quality for purposes for safety on the water, but also as to its potential impact on camp site management. Moreover, the authority exercised by other trip leaders loses a part of its moral foundation by ricochet.

Yet the transition of leadership from one figure to another is rarely automatic. The task of confidence-building to gain participants' acceptance of new arrangements is a subtle and ongoing process which places a premium on interpersonal skills as well as outdoor expertise. 'It follows,' Macdonald argues, 'that whatever the original allocation of decision-making authority, and whatever the leadership dynamic at the outset of the trip, tacit accommodations resulting from the ongoing interaction of trip members shapes and defines how the allocated authority is actually exercised.'[21]

Less elaborate observations on leadership confirm the significance of style in the choices made by those in charge. A crude but insightful classification by the author and journalist Marni Jackson distinguishes two types of canoe trip guides. One she characterizes as 'the neo-Nazi, more dude-than-thou type,' a leader most likely to impose the discipline of daily mileage targets and to insist on rigorously scheduled campsite preparations. Guides of this ilk are inclined to regard fire-starting, bannock-making, and packing as activities to be performed in only one way, with any deviations constituting unpardonable error. The contrasting leadership alternative is a guide who 'settles into nature like a huge beanbag chair and lets the group find its own style and pace.'[22]

Leadership, of course, is only one of the talents the canoe trip has been expected to nurture and develop. Comparable illustrations exist to suggest how other characteristics can be tested and refined. Mike Jones, an outstanding British expedition canoeist until his death on Pakistan's Braldu River in 1978, emphasized the role of ingenuity in dealing with the challenges presented by canoe travel:

I find it a fascinating experience tackling problems, coming up with solutions and developing the skills and experience to see them through to fruition. Each problem requires its own special approach, whether it be puzzling out how to mount a camera on a canoe or persuading a major sponsor to part with a large sum of money. It's time consuming and sometimes it involves the tenacity of the badger and others the finesse of the smoothest of diplomats.[23]

Jones and his associates derived considerable satisfaction from completing a series of demanding expeditions around the world. Versatility and determination seem to have been central, along with the message that a carefully planned and deliberate approach to risk and adventure is more likely to result in success – not to mention survival.

After considering evidence about the lessons that can be drawn from the canoe trip experience, it may still be appropriate to ask, How many of the virtues taught are also learned? Again, this question cannot readily be answered, although one intriguing sample invites examination. In the 1920s, when Hedley S. Dimock and Charles E. Hendry inquired into the 'purposes and objectives of 73 boys as indicated in their statement of the biggest things a boy gets out of camp,' they found that leadership ability, respect for elders, cleanliness, learning obedience, and the love of God secured fewer than six endorsements each. At the other end of the spectrum, thirty-nine campers mentioned the development of swimming, canoeing, and campcraft skills. 'Mental abililties,' including self-confidence, reliance, and initiative, produced a respectable twenty mentions, at the top end of a central clustering of purposes and objectives also involving courage, an appreciation of nature, fellowship, and sportsmanship. Only fifteen participants found the 'general values' of 'better character, citizenship, morals etc.' worth pursuing.[24] These answers seem indicative of a general inclination on the part of boys, well, to be boys – in their own way, notwithstanding the adult agenda, whether hidden in the demands of an industrial economy or explicitly articulated in a way that camp promoters felt might appeal to those most likely to sign the cheques and pay the fees.

Despite the uncertain evidence of past performance, or perhaps with a view to increased effectiveness, the objective of 'character building' was formally proposed for addition to the constitution and by-laws of the Canadian Camping Association in 1947 as one component of the organization's educational mandate.[25] The thrust of the camping movement, at least by the 1940s, had been redirected towards what Hedley Dimock, a leading commentator, described as 'social orientation and responsibility.' The small group – a chacteristic of camp organization, and of the canoe trip in particular – had emerged as central to the mid-century definition. 'The program of the organized camp,' Dimock asserted in 1950, 'consists of the experiences that are indigenous to group living in the out-of-door setting.' You could do a lot of things in the outdoors, from joining in conferences through participating in athletic programs to convalescing, but ultimately 'the process of living together in groups out of doors is the major content of the camp "curriculum."' The underlying purpose, though, had shifted in reaction to the depression, the rise of fascism, and war: 'The concept of democracy and its significance for camping took on both a deeper and more urgent meaning.'[26]

In the years to follow, providing opportunities for character development and an awareness of social responsibility remained part of the camping community's objectives. In the 1960s, along with skills training, fun, and adventure – among other goals – day camps were expected to facilitate the personal growth of campers. This could involve, for example, opportunities for 'the development of self-reliance, individual initiative and positive values for living.' Social growth, by which was meant the 'ability to get along with others, sense of responsibility to others and understanding of groups and individuals of varied background,' was also to be promoted. In addition, camps were charged with furnishing experiences that could enhance physical and mental well-being and with encouraging 'spiritual responses to camping experiences.'[27]

Meanwhile, the Outdoor Education Committee of the Canadian Camping Association pursued related themes in a brief on the values of outdoor education. In addition to the many possible contributions of camping to the preparation of teachers active in the educational system, the importance of making children aware of 'their roots in the soil, their dependence on the wise use of nature for survival' was to be stressed. Echoing a long-standing theme, the brief argued that if 'the evils of urbanization are to be combatted, contact with nature seems to be an essential ingredient.'[28] The authority of Bruce Hutchison, the well-respected journalist, was invoked:

The underprivileged generation of affluence, travelling in a costly automobile, may get no closer to Canada than a public roadside camp, with hot running water and firewood cut at the taxpayer's expense, and will go home in the pathetic belief that it has been camping. If I had any influence on national policy, the state would put all Canadian children in a real camp for at least a month each summer. That would be the best possible investment in health, sanity and true culture. It might even stave off a revolution against the Great Society whose beneficiaries are beginning to find its imperfections already, as any old wilderness man could have told them in advance.[29]

Once again, a vigorous exposure to the wilderness was promoted as an antidote to a rearticulated sense of moral decay. Affluence had become an evil to be combated, for it was being taken for granted; life was being handed to people on a platter, and they were losing touch with self-reliance, effort, and the experience of doing without. Naturally there were positive and independent features of outdoor life, but the experience was still promoted as an antidote to the debilitating consequences of urban civilization.

One variation on the summer recreation theme has been offered, for much of the twentieth century, through the junior ranger program of the Ontario Ministry of Natural Resources and its predecessors. Arthur Lower, at twenty, was one of those for whom the early summer ranger program provided a first exposure to the northern wilderness. 'After a year at college,' recalled one of Canada's most influential historians in his autobiography, ' I found myself plunging into the wilderness, already hundreds of miles from the familiar.'[30] In 1989 some nine hundred jobs were available at about thirty-five summer ranger camps across northern Ontario, where seventeen-year-olds (both young men and women by this point) could combine a serious working day with training in outdoor skills and a modest level of fishing and paddling. Work assignments might include tree planting, fish stocking, cleaning public campsites, or clearing portage trails. As one supervisor explained, 'We teach them what it's like to physically work and that, yes, there is life beyond the city.'[31]

Another modern variant of the notion that camping is the ideal summer experience may be the sense that the experience can provide an indirect form of advancement. The columnist Roy MacGregor – not Rob Roy MacGregor – suggests that in the age of 'power parenting,' the experience of the canoe trip, campfire gatherings, and Indian lore are clearly secondary to an underlying concern – contacts. 'It is not this coming summer that concerns the Power Parent, but the seasons that will follow that summer 15 or 20 years down the road when this summer's happy camper finally graduates from the Right School.' Only recently have these parents realized that 'the critical connections in more successful lives had been made in places that were cleverly disguised by rustic names and backwoods addresses.'[32] Cynicism aside, the fellowship of the outdoors has helped to shape the outlook of generations, embedding contacts in a wider sense of community.

Although canoeing has had to contend for some time with other current fancies in the camping movement, and must now compete with contemporary fashions such as hockey, computer training, horseback riding, and water-skiing, the attraction of the traditional summer remains strong. Of approximately a hundred thousand young people who attended private summer camps in 1988, some seven thousand were of foreign origin. They came – as one observer remarked – 'because an authentic summer camp experience is equated with Canada in much the same way that Switzerland is linked with finishing school.' Companies specializing in Canadian summer camp promotion for the international market exist, notwithstanding the problems of transition encountered by some participants: 'Kids from some cultures take time just getting used to the fact they can run around and get dirty.'[33]

The ambitious business leaders who have supposedly been sending their offspring to learn the survival skills of corporate culture in the wilderness bear a remarkable similarity to the professional and industrial leaders who continue to fish and portage their way back to a state of health and contentment with the competitive environment of their daily lives. Canoeing still offers significant attractions to the harried corporate executive or professional, who faces relentless pressure in the demanding world of modern business. Paul Rush, a former publishing executive, realized his dream of getting away from it all by taking a solo wilderness trip 'to get things in perspective and shake off the layers of executive stress.' During a mid-portage snack, Rush reflected on the meaning of his adventure: 'I got out here on my own. I have food and fuel and transportation (my arms and a canoe), shelter. I am sufficient.' Relishing the pleasures of temporary solitude, he noticed that as 'the sun goes down and stars come out and the darkness creeps to the edge of the campfire the phone never rings. No directives come down from the 40th floor, no discord bubbles up from the gang in the shipping room.'[34]

So alongside a notion of the canoe's role in bringing about individual transformation, which has been present from the very creation of the Canadian summer boy around the turn of the century, an idea of its contribution to the restoration of troubled spirits has persisted. Somehow this versatile watercraft has managed to keep afloat despite the heavy burden of the contradictory cultural baggage that enthusiastic admirers have piled between the gunwales. And, despite the impression that most of its paddling passengers are male, the canoe has also been a remarkably popular means for women to visit the outdoors.

6

Women and Wilderness

The potential for character-building encounters with rugged terrain and challenging whitewater, while widely regarded as enhancing the attraction of recreational canoe travel for young men, appeared to be of more limited utility for earlier generations of women paddlers. Indeed, to the extent that the canoe trip was regarded as a contest with nature, women were actively discouraged from participating at all, for to tempt fate in the wilderness – to compete or struggle against elemental forces – was variously perceived as too dangerous and as unfeminine, not to speak of the effect that meeting adventurous women in the wilderness might have on the self-esteem of the 'summer boy' pursuing manliness in the company of his peers. Accordingly, whatever the physical challenges, canoeing for women has been intimately connected with a broader concern about female self-development in a social context that has rarely been supportive. Thus, in addition to the direct enjoyment of the waterways, women paddlers have savoured the particular satisfaction of doing something they were expected not to do.

In the early nineteenth century, Susanna Moodie reported some success in her personal endeavours to master the light cedar canoe her husband had purchased, claiming, in fact, to have become 'quite proficient in the gentle craft.'[1] Anne Langton was another English settler who expressed enthusiasm for the Canadian watercraft that was so much a part of the pioneering experience in the Peterborough district: 'I rather prefer a canoe ... I can take a paddle, and at least flatter myself that I do some little good, which is more agreeable than sitting in state at one end of the boat and having nothing to do but observe my companion's exertions.' Having made some headway with her own paddling, she no doubt suffered all the more when her brother John, a settler on Sturgeon Lake who would later chair Upper Canada's first Board of Audit, imposed his own version of security upon her: 'But my canoeing days are over,' she lamented. 'John does not like the responsibility of taking me out in one, and thinks it altogether an unfit conveyance for so helpless a being as a woman.' Native women, as one of Langton's contemporaries observed, appeared to be less restricted. 'The Indians on the shore ran backwards and forwards on the beach ... leaping into the air, whooping and clapping their hands,' Anna Jameson reported of the efforts of male spectators to exhort Native women paddlers to exert themselves to the full during a race. The arrival of the victorious canoe at the landing-place produced a scene suggesting that 'all had gone at once distracted and stark mad. The men, throwing themselves into the water, carried the winners out in their arms, who were laughing and panting for breath.'[2]

In the final decades of the nineteenth century, rowing or canoe club regattas and other organized events occasionally provided opportunities for the participation of women. E. Pauline Johnson (Tekahionwake), born on the Six Nations Reserve near Brantford, Ontario, to an English mother and a hereditary Mohawk chief, was not yet a literary phenomenon when she chronicled canoe camps, regattas, and other club events during the 1890s. As Johnson reported, women were actively involved in the program, or at least as actively involved as most cared to be. 'It is a nice thing to be a lady canoeist. All the men in camp revere you, and if you are a very good paddler, they may do you the honour of imposing on you.' Some women in Johnson's circle took pride in their knowledge of boat building, of the racers and cruisers, not to mention the rules of competition. Such accomplishments may have come at a price, however, for 'the girls who never paddle but loll gracefully with their backs to the bow, while they play the mandolin and look tender things across the center thwart, have much the best time of it, and somehow they always have the best cushions.' Conversely, more physically capable women – those whose paddling skills were fully equal to those of their male colleagues – were 'expected to kneel on a slidy oilcloth affair about as thick as a knife blade, keeping [their] temper angelic and serene the while.'[3]

Women paddlers were in particular demand on two occasions. First, when one of the more indolent male paddlers felt the need of an outing, the capable female canoeist would be astonished by the 'rapid growth' of his affection as it 'springs forth into flower.' The appearance of a long cruise on the program was also guaranteed to increase the popularity of the more athletically inclined women, who were thereupon 'sought by every masculine member of the camp, and the honour of [their] company begged, nay, supplicated for.'[4]

Johnson's writing took a somewhat different focus in 1893, when she inquired into an apparently widespread Canadian prejudice against 'the ladies across the border.' American girls were charged with being 'delicate, petted exotics given to bon bon eating, extravagant toilets and indigestion.' Yet Johnson found them to be 'the finest paddlers, the most sensibly gowned, healthy-appetited girls at the meet.' 'It is a positive treat,' she continued, 'to see the little Yanks run out their canoes in the teeth of the rollicking breeze to ride the treacherous old river in racing craft that Ford Jones or Harry McKendrick would not despise. Like time and tide they wait for no man, but are as independent, fearless and tanned as any boy in camp.' Not only were the Americans singled out for praise, 'La Canadienne' was the target of merciless scorn: 'We see La Canadienne living under canvas, it is true, but she dresses in silken blouses, wears tulle veils, carries la-de-dah walking canes and comparatively few of her ever attempt to paddle forth without a gentleman, and oh! everlasting disgrace, some of her cannot even steer a canoe.'[5] Women who had mastered the paddler's arts underwent something of a transformation over the course of the summer season. Back in town, and even outfitted in her best urban finery, Johnson's 'canoeing girl' would persistently re-emerge in the memory and imagination of knowledgeable observers:

You go to church the first Sunday you are in town, and across the aisle sits Jennie, prinked up in a French challie trimmed with velvet, a flower garden on her head, and gloves on those dear little hands you helped to brown the day you and she went fishing alone up the river. And then this object that is propped up in the pew like a fashion plate fades slowly away, and you see her as she was last week 'up north,' perched on a rock, with her heels hanging down a good half foot below a jaunty sailor dress of blue serge and white braid, it is open at the throat with a big silk tie knotted under the Byron collar, and her pretty little face with its sun kissed nose laughs out at you from under a scarlet Tam o' Shanter.[6]

Johnson regarded 'the canoeing girl' as 'the most laughter-loving, unconventional, sunburnt maiden that the physical culture faddist could desire to see.' Enthusiastic endorsement led her into the realm of prediction, with the assertion that 'without doubt, canoeing is the coming outdoor pastime for girls.'[7]

This positive forecast about the impending popularity of women's canoeing proved somewhat optimistic. It was a further decade before Northway Lodge, Ontario's first private camp for girls, was opened, in 1905.[8] Four summers later, the National YWCA operated its first schoolgirls' camp at Geneva Park on Lake Couchiching, and the program soon expanded significantly.[9] Despite early beginnings and modest participation by women in organized paddling over the years, it was also a long time before wilderness travel and recreational canoe tripping involved women in significant numbers. Explicit discouragement and a variety of social impediments remained the order of the day.

The case against women in the wilderness took several forms. Certain terrain was 'no country for women'; other trips 'could not be done.' Additional deterrents appeared still more fundamental. Leslie Glendower Peabody, a turn-of-the-century canoeist whose paddling experiences had taken her from a Florida bayou to the coast of Maine, was sharply critical of the 'insidious seed planted and guarded over by our grandmothers – the idea that physical development coarsens a woman.' Her own view, firmly expressed in the essay 'The Canoe and the Woman,' was that 'the lightness of the sport puts it easily into woman's kingdom. All the movements are to round the body out and forward, and to expand the lungs at every stroke. It is a splendid training for the muscles of the arms, back and waist.'[10] Many other women, even committed paddlers, remained unpersuaded, thereby suggesting that women truly were limited in their ability to contend with the physical rigours to be encountered in canoe travel. Kathrene Pinkerton, for example, imagining a 'hat, gloves, bag and a dozen smaller articles' to be standard equipment for women on the trail, urged her contemporaries before the First World War at least to minimize the inconvenience they were likely to occasion on the portage. 'About the only way a woman can assist on a portage,' she advised, 'is by collecting and caring for her small possessions and not causing trouble.'[11]

Self-deprecation and even ridicule were commonly used deterrents. 'Earthworms,' a 1920s account of one family's fishing and canoeing vacation, graphically portrays the differences between young Bob, the 'hope of the family,' who is a 'born camper and a keen fisherman,' and his older sister Dulcie. She finds the space allotted to earthworms in the family's packs and suitcases disproportionate with respect to her wardrobe requirements. In response to her father's insistence that 'fussy clothes' are out of place in the backwoods, Dulcie protests that this is hardly true if you want 'to spend a day with friends at the Highland Inn among the smart city guests.' Indeed, the guide might even prove to be a 'young, handsome and very intelligent university student.' Happily for Dulcie, at least in the short term, her mother has managed to smuggle along a muslin dress and a sports hat – crushable, 'but most bewitching.'[12] This portrayal of women paddlers as essentially ornamental was hardly promising in terms of their wider participation in canoeing.

The threat of serious discomfort and indeed of danger, combined with the belief in women's physical deficiencies and temperamental limitations, presented a formidable obstacle, the more so as these attitudes were directed to much more than paddling and canoe travel. Late nineteenth-century opinion, often resting upon rationales emanating from the highly influential and male-dominated medical profession, emphasized fundamental differences between men and women, differences ultimately rooted in women's reproductive function. Women, essentially created for child-bearing, were presumed to be best suited by nature for a domestic role. They were less capable than men in physical labour outside the home. Participation in strenuous activity – including, of course, 'manly' sports – was not only unnatural, but also threatening to vital reproductive machinery.[13] In the early 1900s, research challenging these assumptions began to appear. New findings suggested the beneficial effects of exercise on overall health and the potential for training and conditioning to improve performance. But earlier attitudes remained widely influential.[14]

These constraints surrounded other sports and have been remarkably persistent through the twentieth century at the domestic and international levels. Women faced exclusion or were generally not encouraged to participate. When they did so, they were not encouraged to excel. Limited access to financial support, training, and specialized equipment undermined their endeavours, and their involvement was never given the social acceptance and approval that male involvement enjoyed. Restrictions on the time available to women, especially in consequence of their domestic responsibilities, were also severe. Role models were virtually non-existent or unknown.[15]

Efforts to promote women's participation in recreational canoeing against these obstacles have been supported by two principal streams of thought, evident from at least the turn of the century. One of these has rested on the claim that canoeing appeals to women for more or less the same reasons that it appeals to men, and that they should be equally entitled to pursue any inclination they might have to enjoy the sport, with all its physical attractions and spiritual rewards. From this perspective, the preoccupation with physical differences between men and women has brought about unfair exclusion, for those differences, if not entirely irrelevant, have certainly been exaggerated. According to the second current of thought, women would indeed approach canoeing from an entirely different perspective, based on values that either are distinctively feminine or have been most commonly associated with women. Not only should women have opportunities to pursue and develop their interest, but the entire activity would benefit from the transformation their more active involvement would help to bring about.

Isobel Knowles, an experienced East Coast paddler, described the canoe as 'the primal form of water-craft.' Conscious of what she called its savage origins, she found that 'all the savage in me, all the instinct of revolt, bubble forth as I paddle away from civilization.' As a testing-ground of resourcefulness and the capacity to rise to the challenge of the elements, the canoe trip could serve men and women alike. In 1905, *Cosmopolitan* carried Knowles's 'Two Girls in a Canoe,' featuring the drama of unexpected rapids, a treacherous eddy, and a near upset on Quebec's upper Gatineau River. As the frail craft 'boiled down between the boulders' with 'the current sweeping us on at a rate of fully fifteen miles an hour,' the more experienced of the two women lost her paddle. However, her novice companion, untrained before the expedition began, rose to the occasion and delivered the craft to safety. 'Plainly the river and the forest were in her veins, and the craft of the paddle had come by inspiration. The hesitation of the city-born was dispelled, and with skillful stroke ... she steered safe through the boiling waters of the second pitch.'[16] A wilderness challenge thus stimulated a young female urbanite to acquire new skills and gave her the confidence to use them, just as the crucible of outdoor adventure was intended to transform boys into men.

Several years before Knowles's recollection appeared in print, Ella Walton advanced the view that 'primitive instincts are the same in a woman as in a man, and the woman who will best enjoy life is she who follows most closely in the footsteps of her gentlemen friends and relatives.' A woman who did so, she believed, would readily enough overcome the effects of the social confinement and conventional expectations which were the underlying source of differences. Such a woman would 'forget to be nervous and hysterical, and gain a self-reliance and courage that years of travelling and mixing with the world cannot give.' Walton's advice was to abandon socially constrainting sports such as golf and tennis in favour of 'fishing, hunting, camping, exploring, getting sunburned and dirty.' In the company of the 'rough and hardy, but interesting trapper, guide or fisherman' a woman can feel safer than with 'the polished men of society and learning.'[17]

Other women with canoeing experience explained its significance for them. Kathrene Pinkerton said she had learned 'to love the northland and to feel its lure, as men love it and feel it.' Canoeing thus provided women with 'another of those rare planes upon which they can meet men as comrades' and permitted a degree of mutual understanding and respect not otherwise attainable. Lest this prospect appear too disorienting, Pinkerton assured her readers that there would be no 'corresponding loss in womanliness, even though the woman ceases to expect the usual little attentions made difficult by the toil of portage and paddle.'[18] Pinkerton's reformist agenda clearly was moderate, both in its objective of preserving womanhood and in her acceptance of the rarity of the equality that canoeing seemed to offer.

Canoeing was not a frivolous activity, and certainly not something to be approached casually. There were risks to be considered, as Jeannette Marks, the author of *Vacation Camping for Girls*, indicated in a carefully worded passage that was simultaneously an invitation for women to take up paddling and a warning about the consequences of doing so. The source of the canoe's charm was to be found in its delicate lines, in 'its lightness, its grace, its friskiness, its strength, its motion, its adaptability to circumstances.' But the charming little watercraft might act 'like a demon,' something women would do well to remember: 'The canoe is always high spirited, and, with high spirited things, whether they be horseflesh or canoe, it does not do to trifle. The girl who expects to take liberties with a canoe has some dreadful, if not fatal, experiences ahead of her.'[19]

Another perspective on canoeing also served to promote its appeal for women, but did so without reference to the prospect of adventure or physical challenge and other reputedly manly attractions. 'A Lady's Canoe Trip,' written by Mrs Knox for readers of *Rod and Gun* in the early 1900s, described a guided expedition in the Desbarats area of northern Ontario. The author considered the trip a 'fascinating, healthgiving and wholly delightful' outing. Although the guide lost his bearings along a new route, 'we are not far enough inland to be frightened, and the woods are too full of interesting things for us to be cross.' Finding 'new beauty at each turn' of the river, the author intimated that the focus of her enjoyment differed markedly from that of male contemporaries whose exploits revolved around battles with plump trout and wild game. 'We gather some of the great white water lillies that float on the quiet water,' she confided, 'and carry them in our laps as we paddle on.' The 'bushes of greenery that mirror themselves in the clear water' were a source of delight, as were the wild roses that 'make a spot of tender loveliness among them.' Only the quiet camper, she reminded readers, would ever experience some of the pleasures to be had along the route: 'There is a dear little fat chipmunk waiting for you at the camp site, who will come out and trustingly eat the scraps you toss him from your dinner. If you go there, do not spoil his faith in humanity.'[20] Similar encouragement had come in the 1890s from Bergathora, the veteran author of 'A Woman's Outing on the Nepigon': 'If any of my readers are women who love nature deeply, are content with long idle hours, good appetites, and that blessed opiate a fir bed, let them go to the Canadian river.'[21]

Whether the appeal of wilderness travel was to those primitive instincts women shared equally with men or to some gentler, more feminine side of their nature, there might nevertheless be obstacles to overcome. One inventory identified 'three bugbears,' the first being an aversion to sleeping out. This deterrent produced a simple response of the 'you don't know what's good for you' variety, for sleeping out 'is really where most of the benefit comes in.' If women only understood the effects of the night air on nervousness or mental depression, 'they would spend as long a time as possible sleeping outside dust-laden and dusty walls and fittings.' The second bugbear, thunderstorms, and the third, 'the little numberless things that crawl, and jump, and hop,' were also readily enough dismissed.[22] The bugbears, interestingly, are not presented as significant challenges offering opportunities for character-building or as ordeals constituting a rite of passage. Rather, they are minor impediments, on proper understanding not worthy of serious consideration as obstacles to the essential goal of simply enjoying the pleasures of the natural world.

The problem of getting on with it could more easily be resolved by men, for whom guidance and advice, especially the advice of those who had gone before, was readily available. There was a comparative scarcity of literature on women's canoeing in the first half of the twentieth century, and role models were neither plentiful nor always likely to instil a spirit of 'I can do that too' confidence. Whether or not women knew of Mina Benson Hubbard's accomplishments in crossing the Labrador peninsula to reach Ungava Bay via the George River in 1905, few were inclined to emulate her. Some of those who did regretted their ordeal.[23] Yet essays of the kind mentioned here were appearing with notable frequency in the early twentieth century.

Anna Kalland and her companion, Judy, were 'two lone women up the Hudson River in a canoe' for a three-week period in September 1922. Having heard from friends and acquaintances – male – that the trip 'could not be done,' they encountered no insuperable difficulties on the upstream journey. After setting out from New York, and eventually passing through Albany and Troy, they reached their destination at Glens Falls. Muddy and oily in parts, the river was less notable for its scenic splendour than for the activity concentrated along it – barge traffic, railways, commerce and industry: 'We had been seeing the river in real truth: the moving human life all up and down the wide river, new discoveries at every bend; the poignant beauty of the blending of earth and sky and water, and we had been in the midst of it all, tasting the infinite delight of things as they are.'[24] The underlying accomplishment was independence – asserted by their departure, demonstrated by their performance, and, most important, confirmed to their own considerable satisfaction. The message would not have been lost on readers, and may have inspired any number of female vacationers to undertake comparable outings.

The portage trail – an avoidable obstacle on Anna and Judy's Hudson River route – frequently represented a more significant physical challenge. Whereas flatwater paddling by and large allows the canoeist to set the pace, to determine from one stroke to the next how much force to apply, portages are less accommodating. Indeed, depending on one's route, a portage might simultaneously demand both great strength and great agility. And this demand could well occur at a point where endurance, too, was called into question.

The use of guides could reduce the physical labour expected of female participants, as the same practice relieved a good many middle-class fishermen: 'Some of the portages were stony, and some were hot, but we women had nothing to carry, and with our short dresses and stout boots we were very free.'[25] If there was an appeal for some in having guides along to lessen the physical demands of canoe travel, there were also reservations. Kathrene Pinkerton claims to have advised men against the use of guides and easy trips as a means of encouraging their wives to accompany them. 'Guide-paddled and guide-served,' Mrs Pinkerton proclaimed with a determined opposition to what remained a very common practice, 'she will be shut out forever from the real wilderness. Let her learn it as you have learned it. Let her be your comrade, not your passenger.'[26]

Four New York women have left a survivors' account of the nine Temagami portages they encountered during the summer of 1934, with canoes 'eighty pounds on land (two hundred in the air). They were eighteen feet long, underfoot (forty feet long, I swear, overhead).' With the principal portage expert (she had at least seen the feat accomplished) hobbled at the outset by a sprained ankle, the party began at a disadvantage. Finding it 'a struggle to walk a few steps with the canoe' convinced the others that portaging was 'a dangerous and difficult feat.' Just getting the canoe up and ready to carry proved a challenge: 'We tried various ways of getting under the canoe. Prone fall and knee-chest positions didn't work. We deduced from a blur of green paint at shoulder level on a nearby rock that that might be the way to approach a canoe. Finally Marianne propped one end of the canoe there, got under the middle, and heaved it up where it seesawed perilously.' Marianne, the 'headless victim,' struggled on to an eventual collapse, having encountered most of the pitfalls for which a canoe carrier must be prepared:

Did you ever get the high and windy end of a canoe caught between two stout birches? Did you ever raise the forward end of a canoe over a six-foot boulder only to be catapulted by the impact of the rear end against another rock you thought you'd left far behind? Did this happen to you? I hope, by doggy, it did. The worst of carrying a canoe is that it's all so mysterious – you, with your head in total eclipse, the Moby Dick on top driving forward (or sideways) with a will of its own.

Portage number one may have been an ordeal, but lessons from the school of hard knocks were duly learned. 'The first portage took us all afternoon. But our last one! – duffle all stowed, canoes riding blithely, bottoms up. We were all experts by then.'[27] Perhaps the difference between men and women is less likely to be a few falls ascending the learning curve than a ready willingness to acknowledge some initial scrapes and bangs.

While the success of the New York crew might have inspired others to pursue an interest in wilderness canoe travel, opportunities for young women to learn from experience were often systematically discouraged by organized summer camps, where the ordeal of the portage tended to be avoided. Male guides on the girls' canoe trip would do much of the heavy lifting, or a support crew could be dispatched to rendezvous with the expedition at longer or more difficult carries.

When, in 1948, Dr Carter B. Storr, chair of the Preview Committee for Camping Films for the Physical Fitness Division of the Department of Health and Welfare, Canada, circulated for comment a proposal for an instructional film on 'trail camping,' portaging the wood and canvas canoe remained a problematic issue. The Ottawa YMCA inquired about the film's portrayal of portaging: 'Is this section for girls as well as boys? When girls are on trips without a guide (as they often are), they must not choose a route with long portages. On short portages, three girls carry a canoe. Could this method of lifting, carrying and lowering a canoe be shown in one of the girls' scenes?'[28] And apart from the physical challenges of canoeing, concerns about physical security or personal safety might arise.

'It is quite possible,' some women argued with conviction, 'for two or three women to camp alone without a male companion, and perfectly safe. A dog, a revolver, which every woman should know how to use, and camp within call of a house, is enough protection.'[29] Whether or not such security measures were widely used cannot be determined. They were not uncommon, though: Anna Kalland and Judy included in their outfit 'a .38-caliber, mother-of-pearl handled and a beauty; a blackjack and a nightstick lent by a friendly cop.' This equipment was evidently not selected for its utility in combat against mere wilderness.

For those who did go paddling, the experience often left a rich store of memories of shared adventure, an affection for nature, and a sense of accomplishment. The events of a thoroughly charming August day recorded in the diary of a young camper in the summer of 1942 correspond closely with those that formed part of the ideal mid-century canoeing experience:

Granny woke us up at 8 o'clock and made us a delicious breakfast and we were very sleepy because we had been 'up too late.' Quote Granny. We left at 10:15 and paddled and portaged to Wap on Canoe Lake. We were confused by all the hive of people. Took our shirts off and put them on again. Paddled up the Joe Lake Creek. Had lunch at the dam. Went to the store and bought a map of Algonquin Park and peppermints. We tried to go by the river where we should have gone by portage. Hurt our feet. We saw a friendly deer close by. Pushed canoes over rapids, paddled two feet. Met lots of trips 2 Wap and 2 Ahmek. Said 'How, how, how' and nothing else. Arrived at portage ¼ mile to Baby Joe. Portaged into Island Lake and nabbed the first campsite we saw. We swam, ate delicious fish while Camp Northwood paddled hungrily by. Took pictures of a deer which later ate out of our hand. We did not have to pitch our tents as there was a house. Told ghastly ghost stories. Toasted marshmallows and went to bed.[30]

This episode holds up well against analysis that a more recent commentator has offered of the way in which feminine values might be incorporated more systematically into wilderness travel:

Slow it down. Don't have the distance covered and the number and length of portages be the only measure of success. There should be time and energy at the end of each canoe day for other things besides a quick meal and crashing out. Chances for quiet, private time; close-up looking time; hiking time; swimming time; water fights and digressions; star gazing; let's stay here another day time; canoe sailing; good meals; floating lunches and basking in the sun. There should be a focus on the social aspects of a canoe trip – on the times shared together, as a group or in one-on-one situations. In the canoe, on the portage, at the fire. Having a bit more time at the end of a day (and/or in the middle of it) allows for private time to be alone, to find a quietness for whatever your soul is needing then: to walk feeling the moss under your feet; to crouch watching the waves lap the evening shore or an ant carrying a wasp wing over the uneven ground; to write; to think or not to think; to wonder.[31]

Growing numbers of children's camps provided more opportunities for young women and girls to experience the out-of-doors. One of Margaret Atwood's fictional characters claims to be able to identify the veterans of such camps, long after the experience: 'They have a hardness to their handshakes, even now; a way of standing, legs planted firmly and farther apart than usual; a way of sizing you up, to see if you'd be any good in a canoe – the front, not the back. They themselves would be in the back. They would call it the stern.'[32]

As the popularity of outdoor recreational activity expanded further in the 1970s and 1980s, the participation of women in canoeing and wilderness travel increased dramatically. Lighter equipment, notably canoes and tents, and the dehydrated or freeze-dried food supplies that replaced canned goods had certainly reduced the burden of portages and facilitated easier access to remote waterways. More receptive youth camps and outdoor educational programs also helped to account for the surge, but special mention must be made of commercial outfitters, whose regularly scheduled trips – often guided by women as well as men – provided a convenient way to experience the outdoors.

Yet Meg Stanley has cogently analysed the deficiencies of treating the mere involvement of women in canoeing as a satisfactory indication of equality. Her review of explanations given for the participation of women in canoeing and her assessment of ways in which their canoeing experience was modified from that of male paddlers led her to the conclusion that 'the ideas prevalent in society about the appropriate role of women were incorporated into the canoe trip experience.' On the basis of North American periodical and camping literature from the first four decades of the twentieth century, she argues, for example, that conventions concerning femininity exerted a continuing influence and had the effect of 'maintaining certain standards in clothing, limiting the decision-making role of women on mixed trips, devising purposes which fit with socially acceptable roles for girls and women in society, and warning against too great physical exertion.'[33]

In response to such concerns, some organizations have devoted themselves to leading and outfitting wilderness tours designed exclusively for women. One such organization, the Minnesota-based Women in the Wilderness, has sponsored trips in the Voyageurs National Park, through Quetico country, around Lake Superior, and as far afield as Alaska and the tundra of Canada's Northwest Territories. Promotional literature suggests the distinctive approach to be expected:

Our trips aren't for 'character-building,' – they are designed for fun, enjoying the good company of other women and renewing your friendship with Mother Earth. If you are an experienced camper, you'll appreciate the unhurried pace of our trips, the careful planning that goes into them, and our willingness to explore side paths, go for a moonlight paddle, or help you try something you've never done before.[34]

Another elaboration of the current rationale for encouraging women to experience the wilderness on their own is provided by Ruth Goldman, who has been closely associated with the 'Women of Courage' program at the Canadian Outward Bound Wilderness School. She explains how wilderness can provide a valuable woman-centred experience:

First, women do not often go into the wilderness without men. In the act of going out on our own, we are claiming wilderness as a place for women. We are taking up space, breaking traditional stereotypes of where and how women should be confined. Wilderness can easily be a very safe place for women. There are no men (women's greatest predator). Once we know how to take care of ourselves, there is little else to worry about. There are precious few natural 'predators.' Wilderness is removed from the everyday constraints of society. It can truly be a woman-centred space without the intrusions and demands of men and children. Wilderness is a new environment. There are no old habits, nagging voices, or reminders of the past out there. We can choose to start afresh, to explore different undiscovered parts of ourselves. The aesthetics of wilderness are important. The solitude, peace, and beauty can be great sources of strength for us. The sense of being in and living with wildness is energizing and refreshing. Wilderness nurtures us. As women we are in need of this care.

However much these virtues of the wilderness experience are conceived in the context of nurturing and self-discovery, the ultimate objective emerges as a form of empowerment not unlike the transformation of the Canadian summer boy:

There is a strong feeling of self-sufficiency. Women are able to feel independent of the help of men or any other 'experts.' Everything that is needed is carried with the group ... For all women there is an overwhelming sense of competence and confidence to do something previously seen as impossible. This provides each woman with an opportunity to see herself in an entirely different light as a person who accomplishes extraordinary things. For many women these are often physical tasks because women are used to denial of their physical abilities. It is incredibly empowering for a woman to feel her body doing something she thought impossible.[35]

Having gained some experience, women paddlers have been venturing increasingly far afield. Emergency fire-fighting crews working against a blaze in the forests of northern Manitoba were more than a little surprised when seven young women from Minneapolis paddled through the smoke to the evacuated community of Cross Lake. The group, Femmes du nord, who were en route from Norway House to York Factory, interrupted their journey to help the fire-fighters.[36]

But women canoeists are not simply asserting their independence and claiming an equal entitlement to enjoy, alongside men, whatever challenges and satisfaction the wilderness might offer. Their participation now often rests on a new confidence that they belong and that their presence is legitimate. There has been a growing conviction that women have a distinctive and important perception of and attitude towards nature. As more people have sought out increasingly rare sanctuaries and landscapes threatened by economic development, women have been inclined to reflect and argue that the losses would have been less severe if the male preoccupation with growth, conquest, and the domination of nature had been moderated. Moreover, as the woods and waterways as well as the mountaintops have become more crowded with solitude-seekers, women have offered advice on lowering the impact. *How to Shit in the Woods*, an instructive treatise on a topic that – apart from a vast Boy Scout literature on the trench latrine, and the elaborate instructions of campcraft pioneer Horace Kephart – has often been neglected, is an example.[37]

Another recent phenomenon is the search for archetypes or forerunners of the current generation of women paddlers whose accomplishments can continue to inspire and enhance. Anna Jameson, an author and the wife of Robert Jameson, whose appointment as attorney general of Upper Canada occasioned her North American travels in the 1830s, is among the earliest of the candidates. Her journey around Lake Huron, accomplished largely by bateau, included some canoe travel and provided Jameson with a claim to be the first European woman to run the rapids at Sault Ste Marie. The northern journeys of Elizabeth Taylor in the late 1880s and early 1890s, as well as Florence Tasker's travel a decade later down the Missinaibie and Moose rivers en route eventually to Fort Chimo on Ungava Bay, are also worthy of note.[38] However, most attention has been devoted to the accomplishments of Frances Anne Hopkins and Mina Hubbard.

Frances Anne Beechey, the daughter of Rear Admiral Frederick William Beechey, arrived in Canada in 1858 at the age of twenty as the wife of Edward Hopkins, the chief factor of the Montreal Department of the Hudson's Bay Company. During a twelve-year stay in Canada she travelled extensively in the vicinity of Ottawa and Montreal, and on occasion journeyed by steamer and canoe as far inland as Fort William and Nipigon. With sketchbook in hand she carefully recorded her observations of the closing era of the fur trade, and took in details of the lives of the voyageurs which subsequently appeared in the large oil paintings for which she is now best known. 'All Hopkins's major canvases, and many of her watercolours and drawings,' notes Robert Stacey in a recent assessment of her work, 'feature canoes and canoe travel, and none of these works could have been conceived, much less completed, without the aid of the mode of transportation she so faithfully delineated.'[39]

Frances Anne Hopkins's canoeing credentials are sometimes dismissed on the ground that her canoeing experience was largely or entirely a derivative of her husband's business travel. Not having chosen independently to go, and not having been in charge, she has been seen as somewhat less inspiring and worthy of admiration than she might otherwise have been. A more generous view acknowledges a unique contribution of incalculable value:

For women, independent travel, especially by canoe, was almost unheard of at that time, nor would many have considered it an option ... Frances Anne Hopkins, aided by her husband's encouragement of her artistic endeavours, seized the opportunity that presented itself not only to travel by canoe, but to become the only woman artist to actively pursue the canoe voyage scene.[40]

If there is any reason to call into question Frances Anne Hopkins's status in canoeing circles, none so far has been suggested in the case of Mina Hubbard, whose reputation rests on her personal resolve to undertake her own journey through Labrador; her contribution to exploration; and her success in thereby besting Dillon Wallace, a man who she believed had injured the reputation of her late husband, Leonidas, after surviving the expedition that took his life.

Notwithstanding some measure of discouragement and despite recent perceptions, the active participation of women in recreational canoeing goes back a long time, and that participation perhaps requires a word of explanation. One question that emerges from the story of women and canoeing is whether or not the activity is an exception to the general pattern, in which sport has been charged with reinforcing stereotypes and the sexual division of labour.

Certain distinctive characteristics of recreational canoeing may be relevant. Much of the activity – arguably not a sport at all – takes place in settings beyond the range of conventional supervision and authority. That in itself promises a relaxation of norms, and opportunities to depart from traditional expectations. Moreover, despite some organizational structures, especially in relation to camping and competition, recreational canoeing remains a very informal, unstructured activity largely free from institutional constraints. Thus, participants are fairly well insulated from social strictures and pressure to conform to community expectations.

As for access to the sport, practice and training are obviously worthwhile, but equipment is easily obtained and the essential training – certainly the training for a flatwater holiday – is quite limited. Moreover, just as recreational paddling can accommodate participants with different degrees of physical strength, so it distinctively combines a need for strength and exertion with a need for balance and coordination.[41] All these factors suggest that in canoeing women might have found – despite social pressures to conform to existing norms – significant opportunities for personal fulfilment in experiencing the pleasures of the natural world.

7

Rock Dodging and Other Perils

The idea that 'rapids are to canoers what fences are to fox hunters'[1] has been expressed on more than one occasion to suggest that a thrilling encounter with whitewater was for many – as it remains for some – the central appeal of canoeing. Indeed, whitewater rivers have frequently proved irresistible to paddlers in their vicinity. In New England, for example, residents have long enjoyed a wide range of choice among many regional streams. These comparatively accessible waterways have offered excitement for the novice and continuing challenges for more experienced paddlers. The early European settlers of northwestern Ontario's Thunder Bay district could not so readily reach the many streams and rivers of their thinly settled region, but a day's outing on the Kaministikwia River nevertheless became something of a local ritual: 'One of the joys hereabout is to run the many rapids of this river, in a canoe, and under proper conditions it is a pleasure likely to last for some years.'[2] Like a good many early visitors to the rural outdoors, these settlers welcomed the challenge presented by the powerful river.

Yet a certain amount of initial hesitation at the top of the rapids was not uncommon; in fact, it was a normal reaction, often noted by summer travellers. Albert Bigelow Paine reported that prayer was the first step in his encounters with turbulent Nova Scotia waters at the beginning of the twentieth century. Having thus made peace with the world before taking the plunge, and after surviving the first few rapids, he wrote, '[I] presently gave myself up to the pure enjoyment of the tumult and exhilaration, without disturbing myself as to the dangers here or hereafter.'[3]

A more prudent inclination, even among those captivated by what a French participant described as 'l'enchantement des rapides,' was to emphasize the hazards of a momentary lapse of attention in an unstable medium where the force of the current and the rock could be unforgiving.[4] Mina Hubbard found herself drawn to rapids along the course of her 1905 journey through Labrador, and was repeatedly warned by George Elson and the other guides accompanying her of the danger that inattention along the shoreline could bring. 'I promised to be careful,' she noted,

but not to keep away altogether, for they grew more and more fascinating. I wanted to be near them and watch them all the time. They were so strong, so irresistible. They rushed on so fast, and nothing could stop them. They would find a way over or around every obstacle that might be placed before them. It made one wish that it were possible to join them and share in their strength.

Her description of the rapids on Quebec's George River does much to explain the continuing appeal of that waterway, now more accessible through modern transportation:

There were long stretches of miles where the slope of the river bed was a steep gradient and I held my breath as the canoe shot down at toboggan pace. There was not only the slope down the course of the river but where the water swung past long points of loose rocks, which reach out from either shore, a distinct tilt from one side to the other could be seen, as when an engine rounds a bend. There were foaming, roaring breakers where the river flowed over its bed of boulder shallows, or again the water was smooth and apparently motionless even where the slope downward was clearly marked.[5]

If the risk of accident, injury, or even death has deterred some paddlers, for countless canoe trip participants this was precisely the attraction, a source of exhilaration.

Grey Owl, as the Englishman Archie Belaney restyled himself following a period of metamorphosis in the northern forest, was a still more effective popularizer of the theme of challenge, risk, and adventure.[6] In *Tales of an Empty Cabin* he wrote of the Mississauga (Mississagi), a river where 'rapid succeeds rapid in quick succession.' This river, where well-established portages signalled potential difficulty and cautioned travellers, was not considered dangerous despite its numerous stretches of whitewater:

Most of them we run, some full loaded, others with half loads, saving a lot of work on portages. A few are more in the nature of low waterfalls, or else too filled with stones, and are impossible. There is a marvellously picturesque cataract, running through a chasm in a series of chutes and sudden drops, that is worth the trouble of going off the portage to see. This spot is known as Hell's Gate. The old rapid is too dangerous to run with any load, and the canoes go down empty.

At the more challenging rapids, less experienced canoemen were urged to seek adventure from the shoreline, where they might contemplate the consequences of misadventure from a position of greater security:

In such spots, brother, we leave you on the shore, and I think that the skill and dare-devilry, the utter disregard for personal danger with which a good canoeman flings (there is no other word) a good canoe from place to place through a piece of water in which it seems impossible that anything could live, will furnish you with a spectacle that you will be a long time forgetting. And you may sometimes, too, remember the narrow plot that is a grave, surrounded by a picket fence, at one of them. A man was drowned here a few years ago, an old, experienced trapper, who made perhaps this only one mistake in all his life. Some rivers have their private graveyards, to which they add from time to time.[7]

Small wooden crosses no doubt satisfied those canoeists whose sense of excitement required some confirmation of the presence of danger. Less skilful – and certainly less respectful – paddlers may have found other ways to enhance the intensity of their wilderness experience.

In James Dickey's novel *Deliverance*, Lewis advises Bobby on the subject of liquor: 'Bring all you like. In fact, the sensation of going down whitewater about half drunk is not to be missed.'[8] Other fictional accounts have reinforced the sense of adventure involved in whitewater canoeing. Robert Pinkerton's novel *White Water* refers frequently to river work, and is in some sense an apology for the risk-taking indulged in by some of his characters: 'White water lad, ain't you? Go to it, son, while you can. White water. I know. Never portage unless you have to, and then take a chance. Only ...'[9] For another fictional hero, Esau Gillingham in Harold Horwood's *White Eskimo*, the Ten-Mile Rapids represents 'one wild, continuous ride on the Okak River, a test of nerve and skill that went on and on, hour after hour, hardly a moment when death was more than a second away.'[10]

For the most part, actual paddlers have seemed more inclined to prefer a level of excitement falling somewhat short of imminent peril. Anna Jameson found whitewater canoeing in the company of a skilled and experienced guide thoroughly stimulating, indeed possibly the equivalent of an alcoholic intoxicant. After shooting some three-quarters of a mile of rapids at Sault Ste Marie in a small canoe paddled by a local Indian guide, she recommended the experience as 'an exercise before breakfast' and confessed enthusiastically that 'two glasses of champagne could not have made me more tipsy and more self-complacent.'[11]

The government officials who edited *Camping in Canada* referred to 'the breathtaking dash through the white water of wild rapids,'[12] and in 1924 the magazine *Saturday Night* reminded anglers that the Nipigon country also offered 'rapids to shoot, taxing the dexterity of the most expert to guide the canoe through the maddened, boiling waters without a spill.'[13]

Numerous accounts of canoe trips now treat rapids as a more or less routine element of the expedition, one that simply causes the heart to beat a little faster. In *Where Rivers Run*, the story of a transcontinental honeymoon canoe-trip, Gary and Joanie McGuffin capture the experience well:

Angling the canoe toward shore, we propelled it forward with short, savage strokes. We just nicked the swirling wave below the ledge before bursting into the sluggish backwater. A moment later we were sucked back into the hungry current which rushed furiously toward a second ledge. Just as it appeared that we would go hurtling into that foaming maelstrom, we exerted a few pry and draw strokes, miraculously sideslipping disaster by a hair's breadth.

However frequently the honeymoon paddlers repeated their encounters with rapids, they remarked that the intense combination of their skills and the rampaging forces of nature 'never ceases to excite us.'[14] For the McGuffins, as in so many other recollections of whitewater experience, rapids have been a reminder of the presence of risk, a reminder that variously serves to attract the adventurous and caution the prudent.

Denis Coolican, the author of a series of newspaper articles that first drew widespread public attention to Eric Morse's group of voyageurs in the 1950s, recalls short runs on the Gatineau River near Ottawa in exactly these terms. The rapids, he recollects, were 'something you were warned against by your mother but encouraged to do by your father if anyone ever suggested it.'[15]

Mishaps have always occurred, and were sometimes discussed for the benefit of future travellers. 'Running the Rapids with an Amateur' was typical of articles designed to give inexperienced canoeists warning and advice. Here, the 'old hand' lamented his experience on Nova Scotia's Tusket River with 'a fellow who did not understand the game of shooting a rapid.' Despite careful scouting of the river, when the decisive moment arrived, 'Bob got rattled, and … gave a fierce stroke in the wrong direction, when with a sickening crash, we fouled the ledge – just a second of suspense – and the raging waters closed over our heads.'[16] The 'old hand' lived to tell the tale, and we can only hope that Bob learned his lesson. Such encounters perhaps even have added to the appeal of whitewater rivers.

For recreational paddlers as a community, the challenge has constantly been to maintain enough sense of actual danger to preserve the allure of canoe travel for those to whom a modest dose of danger is attractive, without alarming onlookers to the point that regulations become prohibitive, or that fear undermines enjoyment. Deaths associated with canoeing in Canada, not all involving rapids, amounted to 43, 39, and 26 in the years 1991, 1992, and 1993 respectively.[17] Risk thus remains a consideration canoeists have had to address in defence of an activity they enjoy. The responses have been varied. Canoeists have repeatedly found themselves defending their chosen watercraft and redirecting blame for accidents away from the vessel and towards its inexperienced or unqualified occupants. They have produced increasingly elaborate instructional procedures, and they have often incorporated measures to comply with regulations intended to increase their safety. These measures remain supplemental, however, to an awareness of the actual perils that canoe travel might present. Short of firsthand experience of a tragic mishap, cautionary tales such as Bob's adventure with the Tusket River have served as the best reminders to recreational paddlers of what they are expected to take precautions against.

In some respects, cautionary tales, whatever their instructional merits, have served to safeguard recreational canoeing and the watercraft itself from the criticism which has inevitably arisen in the wake of fatal accidents, whether or not these involved whitewater. Robert Pinkerton, the author of the novel *White Water*, was also the author of the early manual *The Canoe: Its Selection, Care, and Use.* In it he acknowledged the potential for tragedy but attributed many accidents to carelessness and ignorance. Pinkerton's perspective was eventually adopted in the well-known proposition 'Canoes don't cause accidents, people do,' and similar assessments were made by numerous other commentators. Ronald H. Perry, in his influential classic *The Canoe and You*, made the point that 'a love for the canoe depends to a great extent on the paddler's ability to manage it.'[18] A properly managed canoe is 'as safe as any other vehicle of transportation,' but the craft is sometimes involved in accidents 'when unqualified people are in charge.'[19] Waldemar Van Brunt Claussen, the national canoeing adviser of the American Red Cross and the Boy Scouts of America, was also anxious in 1931 to counter the widespread impression that the canoe was a treacherous object, and in particular to forestall pressure, in the wake of numerous accidents, to ban canoes or to confine them to 'placid shallow park lakes.' He directly confronted the notion that the canoe was 'endowed with an especially malignant nature' or designed so as to cause destruction to unsuspecting victims attracted by its grace and beauty. The canoe, he insisted, was not treacherous: 'Even in the hands of an ignorant owner it will, in case of upset, remain floating on the surface of the water ready to lend the buoyance [sic] of all the wood in its construction for support in exactly the same manner as would a life preserver under similar circumstances.'[20] The challenge facing Claussen as a defender of the canoe in the early 1930s is best understood against the backdrop of a disaster that only a few years before had inspired a good deal of reflection about water safety, particularly where children were involved.

On a July evening in 1926, a crew of fifteen boys and their leaders from the Brotherhood of St Andrew Leadership Camp on Balsam Lake, Ontario, set off to pick up supplies in nearby Coboconk. They paddled a round-bottomed semi-racing canoe, thirty feet in length with 'torpedo' decks and splash rails. When a sudden squall unbalanced some of the paddlers, the craft capsized and eleven members of the young crew perished in the succeeding hours of darkness.[21] The short- and long-term legacy of Balsam Lake was a heightened concern for safety in institutional canoeing circles, along with a particular apprehension about the actual craft involved in the tragedy.

Correspondence and advice concerning the tragedy reached the desk of the provincial attorney general almost immediately and led to a formal inquest into the incident, a general inquiry into the canoe safety practices at Algonquin and Temagami youth camps, and discussion with federal officials about possible reform measures, including regulations to require night lights on canoes and annual licensing of all small vessels.[22] While the summer camps were cooperative in their replies, there was considerable resistance to the notion that regulations could make canoeing entirely safe, that is, risk-free. Common sense and continuing care were seen as the only appropriate basis of confidence. A.L. Cochrane of Camp Temagami was firm in his insistence that effort rather than rules was the only course: 'My experience has been that printed rules are of little value with unthinking boys. It is only by the most careful and constant supervision, and frequent verbal reiteration, that rules for the safety and well being of a camp in general, can be understood and enforced.'[23]

Summer camp accidents had indeed been rare, yet other incidents took place and were widely reported in the media. In the year immediately following Claussen's handbook, the *New York Times* reported canoe accidents and drownings – including several multiple fatalities – in Chesapeake Bay; at Silver Lake, Massachusetts; at Squam Lake, New Hampshire; at Scudder's Falls, New Jersey; on Lake Champlain; at Beaver Dam Lake in Wisconsin; and close to home at Redman's Neck, New York City. Seven other U.S. canoeists were reported as missing and believed drowned in the same year.

Tragedies on the water cast recreational paddling in a bad light and gave rise to pressure for regulation and restrictions such as those Claussen hoped to avoid. The alternative to curtailment of the activity was an emphasis on the message that basic training in certain essential skills could reduce or eliminate accidents and fatalities. In such circumstances, concern about the process of training, including the development of whitewater skills, was natural.

How were the art of paddling and the skills needed for wilderness travel acquired or transmitted from experienced paddlers to novices, as growing numbers of people became attracted to a canoe vacation? In *Camping and Canoeing*, James Edmund Jones, a Toronto lawyer who travelled from the 1890s with a group of paddlers known as the Aura Lee Club, provided sensible basic suggestions: paddlers were encouraged to examine the rapids in advance, to space canoes out in the rapids, and to lash in guns and other heavy articles of baggage. He was insistent, however, that canoeing could be properly learned only by experience. Jones recalled his father's advice that mankind fell into three classes: 'The first, a very limited class, who learn by other persons' experience – the wise; the second, an inconsiderable number, who learn by their own experience – the mediocres; the third, the large majority, who never learn at all.'[24] Jones senior's definition of the basic categories may be more reliable than his assessment of the numbers therein and his judgment as to the merits of those in each group.

Some vacationing travellers first learned paddling and experienced rapids – upstream and down – in the school of hard knocks. The vast majority, of course, lived to tell the tale, generally a little wiser if not necessarily proficient. The artist A.Y. Jackson, for example, told this story of an early encounter with the waterways around Georgian Bay:

My companion was a very cheerful, careless fellow, as inexperienced as I ... We were paddling against some swift water at a bend in the river. Westengard was paddling bow, rather indolently, and the current caught the bow, swung it sideways, and over we went. We swam around getting all our stuff ashore, retrieving the canoe, and getting it righted. As we were thus engaged another party came down the river. We tried to look unconcerned, as though this was normal practice with us, but they were not fooled. A few miles further up-river, at a portage, we decided to camp and dry our stuff. We made a big fire and unpacked everything.[25]

Having somewhat increased his attentiveness as a result of direct exposure to the water, Jackson pursued his whitewater career in the rapids of the Mississagi with his friend and the patron of the Group of Seven, Dr James MacCallum.

At the turn of the century, Robert Pinkerton published an insightful article, 'The Canoe – Half Stolen,' in *Outing* magazine. He recognized that paddling techniques had been neglected when canoe design was adopted from the Native peoples of North America. Few twentieth-century paddlers would have enjoyed the opportunity afforded young Archie Belaney to learn from Indian canoemen the paddling skills which contributed to his transformation into Grey Owl. As late as the 1930s, however, Eric Morse and his companions studied Indian paddlers to improve their own abilities in whitewater. 'Keeping behind the Indians, and imitating them,' Morse explained, 'proved to be an excellent whitewater "primer."' The central lesson Morse derived from his observations was the importance of back-paddling to increase the time for judging the rapids and steering around obstacles.[26]

Some early recreational paddlers learned canoeing skills as junior staff with government forest fire–ranging crews, although the ranks of long-time rangers and canoemen were thinned by the First World War. Often the new recruits were students, summering on the job in various northern districts. Howe Martyn, a graduate of the University of Toronto and Oxford University whose later business career kept him in England, recalled appreciatively that 'the danger period of fires is three months in the summer coinciding nicely with vacations from Canadian universities.' As a student at the University of Toronto, he had found that neither his youth nor his inexperience was a significant disadvantage with the ranger service, for there was no lack of work to be done. Cash income after expenses was small, but the other attractions were clearly compelling:

It was outdoor life twenty-four hours a day, full of vigorous exercise without strain, as healthy as could be found. Vast areas had to be closely watched, giving employment on a considerable scale. Beyond all this, there was extraordinary experience to be gained, in uninterrupted, isolated months in the wilderness practically spent in a canoe.[27]

Perhaps the attraction of this form of summer activity was conveyed to others by works such as Richard Garwood Lewis's *The Romance of Fire Ranging*, or films like *Spare Time* from the Ontario Motion Picture Bureau. The historian A.R.M. Lower was certainly among those who appreciated their early twentieth-century experience as fire rangers. For four summers, from 1910 to 1913, Lower worked as a fire ranger at either Nipigon or the Matagami Forest Reserve, and then he enjoyed one final year in the north as an itinerant researcher for the federal Department of Fisheries.[28]

Omond Solandt, a distinguished scientist and public servant, was another twentieth-century paddler who acquired at least the basics of his familiarity with a canoe as a summer ranger in the Temagami Forest Reserve. While living with his parents in Toronto, he had occasionally rented a canoe in the course of family holidays at Geneva Park. From summer jobs at Geneva Park, Solandt graduated, after high school, to employment with the Department of Lands and Forests at Temagami, where canoes were much in evidence. However, the nature of his work as a radio operator and assistant to the chief ranger of Ontario's most popular forest reserve was such that he never claimed to be more than a competent flatwater paddler.

The background to young Solandt's association with the canoe is of some interest in light of his later involvement in the crew of 'voyageurs' who paddled so extensively with Eric Morse from the mid-1950s. Both of Solandt's parents had been avid paddlers whose experience of canoeing illustrates the continuity of the tradition from commercial to recreational canoe travel. Solandt's mother, an Ottawa native, spent many summers 'up the valley' at Lumsden's Mills, where Alex Lumsden, a lumber baron of the turn of the century, entertained a handful of close friends and associates at a small hotel with ready access to water and canoe country. She became a keen canoeist, probably a keener one than the young minister who became her husband. The Reverend Mr Solandt, having recently graduated from theological studies at Queen's University in Kingston, began his canoeing career as a student minister in the vicinity of Cobalt, Ontario, where a large population of miners, prospectors, and other itinerants was presumed to be in need of his services. The family then settled in Winnipeg. For the cost of a land survey, the Solandts obtained a small – and not very accessible – lot on the shores of Pistol Lake near Minaki. Here the canoe was very handy indeed.

Despite the association and basic familiarity with canoeing in his background, however, for a decade in England as a scholarship student in pathology, an intern, a resident, and a wartime practitioner, Dr Solandt did virtually no paddling at all. In fact, when Eric Morse and the journalist Blair Fraser first invited him to participate in a wilderness expedition, Solandt acknowledged that he 'was about 41 and hadn't been on a canoe trip.' The attraction for a former Temagami ranger was almost immediate, however, and Solandt became a keen and regular participant in Morse's outings and expeditions.[29]

Aside from the summer forest ranger program, a few youth camps and some canoe clubs were sources of instruction, and information was also to be found in a few early manuals and such outdoor magazines as *Rod and Gun, The Illustrated Canadian Forest and Outdoors,* and *Field and Stream.* One of the more comprehensive instructional canoeing manuals of the interwar period observed that 'there is nothing to compare with the thrill of running a fast rapid'; nevertheless, the author advised paddlers not to run rapids for fun 'unless you are an expert or are paddling with one.'[30] One could follow this injunction and still get on the water. More restrictive advice, amounting in effect to a 'Catch-22,' came from Ron Perry in the popular handbook *The Canoe and You.* 'Shooting rapids,' in Perry's judgment, 'should be attempted only by those who have had considerable experience, and never by amateurs or young people.'[31]

For those determined to contend with whitewater, instructional literature stressed the importance of studying the rapids before a descent. In *Small Watercraft,* a 1931 manual approved by the Canadian Boy Scouts and Girl Guides Association as a handbook for members seeking merit badges, Richard Garwood Lewis was emphatic that one should 'never under any circumstances' run an unfamiliar rapid without first checking its entire course from the shore.[32] In an earlier article he had simply noted the usefulness of standing at the top of a set of rapids for a good view of the route: 'Under ordinary circumstances only a fool stands up in a canoe, but you seldom see a northern Indian start to run any rapid without first standing up in his canoe to take a mental snapshot of the channel just before he enters the swift water.'[33] However, suggestions for reading the water to identify a safe course around obstacles were seldom fully elaborated. Canoeists were expected to identify the location of dangerous rocks and currents, but rarely given any precise instruction about how to do so.

Those fortunate enough to be associated with local canoe-tripping organizations had the distinct advantage of being able to learn from more seasoned paddlers. An outstanding example was the Appalachian Mountain Club, whose novice members were brought along over the course of a season through a series of training runs on easy stretches of familiar rivers. Experience was supported and reinforced by analysis on the blackboard and, at least as early as 1935, by the use of films.[34] Canadians might have benefited from such instructional films as Reg Bloomfield's 1934 classic *Canoeing*, in which whitewater techniques, among other skills, were expertly demonstrated by an international champion.

Of course not everyone tempted by the thrills of rock dodging had the advantages of systematic instruction. Dr N.A. Powell has left a straightforward observation on the predictable consequences of failing to master one of the central lessons: 'The rapids we try to divide into two classes: – those which can be run and those which cannot. That mistakes are made in relegating certain of these to their proper class, is demonstrated by wrecks of canoes to be seen in a number of places.'[35]

For many people, apart from those simply willing to take their chances, the decision about what could be run in a canoe and the choice of a suitable route became intimately connected with consideration of the technique to be used. Speed and steering in rapids were subjects of particular interest to those who contemplated Grey Owl's heroes 'flinging' themselves into the turbulence, as Eric Morse's mid-century enlightenment in the presence of some Indian canoemen will have suggested. The relation between the speed of the canoe and the speed of the current was recognized as an important factor in maintaining control, although inconsistent advice had been available over the years as to whether a faster or a slower approach was more appropriate.

'Rob Roy' MacGregor encouraged a fast approach to rapids in some of his early advice on rocks and currents in *A Thousand Miles in the Rob Roy Canoe on Twenty Rivers and Lakes of Europe*. Ultimate proficiency, MacGregor sought to persuade his readers, would enable the canoeist 'to steer without thinking about it, and therefore to enjoy the conversation of other people on the bank or the scenery, while he is rapidly speeding through rocks, eddies, and currents.'[36] Travelling faster than the current in order to maintain some control on steering became a well-established practice. However, the alternative technique of back-paddling to go slower than the current was also recognized, as *The Field* insisted in 1892, the year of MacGregor's death: 'The one great feature as to the canoe is that she must be capable of being "shifted" sideways across the stream by back or knife-edge strokes of the single-bladed paddle.'[37] 'The slower speed,' explained Elton Jessup for an American audience in *The Boy's Book of Canoeing* in 1926, is the safer of the two although not always as practicable ... In many instances, you can check your speed as needed by backpaddling with vigorous 'shove back' strokes. In extremely swift water, however, paddles haven't the power to hold you back. Therefore, your only alternative in such conditions is in getting steerage way by travelling faster than the current.[38]

Richard Garwood Lewis also expressed a preference for travelling more slowly than the current. He explained to the Scouts and Guides and other readers of *Small Watercraft* that it was neither necessary nor advisable for the canoe to travel faster than the speed of the water to maintain steerage. 'If the current is slow and obstacles can be seen well ahead the canoe can be paddled faster than the current and steered around obstacles as in still water.' Faster water or the presence of underwater hazards or snags made slower travelling preferable.[39] The actual principles of steering in fast water were sufficiently understood in the 1920s that Lewis advised paddlers seeking to avoid an obstacle 'to actually drag the canoe sideways into a part of the stream which is passing the obstacle unhindered,' and he explained the combined use of draws and pries to accomplish this feat.[40]

Similar recommendations on speed and steering were to be found in American canoeing literature dating back at least to the First World War. Warren Miller, who served for several years as editor of *Field and Stream*, acknowledged in a 1918 publication that opinion was divided on the issue of speed in rapids. But his own preference – no doubt influential – for the slow style was presented emphatically: 'In swift water full of rocks and snags the principle to aim at is to keep the canoe going slower than the water is flowing.'[41]

Back-paddling is a much more deeply rooted practice among recreational paddlers than some modern accounts would seem to indicate, but for a variety of reasons it has never been a universal preference. The canoeist's typical inclination to enjoy this outdoor pastime in isolation limited his or her opportunities to observe other ways of doing things.[42] Moreover, a number of influential writers continued to encourage speed. In the United States, Calvin Rutstrum insisted: 'Once you have made up your mind to run the rapids, your approach to them should not be slow – but fast – from the quiet water. The speed of the canoe must be faster than the rapids if steering control is to be had.'[43] William Bliss asserted a personal preference for giving the canoe a little extra push at the top of a drop in the water in order to ensure that the stern would clear, although he acknowledged to his English readers the virtues of back-paddling in 'a rock encumbered rapid.'[44]

John W. Worthington went beyond many of his interwar contemporaries both in recognizing that 'a canoe, like the well-known pin, may be pointed one way and headed another' and in describing such manoeuvres as the eddy turn and the pivot.[45] His advice, first circulated through the bulletin of the Appalachian Mountain Club, was soon made widely available to New England paddlers,[46] so interwar canoeists unquestionably had access to certain essentials of modern whitewater technique. Yet it is difficult to estimate how widely modern paddling fundamentals were appreciated and practised during the first half of the century. C.E.S. Franks, in *The Canoe and White Water*, goes so far as to suggest that whitewater skills, having been abandoned by organized children's camps, were effectively lost until the 1950s, when Eric Morse and his crew inspired a wider interest in wilderness travel. The necessary techniques, Franks argues, were reintroduced to Canada by British and European canoeists, who immigrated in significant numbers after the war. These new arrivals provided 'the real stimulus to modern white water techniques,' which were developed and refined by competitive kayakers. The situation, in fact, appears to have been a good deal more complicated than this model of loss and rediscovery via European immigration might suggest.[47]

Whoever taught what to whom, the published instructional materials demonstrate a lively concern for the further refinement and dissemination of skills. They also suggest some sense of responsibility or community linking more experienced paddlers with interested novices. The relatively informal instructional publications on paddling both encouraged and facilitated physical access by urban residents to the waterways, where whitewater served as the gatekeeper on certain routes. If you were not prepared for rapids, you would not enter these pathways. So, as Bill Mason later put it, 'the rapids and falls always have been the lock and bar to this secret world.' Only those prepared to acquire the skills and put in the effort needed to pass through the barriers presented by whitewater and difficult portages would ever enjoy it.[48]

Through films, books, and, later, his *Path of the Paddle* video series, Mason personally made a major contribution towards enhancing the skill level and thus the safety of recreational paddlers. Part of his teaching involved a new vision of rapids: 'To understand rapids and really get to know what they are and how they work, it helps to think of them as a living, breathing organism, like a wild animal.' Depending on conditions, he suggested, a given set of rapids might be 'as gentle as a lamb or as wild as a rampaging rhinoceros, as playful as a kitten one moment and as deadly as a man-eating tiger the next.'[49]

Wilderness travel, including whitewater travel, underwent a major period of expansion in the 1970s and 1980s, when whitewater recreation reached new levels of popularity; camping and remote canoe trips became highly marketable activities. It is not inappropriate to suggest that an industry emerged, catering to what has been called the 'life enhancer' sector of consumer tourism. Forty per cent of respondents to a Harris survey of fifteen hundred vacation travellers placed themselves in such a category, reporting their self-perception as risk-takers who look for adventure and excitement in a vacation, as well as for opportunities for learning and personal development.[50]

Canoeing and kayaking were clearly central elements of the adventure travel movement, which enjoyed popularity among almost all age groups as well as government support. A group of Metro Toronto seniors, aged sixty-three to seventy-eight, and variously described as 'brave,' 'intrepid,' 'courageous,' and 'passionate,' participated in a five-day whitewater canoe trip on Ontario's Madawaska River. Tested in advance for fitness, six Brave Senior Warriors and an equal number of staff took the river's challenge in stroke. Such exhilarating journeys soon became regularly available.[51]

Those less inclined towards the training in paddling techniques that constitutes one element of the personal development of adventure tours could proceed directly to the experience of risk-taking in rubber rafts. The whitewater rafting industry is reportedly a multimillion-dollar business in eastern Canada, with an impressive level of additional activity taking place in British Columbia. Twelve drownings in three separate accidents in British Columbia during the 1987 season provoked some inquiries and the implementation of guidelines and regulations. Candidates for guiding certificates are required to pass both written and practical tests and must also demonstrate familiarity with the rivers they plan to run prior to taking clients on them.[52]

'Rafting for everyone,' also offered as 'sportyaking,' has expanded significantly. In Quebec, for example, New World River Expeditions has introduced one- and two-day outings on the Rouge, the Batiscan, and the Jacques Cartier rivers with 'personable' guides and elaborate camping facilities to heighten – or to reduce – the adventure. At the end of a day on the river, participants can complete their escape by lounging at poolside or relaxing in a hot tub. Rafters concerned about getting bushed in the Rouge wilderness might take comfort from the Polynesian bar, which 'brings the tropics North with a wide selection of exotic drinks.' Anyone truly determined to enjoy an extended season of whitewater adventure is encouraged to contemplate 'heli-rafting' on the 'pulsating' Batiscan River. Strobe lights, one assumes, are optional.

For Mike Jones, happiness could be summed up as

struggling against the huge elemental pounding waters of some strange river, being rushed, hurtled, jolted and thrown about the boat with every muscle of the body and every fibre of the mind fully stretched for survival, as one hurtles excitedly through the swirling waters where no one has travelled before ... At the end of the day, peace, quiet, warmth, food and friendship.[53]

Jones recognized and accepted the risks involved, although he calculated the likelihood of a fatality for an experienced paddler to be quite remote.

In Britain, for the seven-year period from 1970 to 1976 the tally of canoeing fatalities – not all involving whitewater – averaged ten deaths annually. 'When you think that most of these casualties were not experienced canoeists but individuals who went out unsupervised,' Jones argued, 'you can see what a non-lethal sport it is. There are only about two or three deaths a year of experienced canoeists.'[54] Jones, the author of *Canoeing down Everest* and the man who made these encouraging statistical observations about canoeing fatalities in Britain, was a highly experienced expedition canoeist when he died on Pakistan's Braldu River in 1978. Jones met his death while attempting to save the life of a canoeing companion, a not unfamiliar end among canoeists.

The dramatic deaths of experienced paddlers are solemn and sobering milestones for other adventure-seekers. Like Balsam Lake and the 1978 tragedy in which thirteen boys from St John's School in Claremont, Ontario, perished in the open waters of Lake Temiskaming, deaths such as Mike Jones's are embedded in the consciousness of contemporary canoeists. The deaths of Art Moffatt in 1955 and Blair Fraser in 1968 left their marks on an earlier generation of wilderness travellers.

The Vermont-based Moffatt was a veteran northern guide and naturalist when he recruited five younger companions to join him on an expedition from Stony Rapids, Saskatchewan, via the Dubawnt River system across the Barren grounds of Canada's Northwest Territories and down the Thelon River to Baker Lake. An editor of *Ski* magazine, Moffatt himself may have had a hand in the *New York Times* story announcing the trip in May 1955. The party had successfully covered the better part of the difficult nine-hundred-mile route, but was running well behind schedule when, on 14 September, disaster struck. Misjudging the rapids above Marjorie Lake, Moffatt and his canoe partner, Joe Lanouette, floundered through two small falls, swamping in frigid water. The occupants of a second canoe were also submerged, and by the time George Grinnell and Pete Franck were able to rescue their four companions, Moffatt's struggle with the bone-chilling river was over. He was only thirty-six. Ten days later, when the survivors reached a small settlement, the *New York Times* had another headline, '5 Reach Baker Lake.'[55]

Blair Fraser had not even begun his wilderness canoeing career at the age of thirty-six. In fact, Fraser was forty-three before he took up paddling, having been challenged at a cocktail party for provocatively asserting that one Precambrian lake was pretty much like another. But having begun, the respected journalist and broadcaster pursued canoeing and whitewater with characteristic energy, incorporating his insights and experiences into many of his widely read contributions to *Maclean's* magazine. Blair Fraser's son Graham, also a journalist, reflected on the attractions of canoeing for his father:

The trips appealed to more than Dad's sense of historic national identity, or his determination to make up for the athletic excitement he had missed in his youth. There was something in the solitude, the awesome geographical force of the surroundings, the physical effort, and, I suppose, the risks involved, that seemed to mesh with the private, unspoken parts of him.[56]

Fraser's death, again in the words of his son Graham, 'had a dignity and suddenness about it that would have appealed to him,' and when he perished in the Rollway Rapids of the Petawawa River in May 1968, many Canadians experienced shock at the loss of a very familiar personality. Canoeists were reminded that the pleasures of paddling were not without peril.

8

Getting Organized: Clubs and Competitions

The most evocative images of the canoe feature the open or Canadian craft in a wilderness setting. Whether a classic artefact of traditional aboriginal life, a commercial vehicle used by adventurous fur traders and explorers, or, more recently, a recreational vessel in the hands of summer vacationers, the canoe seems most at home in the rugged granite land-scape of the Northern Shield country, in fast and open water, or resting quietly at some remote campsite. But to ignore the extensive history of canoeing as an urban pastime, as an intensely social activity, and as a competitive sport would be to overlook much of the story of this versatile watercraft. Several different traditions and influences lie behind the present state of organized paddling or sport canoeing, aptly described by C. Fred Johnston, the historian of the Canadian Canoe Association, as the use of canoes 'to sprint short distances, to agonize over marathon distances and to manoeuver deftly over slalom gates suspended over white water.'[1]

Elements of competitive canoeing were firmly established in aboriginal and fur trade experience, as nineteenth-century travellers reported. In 1829, while travelling through Canada, John Mactaggart observed 'fifty canoes in the smooth broad lake, voyageurs fancifully adorned, the song up in full chorus, blades of the paddles flashing in the sun, as they rapidly lift and dip.'[2] And while visiting Manitoulin Island in 1837, Anna Jameson watched thirty canoes, 'each containing twelve women and a man to steer,' dart off at the start of a race 'with a sudden velocity, like that of an arrow from the bow.'[3] In the course of their trip to the west coast in 1876, Governor-General and Lady Dufferin witnessed similar events. At Nanaimo, British Columbia, for example, Lady Dufferin saw Indians participate in 'some excellent races, four or five of the large canoes in a race, the men rowing, or rather paddling with all their might – eighty strokes a minute –

leaving quite a sea behind them.'[4] In the 'off-season,' with ice still very much in evidence along Quebec's St Lawrence shores, the midwinter crossing of twenty or thirty canoes was a remarkable event:

The canoe is launched into the water, where there is an opening; the people are provided with ropes, boat-hooks and paddles. When they come to a sheet of ice, they jump out of the canoe upon it; draw the canoe up after them; push it to the other side of the sheet of ice; launch it into the water; paddle till they come to another sheet of ice, again haul up the canoe, cross the ice, and again launch. This continues until they reach the other side.[5]

The formation of canoe clubs and the development of organized canoeing in urban centres throughout North America – and indeed beyond – can be attributed to this Native and voyageur legacy in combination with other influences. The military contributed an administrative structure that could readily be adapted to the organization of an event such as a regatta. Military regattas, held occasionally on Canada's east coast during the 1700s, had become more or less regular events by the early decades of the nineteenth century and provided opportunities for audiences to observe a variety of aquatic contests.[6] This was true in Halifax, Nova Scotia, for example, where the first recorded regatta was staged in 1826 to mark the visit of Lord Dalhousie, then governor of Lower Canada. Crews from British vessels participated in a series of cutter races in Halifax harbour, but were overshadowed in the public eye by Micmac paddlers, whose competitive canoeing aroused far greater enthusiasm. In subsequent years Micmac canoe races helped to sustain local interest in competitive paddling, with the result that some regular competitions shifted to the more sheltered and predictable waters of nearby Lake Banook, where competitive paddling for non-Natives began in 1846.[7] What the young John 'Rob Roy' MacGregor might have learned when his father's Highland regiment was stationed in Halifax in the 1830s remains something of a mystery, however.

British officers in the Halifax area were instrumental in the formation of one of the earliest Canadian canoe clubs, the Chebucto Canoe Club. The canoeing tradition in the Halifax-Dartmouth area remained strong for many years thereafter with the establishment of other, later paddling clubs, including the Knockabout Club, Woodside Aquatic, the North Star Rowing Club, the Lorne Amateur Aquatic Club, the Banook Canoe Club, the Jubilee Club, the North West Arm Rowing Club, and the MicMac Amateur Aquatic Club.[8]

Annual regattas also became quite common in the district around Peterborough, Ontario, during the middle of the nineteenth century. These brought together paddlers and canoe-makers, an association that had an influence on both design and styles of craftsmanship. Shortly after the introduction of a Native canoe race for bark craft in 1846, the regattas on Rice Lake began to include log canoe, or dugout, races. The 1849 Rice Lake Regatta schedule included a four-man bark canoe race and a log canoe singles event for Indians, as well as a second log canoe race for '2 White men,' the specifications reflecting established racial relations and the reluctance of amateur sportsmen to compete against those who earned their livelihood in a canoe. Although rowing and sailing continued to figure prominently in the program, the Kawarthas soon enjoyed an elaborate summer regatta circuit involving canoe events on Rice Lake, Curve Lake, Stoney Lake, Chemong, and Little Lake in the heart of Peterborough itself.[9]

In Quebec, the Lachine Boating Club, the Longueuil Boating Club, and the Grand Trunk Boating Club of Montreal led the introduction of canoe racing, sometimes in connection with crowd-pleasing 'war canoe' races staged by nearby Caughnawagas.[10] Comparable developments occurred in the United States.

Leonidas Hubbard – now remembered for his fatal 1903 misadventure in Labrador – left his reflections on the origin and evolution of the Detroit Boat Club in an article which appeared shortly after his death. 'It was in the neighborhood of 1840,' he began, 'that there were so many men who loved the canoe merely for recreation after business and on holidays that it dawned upon them it would be a good idea to club together and build some sort of house down on the river, where they could leave their boats and a change of clothing.' Clubs, Hubbard observed, become rather complex organizations whose origins and primary purpose are surrounded in confusion, yet 'the idea invariably goes back to just that same principle.' Growth, too, was easily enough explained by the statement that 'when the house was built more men wanted to join, and then men became canoeists just to get the privileges of the organization.' In due course, the clubhouse came to serve as a rendezvous point for men with similar interests, and 'the club as a social feature began its growth.'[11] Allowing for a few regional peculiarities, the local foundations of organized canoeing evolved in a similar fashion in dozens of North American communities over the course of the nineteenth century.

Sport canoeing emerged as one consequence of the expansion of a

North American middle class whose members had the resources to afford such activity and the leisure time to enjoy it. The *American Canoeist*, a newsletter that served canoeing enthusiasts by communicating opinion, advice on technological innovations, and information on forthcoming events, confirmed that its readership consisted of 'clergymen, lawyers, doctors, journalists, manufacturers, farmers, merchants, clerks, and men with no calling at all save that of pleasure-seeking.'[12] In this respect, the organizational dimensions of nineteenth-century recreational canoeing were roughly comparable to those of other sports developed in the growing urban centres of North America. 'The real innovators, organizers, and enthusiasts in the field of sport,' the historian S.F. Wise has concluded, 'were neither the aristocratic few nor the labouring many, but the solidly respectable business middle class and its allies in the professions, the universities, and the military.'[13] The energetic participation of these constituencies was a precondition of both the popularity of canoeing as a competitive sport and its organizational stability.

The same groups also contributed a moralizing element in proclaiming the particular virtues of their pastime: 'Canoeing,' insisted the *American Canoeist*, 'is one of the few sports whose bright escutcheon is untarnished with the slightest taint of professionalism; and it still retains its purely amateur elements and characteristics.'[14] It was hoped that that state of affairs would persist. Professionals were unwanted, the *American Canoeist* observed; it assumed that 'every canoeist will join in the effort to keep them out, together with their twin companions, betting and gambling.'[15]

Neither organized canoeing nor a strict code of amateurism was confined to North America. Commentators in the United Kingdom endeavoured to instil the virtues of amateurism into canoeists with firm discourses on the significance of competition for organization:

Canoeing, so far as paddling racing is concerned, has frequently been asked to claim itself as a separate or distinct sport. It may be so, qua sport, but when it comes to a question of racing by paddling – i.e. by muscle and training, quantity and quality of animal force, it enters the category of athletic sport or athletic competition, and must be covered by the recognized rules of such competitions.

Particular attention was given to amateurism as a unifying theme throughout the sporting world. 'Every branch of athletic sport may have, and ought to have, its own technical rules,' the country gentleman's magazine *The Field* acknowledged, 'but the question of amateur status, inter-sports,

is clearly one-and-common to all athletic competitions.'[16] Such sentiments no doubt reflected middle-class Victorian values and shaped the
origins of organized canoeing in Britain.

'Rob Roy' MacGregor, after completing several of his widely publicized
canoe expeditions, contemplated the idea of an English canoe club while
rowing at Kew in the summer of 1866. Very soon after, as recorded in his
diary, MacGregor and a few associates established the Canoe Club, which
held its first paddling regatta for fifteen canoes in 1867.[17] In 1873, with
Edward, Prince of Wales, as member number 57 and the owner of the
vessel *Risk*, the organization became the Royal Canoe Club and entered a
period of rapid expansion. Not much is known of the Prince's canoeing
career; during the course of his visit to Canada in 1860 he had been
presented with a racing dugout by the Strickland family of Peterborough,
and had been an enthusiastic observer of a voyageur pageant at Lachine.[18]

British canoeing evolved along several fronts during the late nineteenth century. Paddlers might aspire to the challenge of the twelve-mile
race on the Thames from Teddington,[19] although other aspects of the
nautical tradition soon asserted their influence. Technical innovation,
especially that linked to canoe sailing, was inspired by Warington Baden-
Powell, the brother of the founder of the Scout movement, whose adaptations of the basic Rob Roy model resulted in the Nautilus, a heavy,
fourteen-foot canoe intended for open-water sailing.[20] On the basis of
their own long-established traditions of navigation and boat building,
various coastal centres contributed canoe designs that were often associated with the characteristic conditions of the tidal and coastal waters to
which the craft would be exposed. The significance of salt water is seen in
the list of early clubs: Royal Canoe Club, Mersey Canoe Club at Birkenhead,
Northern Canoe Club at Newcastle on the Tyne, Clyde Canoe Club,
Eastern Scotch Canoe Club on the Forth at Edinburgh, Hartlepool, Wear,
Sunderland, Ulster, Humber Canoe-Yawl Club.[21] The Mersey club, for
example, was recognized as the point of origin of the 'large-bodied,
beamy canoes' that evolved into 'canoe-yachts,' first abandoning virtually
all their canoe characteristics and then gradually returning to the fold.[22]

The open Canadian canoe – not necessarily manufactured in the country after which it was named – acquired a considerable following in some
parts of the United Kingdom. The owners of open canoes, however,
appear not to have joined the organized clubs in the numbers that
supporters of these fledgling institutions might have hoped for. 'The
growing popularity of the Canadian canoe among us is remarkable,'
observed J.D. Hayward, MD, of the Mersey Canoe Club in 1893; he

estimated that 'there are at least a thousand Canadian canoes on the Thames alone.' Although this number of enthusiasts might benefit the sport generally if the owners of open canoes were to join existing canoe clubs or even form their own canoeing associations, Dr Hayward observed, this had not occurred 'to any appreciable extent.' The clubs and associations were made up overwhelmingly of decked canoe owners.[23]

The British Canoe Association was first formed in 1887; its object was to promote 'cruises and meets, whereby canoeists of the United Kingdom, irrespective of clubs, may unite for the purpose of cruising and camping,' to secure 'reasonable tariffs for land and water transit of canoes,' to procure 'concessions and permissions for the navigation of canals, streams, and lakes, and, in all possible ways, to procure increased facilities for cruising, camping, and exploration.'[24] This organization, before it was eventually disbanded in the 1920s, catered to individuals and thus focused on a set of considerations which were less relevant to their North American counterparts, who were more likely to enjoy untrammelled water access. To *The Field*, which took upon itself the task of heralding the exploits of canoe sailors and, later, cruisers, the want of a national association of canoe clubs with uniform standards was a constant source of disappointment. *The Field* repeatedly exhorted canoeists to adopt consistent design classifications, to increase the availability of opportunities for real racing, and to abandon handicapping, a system which it considered unworkable and condemned as detrimental to innovation.[25]

British canoeists travelling – or cruising – in Europe reported a high degree of enthusiasm for the sport on the Continent as well. Robert Louis Stevenson, a canoe cruiser with very little interest in competitive paddling and a man not yet confident in his literary vocation, recounted in his first book the story of an 1876 trip from the Belgian port of Antwerp to Pontoise, France. En route, Stevenson in the *Arethusa* and a companion in the *Cigarette* were generously hosted by members of the Royal sport nautique in Brussels, where the local preoccupation with competition and technical refinements almost overwhelmed the pair. As his hosts probed, 'En Angleterre, vous employez des sliding seats, n'est-ce pas?' Stevenson squirmed. Describing himself as one 'who holds all racing as a creature of the devil,' he faced a pitiful dilemma. For 'the honour of old England' he struggled to conceal his ignorance and 'spoke away about English clubs and English oarsmen whose fame had never before come to his ears.' On several subjects, though, including the controversial question of the sliding seats, he was very nearly exposed as something other than the genuine article.[26]

Meanwhile, in North America organized and competitive canoeing flourished. The New York Canoe Club, having introduced a racing program for canoe sailors in 1871, saw rivalries develop rapidly with other American clubs as well as with British canoeists who had been inspired by MacGregor's exploits and were keen to test the innovations of Warington Baden-Powell and others against American boats. The British influence was sufficiently strong that Kenneth G. Roberts and Philip Shackleton have argued in a major study of canoe use and design from Panama to the Arctic that 'the widespread popularity of canoeing in the United States in the final quarter of the century did not spring from a home-grown enthusiasm for the watercraft of the Indians. Canoeing as an American sport was imported from Britain.'[27] Some British initiatives certainly inspired emulation, but it is important to distinguish enrichment from conception. International rivalry stimulated developments on both sides of the Atlantic, and each of the major late nineteenth-century participants – Canada, the United States, and Britain – inspired and learned from the others, borrowing technological and organizational innovations and incorporating these into their domestic traditions.

Not unnaturally in the competitive atmosphere of the 1870s, the idea of a general gathering of canoeists eventually surfaced in the United States. Nathaniel Holmes Bishop, a widely travelled paddler from New Jersey, invited canoeists from Canada and the United States to a congress or convention at Lake George, New York, for the purpose of establishing an umbrella grouping. Following the August 1880 event, some two dozen paddlers from the northeastern United States founded the American Canoe Association, thereby providing a further stimulus to organization.

The Lake George congress of 1880 was attended by two Canadian paddlers, Robert Baldwin, a federal public servant from Ottawa, and Thomas Henry Wallace, of Gore's Landing on Rice Lake, Ontario. The participation of Wallace, a hunting and fishing guide, did not appear to raise any immediate concerns about professionalization. However, his open-style canoe, paddled with a single blade, proved somewhat difficult to accommodate in the racing schedule. Permitted to enter two races, Wallace won them both, earning for his efforts a new Rob Roy canoe built and donated by the enterprising J. Henry Rushton. The comparative thinness of the Canadian participation at Lake George was at least partially attributable to prior commitments on the part of some canoeists, notably to the first regatta of the Amateur Oarsmen's Association, which involved many of Peterborough's leading paddlers as well as members of the host Argonaut Club in Toronto.[28] Soon, however, members from north of the border became actively involved in the ACA, contributing to and being influenced by developments within that larger organization.

Nine people gathered on 14 December 1880 at Rossin House in Toronto to form the Toronto Canoe Club, with John W. Bridgman, a portrait painter and amateur mechanic, chairing the organizational meeting. Bridgman, one of only five original members who owned a canoe, claimed to be the first resident of the city to have built a decked sailing canoe from a design by the American builder W.P. Stephens.[29] Eventually, sailing canoes and the events associated with them made inroads in Canada, but of the twelve canoes on the Toronto list for 1882, five were open.[30] Despite a steady influx of new canoeists in the early years, Toronto's total membership initially grew slowly, as many of those who joined either lost interest or soon departed the city, often, it seems, to pursue opportunities in the expanding Canadian Northwest.[31] Twenty-three members were paid up for the 1882 season, but only a dozen or so remained on the books in 1884. That year's membership list included Mrs E. Leigh. She had originally been admitted as an honorary member; later, having established her credentials as an 'actual paddler,' Mrs Leigh acquired full membership status.[32]

ACA regattas at Lake George grew rapidly from the first meeting in 1880, when 35 canoeists and a fleet of 25 canoes constituted the entire assembly. The next year there were some 80 paddlers, with approximately 55 canoes, and in 1882, 145 canoeists attended, with 125 canoes. 'Who says,' the *American Canoeist* demanded, 'that canoeing is not on the high road to popularity?'[33] Indeed, stimulated by competitive rivalry, commercial promotion, and economic expansion, significant growth and organizational development continued for much of the 1880s in both Canada and the United States.

Pursuant to a decision to take advantage of other locations, and on the invitation of Elihu Burritt Edwards, a young Peterborough lawyer who was the ACA's first Canadian commodore, the assembly travelled to nearby Stoney Lake in the summer of 1883. The new hosts introduced a number of organizational innovations, lengthening the gathering to two weeks, 10–24 August, with competition concentrated in a three-day period during the second week. Overall, the first of several ACA gatherings in the Kawarthas attracted nearly four hundred enthusiasts, with three hundred canoes, by no means all of which were entered in competitive activities.

On the basis of the linkage between competitive recreational canoeing and the wilderness tradition from which it had emerged in Canada, the Peterborough organizers added an event to the regatta schedule. Credit for the initiative must go to Dr Campbell Mellis Douglas, VC, of Lakefield, who proposed the new race for the forthcoming ACA regatta on the ground that it 'would prove useful in testing the handiness of cruising canoes.' He suggested that the new event might be called a 'portage race' because contestants would be required to carry rather than drag their canoes about. 'Let the competitors start from the stakeboat,' he proposed, 'paddle about half a mile, then land, carry their canoes round a portage of at least a quarter of a mile ... launch their canoes again, paddle round a turning-buoy moored about a quarter mile off-shore, and return to the stake-boat.' In defence of the idea, Dr Douglas said that 'one of the great advantages of the canoe is that it can be carried around an obstruction, and it would be well to have the quality tested.'[34] Like Thomas Henry Wallace's seemingly anomalous appearance at the 1880 Lake George meet with the simple open canoe of which he was a master, Douglas's invitation to canoeists to pick up their boats was symbolic of the continuing Canadian influence, the merging of traditional North American canoe use – linking the water and the land – into the organization of modern sport; and, of course, it marked a difference from the preoccupation with canoe sailing, racing machines, and canoe-yawls then beginning to dominate discussion in Britain.

The ACA's first commodore, W.L. Alden of New York City, in the spring of 1883 estimated that there were 'about two thousand canoes in this country, each one of which is commanded either by a captain or a commodore.'[35] With 215 members at the end of the previous season, then, the ACA had managed to induct only about one in ten of the potential recruits into its ranks, notwithstanding the enthusiasm of its originators. ACA membership more than doubled during the year of the Stoney Lake regatta, to reach 450 by September 1883,[36] thanks in part to the proliferation of new clubs on the Canadian side of the border.

The May 1883 issue of the *American Canoeist* announced the formation of the Ottawa Canoe Club, an association of twenty members whose fleet 'comprises birch-bark, Peterboro, and Rice Lake canoes, and six decked canoes of various types.'[37] The formation, elsewhere in Ontario, of the Lindsay Canoe Club and the Lakefield Canoe Club was announced just in advance of the Stoney Lake regatta, with each claiming twenty to thirty members.[38] The enthusiasm continued after the summer's events with a new organization 'budding into life' as the Royal Military College Canoe Club at Kingston, under the leadership of Lieutenant Colonel Edgar Kensington, who had attended Stoney Lake in an 'antique birch bark canoe.'[39] The spring of 1884 witnessed the formation of the Deseronto Canoe Club, with fifteen members.[40]

On the basis of active encouragement from *Forest and Stream* and the promotional efforts of J. Henry Rushton, the prominence and popularity of recreational canoeing also surged in the United States. ACA membership reached seven hundred in 1885, and a rival grouping, the Western Canoe Association, came into being. Paddlers eagerly followed reports on the exploits of their most adventurous colleagues. George Washington Sears, a Pennsylvania shoemaker, transformed himself into the woodsman Nessmuk and criss-crossed the Adirondacks in his lightweight *Sairy Gamp*; Dr Charles Neide accompanied by Captain Samuel D. Kendall journeyed three thousand miles to produce *The Canoe Aurora: From the Adirondacks to the Gulf* in 1885; and Nathaniel Holmes Bishop, whose paper canoe voyages of the 1870s had made him famous, continued to attract attention for his travels and opinions.[41]

The very appeal of Nessmuk and his fellow canoe-campers represented a surprising threat to the organizational ambitions of the competitively oriented ACA leadership. Even though the range of vessel types owned by the growing membership of canoe and rowing clubs was extremely varied, a preoccupation with innovation, especially in relation to canoe sailing, became increasingly difficult to reconcile with the outdoor interests of less technologically oriented canoeists. Bishop himself had warned in the immediate aftermath of the ACA's creation that the organization should be led by 'a cruiser' rather than by someone inclined to have 'silk sails, twelve dollar silk stockings, or a water closet on his canoe.'[42] By all accounts, the tension peaked at the ACA's 1886 meet with the acceptance of the sliding seat that had proved so awkward for Robert Louis Stevenson among the Belgians, and the advent of a purely racing canoe. Notable British canoeists found their heavily ballasted Nautilus and Pearl models incapable of matching the rival American vessels *Vesper* and *Pecowsic* in an international challenge cup, but the Americans' potential to attract a broader membership was lost in the victory.

In the words of Atwood Manley and Paul Jamieson, the biographers of Henry Rushton, the ACA's absorption with racing rules and procedures made it from 1886 'one of the factors that changed the sport from a romantic and adventurous pastime to a racing-directed routine and caused a leveling-off of interest.' The canoe, the authors philosophically conclude, 'is not prime material for regimentation.' 'Nor,' they add, 'is the canoeist likely to be a prime organization man.'[43] The organizational challenge took the opposite form in Britain, where, if *The Field*'s portrayal of the situation may be relied upon, no governing body emerged to promote general design standards or a coordinated regatta schedule.[44]

A somewhat different pattern unfolded in Canada, where deeper roots, a more broadly based program of activities, and a comparative shortage of alternative sports sustained the organizers' momentum through the years of American decline in the 1890s and into the early twentieth century. At Toronto, despite the club's uncertain, even precarious, early existence, membership reached 318 in 1900, and by 1908, with 600 members, the TCC claimed to be the largest of its kind then in existence. In terms of canoes, the TCC began with a mere six, stored at the foot of Lawrence Street in the boathouse of one John Clindinning. Several moves later, the 1903 membership owned about 250 canoes.[45] Meanwhile, other clubs in the area, notably Parkdale, Island Aquatic, and the Balmy Beach Club, began operations.

The Ottawa Canoe Club, one of four eventually to open in the Canadian capital, took advantage of the 1890s to establish its headquarters in premises provided by the Ottawa Canoe Club-House Company, the latter incorporated in 1894 specifically to 'erect and maintain a boat-house or aquatic Club building for the purpose of leasing or selling the same.' The incorporators, each of whom initially invested between ten and one hundred dollars in shares of the Club-House Company, included figures prominent in the city's commercial community: David Maclaren, lumber merchant; George Patrick Brophy, civil engineer; George Burn of the Bank of Ottawa; James Dewar Fraser of the Ottawa Electric Street Railway Company; Henri Roy, civil servant; John Alexander Drysdale Holbrook, merchant; and Richard Henry Haycock, insurance agent.[46] Little more than a decade after the original structure was complete, the club was building again, this time an impressive three-storey facility approximately a hundred and sixty feet by eighty feet, complete with a 'lofty' tower.[47] By 1900, $3.50 would purchase an annual membership; this, at least, was young Henry Harper's fee for 'all the privileges of the club.'[48]

The premises of the rival Rideau Canoe Club, along the canal driveway, were in operation by 1905, only three years after the club came into existence with fewer than twenty members. At eighty feet by fifty-five feet in dimensions, the new building occupied less space than the Ottawa Canoe Club facility, yet it was considered 'a model of convenience.' The structure was divided into three flats, the first containing the rowing quarters, dressing-room, and showers, as well as lockers and racks for two hundred canoes. Above this, surrounded by a ten-foot verandah affording excellent views of the Rideau and 'the beautiful driveway of the Improvement Commission,' were to be found the Ladies' Parlor, the Gentlemen's Smoking Room, the Board Room, and the handsome Ball Room. A large dining hall and various service rooms took up the third floor.[49]

Not long after the completion of the Rideau clubhouse, Ottawa became known for the intensity of the rivalry and competition among the area clubs: 'For years, paddling has crowded all other sport to the background during its brief season from the middle of July til the same time in August, in Ottawa.' With several strong clubs and a very active membership, local supporters confidently asserted that 'Ottawa owns more paddlers than any other city in the world,' and in ranking their sport against other competitive endeavours they argued that 'the rivalry can only be equalled in hockey.'[50] This was the atmosphere that eventually produced Francis Amyot, who competed for Rideau Aquatic and then the Britannia Boating Club before becoming gold medallist in the men's thousand-metre singles event when canoeing first appeared as an official competition sport at the 1936 Berlin Olympics.

In smaller nearby communities the passion for canoeing was equally high, even if construction financing was less readily available than in the capital city. In the Rideau Canal community of Smiths Falls, for example, public fundraising events such as outdoor concerts were held to obtain building funds for what ultimately became a fine clubhouse, even if it was not in the Rideau club's league.[51] A short distance away in Carleton Place, another club began life in 1893 as the Ottawa Valley Canoe Association. Also comparatively limited in its ability to compete indoors with the gracious facilities enjoyed by Ottawa paddlers, the Carleton Place club found satisfaction over the years in the successes of its race crews and, eventually, in its status as Canada's oldest continuously operating canoe club.

Canoe club camps, generally of two weeks' duration, were held in various Canadian centres as comparatively local events or, on occasion, in cooperation with the American Canoe Association. During the early 1890s, *Saturday Night*'s reporter on the canoe camp circuit was none other than the aspiring poet E. Pauline Johnson. Her literary career was already under way when she began her series of canoeing essays for the magazine, but it was perhaps the publication of 'The Song My Paddle Sings' in *Forest and Outdoors* in 1892 that brought her work to the attention of significant numbers of North American paddlers.[52]

The Galt regatta in 1890 was very close to home for the young poet, paddler, and journalist. After 'two delightful days and two jolly late-to-bed

nights' over the course of which she was liberally entertained, her enjoyment of the races was clearly heightened by the strong performance of
several members of her party from the Brantford Canoe Club. Galt, she
allowed, had put on a good show, having welcomed 'all the pleasure
seekers, the idlers, the strangers and pilgrims who flocked from near and
far to participate in the summer carnival that has proved a revelation to
outsiders.'[53]

In subsequent years Pauline Johnson ventured farther afield, regularly
attending canoe camps – including the annual ACA gatherings – and
defending her indulgence with the claim that 'there is no prettier contest
on turf or tide than a canoe race.' And, she added for good measure,
there is 'no better man in the world's arena of manly pastimes than he
who manages sheet and tiller, or plies the ashen blade.'[54] In fact, she
demonstrated relatively limited interest in the race details, and her observations tended to highlight the experience of the general participants.

The two-week camps were absorbing affairs; despite the modest hardships and adjustments imposed on them, the men and women who
attended wouldn't have spent their vacation time any other way. They
were prepared to ignore such difficulties as the limited supplies of fresh
meat and fruit, the 'plaguey' flies, and even 'that haunting dread of
finding a snake in your bed every night.' The unpleasant memories faded
rapidly, or seemed somehow unimportant, in the context of the companionship and exhilaration of these extended canoeists' outings. 'You forget
how intensely you suffered from sunburn the first week, or how stuffy the
grey blankets smelt after a shower, and how the tent always leaked over the
corner where your stretcher stood.' Not only did the agreeable features of
the canoe camp compensate for the inconveniences, but, Pauline Johnson
proclaimed, the whole adventure was preferable to any of the alternatives
that might come readily to mind:

Was not your tent infinitely better than the ten by twelve foot box your fashionable
married sister was occupying down on the Jersey coast, where she coaxed you so
hard to join her? Were not your coarse blankets outspread on aromatic cedar
boughs a thousand times superior to a stuffy berth in a hot sleeper or steam boat?
... And that little canoe of yours lying on the shore ready to be packed for
shipment, was it not worth all the carriages at a fashionable watering place? Was
not your paddle more precious than steaming, harness-hampered horses, the
gunwales curving lines more shapely than a lumbering victoria or a nobby two
wheeler?[55]

In the varied program of canoe clubs in Canada, participants could find a mix of camping, companionship, and competition, including – as Pauline Johnson's reports confirm – some occasion to use the sheet and tiller. But the clubs, notably those in smaller centres, were never much attracted to the gadgetry demanded by the poor man's yacht. If the 1905 Orillia Regatta program is in any way representative, a highly competitive and entertaining day might unfold with barely a sail in sight. The challenging singles, tandem, three-, and four-paddle races were combined with the diversion offered by crab and gunwale races, upset doubles, the flip, and an event known as the fat man's race, for contestants with unspecified qualifications. A war canoe race rounded out the program.[56]

The canoe used in this last event, one which Toronto paddlers claimed to have originated in 1889, was regarded as a descendant of the freight canoes of fur trade days, although it also came to be known as a club canoe. Romanticizing the war canoe phenomenon from across the Atlantic, *The Field* remarked in 1899 that 'nothing grander or more vivacious can be seen or imagined than a hot, close race between, say, half a dozen war canoes, but it needs club against club to breed real excitement, and this they do in America.' Such was the appeal of the war canoe that one firm of builders had seven on order at that time.[57]

Roberts and Shackleton have noted the democratic influence of the club canoe in attracting younger paddlers who would not have been in a position to afford a craft of their own. They also remark upon the socializing influence of these vessels, in which a smaller club might actually install most of its membership. Women, it should be noted, were also active in the war canoe rivalry that grew up between canoe clubs.[58]

There may well have been limits, however, to the virtues of communal paddling. Leonidas Hubbard described the war canoe as struggling for a place in the Canadian clubs and at Detroit. At thirty feet and paddled by a crew of eight, the vessel, he explained, was 'a sublimated North canoe such as the fur traders used in their palmy days.' Primarily for racing, the war canoe, as Hubbard had observed, particularly at Detroit performed other functions:

On Saturday afternoons and on holidays, it leaves the club house. There are seven paddles, but fourteen cushion seats. At the side of each paddler is the omnipresent parasol, and the party of fourteen passes under the bridge. Down the river are docks, and beyond the docks is a road that runs along the Canadian shore. It is an old, old road, bordered with ancient trees, and along its side, among the trees, are quaint old farm houses that date back to the French regime. And here and there is an ancient French tavern, whose keeper has learned that serving suppers of fish and frogs and chicken at fair prices to city people is better than serving cheap meals to chance passers-by. From ten to thirty miles below the city the war canoe lands and the canoeists saunter up the road to an inn among the trees, and sit about in the shade watching the ships go by while François is cooking the chickens. After the supper, maybe the launch from the club comes and tows the war party back through the moonlight.[59]

Hubbard was not alone in querying the contribution of the war canoe, for a later dockside observer of the Toronto Canoe Club's training efforts remarked that any number of lads 'like to take a single down to Sunnyside and pose for the girls.' Visitors, however, would be disheartened to see paddlers 'lying around the float waiting for the war canoe to go out, when they might be out improving their style and condition generally.'[60]

In 1900, as the canoe club phenomenon was thought to be on the wane in the United States, the sustained popularity of the sport in central Canada was such that steps were taken at Brockville to establish a Canadian Canoe Association. In addition to three Brockville area clubs – the Rowing Club, the Bohemian Athletics Association, and the YMCA Boating Club – the original charter members of the CCA were the Ottawa Canoe Club, its neighbour in Britannia, the Grand Trunk Boating Club of Montreal, the Lachine Boating Club, and clubs from Kingston and Carleton Place.[61] After years of hectoring British and American canoeists about the need for a uniform system of classification if international canoe racing was to have a future, *The Field* welcomed the formation of the Canadian organization with the thought that it had a new lever to exercise in its own campaign.[62]

Whether or not *Outdoor Canada* was correct in informing its readers in 1908 that 'in Canada canoeing has been for many years the foremost aquatic sport,' it was certainly not incorrect in emphasizing the extraordinary popularity of the canoe. Paddling then enjoyed a wide following among thousands of individuals, including the members of nearly fifty clubs which had grown up in towns and cities across the country. Many, though not all, of these organizations had been established in the years following the creation of the CCA.

The CCA's original list of member clubs raised some doubt about its claim to represent the interests of canoeists across Canada. Not only the Toronto club, with its several hundred members, but a number of other communities in which organized canoeing was firmly entrenched were unrepresented at the CCA's founding.[63] One of the clubs originally excluded by geography from the CCA was Winnipeg, where an organization began with fourteen members in 1893. The Winnipeg club's regional isolation from the central core is illustrated in its regatta circuit, which included Fort William, Minneapolis, and Duluth. Distances and the costs and complications of travel limited the participation of this and other 'regional' clubs in the central Canadian competition schedule. Thus, when Winnipeg at last affiliated with the Canadian Canoe Association in 1912, the club remitted its fees 'only on condition that our crews be allowed to compete in the final regatta without having to take part in the elimination trials.'[64] Halifax-Dartmouth was another regional centre where highly competitive paddling enjoyed an immense popularity within a comparatively localized circuit.

Although racing and regattas remained the principal attractions of club programs, many urban-centred canoe clubs also promoted touring and camping activities for those of their members who were more inclined to view themselves as devotees of the outdoors than as athletes. A commentary on the Toronto club stressed that 'cruising and camping are leading features ... and many of the men have their complete outfit, carried in the canoe, for shelter, food and sleep.'[65] There was also some interest in canoe tripping under the auspices of the Winnipeg club, as members were encouraged to make use of suitable water routes in the surrounding area. Winnipeg established a 'Voyageur Section' in 1927 in order to promote 'paddling hikes during the holidays' by providing information on equipment and on suitable routes through the rivers and lakes of northern Manitoba.[66] It was not surprising, then, that Eric Sevareid and Walter Port were 'taken right into the "family" of more than a thousand members' when they paddled through a few years later en route to Hudson Bay.

One of the highlights of the annual program for Winnipeg canoeists was a sixty-five-mile outing from the Winnipeg clubhouse to Lower Fort Garry and return. 'The idea behind this race is to promote the use of the canoe for holidays and long trips, and to make the conditions of the race similar to actual conditions on the trips.'[67] Whatever the intent, this particular event became increasingly competitive. In 1936 the *Winnipeg Free Press* noted several changes that had become evident over the years:

It is no longer a weekend jaunt – it is a race against minutes that does not even allow time for a chocolate bar. There are no less than ten of the newer faster type of canoe in Winnipeg, this being a large factor in the lowering of the record time about 45 minutes. Detailed care is taken in selecting paddles, equipment, running the portage, and so on.[68]

Long-distance racing for open canoes frequently highlighted the canoeing season in other parts of the country as well. In Alberta, a Banff-to-Calgary run took place at various times during the 1920s. In June 1914, a two-hundred-mile race down the Ottawa River and the Lièvre attracted nine entries. The winners, Robert Gamble and Fred Thompson of the Rideau Aquatic Club, completed the course from Mont Laurier to Ste-Rose in under sixty hours, including two compulsory rest periods of nine hours and an unscheduled three-hour delay. Participants more or less unanimously expressed their unwillingness ever to take on such a course again.[69]

The Ottawa River event and many other regular activities of the organized canoe clubs were abandoned for the duration of the First World War, but rebuilding was soon under way. The Ottawa–New Edinburgh Canoe Club undertook to revive its traditional two-hundred-mile race in 1919 and invited Prime Minister Robert Borden to preside over the start of the event: 'Canoeing is distinctly a Canadian national sport, and the Two Hundred Mile Canoe Race, taxing as it does to the utmost the strength, endurance and skill of the competitors, easily ranks first among the athletic events of the world.'[70] The rigours of such an event were questioned in the 1920s, and some controversy arose as to whether the CCA's Graham-Browne 200 Mile Canoe Race trophy could be awarded to the winners of a less arduous contest. 'Experience,' asserted advocates of the shorter course, 'has proven that the 200 mile race is too exhausting for amateurs and a number of athletic and aquatic experts have agreed that a 100 mile race would be much better and yet serve the same purpose.'[71]

An event of roughly this length, generally from La Tuque to Trois Rivières, along the St-Maurice River immediately became a highlight of the summer season for members of the Radisson club after its formation in 1934. Each August teams of canoeists raced down the historic valley of La Mauricie. Close races, sometimes involving more than fifty canoes and contestants from the United States as well as Canada, were immensely popular with local residents and visitors alike.[72]

From the introduction of canoeing as an Olympic discipline in 1936, international competition has been a recurring source of inspiration for various campaigns to upgrade the performance levels of Canadian athletes. Early successes, notably Frank Amyot's triumph, were followed by disappointment as European competitors increasingly set the standard. Thus, reports from the Lake Albano canoe and kayak events near Rome were accompanied by a call for 'a national re-awakening in respect to the value of mass participation in this and other amateur sports in order that Canada can compete on more equal terms with the athletes of other countries.' The Europeans' successes suggested that their training camps and the combined support of government and industry were worthy of emulation in the form of an 'all-out effort.'[73]

Advice on training received greater emphasis in the canoeing literature of the early 1960s. Exercise regimes, dietary considerations, and fitness programs became the focus of efforts to enhance the quality of Canadian paddlers. The physical activity included off-season drills, weightlifting programs, and isometric exercises. The relation between 'stomach puffing' and successful paddling deserves particular attention as a Canadian corollary to Caesar's dictum that an army marches on its stomach:

Lie on your back, feet flat on the floor with the knees up. Place 10 lb. weight over stomach, holding it lightly in place with the hands. Then, pull your stomach in as far as possible, hold for 2–3 seconds and then puff your stomach out as far as possible, making the biggest mound possible. Start slowly and gradually do the exercise faster and faster, making sure to pull in and puff out as far as possible each time.

In case the regime was not sufficiently exhausting – even in contemplation – hopeful young paddlers were admonished: 'Do until thoroughly tired. When you can do it for two minutes without trouble add more disks.' The advocates of this activity referred to it as 'a form of healthful internal massage as well as ... a strengthener.'[74] The young paddlers may have wanted strong stomachs for other reasons as well, as the same training pamphlet that prescribed stomach puffing recommended four to five bags per pint of tea in the pre-race meal.

Ironically, as the appeal of canoeing as a competitive sport grew, attention shifted from the original craft to vessels featuring a more innovative design oriented towards performance. That was particularly true of canoe sailing, but a similar shift was not unknown among competitive paddlers, who remained as the mainstays of canoe clubs after wilderness canoeists abandoned organization. The outstanding athlete emerged as the focus of attention in an activity held on a course rather than on the pathways – including the portages – of the voyageurs. But canoeing never did draw crowds, at least not in the manner of major spectator sports, and soon clubs were struggling to maintain their place in the lives of communities whose accelerating passion for the automobile was diverting them from the waterways and shorelines.

Survival strategies, in both Canada and the United States, often involved diversification away from the competitive core. Even in its heyday, the Toronto club boasted some of the finest whist players in the country and a hockey team that 'did itself no dishonour.' Balmy Beach also had an outstanding record in a range of athletic endeavours and was noted for the scope of its social programs. Winnipeg added golf, tennis, and a range of outdoor sports facilities to retain the loyalty of its membership, but eventually succumbed.

The American Canoe Association's efforts sustained a two-week national meet for many years, but alongside canoeing itself the divisions became deeply involved in dinners, smokers, and other social functions. In due course – even after the virtual disappearance of the sailing canoe races that had inspired such interest in the later years of the nineteenth century – the competitive core experienced further specialization and fragmentation as flatwater racers, slalom paddlers, and marathon paddlers defined their particular interests with greater precision.

Once again, in a manner somewhat reminiscent of the design revolution led by Warington Baden-Powell, W.P. Stephens, and their contemporaries, it became of considerable importance to determine who was paddling what kind of boat. The desire to avoid unfairness among competitors in remarkably intense canoeing contests forced early organizers to formulate classification schemes for the various watercraft then in use. Ultimately, devotees would be inspired to contemplate the essential nature of the canoe, a craft whose basic characteristics might not seem to occasion controversy. But even discussion of the nature of the canoe was caught in the charged intellectual atmosphere of the nineteenth century, when British imperial expansion and Darwinian ideas about the survival of the fittest formed a backdrop for so many controversial debates.

9

What Kinda Boat Ya Got?

The vessel that some have regarded as 'the little savage princess of boats'[1] or endearingly labelled a 'magic little craft'[2] has not always been the object of admiration. Fundamental attitudes towards the canoe, both favourable and unfavourable, have shaped commentators' perceptions and their views as to whether mastery of this small watercraft was an art held in high esteem or an activity to be disdained. In the 1880s, Charles Ledyard Norton captured the spectrum of opinion when he considered the impressions of the readership of *Hour* magazine: 'Do *Hour* readers know what a canoe is? Most of them will reply: "Yes, certainly, we know. It is a boat made of birch bark, or hollowed from a log – a rough affair made by savages, and mostly used by them."' Against this disparaging view Norton set out what he imagined to be the other extreme. For this latter class of readers, 'a canoe in the civilized acceptation of the term is a beautiful piece of builder's art, shining with varnish, finished like cabinet work, with brass or nickel fittings, and carrying an amount of canvas that makes a sailor wonder how she keeps right side up.'[3] Even from this perspective, however, the craft hardly enjoyed unequivocal endorsation, for its use was widely seen as perilous: 'A young man ... was drowned just below Folly Bridge by the over-setting of a dangerous kind of boat called a canoe, much used for pleasure till forbidden by the Governor of the university.'[4]

Even 'Rob Roy' MacGregor, Cambridge graduate and barrister of the Inner Temple, had not escaped adverse commentary on his mid-Victorian waterborne exploits. The charges included a certain amount of criticism of his chosen watercraft. One of MacGregor's better-natured critics described the canoe as 'a broad, clumsy, flat-bottomed "funny" with the outriggers removed.' MacGregor himself, the vessel's paddler, was described as an aquatic centaur, 'his lower part being a boat, and his upper a wandering Englishman!' Critics further suggested that 'as the constrained position of the legs produces continual cramps, it would be an improvement to have the legs amputated.' This line of analysis eventually led one very sceptical observer to remark that 'mortals of less buoyant spirits might get tired of sitting in a damp tub, paddling in a confined attitude, and being confined to watercourses as the only available routes.'[5]

MacGregor, certainly a formidable and energetic publicist, responded to his detractors with an inventory of the functional advantages of the canoe. The canoeist, he argued, 'looks forward and not backward as he sits in his little bark,' with the consequence that the course ahead and the surrounding scenery were always in view. For manoeuvrability and portability the canoe was unsurpassed:

With one powerful sweep of his paddle he can instantly turn the canoe, when only a foot distant from fatal destruction. He can steer within an inch in a narrow place, or press through reeds and weeds, branches and grass; can hoist and lower his sail without changing his seat; can shove with his paddle when aground or jump out in good time to prevent a decided smash. He can wade and haul the light craft over shallows, or on dry ground, through fields and hedges, over dykes, barriers, and walls; can carry it by hand up ladders and stairs, and can transport his boat over high mountains and broad plains in a cart drawn by a horse, a bullock, or a cow.

Strength, versatility, and stability were further virtues of MacGregor's craft, with comfort and elegance noted as distinguishing features:

For comfort during long hours, for days and weeks of hard work, it is evidently the best, because you lean all the time against a back-board, and the moment you rest the paddle on your lap you are as much at ease as in an armchair; so that while drifting along with the current or the wind you can gaze around, and eat or read, or chat with the starers on the banks, and yet, in a moment of sudden danger the hands are at once on the faithful paddle ready for action.

MacGregor's defence of the canoe concluded with reference to the varied uses to which it could be put, and to certain economies enjoyed by its devotees.

Finally, you can lie at full length in the canoe, with the sail as an awning for the sun, or a shelter for rain, and you can sleep in it thus at night, under cover, with an opening for air to leeward and at least as much room for turning in your bed as sufficed for the great Duke of Wellington; or, if you are tired of the water for a time, you can leave your boat at an inn – it will not be 'eating its head off' like a horse; or you can send it home to sell it, and take to the road yourself, or sink into the dull old cushions of the 'Premiere Classe' and dream you are seeing the world.[6]

According to MacGregor's biographer, some critical observers were unpersuaded, arguing, for example, that 'it is a mistake to paddle where you can go in a steamboat,' or that the canoe was 'only meant for water impracticable for other kinds of boats.' Still more intemperate protests were directed against 'the claims of an upstart phenomenon of our days to share in the unapproachable merit really possessed by the gig as a boat of pleasure. We denounce, abhor, scout, and scorn the notion that the canoe is anything of the kind.' The canoe had its own legitimate uses and was admittedly 'highly commendable in its own sphere.' But that sphere was a narrow one; the canoe was to be confined to waters 'where nothing else can navigate.' It was relegated to this status on the ground that it was 'the invention of savages, dwellers on savage waters whose shallowness and rapidity would be destruction to regular craft.' Necessity rather than choice or pleasure was the justification for employing this 'imperfect, unscientific, uncomfortable imitation of the true boat.' The critics concluded that 'it is a species of mockery of boating to go on expeditions of length and cost in a craft whose only method of propulsion is based on the most wasteful expenditure of man's powers ever invented.'[7]

Such intense hostility represented more than casual disapproval of an unfamiliar vessel. The roots of the criticism lay in deeply held convictions about the relative limitations of indigenous peoples and, by corollary, the inadequacy of their technical accomplishments.[8] Extreme nineteenth-century views on the merits or failings of the canoe thus echoed a more fundamental controversy about the relationship between the new world and the old, between advanced societies and their pre-industrial counterparts, indeed, about the nature of progress.

Although the acknowledged inspiration for MacGregor's career as a canoe traveller was an india rubber boat, he was quite familiar with the Native craft of North America, where his father had been stationed as commanding officer at Halifax, and where as a young man he had later paddled several variations.[9] His own early inquiries into the mechanics of marine propulsion and his professional experience as a patent lawyer provided further foundation for his pronouncements. 'The true Indian canoe is made of bark,' he reported in 1859 after visiting New Brunswick. Although he initially found the craft 'easy to manage,' manoeuvring around the mill-races and the magnificent falls in the Ottawa area proved more challenging, and he discovered it was 'rather a delicate matter to urge my little bark canoe along.'[10] Other watercraft in the canoe category had proved even less satisfactory. In a four-passenger dugout fashioned by French settlers, MacGregor made good progress up the beautiful Tamaraska, but the vessel proved highly unsuitable for a crossing of Lake Tameasquota. Wind on the lake nearly filled the canoe with water, making the efforts of the crew to bail it out almost useless. After landing three times to restore the craft to seaworthiness, MacGregor concluded that a canoe was 'a very bad sort of boat when there is the least wind.'[11] MacGregor was mechanically inclined, and such unsatisfactory experiences in aboriginal bark canoes and settlers' dugouts presumably nurtured a predisposition on his part to effect improvements in the design and construction of the recreational vessel he would do so much to popularize.

Diversity of craft within the canoe category such as MacGregor had noted during the course of his travels was occasionally remarked upon, although for most purposes the variations appeared to be inconsequential. For W.H. De Puy, the energetic compiler of *The People's Cyclopedia of Universal Knowledge*, the canoe was either a 'boat made of a hollow trunk of a tree, or the bark shaped and strengthened.' Canoes ranged in size, up to those 'large enough to carry 20 or 30 hogsheads of sugar.' They might be decked or equipped with sails of rush or silk grass. Generally open boats, the cyclopedia's canoes were customarily 'rowed by paddles, and steered by an oar.' Minimizing any possible gulf between canoes and kayaks, the cyclopedia concluded its definition with the observation that 'near sea coasts canoes are often made of wooden frames, covered with seal skins, which are also drawn across as a deck, with only a hole left for one man to sit in.'[12]

Readers of Samuel Johnson's *Dictionary of the English Language* as originally published in 1755 could hardly have detected the seeds of later intercultural controversy in its brief definition of a canoe as 'a boat made by cutting the trunk of a tree into a hollow vessel.' Subsequent revisions of the dictionary in 1818 and 1827 preserved the innocent simplicity of the original definition while adding new illustrative references and the etymological observation that previous spellings had included 'cannow.'

The definitions perpetuated by the *Oxford English Dictionary* illustrate the early divergence of opinion, later to become widespread, on the nature and merits of the watercraft. On the one hand, the dictionary defined the canoe as 'a kind of boat in use among uncivilized nations.' It associated the origin of the word with the hollowed-out craft of the West

Indian aborigines and noted that the word had been extended to apply to similarly constructed vessels used by 'other savages' or 'pre-historic men.' More generally, but in the same vein, the *OED* defined the canoe as 'any rude craft in which uncivilized people go upon the water.' On the other hand – to accommodate the growing enthusiasm of modern cultures for the canoe as a pleasure craft – the *OED* explained that the canoe 'in civilized use' was 'a small light sort of boat or skiff propelled by paddling.'[13]

The inclination to credit aboriginal boat-builders with commendable inventiveness and craftsmanship, though rare in literary circles, was not entirely absent. C. Stansfeld-Hicks, the English author of the treatise *Yachts, Boats, and Canoes*, declared in 1887 that the design and construction of the birch-bark canoe rendered it 'most beautifully adapted to the purpose for which it is used.' Whether even the most expert of naval architects would be capable of producing 'a design more calculated to fulfil every detail of requirement than is shown in this of the rude savage' was a matter of some doubt. The modern canoe, Stansfeld-Hicks argued, developed from its precursors through a process of Darwinian evolution:

Those craft most suited to the purpose for which they are used have been handed down from generation to generation without change by their savage owners, until civilized man, taking the general idea, altered it to suit his particular requirements and the materials at his disposal, making a construction possibly more convenient for himself and the conditions under which he intended to use it, but not necessarily improving on the original structure as intended for its particular uses.[14]

Not many years after this formal acknowledgement of the distinctive virtues of aboriginal watercraft, English readers of *The Field* were reminded by the discovery of what the magazine described as an 'ancient canoe' that they, too, might lay claim to indigenous status. A prehistoric dugout, unearthed on the banks of the Clyde at Dumbarton, Scotland, in the late 1890s, inspired one correspondent to muse about 'this curious connection between the Indian canoeists of today and their ancient British prototypes of many centuries ago.'[15] However, there is no evidence to suggest that this occasion for emphasizing the common humanity of waterborne civilizations marked a fundamental shift in attitudes.

The Funk & Wagnalls *New 'Standard' Dictionary of the English Language* resorted in 1949 to a series of definitions to preserve cultural distinctions. The canoe was, first, 'any boat propelled by paddling.' One set of such watercraft included 'any small craft in use among savages,' a category illustrated with reference to the kayak, oomiak, birch-bark canoe, bull-boat, and dugout or pirogue. Alternatively, Funk & Wagnalls noted 'very light pleasure boat(s).' These were 'pointed at both ends, propelled by a paddle and usually fitted with small sails.'

A *Dictionary of Canadianisms on Historical Principles* managed to finesse the cultural gulf in 1967 with this workable and diplomatically worded composite: 'any of the various light watercraft propelled by paddles, including the birchbark canoe ... and more modern craft of similar design.' While less illuminating than many of its predecessors, this definition could at least claim the quality of inclusiveness. Ken Roberts and Phil Shackleton, the authors of *The Canoe: A History*, have responded in somewhat technical terms to an understandable impulse to define their subject. Braving the waters of definition they cautiously advance this formulation: 'An all-encompassing definition must be a general one: a canoe is an open watercraft of hollow form, generally shaped at each end to improve its hydrodynamic qualities, and designed originally to be propelled by one or more occupants, facing forward and using paddles or push-poles.'[16]

Precision has not always been essential; recently, lovers of the canoe in any of its forms and variations have generally accommodated the preferences of their fellow enthusiasts. Tolerance, however, has not been universal. In some circumstances precise definition serves to delineate the boundaries between permitted and prohibited activity. Chief among such settings is the racing environment, where the possibility of competitive advantage and of unfairness are inherent in excessive flexibility.

Not surprisingly, a vigorous debate emerged about the characteristics of watercraft that would be accepted in the various competitions the popularity of which was peaking in the final decades of the nineteenth century. In the United States any number of scribes weighed in with proposed definitions and classification schemes, for several of which they sought official endorsement:

A canoe is a boat, sharp at both ends, and capable of being efficiently propelled by one man, wielding a double-bladed paddle. These conditions necessarily limit her length, breadth, and weight. She may carry sails of any shape or size, and may be built of any material; but she must be, above all, a single-handed craft, managed by her crew of one under any and all reasonable circumstances.[17]

Revisions to the American Canoe Association's regulations as advocated by the regatta committee in advance of the 1883 event would have clarified the reference to two sharp ends by insisting that there be 'no counter, stern or transom.'[18]

British canoeists also became embroiled in the controversy. Dr J.D. Hayward cited the Mersey Canoe Club's definition as 'about the most defective with which I am acquainted.' Mersey officials defined a canoe as 'a decked boat not exceeding club dimensions (not exceeding 18 feet in length or 3 feet beam), the means of propulsion to be by paddle or sails only by one person facing forwards.' 'In the first place,' Hayward lamented, this pronouncement 'excludes all canoes taking a double crew, although most of these are considerably within the above dimensions.' A further defect was the exclusion of Canadian canoes, on the grounds that these were not 'decked boats.' The 'still greater vice,' Hayward concluded, was 'the omission of any reference to the necessity of a sharp stern.'[19]

Innovations and refinements of the Rob Roy and other basic designs multiplied the variety of watercraft in competition and complicated the process of classification. The range of experimentation throughout the 1870s and 1880s is reflected in W.P. Stephens's survey of models and designs for the amateur boat builders of 1885. Changes and improvements had been so numerous that the names of early canoe types – Nautilus, Rob Roy, Shadow – could 'convey no definite idea of the boat's model and dimension.' Stephens reported the existence of nine models named Nautilus and six named Pearl as a prelude to his own taxonomy, based on 'the relative proportions of their paddling and sailing qualities.' This approach led him to propose the categories of Paddling Canoes, Sailable Paddling Canoes, Sailing and Paddling Canoes, Paddleable Sailing Canoes, and Sailing Canoes.[20] But the fact that these rather loose labels were not adopted suggests that they were judged unlikely to prevent abuse, to reduce confusion, or, if the following warning was an accurate reflection of the resale market, to facilitate entry and exit into sport canoeing:

A canoeist seldom wakes up to the fact that his own club is not all in canoeing, and that no two clubs at present abide by the same classification rules or definitions, until he has a valuable canoe for sale; it is then he finds how narrow the market he has before him, especially if his club rules have cramped his craft into a particular type of boat useless for purposes other than his particular club's racing.[21]

As U.S. canoe clubs, especially those preoccupied with competitive sailing, experienced a period of decline in the late 1800s, a modest upsurge could be detected in the intensity of another vigorous controversy about basic style and design. Refinements and technical distinctions within the competitive canoe category attracted less attention than formerly, and debate turned instead to the essential differences between – and the comparative virtues of – the open Canadian model (as commercial adaptations of the aboriginal birch-bark craft came to be known) and any variation of the closed or decked version. As each of the two basic designs had become firmly associated with distinctive traditions and styles of use, the outcome had a significant potential to influence the nature of modern recreational canoeing.

The closed canoe, often resembling a kayak and still commonly known as the Rob Roy after MacGregor's famous mid-century vessel of this type, had aroused enthusiastic interest in the United States and Britain. With modifications it had become especially popular among canoe sailors. This model made only modest inroads into Canada, where a distinctive tradition of design and use persisted and eventually triumphed. The differences lay in the Canadian preference for an open two-paddler canoe, a craft better suited to fishing, camping, and wilderness travel. In Canada the open canoe was also supported by the experience of history.

One explanation offered for the slower and less dramatic rise in popularity of open Canadian canoeing as a recreational activity referred critically to John MacGregor's influence on the British and American tradition:

If 'Rob Roy' McGregor [sic] had not been able to transform his no doubt very ordinary cruises on the Baltic, the Elbe, the Danube, the Rhine and the Jordan, into one of the most delightful series of books of travel in the English language, would his civilized Kayak, by her own merits, have ever become the most famous of small boats, or produced the school of English canoeists? Not only has the Canadian canoe been deprived of all the advantages resulting from the efforts of a single inspired and gifted inventor, but it has never been blessed with a prophet.[22]

Although the closed canoe enjoyed the support of racing enthusiasts, the Canadian canoe ultimately established its position as the most satisfactory overall model for camping and wilderness travel. The open canoe eventually became the most popular model in Britain and the United States as well, where it had always had devoted advocates. W.S. Holden of Liverpool, England, wrote after visiting the United States in the early 1880s,

If I, an English canoeist, may express an opinion on the canoe most adapted for real canoe life in your land of lake, river, and forest, I should say the Canadian canoes, as built by the Ontario Canoe Company, are those most likely to be the ones generally used in the future, lightness being an essential where portages have often to be made under circumstances which preclude extraneous help.

'To me,' Holden concluded, 'it appears that the single bladed paddle is the poetry of motion and that for canoeing the pure type of the original canoe is the one to be followed.'[23] Indeed, the Canadian canoe was to be found with increasing frequency on English waterways into the early years of the twentieth century. Even *The Field* finally relented, broadening its coverage away from the racing circuit in order to carry regular notes on English river trips for paddlers. The magazine insisted, nonetheless, that local cruising was a derivative of club-centred competitions, and not an underlying attraction in itself as in the North American context.

During the height of racing's early popularity, a few American commentators had urged the importance of taking cruising into account when settling upon the design of the canoe. They seemed inclined, however, to accept that adaptations of the decked model would serve the purpose. In *Sports and Pastimes of American Boys*, for example, Henry Chadwick accorded pride of place to suitability for cruising, while accepting the merits of versatility:

The true object for which the canoe is built is cruising. Hence she is made so light that she can be carried around obstacles by the canoeist; so strong that she will bear the rough work of running shallow rapids; so seaworthy that she can brave the rough waters of large lakes; so commodious that her owner can sleep on board of her and carry plenty of stores, and so beautiful that every stranger will admire her and be proud to aid the lofty purpose of the canoeist.[24]

For Chadwick, a canoe unfit for cruising was not really a canoe at all, however suitable if might be as a sailboat or as a paddling machine.

The distinctions between canoe sailing and canoe camping were sufficiently understood that one contributor to the American outdoors journal *Forest and Stream* could assert in 1890, 'Canoeing in the States is essentially different from that in Canada.' Contemporary opinion was probably not so firmly divided; the canoeing volume in the widely circulated Spalding's Athletic Library series considered the Canadian open canoe models, in contrast to the decked or closed one-man British or American sailing canoe, to be the 'best general cruising boat.' The view that the open wooden canoe was a Canadian innovation was widely understood in the early twentieth century. 'The wood canoe is essentially a

Canadian product although it is now beginning to be made rather extensively in this country as well.'[25]

At least one early commentator felt that it was important to make an aesthetic distinction between canoeing and boating, which might – to the casual observer – appear to accomplish similar ends. 'Boats are for work,' John Boyle O'Reilly confidently avowed, adding definitively that canoes are for pleasure. 'Boats are artificial; canoes are natural. In a boat you are always an oar's length and gunwale's height away from nature. In a canoe you can steal up to her bower and peep into her very bosom.'[26] In this way, the recreational focus shifted away from the craft and towards the pleasurable activity of vacation travel and the exploration of nature rather than of uncharted geography. The canoe emerged as a companion, and to the possible annoyance of women contemplating the sport, a female companion with very modest demands who serves best when once mastered by the male adventurer:

The canoe is not a fickle, but a very shy and modest little puss, and she must be long and faithfully wooed – gently withal – before she is won. Once conquered she is docility itself, and obedient. A more faithful traveling companion you cannot find. She will show you the choicest bits of nature, un-got-at-able except with her aid.

This, alas, was not all, for this glowing praise for the canoe continued at some further cost to the dignity of women:

She will shelter you miles from civilization, will carry you and your luxuries and necessities down rivers, across lakes, along the sounds and bays of the coast and will ask very little in return – a coat of varnish twice a year, a few brass screws now and then, a little care of her and nothing more.[27]

The transition of the canoe from working vessel to pleasure craft involved some loss of status in certain contexts. For example, it has sometimes been necessary to ask whether the presence of canoes satisfies the legal tests for determining if a particular waterway is to be classified as navigable or non-navigable, as a means of determining its public character. Such determinations are more than mere judicial pronouncement on the character of a particular waterway; they are made to settle questions such as whether or not the public has access to the waterway, who owns the underlying bed, and which legal rules apply. But canoeists have known from the time of Chief Justice Shaw of the United States Supreme Court in the 1830s that the object of their personal enjoyment is not highly regarded in all circles. It is not, Shaw remarked, 'every small creek in which a fishing skiff or gunning canoe can be made to float at high water which is deemed navigable, but, in order to give it the character of a navigable stream, it must be generally and commonly useful to some purpose for trade or agriculture.'[28] Unimportant, perhaps, in the eyes of some influential early observers, the canoe – whatever that actually is – nevertheless managed quite well to preserve and extend its following.

Devotees of the open canoe forthrightly championed their chosen watercraft and generally celebrated their understanding of its origins and historical uses notwithstanding the sentiments embedded in dictionaries or the opinions of U.S. Supreme Court judges. Thus, the so-called primitive and civilized usages converged to a degree; the conflict of status between aboriginal peoples and advanced societies was gradually recast as tension between the natural and the artificial. Those who had taken the trouble to inquire into aboriginal methods of canoe construction were most inclined to express admiration for the builders. They were appreciative rather than dismissive of their predecessors.

In its service to successive generations, as an artefact of continuity between civilizations, or as a link between an incessantly intrusive species and the natural environment, the image of the ideal canoe has changed character again and again.

The birch canoe was the supreme product of the red man's ingenuity and skill, and the white man, backed by centuries of training in the arts and crafts of civilization, has never been able to invent so good an implement for the purpose for which it was designed, nor with all his experiments has he ever improved upon the Indian model.[29]

Those were Dillon Wallace's thoughts in 1910, but devoted readers of Longfellow's *Hiawatha* would hardly have taken issue with this sentiment:

Thus the Birch Canoe was builded
In the valley, by the river,
In the bosom of the forest;
And the forest's life was in it,
All its mystery and magic,
All the lightness of the birch tree,
All the toughness of the cedar,
All the larch's supple sinews;

And it floated on the river
Like a yellow leaf in Autumn,
Like a yellow water-lily.

Mournfulness eventually displaced disparagement as a characteristic sentiment among recreational paddlers who contemplated the passing of the aboriginal bark canoe. 'Years ago,' explained one visitor to the Nipigon district, canoes were overwhelmingly of the birch-bark type. They harmonized completely with the local environment, and were 'admirably adapted to their requirements and to the character and contour of the country, dovetailing with their natural surroundings and blending harmoniously into the land and water scape.' The traditional Native watercraft was so much a part of the landscape that 'like the sky and hills and river, they seemed a part of it, and were the aesthetic thing for the northern wilds, proper and becoming.' In function, the birch-bark canoe was responsive to necessity; in manner of construction, it was natural: '[Canoes] were necessary when the Indian, the pioneer and voyageur were living off the country, and there were thousands in the making, scattered throughout the forest, hanging on trees like Christmas gifts.' Even the building process, which later generations would find intriguing, was part of the natural order of things:

The builder had only to select the one he fancied, and none save the choicest were taken. The roots of the young spruce furnished thread for sewing the birch sheets, cedar and spruce the ribs and flooring, tamarack the crossbars, and there was pitch from the pine for covering seams and preventing leakage. A little juggling with knife and hatchet, a little twisting and turning, quite a simple matter for the expert, and lo, the poor Indian had fashioned a beautiful canoe, buoyant, symmetrical, graceful and somewhat resembling himself, with its high cheek bones and complexion.[30]

Indian-made birch-bark canoes were used so frequently by late nineteenth- and early twentieth-century recreational paddlers that James Dickson in the 1880s believed it would be helpful to set out elaborate instructions on repair techniques for aboriginal watercraft. Some years later Robert Pinkerton still felt that recreational paddlers would benefit from his advice on purchasing a craft. 'In the first place, never buy a canoe an Indian makes to sell. He wants ten dollars for it. Pay two more and get one he made for himself. It is two hundred per cent better. The difference which the Indian considers to be worth two dollars is really astounding.'[31]

But although the traditional craft retained some appeal even after 1900, its decline was unavoidable as the popularity of recreational wilderness travel surged. Many of those who experienced the transition now felt the rupture of a direct link with the Native craftsmen and the important sense of continuity that this physical association with the aboriginal watercraft symbolized. Close associations between one generation of paddlers and its predecessors persisted through the twentieth century, as birch-bark gave way to wood and canvas, as these classic craft later gave way to aluminum, fibreglass, and more modern materials, and as craftsmen gave way to builders, who in their turn faced competition from large-scale manufacturers.

10

The Craft and the Craftsman in Transition

For a century and a half, successive generations of wilderness travellers and recreational canoeists have watched the canoe emerge from the craftsman's shop or the builder's factory in a variety of new materials. Birch-bark vessels acquired from aboriginal craftsmen, building for themselves or for sale, were superseded by handsome wooden vessels. These in turn gave way to less costly and somewhat more utilitarian canvas-covered watercraft, which effectively symbolized the idea of canoeing for over half a century. Following the Second World War, new materials appeared with astonishing frequency, beginning with aluminum and fibreglass. Each of these transitions corresponded with changes in the nature of manufacturing and, more important, in the nature of canoe use.

The transitions also provided the occasion for wilderness paddlers to reassess personal preferences and to reflect – often wistfully – upon the evolution of the tradition to which they belonged. One former birch-bark devotee openly discussed his transformation from an unquestioning admirer of the aboriginal craft to a paddler more willing to enjoy the advantages of new models: 'I, too, once worshipped at the shrine of the birchbark; knelt in spirit before the creation of the Indian; believed in Longfellow's panegyric, and scoffed at those practical men who hinted at any imperfections in it. But I have had a change of heart.'[1] In 1914, Robert Pinkerton summarized the disadvantages of the vanishing birch-bark craft:

You will have to travel much more slowly with the same expenditure of energy, and you must always carry a can of pitch wedged in the bow. Your craft will be harder to handle, especially in a wind, and, unless you rig some sort of low seat, you must kneel in the Indian's position when you paddle.[2]

The new watercraft, generally of cedar or basswood, could be made lighter than a birch-bark canoe of similar length and capacity. And the birch-bark would soak up more water in the course of an extended trip. The hollows of a birch-bark canoe were 'highly prejudicial to speed,' so that 'given equally good men in a cedar and in a birchbark canoe ... on still water the former will draw away from the latter one foot in every ten.' The author of these remarks, among others who publicly debated the minor technological revolution, had some misgivings about the suitability of the wooden canoe for work in rapids, but agreed that the fault could be remedied.[3]

Not every observer conceded that all the advantages were on the side of modernity. For Edwin Tappan Adney, a young artist and journalist at a comparatively early stage of his lifelong passion for bark canoes, the passing of the North canoe around the close of the nineteenth century marked the end of an era, 'a passing which will ever be looked upon with regret by lovers of wild and picturesque life.'[4] The debate continued even into the 1930s, with loyal traditionalists still willing to argue that '[a] properly made Indian birch bark canoe will ride waves better than a manufactured one the same size,' or that it 'bounces like a cork and manages to stay on top.'[5]

If Longfellow saw the natural grace of a water lily when he looked at bark models, other imaginations added their own visions of the canoe. Arthur Silver saw the canoe as 'the very soul and poetry of motion,' a serenely resting craft that was 'calm as the iris that broods over the raging cataract.'[6] The birch-bark canoe later struck one devoted admirer as 'trim and pert,' as riding the waves 'with the sensitivity of a duck.'[7] Nevertheless, the traditionalists themselves were forced to acknowledge that 'even the Indians do prefer a canvas covered job,'[8] and as early as 1900 Tappan Adney had noted the problem that 'younger and more progressive Indians ... having learned from white men the commercial value of time, had acquired the habit of throwing things together with nails and tacks, instead of patiently split sewings of root and fibre.'[9] In other words, the authentic, archetypal birch-bark canoe was losing its pedigree; a certain shoddiness was becoming apparent to more astute observers, although whether to ascribe the perceived deterioration to Western technology or to the voluntary adoption of that technology by Native builders remains a matter of contention in some circles.

What had replaced the aboriginal canoe, gradually at first from the mid-1800s and then in overwhelming numbers in the final decades of the nineteenth century, was the product of another set of forces, the handiwork of an immigrant tradition of craftsmen later supplemented by still more entrepreneurial associates. The evolution of this 'Canadian'-style recreational canoe is an intriguing question; the subject of its origins and development has piqued the interest of a good many paddlers over the years. No doubt the debate – like the one on the merits of boiled campfire coffee – will endure along the waterways for some time to come.

Charles Ledyard Norton, writing for the *American Canoeist* in the 1880s the essay 'My First Canoe,' reflected that it would be of interest 'to fix the date when the first departure was made from the birch, and the more perfect structures of basswood and cedar began to be constructed.' He urged Canadians to take up the inquiry and to secure the necessary information 'before the "oldest inhabitant" forgets or dies.'[10] Norton's phrase 'more perfect' was offered without elaboration; it embodies at least a generous admiration both for the immigrant craftsmen who began commercial production of wooden canoes for recreational use and for their predecessors, aboriginal and immigrant builders of bark boats and dugouts.

The lengthy essay 'The Canadian Canoe' in *Forest and Stream* credited the Strickland family of Lakefield, Ontario – and George Strickland in particular – with making great advances during the 1850s.[11] By his own admission, George Strickland's first attempt at dugout canoe–making in 1853 resulted in an object that 'looked more like a hog-trough than a boat.'[12] His efforts were by no means unique, however: dugout craft were widely observed in the early years of the nineteenth century.[13]

As Strickland's handiwork improved, the outcome was a trim dugout sharing the shape of the popular birch-bark boat, but not its lightness.[14] At local regattas Strickland enjoyed considerable success, racing his *Shooting Star* against other elegant and surprisingly refined dugout models. Regattas held in the Peterborough district at Little Lake and Gore's Landing directed attention towards speed, but the enthusiasm of local residents such as Thomas Gordon and John Stephenson for hunting and fishing in the small lakes of the back country placed a premium on portability that the dugouts, however sleek, could never satisfy.

John Stephenson and Thomas Gordon have been credited jointly with the introduction of a manufacturing technique that set canoe builders on a new course. They were certainly among the very first builders to assemble cedar and basswood canoes, and as one diligent inquirer remarked after years of investigation, 'the fact that the two leaders were friends who enjoyed the "mystique" of the hunt together and must have spent many an evening by the fire talking canoes and swapping ideas surely leads to a reasonable conclusion that Stephenson and Gordon share the distinction of inventing the Peterborough canoe.'[15] Stephenson patented a number of subsequent innovations derived from continuous refinement and experimentation, while other Peterborough-area builders such as William English and Dan Herald of nearby Gore's Landing, who took credit for the Herald Patent Cedar Rice Lake Canoe, were soon making their own craft.[16]

The basic Peterborough or Rice Lake canoe was typically built of basswood or cedar in lines that are still familiar today. The standard model was approximately sixteen feet long and about twelve inches deep with a thirty-inch beam, but to facilitate shipment, canoes of various sizes were built to nest within each other. Dan Herald's highest-priced canoe, a seventeen-foot craft, sold in the United States for forty-five dollars in 1878. As described by a contemporary observer, Herald's canoes were 'smooth inside and out, and have no ribs, being constructed with double skins or planking. The outer one runs longitudinally, and the inner one transversely, and they are firmly rivetted together.'[17]

'Stephenson of Peterboro, Canada,' reported the *American Canoeist* in 1882, 'is busy filling an order for fifty of his beautiful cedar rib canoes to be exported to England, where they are attaining great popularity.'[18] And the early paddlers' magazine soon added that this pioneering builder and innovator had 'just sent to England a very pretty canoe with a removable deck.'[19] Within months, however, Lieutenant Colonel J.Z. Rogers bought Stephenson's business and was 'going to push it with vigor.' The Ontario Canoe Company – as Rogers's operation was originally known – acquired a large building for the purpose and expected to employ a number of workmen.[20] With Rogers's entrepreneurial skills contributing to the financial success of the newly expanded venture, Stephenson's talents were appropriately directed towards design and craftsmanship. A decked canoe with longitudinal ribs and sides lower than the Peterborough's soon came into production. A half-decked canoe, the Juniper model, followed shortly afterwards.[21] Within a few short years, style and model variations had proliferated to the point where Ontario Canoe was offering customers 120 choices.[22] Fire destroyed the Ontario Canoe Company operations in 1892, and from the embers emerged the Peterborough Canoe Company, in which Rogers retained a continuing interest until his death in 1909.

In the United States, the early builders included the New Yorkers James Everson of Williamsburgh, W. Jarvis of Ithaca, George Roahr of Harlem, and Walters and Sons of Troy. J.F. West of East Orange, New Jersey, E.H. Gerrish of Bangor, Maine, and the Carleton Boat and Canoe Company of

Old Town, Maine, were also building in the 1870s. B.N. Morris of Veazie, Maine, began production in the next decade, competing with existing Maine builders and, later, others such as Kennebec of Waterville, E.M. White of Gilman Falls, and the Old Town Canoe company of Old Town.[23] J. Henry Rushton of Canton, New York, combined a talent for construction with promotional acumen. His own canoes, as he was quite willing to remind his prospective clientele, were the product of continuous refinement, and, by implication, worth the price. As Rushton explained, 'A fine canoe is never the result of chance. The designer or builder does not go to bed at night, and awaken in the morning to find his craft ready for the water. Neither is his first attempt likely to be quite successful. Little by little the canoe approaches perfection.'[24]

In addition to the proliferation of wooden canoe builders in the final decades of the nineteenth century, a notable development in open canoe construction was the introduction of canvas as the covering skin. The canvas-covered canoe, when production finally expanded, was a less expensive and therefore more widely accessible watercraft which rapidly became the standard for wilderness travel, latter-day prospecting, and exploration, as well as for the youth camps. The replacement of birchbark by canvas was popularly assumed to be the key process in the design transition to the craft that epitomized recreational paddling in the first half of the twentieth century.[25]

Credit for pioneering the canvas cover has been given to a number of contenders. In northern Canada something resembling the conventional wood and canvas canoe was being developed directly from the birch-bark model, which some claimed was occasionally built with a canvas cover. Other commentators credit Indians with the innovation. Thus, Dillon Wallace remarked in 1910 that 'if tradition says aright, it was an Indian who first substituted canvas for birch bark, at a time when, because of depleted forests, bark was no longer obtainable.'[26] Another account of the transition maintains that John Edwards raced a canvas-covered woodframe canoe in an 1857 regatta in Peterborough. 'This lightweight racing canoe represented the first appearance of a construction method that would dominate canoe building by the turn of the century.'[27] Wood and canvas canoes – in very limited numbers – were commercially manufactured in Maine in the 1870s by E.H. Gerrish of Bangor, while B.N. Morris's Veazie Boat and Canoe Company entered production in the early 1880s, soon to be followed by E.M. White of Gilman Falls.[28]

It is, of course, possible that canvas covering was introduced independently in several locations, with no one centre entitled to exclusive credit for originating the use of the new material or for the important innovations that facilitated production. Gerry Stephenson argues, however, that his ancestors travelled from Peterborough to New England after the use of canvas began in Peterborough and before it seems to have begun in Maine.

Whatever the precise chronology, the products of at least three streams of technological development for cruising canoes were evident by the 1870s: the all-wood open canoe, the decked model with its various adaptations to competitive sailing and cruising, and the canvas-covered craft. These differed one from another in the degree of difficulty each presented to the builder and in their cost in a growing market. When the manufacture of the canvas-covered canoe on an inverted form had been mastered, the price of a very serviceable open canoe fell, broadening participation in the sport.

Important changes in canoe building took place in the years preceding the First World War, when the birch-bark canoe was permanently displaced as a North American recreational craft by cedar, basswood, and butternut canoes constructed by a multitude of small canoe companies, and then increasingly by the canvas-covered models, which were beginning their own extended period of popularity. Not surprisingly, turn-of-the-century canoeists debated the desirability and appeal of the innovations they were able to observe. As early as 1910, Dillon Wallace noted that 'canvas, it is true, has taken the place of birch bark as a covering, but shape and lines have undergone no change.'[29]

Nor did the all-wood models disappear immediately when canvas-covered boats became available. Some builders (Rushton provides an important example) were engaged in producing both types of open canoe simultaneously. In 1906, a year of record production, Rushton's output included 750 Indian Girls alongside more than 150 all-wood canoes.[30]

For wilderness travel, canoeists were urged to use the canvas-covered canoe, a model combining greater protection and strength with design features adapted to rough country. 'The standard guide or tourist models of most manufacturers are designed to meet the varying conditions of travel in the north woods and are almost always the most satisfactory in the long run.' Readers of the May 1927 edition of *Forest and Outdoors* were advised:

When new and dry, a canvas-covered canoe is usually lighter than an all-wooden canoe and, being easier to keep watertight, it usually retains its lightness for a longer time. If it does get thoroughly waterlogged, it becomes a veritable backbreaker on the portages. Repairs are easily and quickly made. Small punctures can be stopped with a daub of hot pitch, ironed out with a heated knife blade. Larger cuts or tears require patches ... Being constructed somewhat like a basket, the canvas-covered canoe is flexible and will stand some very hard knocks that would split the planks of an all-wood canoe.[31]

Yet the all-wood version was still thought to withstand more 'scraping, grinding and scratching' than the canvas model and was sometimes even preferred for shallow rocky streams or for spring and fall travel, when thin, hard ice might be encountered. Ultimately, though, the cost differential and the difficulties of repair made it impossible for these models to maintain market share in competition with their canvas-covered rivals.

The increasing popularity of the canvas-covered canoe stimulated discussion about equipment maintenance. James Edmund Jones had commented on the question in his 1903 guidebook *Camping and Canoeing*, citing the difficulty of repairing birch-bark as an important factor in the attractiveness of other models. Articles on the repair of the canvas covered canoe became common in the sportsman's magazine *Rod and Gun* and elsewhere. C.F. Paul of the *Montreal Star* described his somewhat unorthodox application of two new strips of canvas to a canoe:

I began by tacking this canvas along the keel, beginning at the centre of the boat and working both ways. I found that by soaking the canvas with water I was able to stretch it better with the pliers than when dry, so kept it wet throughout the operation. After tacking the full length of the keel, – that is up to where the bend begins toward the bow and stern, – I stretched it tightly toward the gunwale, tacking it to the side of the boat close to the gunwale and on to the gunwale itself.[32]

Recounting her experience in re-canvassing the smaller Rob Roy canoe, Helen Merrill of Toronto noted that 'the second cover adds not a little to the weight of the canoe, and for this reason a light weight canvas is advised.'[33]

Developments in the design and style of canoes around the turn of the century were accompanied by changes in the commercial dimensions of the canoe trade and in the structure of the canoe manufacturing industry. Numerous American builders such as Old Town, Morris, Rushton, Racine, and E.M. White were either well established or were developing their reputations during the same era.

Recreational canoeing encouraged – as did the extension of mineral prospecting into Canada's Northern Shield country – the proliferation of canoe-building firms. In Ontario, for example, canoe-building enterprises varied in nature and size from small, craftsman-owned and -operated companies exclusively devoted to canoe building to larger operations in which canoe manufacturing was carried on alongside a comprehensive boat-works including the making of skiffs and motorized launches. A listing of Ontario canoe-manufacturing companies whose advertisements appeared in turn-of-the-century periodicals includes the following: the J.H. Ross Canoe Company, Orillia; the Lakefield Canoe Building and Manufacturing Company; the H.L. Bastien Boat and Canoe Works, Hamilton; the William English Canoe Company, Peterborough; the Peterborough Canoe Company Limited; the Capital Boatworks, Ottawa; the Canadian Canoe Company Limited, Peterborough; the Walter Dean Company, Toronto; H.E. Gidley and Company, Penetanguishene; the H. Ditchburn Boat Manufacturing Company Limited, Gravenhurst; J.W. Stone Boatworks, Rat Portage (Kenora); and the Toronto Canoe and Boat Company.

Canoes manufactured in Toronto were available from the T. Eaton Company at least as early as 1901, when the rapidly growing department store's first issue of the *Summer Catalogue* appeared. The sixteen-foot basswood model was modestly priced at $25 with paint or $32 for a varnished finish. Cedar or butternut craft of the same design were somewhat more costly. A good bird's-eye maple or cherrywood paddle could be obtained for $2. The William English design, the distinctively styled Sponson with gunwale-length flotation chambers,[34] and the American-manufactured Old Town had been added to Eaton's canoe selection list by 1914.

In Fredericton, New Brunswick, the Chestnut Canoe Company was incorporated with an authorized capital stock of $48,000 in 1907, after several years of successful operation as R. Chestnut and Sons, an offshoot of a family hardware store originally established when the Chestnuts arrived from Ireland in the 1830s. Remarkably, in 1905 the Chestnut firm obtained a Canadian patent for the wood and canvas construction technique which it employed, though which it had certainly not invented. Indeed, it appears that Chestnut developed its own product line after closely studying a Morris craft that W.T. Chestnut brought to New Brunswick in 1897.[35]

The financial demands of expanding production and of slower-than-anticipated sales growth precluded dividends until 1911, when a modest 5 per cent dividend was declared. By 1913 the prospering Chestnut company had authorized a 10 per cent dividend and a five-hundred-dollar bonus for the managing director. So optimistic were the directors that in the early months of 1914 they empowered H.G. Chestnut to investigate European market potential and to establish production overseas. The outbreak of war undermined the initiative, but the Canadian canoe certainly retained a substantial following on the Continent and in Britain. As early as the 1890s, Lakefield builders were shipping six hundred canoes in a season to England, and any number of recreational paddlers were enjoying the canals and natural waterways of the Continent. In addition to sales to the established European market, the Chestnut company subsequently allocated $350 for advertising in the United States, but it is not clear whether this was a further attempt at expansion or a means of reducing a temporary lag in sales resulting from Canada's involvement in the war.

In the early 1920s the organization of canoe manufacturing in Canada underwent something of a transformation. The network of small builders, sometimes individual craftsmen, which had existed prior to the First World War was replaced by an environment dominated by a few major firms – including Chestnut and the Peterborough Canoe Company. The latter, formed after the destruction of the Ontario Canoe Company plant, absorbed the William English Canoe Company in 1914 and then, in 1923, entered into an arrangement with the Chestnut interests.

Peterborough and Chestnut agreed to the formation of Canadian Watercraft Limited, a holding company which controlled the two firms.[36] Another Peterborough firm, the Canadian Canoe Company, entered the consortium in 1928. Despite the consolidation of ownership, Peterborough, Chestnut, and the Canadian Canoe operation continued to manufacture under their own names throughout the 1930s. In the late 1940s, *Forest and Outdoors* explained the significance of what it called a 'federation': the consolidation was beneficial for the public because it permitted a greater degree of mechanization and specialization. Chestnut's production was exclusively devoted to canvas-covered canoes, while the Peterborough Company made only cedar craft. *Forest and Outdoors* reported that the Canadian Canoe Company still made both types, 'but it seems likely that in time they, too, will specialize.'[37]

Of course, not all the smaller companies disappeared through consolidation; the famous Loretteville Huron canoe, for example, continued to be available from Gagnon and Jobidon in Quebec.[38] However, canoe builders – large and small – would eventually face new challenges as a further revolution in materials got under way in the aftermath of the Second World War.

The evolution of canoe design and manufacturing practices, including experimentation with new construction materials, continued through the first half of the twentieth century, even as the canvas-covered models moved to seemingly unchallenged dominance in the marketplace and in the affection of canoeists. James Edmund Jones reported in 1920 on his experience with a galvanized iron canoe designed for six paddlers. This vessel, twenty feet in length and complete with air bulkheads at each end, proved more satisfactory than Jones and his companions had anticipated, but was destined for neither commercial production nor popular acceptance. An earlier experiment with metal canoes, using aluminum, in the 1890s, had also proved short-lived because of corrosion and deterioration, although even then it was predicted that the light weight of the product would ensure its eventual appeal.[39]

A seventeen-foot, thirty-three-pound aluminum canoe was commercially available in the United States in the 1930s from Frank E. Beers of Los Angeles, and the Aluminum Company of America developed prototypes in the same period. Even enterprising do-it-yourselfers were initiated to the wonders of a home-built aluminum canoe as early as 1936.[40] No less 'woodsy' a figure than John R. Rowlands was won over by the aluminum construction, and he offered an endorsement in his classic 1948 memoir *Cache Lake Country: Life in the Canadian North Woods*. He reported that although a few Indians still favoured birch-bark, 'most of the canoes that carry the Indian families across the lakes and up the rivers to their winter homes are made by white men.' His personal preference, however, was for aluminum. 'I've come to believe that the canoes made of light thin metal that can be molded into sweet and easy lines come closer to the birch bark craft than any other in weight and carrying capacity.'[41]

Whitewater enthusiasts in particular welcomed the 1945 announcement by the Grumman Aircraft Engineering Corporation that four sizes of aluminum canoes in two weights – light and standard – would be commercially available for the following season.[42] North American whitewater paddlers, eager to renew their acquaintance with familiar rivers after the end of wartime hostilities, were keen to assess the performance of the latest watercraft.[43] The Grumman product was well received, and the popularity and durability of this innovation was such that a number of established builders were forced to offer their own aluminum craft.

Traditionalists, in a process that has been frequently repeated, now came to be redefined as those devoted to the 'old style' canvas-covered craft. Bill Mason, for example, retained a lifelong attachment to the canoes of his youth, as did the popular Algonquin Park guide Omer Stringer, who simply preferred the 'feel' of wood and canvas. Stringer, the son of a park ranger, developed his reputation as guide, teacher, and canoe stylist in a lightweight modified Chestnut, and it retained his eternal loyalty.[44] Other wood and canvas paddlers may have scoffed at, lamented, and resented the metal competition in much the same way that those who first mastered the paddler's arts in birch-bark reacted with scepticism to all-wood canoes and mass-produced canvas copies. They wistfully recalled the real thing, but then generally came to accept the virtues of new materials. Eventually, the best of the aluminum canoes won most paddlers' respect, if not necessarily their affection. When the aluminum canoe in its turn was displaced by still more high-tech craft, the cycle of nostalgia repeated itself:

I thought I was the only one attached to an old, beat up *Grumman*. It's seldom used anymore, as I have gone to a canoe made of Kevlar. I'm pushing 50, and that 76-pound *Grumman* came down hard on me one morning last summer when I tried unsuccessfully to jump a small creek. But the 20-plus years of fond memories that are conjured up whenever I look at it are reason enough to keep it. Those old 'beaters' are as maligned as they are forgiving. My *Grumman* cost me $235 brand new, and I don't think I've ever made a wiser purchase in my life.[45]

The problem of weight was a recurring challenge to designers. James Edmund Jones's iron canoe had lacked the lightness of aluminum and was highly unlikely to be praised for buoyancy and sensitivity on the water. The weight difficulty at least was ingeniously circumvented by a design feature allowing Jones's twenty-foot model to be packaged in two seventy-pound sections. Further adaptations of this sectional approach to canoe building proliferated in response to technological changes in other fields.

Advances in aviation adopted for civilian use by the Ontario government after the First World War greatly facilitated surveillance of the province's vast forest regions and aided fire-fighting in remote districts. Nevertheless, fire rangers were still required to travel by canoe along the northern waterways, and the early aircraft, which did not take off easily, were often incapable of transporting conventional models into the wilderness interior. This problem was solved in the 1920s by the construction of sectional canoes, the parts of which could be fitted inside one another for convenient shipment in a small plane. Some of these compact canoes were manufactured for the Department of Lands and Forests in Sault Ste

Marie, where the Ontario Provincial Air Service was based after 1924.[46] Walter Dean, a Toronto canoe builder who patented a 'portable sectional canoe' in 1898, had been ahead of his time and too far ahead of flight to earn credit for his innovation.[47] In addition to a sectional model, the Chestnut Company's Labrador model was designed to conform to the existing limits and possibilities of air travel: 'A feature of this canoe is that it has been well constructed with a straight top so that it will lash to the underbody of a hydroplane, cabin type. The ends or hoods of the canoe are detachable and can be secured inside the hull for transport.'[48]

Convenience or compactness was apparently desired even by recreational canoeists, for experiments were also made with collapsible models. Reporting U.S. and Canadian patents from as early as 1883, the Ontario Canoe Company offered a 'folding canoe' of its own manufacture in sizes ranging from seven to fifteen feet.[49] These were attractive because of the comparative ease with which they could be transported by train and, later, in the increasingly popular automobile.

One observer somewhat caustically described the folding canvas canoe as 'specially designed for people who are willing to try anything once,' and told this story of a camper:

The ranger on duty examined his permit and fishing license, and then asked, 'Where is your canoe?' 'Right here', replied the camper, touching with his toe a long cylindrical bundle that lay beside his bed roll. 'It's a folding canvas canoe that weighs only twelve pounds and folds into a bundle, as you see, forty-eight inches long and six inches thick. It can be put together in half an hour without tools and folds up in ten minutes.'

'Oh!' said the ranger, and I must give him credit for the fact that there was not the slightest trace of scepticism in his tone or manner. Like most woodsmen, he was always most considerate of other people's feelings, no matter what he might think of them. He showed the camper the canoe landing just above the falls and even helped him to carry his outfit from the station platform. 'Would you like me to help you put your canoe together?' he asked politely.

'Oh, no, thank you. I watched the man that sold it to me put it together in the store and I know just how it goes.'

'Quite', replied the ranger in exactly the same manner and tone of voice as before.

The camper unfastened the bundle and opened out the canoe and its framework. He apologized for having to borrow a screwdriver to loosen a screw that had been fastened too tightly and then borrowed a monkey wrench to loosen a bolt that seemed to jam a little. He managed to get the frame set up, all but one end which did not seem to fit as well as it should. When he forced it, the other end came apart again, so the ranger held it in place for him. Two small bolts were missing at one joint, so the camper borrowed some wire and a pair of pliers and wired it firmly together. The ranger began to take more interest in what to him was an interesting problem, and I came in toward the end of the struggle and helped a little myself. By noon, four hours later, the canoe was completely set up and ready to be launched. We carried back to the ranger's shack, the Hudson's Bay Store and the sectionmen's toolhouse a monkey wrench, two screwdrivers, a pair of pliers, a claw hammer, a ball pene hammer, a cold chisel, a platelayer's sledgehammer and what remained of a coil of fence wire.

'Of course', he said, 'this is the first time I have ever put it together myself. Next time I ought to be able to do it inside the half-hour easily.'

The ranger and I were politely silent.

If this was not enough to cast doubt on the virtues of the collapsible canvas model, the story's conclusion eliminates all uncertainty:

The canoe was soon well out in the current, and while it was doing its best it must have felt that it had fallen down badly in failing to assemble itself in the allotted half-hour, for it suddenly proceeded to fold up all by itself, without tools or assistance of any sort, and made a complete job of it with nine minutes and fifty seconds to spare out of ten minutes guaranteed in the advertisement.[50]

Folding canoes retained a more devoted and more expert following in Europe, where their compactness and portability was an extremely attractive feature. Europe was also the setting for the revival of closed canoe or kayak paddling after Henry George 'Gino' Watkins returned from Arctic travel with a passion for Eskimo rolls.

Another technological development to alter canoe design during the interwar years was the proliferation of outboard motors. 'Ozark' Ripley sought to persuade readers of *Forest and Outdoors* that, despite the uncertain performance of early models dating from Evinrude's turn-of-the-century innovation, the outboard in 1928 was a useful and reliable asset for canoeists:

Nowadays, when a fellow wants to make a trip into the faraway places, going by train or auto, he can take this little indispensable, certain performer with him, store it under his berth, strap it to his car and, when he arrives, stick it on in a few minutes to most any kind of boat or canoe and get going without any further perfunctory or subsequent arrangements.[51]

Johnson, Evinrude, Elto, Caille, and Lockwood motors were all available in the 1920s, and engine manufacturers offered a bracket by which the outboard motor could be attached to a canoe. This arrangement was considered to be 'fairly satisfactory, although the thrust of the motor is not directly behind and in line with the centre of the canoe.' The square-ended canoe with a transom for mounting a small motor appeared and was, on occasion, described as the outboard canoe. One centre of manufacturing for this craft was the Canadian Canoe Company plant in Peterborough, where the Outboard Marine Corporation of Canada produced motors. The Peterborough Canoe Company was actually a distributor for the Canadian Johnson Motor Company, Limited.

The mid-century adaptation of the canoe to accommodate an outboard engine has been only the latest product of a surprisingly enduring vision of mechanized canoes dating well back to the 1800s.[52] One of the most recent offerings, the Electra-Ghost canoe, appears the ideal solution for anyone whose idea of canoeing does not include constant paddling. This craft, with 'up to 30 hours of battery power,' promises to 'take you beyond comfortable paddling distance' and is a 'natural for those who desire clean, quiet, motor-driven convenience and the graceful beauty of the canoe form.'

Fibreglass joined aluminum in the production lines, with even lighter and more durable modern materials, such as ABS and Kevlar, to follow.[53] These were serviceable watercraft with a remarkable appeal to a growing constituency of canoe-users, and they were especially popular with commercial tour operators, who simply could not have introduced so many novice paddlers to challenging waterways in the older models. Kayaks for coastal touring and other highly specialized craft – often at highly specialized prices – also proliferated. Most of the senior all-wood and canvas-covered canoe companies had ceased production, having lost their ability to deliver a competitive mix of craftsmanship and convenience.

Interestingly, however, the commercial dominance of high-tech canoes in modern, if not necessarily space-age, materials set the stage for a revival of old-style watercraft. Admirers of the traditional canoe and a number of independent builders inspired what has justly been called a 'quiet renaissance.'[54] Not only were wood and canvas canoes being lovingly restored by their owners or by independent craftsmen, but passionate builders such as George Dyson on Canada's West Coast and Henri Vaillancourt in New England were devoting themselves to the reclamation of threatened arts. While Dyson became preoccupied with the traditional Aleut baidarka,[55] Vaillancourt dedicated his energies to the birch-bark craft with which the love affair had begun.[56] Working with an axe, an awl, and a crooked knife, he builds a handful of exquisite bark canoes each year.

In some respects the revival of interest in traditional watercraft and canoes reflects the attraction to craftsmanship in an era otherwise dominated by technology; small-scale production based on unique personal skills and carefully mastered techniques provides an appealing contrast to assembly-line manufacturing. More generally, the renewal of interest in wood, canvas, and bark watercraft can be associated with late twentieth-century environmentalism and a renewed respect for the aboriginal residents of North America and their long-standing relationship with its lands and waters. Canoeists' interactions with Native North Americans and with the landscape itself are explored in the remaining chapters.

The canoe party shown here in a lagoon in Etobicoke, Ontario, illustrates the leisurely character of recreational paddling as a late nineteenth-century pastime. (Photo by John Boyd, National Archives of Canada)

A CANADIAN SUMMER BOY

The 'Canadian summer boy' emerged in the early decades of the twentieth century as an idealized character based on the experiences of children at summer camp. The young canoeist embodied the virtues that camping and the outdoor life along the waterways were thought to instil.

The woman pictured in *Water Lilies*, a woodcut by Walter J. Phillips, is the artist's wife, Gladys. The image suggests an intimacy in the relationship between the woman in the canoe and the natural setting in which she is portrayed. (Courtesy of John Phillips)

This postcard suggests one of the ways in which the canoe established its place in popular culture.

Not a bad way to spend a summer evening. Idleness has its virtues.

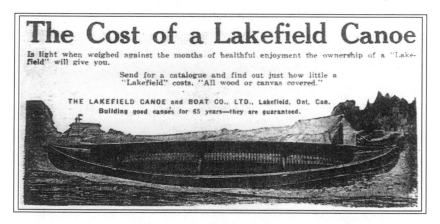
The Rice Lake Canoe Company and the Lakefield Canoe and Boat Company were renowned manufacturers of high-quality canoes in the Peterborough district of Ontario. Their catalogues were elaborate, detailing the many styles and refinements available.

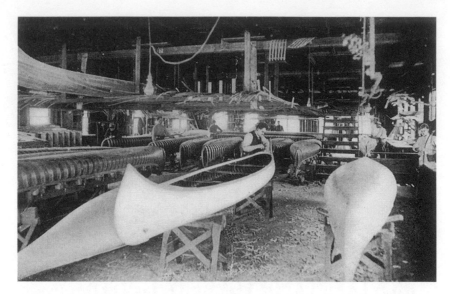

The Morris Canoe Company of Veazie, Maine, was one of many prominent early canoe-manufacturing operations in the eastern United States. Wood and canvas canoes took their shape from moulds in the workshop, as shown here in a photograph from a Morris catalogue dated around 1908. (Courtesy of the Wooden Canoe Heritage Association)

The Chestnut Canoe Factory in New Brunswick was a major supplier of canvas-covered canoes to Canadian and overseas markets. (Courtesy of the New Brunswick Provincial Archives / P5-422)

The canoe and the float plane have had an intertwined history through much of the twentieth century. Here, a collapsible canoe is about to be loaded into a Fokker Universal G-CAIX for transport. Many contemporary northern canoe trips begin or end with similar flights. (Courtesy of the Western Canada Aviation Museum / OS6125)

Although some paddlers resent the portage, these trails provide essential linkages between waterways. Long carries and heavy loads once made the use of professional guides an attractive proposition. (Courtesy of the Ontario Archives / 5.15475)

Smiths Falls, Ontario, was one of the many smaller communities in which competitive canoeing thrived in the context of an association of organized clubs. The regatta circuits generated interesting rivalries, especially in war-canoe events, which were often seen as highlights of the race agenda.

Edwin Tappan Adney devoted years of research to the painstaking task of documenting bark-canoe designs and crafting models such as those displayed here. Much of his work is now located at the Mariners Museum in Newport News, Virginia. (Courtesy of the New Brunswick Provincial Archives / P93-CA2)

Although late twentieth-century paddlers might generally be inclined to see themselves as committed environmentalists, the canoe has a long history of use in resource exploitation. Hunters and fishers have often sought their prey in a canoe. Their recreational pursuits may be seen as an element in the long social transition from the era of exploration and the fur trade to the modern period of paddling for pleasure. (Courtesy of the Lake of the Woods Museum, Kenora, Ontario)

Ice-canoe racing across the St Lawrence from Quebec City is a long-established ritual. (Courtesy of Mike Beedell)

Sea kayaking has developed an enormous following around the world. Here, a few paddlers pause for a moment in a kelp bed in Clayoquot Sound, British Columbia. (Courtesy of Suzanne J. Buhasz)

Trailer transport is a remarkably common feature of modern recreational paddling, no matter what destination canoeists or kayakers have in mind. En route to the 'drop off,' eager anticipation combines with no small measure of trepidation at the uncertain prospects ahead. On the return journey, after an experience of 'exhaustion and fulfilment,' few but the driver are likely to remain awake for long. (Courtesy of Steven T. Repucci)

The ancient tradition of Dragon Boat racing has grown in popularity among North American paddlers, particularly in the Vancouver area. Participants are often attracted to the sport by the opportunity to try out one of the boats that the Toronto Chinese Business Association makes available. (Courtesy of the National Capital Dragon Boat Race Festival)

The opportunity to experience history has become a powerful attraction for museum visitors, many of whom have enjoyed the chance to sit in the place of early voyageurs at Old Fort William. Yes, Virginia, there was a fur trade! (Courtesy of Old Fort William)

11

Native Impressions

If aboriginal people had had no further involvement in the evolution of recreational canoeing than to provide a designer's guide for the original watercraft, that contribution alone would be of inestimable importance. But to focus exclusively on the material prototypes would be to ignore other vital and continuing dimensions of the Native relationship to recreational canoe use. Aboriginal people not only built many of the craft actually used by early holiday paddlers, but also served as guides, as teachers, and indeed in some respects as models. Native and non-Native canoeists formed sometimes curious and even jarring impressions of each other. And, although much has changed during the course of the historical interrelationship, the canoe in its varied forms remains a significant element of Native society and self-understanding.

The design and construction of aboriginal watercraft have long been a source of fascination to observers, who have frequently recorded their admiration for the builders as they sought to understand intriguing aspects of the intricate processes of construction. One of the most recent observers to be captivated by the mystique of the aboriginal birch-bark canoe is David Gidmark, who first encountered the traditional watercraft at close hand on Lake Superior in 1976 and subsequently spent nine years in anthropological field studies of Algonquin communities in western Quebec. Generalizing on the basis of his own reaction, Gidmark commented: 'To see the original technology of the canoe was always a striking experience for uninitiated people. It was as if the large single sheet of birch bark, the hand-carved ribs and gunwales so skilfully and exactingly placed, and the binding with spruce root split by hand, crystallized in many people's minds the mystery of the Indian culture.' Traditional skills and a relationship with nature seemed to be embodied simultaneously in the canoe. 'A person seeing a birchbark canoe for the first time could envision that the builder had, in effect, gone into the woods with only a knife and an axe and come out with this splendid water craft. Not only was the birchbark canoe built from its environment, it was even part of the environment in the visual sense.'[1] Having become a canoe builder himself, Gidmark remains committed to a tradition that links his craftsmanship with Native teachers and predecessors in the Algonquin birch-bark tradition.

Henry Wadsworth Longfellow provided Hiawatha with all the advantages of a good press agent. As a partial consequence of the American poet's enthusiasm, his subject's birch-bark watercraft comes almost automatically to mind when the accessories of the romanticized canoe trip are envisaged. Accordingly, juxtaposing non-Native reflections on West Coast dugout vessels with David Gidmark's celebration of the birch-bark canoe serves as a reminder of the diversity of Native watercraft.

Kenneth Brower, the biographer of the builder and designer George Dyson, whose fascination with the Aleut kayak, or baidarka, contributed to something of a resurgence of this style, had reactions comparable to Gidmark's when he reflected on West Coast Native watercraft in the University of British Columbia's renowned museum of anthropology. 'The success of Northwestern art,' Brower concluded, 'was in the grace of its curves, and that grace reached apogee in the canoes.' Pondering the original inspiration for the graceful and functional lines, he inquired:

Was it the glacier-shaped curve of the fiord headlands? Was it the curve of the lens clouds, or the dorsal curve of a fleeing whale? Or could it have derived from the canoe lines themselves? Maybe all Northwestern art began in that pragmatic solution to the problem posed by the waves. It was a happy solution, certainly, both in form and function. The designers of the clipper ships had thought so, and had let it influence them in lofting their bow lines.[2]

For his part, Dyson, too, has been absorbed in the quest for understanding the purpose of the particular intricacies of design that mark the baidarka, arguing that 'the existence of a particular form or feature of the baidarka implies the existence of a particular function, however resistant to explanation that functional purpose may be.'[3]

Long before Dyson, Brower, Gidmark, and other late twentieth-century observers speculated about an intimate, continuing association between North American aboriginal peoples and the canoe, commentators had lamented the decline of that very tradition. Late nineteenth- and early twentieth-century concern for the plight of the 'vanishing' Indian (a sentiment associated with the widespread assumption that European occupation of North America would inevitably result in the demise of Native cultures) frequently included reference to the disappearance of aboriginal watercraft. 'The red man with his birch-bark canoe is as much an integral part of this northern wilderness as the black bear itself,' remarked Arthur Silver. 'After he has succumbed to that strange sickness which civilization has brought on his race, the rivers and forests will scarcely seem the same.' Continuing his lament, Silver reflected that few people were familiar with the delicate beauty of the birch-bark. 'It is made only by the Indian,' he remarked, conceding that in this respect 'the white man has never equalled him.'[4] Dillon Wallace was somewhat more optimistic about the prospects of the canoe than about the prospects of its aboriginal builders when he pronounced solemnly in 1910: 'The canoe is all that remains of the primitive Indian and his life. This one product of his inventive genius and artistic instinct he conferred as a valuable heritage upon the race that displaced him.'[5]

Filmmakers equally shared a fascination with indigenous North American watercraft and some sense of foreboding about the future of the tradition it embodied. In 1914, Edward S. Curtis filmed *In the Land of the Head-Hunters* during the course of his work with the Kwakiutl peoples on the tenth volume of a photographic record of the Indians of North America. He experienced some difficulty in obtaining the canoes he needed for the production, as planked sailboats and gas-powered vessels were already in common use. Only about six canoes, the largest of which was some fifty feet in length, actually appear in Curtis's film. By disguising these remaining vessels, however, he was able to create the impression of the much larger fleet that would have been typical only a few years previously. Students of film history emphasize that the canoes are the most spectacular artefacts in the classic film, and that the canoe scenes remain the most popular, 'especially those of a great canoe racing by with the masked Thunderbird dancer "flying" in the bow, and the approach of the wedding party with Thunderbird, Wasp, and Grizzly Bear dancing to the beat of the paddles on the gunwales.' The description, provided by Bill Holm and George Irving Quimby, the biographers of Curtis, continues: 'The tiny canoes used by Naida and Motana are beautifully buoyant and graceful. There is an ease born of familiarity and long experience with which the hero handles his little one-man craft. Warriors work their great canoe around a rocky point or leap aboard in the surf and race across a choppy bay with casual skill.'[6] Another filmmaker, Robert J.

Flaherty, was first sponsored in his explorations of the mineral potential of northern Canada by the railway magnate Sir William Mackenzie, before he eventually emerged as the creator of *Nanook of the North*. The 1922 story of a far northern Inuk who hunted massive walrus from his fragile kayak eventually won acclaim from North American and European audiences, encouraging Flaherty to record his observations of man's relationship with nature in several other films.[7]

Only occasionally were recreational paddlers (and cinematographers, for that matter) able to distinguish the disappearance of traditional watercraft and the decline of their builders from the future of aboriginal communities. 'Now the white man is making as good a canoe,' argued an early twentieth-century tourist, 'and the Indian of the Nepigon at least recognizes and concedes its merits.' In consequence, he concluded,

the picturesque birchbark, after playing well its part, is gradually disappearing ... Though apparently incongruous, the new order now is a wooden boat and store clothes for the Indian, and his old canoe will disappear like the tomahawk, the moccasin, the bow and arrow, the scalp-lock and other primeval necessaries and luxuries.

What might be expected to endure, however, was the Native's 'old-time skill with the paddle; and more power to his elbows.'[8] This final comment reflected the fact that the transfer of watercraft technology had been accompanied, at least to some degree, by instruction in the technique of canoe travel – the skills of paddling, poling, and portaging – as well as the ancillary arts of camping and woodcraft.

The educational transfer was neither complete nor universal. Nevertheless, any number of canoeists spoke with affection and admiration of their Indian teachers, who through example or by means of more formal guidance and instruction passed on techniques and insights. As a young boy on the Lake of the Woods, the future socialist intellectual and international relations specialist John King Gordon was advised by his father, Ralph Connor, to study the Indians to learn paddling. He did so, and later recalled the experience:

They were a familiar sight in those days, paddling in their birch bark canoes, usually close to shore. The man would be paddling in the stern, the woman seated in the bottom of the canoe in the bow. In the centre usually three or four children. They paddled with a quick stroke, easily, rhythmically, upper hand low, a slight rotary motion of shoulders and back. And at the end of the stroke of the man in the stern, a slight drop of the shoulder to correct the run of the canoe.[9]

Robert Pinkerton formulated one of the more elaborate accounts of the merits of Native paddling. He argued that in adopting the technology without the technique, the white man had missed a good deal. 'We watched the red man build his craft and saw the finished product, but we never waited to watch him paddle it.' In consequence, he lamented, 'we lost half the prize.'[10] Pinkerton did not necessarily advocate use of the low sitting position widely favoured by aboriginal paddlers in birch-bark craft, but he expressed admiration for its contribution to stability and leverage. In *Cache Lake Country*, John R. Rowlands credited an Indian leader with teaching him, in his words, 'to use my eyes and my nose and my ears in ways only the woods people know,' and said, 'It was the Chief who showed me how to handle a canoe like an Indian with the short stroke that begins at the waist and ends with a thrust from the shoulders and never tires.' These lessons culminated in what Rowlands regarded as the proudest moment of his early years in the outdoors, 'when I was taken for an Indian because of the way I worked my paddle.'[11]

P.G. Downes, a Boston schoolteacher and northern traveller of the 1930s, was another paddler to whom comparisons of his own skill and understanding with that of the Native northerners meant a great deal: 'How could I not go back to the big lake, where one evening, with sizzling moose heart on a stick, an old Chipewyan said, "Stay with us. It is strange for one so white, but you know some things that only old men should know. Maybe you are a born-twice and used to be here among us once?"'[12] Kamil Pecher, in the course of the journey by kayak through northern Saskatchewan described in *Lonely Voyage*, was another modern voyageur who acquired what one sympathetic commentator called 'the indigenous mentality.' During his wanderings along six hundred miles of waterway, Pecher realized that he no longer needed to 'strive for achievement.' Having renounced the 'white man's way,' which was 'to conquer or be conquered,' he moved closer to the Native approach, which he understood as 'to yield to the natural forces and live in harmony with them.'[13]

A sense of alienation from one's own cultural origins, or even renunciation of these in favour of some idealized vision of aboriginal societies, is apparently not uncommon among non-Native observers of the Native peoples. Robert F. Berkhofer, Jr, seems to suggest that any number of anthropologists, writers, artists, and modern social philosophers have been attracted to Indian cultures 'as manifesting the wholeness of man, the humanity of interpersonal relationships, and the integrity of organic unity.'[14] As Kamil Pecher's experience suggests, canoeists have not been immune to the allure of another way of life, especially one seemingly in keeping with the natural environment that is so much a part of the paddler's summer world. How realistic it is to undertake such inter-cultural leaps is certainly a matter of debate, yet the appeal of these transformations is often noted.

Reverence for the Native woodsman as guardian of a tradition of wilderness and canoeing skills and environmental insights is the backdrop against which a number of somewhat disorienting inter-cultural encounters have been recorded. Eric Sevareid, despite 'canoeing with the Cree,' may simply have been recording his youthful observations, but he seemed less than overwhelmingly impressed by the Native paddlers he encountered en route to York Factory in 1930: 'Swinging long, crude, hand-made paddles, the two men sat on small cross boards, exerting all their energy on deep strokes, during which they grunted heavily and jerked back and forth. One or two strokes on one side and they would swing the paddles in an upward arc to the other side.' Sevareid seemed equally critical of the Native canoe, which was as long as his own, 'but wider and much heavier.'[15] P.G. Downes, despite his appreciation for Native society, recorded what he took to be an anomalous aboriginal opinion on the relationship between paddling and progress, the latter symbolized by the outboard motor: 'I remember a conversation I once had with an Indian named Charles on this matter. With a naivete not found in white people, he said to me: "You must be very poor to travel so far up here with no engine."'[16] But Downes's experience was hardly anomalous.[17]

At least by the 1940s, a division of opinion was emerging on the Indian's credentials as canoeist and conservationist. The Ottawa YMCA reacted favourably to the suggestion that an instructional movie on 'trail camping' should include a sequence recalling the Native association with the canoe:

The Indian legend on birch bark seems to be a fitting beginning. It shows that Trail Camping was part of their daily life, and that their existence depended upon their skill and knowledge of woodcraft. In the same way, the health and happiness of campers on trips will depend on their camping skills, and on their knowledge and understanding of the joys and perils of travelling through woods and lakes.[18]

In contrast, a representative of the Boy Scouts Association, having personally discerned what he took to be some deterioration in Native camping practices, was much less enthusiastic about the educational value of Indian legends.[19]

Eric Morse, later traversing some of the general territory in which P.G. Downes had taken so much delight, conveys the impression that the views of the unidentifed Charles were not uncommon:

Those Indians less practised in guarding their real thoughts expressed surprise at seeing a group of white men, all paddling, and most of the Indians seemed quite puzzled by the complete reversal in our roles: the Indians with outboard motors, the whites paddling. So used had they become to regarding the canoe as a vehicle of work that its recreational use seemed beyond their grasp.[20]

Tony Sloan, the author of *Black Flies and White Water*, recalled the same perception on the part of a guide, who expressed amazement that white men would 'work like hell all year at a job you don't like so you can go on holidays and live like an Indian for two weeks.'[21] As traditional communities elsewhere have adopted modern technology, similarly incongruous moments have been recorded. Twyla Wright and her companions, who first visited the Sea of Cortez by kayak in 1977, watched Seri Indian fishermen harpooning stingrays from their motor launch. When the kayakers paddled out to view the catch, the Seris laughed at the little boats and called them simply shark bait.[22]

While these somewhat bemused recollections may have given rise to a certain degree of self-questioning on the part of the vacationing paddler, many earlier – and highly judgmental – reports were devoid of doubt. David T. Hanbury, the author of the classic *Sport and Travel in the Northland of Canada*, had no shortage of opinion and advice concerning the Natives he employed and otherwise encountered in the course of his journeys.

I have learned from experience that an expedition to the north has the better chance of success the fewer white men are connected with it. In travelling over the 'Barren Ground' one cannot have more suitable companions than the natives of the country. A white man there is in a strange land, and, however willing and able to stand cold, hunger, and fatigue, he is a novice in this experience. The conditions and work are unfamiliar to him, and if he were to meet with a bad accident, or to fall ill, or to lose himself in a fog, his misfortune would probably be the ruin of the expedition.

Hanbury then reviewed the attractions of 'Husky servants,' as he referred to the Inuit, who travelled with their families so that they never departed from their customary way of life and were 'always at home.' He found the Inuit extraordinarily helpful assistants as well as 'hard-working, honest, good-natured, and cheerful companions.' They were, he continued, 'unwearying on behalf of one who treats them well.'[23]

At the same time, Hanbury criticized Indian guides and assistants unreservedly, claiming that he 'never yet was accompanied by an Indian who did not threaten to leave.' Hanbury reported a litany of excuses offered by his Indian assistants: 'anxiety about his wife and children, ignorance of the country, the danger of being lost, the dilapidation of his footgear, or, finally, the state of his health.' Advance payments were said to be extremely hazardous, as only by threatening to withhold pay could Hanbury induce his guides to fulfil their contractual obligations. The denunciation continued with a harshly critical description:

The Indian is morose, even sullen, rarely smiles, and of late years has acquired a slovenly, swaggering way of going about. When one arrives at his camp and proceeds to pitch his tent, the Indian never offers a helping hand. Pipe in mouth, he stands sullenly looking on, his hands thrust deep in his trousers' pockets. The contempt which he nourishes in his heart for the white man is expressed on his countenance.[24]

A good many early summer-travellers were also entirely forthcoming with socio-economic observations of dubious accuracy. The historian Agnes C. Laut, for example, travelled much of the Saskatchewan River. In the early 1900s, this author of *Lords of the North* (1900), *The Story of the Trapper* (1902), and *Canada: The Empire of the North* (1909) remarked in the vicinity of old Fort Pitt: 'Literally, and in terms of dollars and cents, the Indians on these reserves are better off than the average wage-earner among white men.' She noted that hay was available in abundance for the use of horses and cattle and that game was plentiful. A good hunter, she estimated, might readily secure seven hundred dollars' worth of fur over the winter; that is, she added, 'he can if he works; but like the Socialist, your Indian does not believe in laying up store for the morrow, which explains why he is so often in debt to the fur company and so often falls back starving on the mission when illness comes or the hunt fails.'[25]

Whatever the merits of this opinionated estimate, wilderness travellers, such as Laut herself, and outdoor vacationers represented a further source of income, especially in regions where reliable maps were slow to appear or where safety required an intimate familiarity with local weather systems or tidal movements. New seasonal employment opportunities for guides also became available at the youth camps, lodges, and resorts of the Canadian northland. Fishermen, hunters, and camping parties arranged, either privately or through their hotels, for the services of guides – often local Natives – on a daily or weekly basis. Ordinarily, two or more fishermen would share a guide during a day's outing from a resort base. Camping parties, particularly those embarking on extended trips, were advised to hire generously:

A canoe and guide should be provided for each of the party, and an extra guide with canoe to carry supplies, cook and attend to camp, leaving the 'sports', as those visiting the country for pleasure seem to be invariably called, and their personal guides, free to get away from camp in the morning or come in late at night, without the domestic economies being upset thereby.[26]

'There is something fine and inspiring about a portage,' mused Albert Bigelow Paine, who was impressed by 'the fascinating thought that you are cutting loose another link from everyday mankind – pushing a chapter deeper into the wilderness, where only the more adventurous ever come.' He was particularly enthralled by the carefree feeling associated with 'having one's possessions in such a compass that not only the supplies themselves, but the very means of transportation may be bodily lifted and borne from one water link to another of that chain which leads back ever farther into the unknown.' The convenience of it all was of course attributable to the distribution of the load, for, as Paine experienced the Nova Scotia portage, it was 'the business of the guides to transport the canoes, the general outfit, and the stores,' while fishermen retained responsibility for their sporting equipment.[27]

Not everyone welcomed the presence of a guide, for there might be disadvantages. After reviewing menu items for a trip in Quetico country, Florence Jaques was forced to admit that she was facing 'what the women's magazines might call a Meager Menu.' A guide would have permitted a far higher degree of luxury, 'with canned vegetables and even an oven.' But a guide would have brought civilization into the canoe country around Lac la Croix: 'We would have a buffer between us and the wilderness. As it is, we're facing nature as I, at least, never have before in my life.'[28] 'For the guides' part,' argues the historian Patricia Jasen, 'dignity was maintained through meticulous, perhaps even exaggerated, attention to the details of their work and through their superior knowledge of the wilderness – the reason, of course, for their employment in the first place.'[29]

In terms of income, guiding certainly had some important attractions.

In comparison with other employment possibilities such as fishing or work in construction and the forest industry, for example, guiding had the potential to be a highly remunerative, if seasonal, occupation. A guide's daily wage of two dollars, common during the 1880s and 1890s, was well above other wages in many parts of the northern wilderness. Baedeker's 1907 edition of the travel guide *The Dominion of Canada* indicated that the daily rate for a Temagami guide and canoe was between $3 and $3.50.[30] Paying up to $5 for the experience, late nineteenth-century tourists in the Sault Ste Marie area would often have enjoyed the same run through the St Mary's rapids that had appealed to Anna Jameson in an earlier era.[31]

When the first set of regulations applicable to Ontario forest reserves included a licensing requirement for guides with a fifty-dollar penalty provision, guiding became one of the earliest features of the tourist industry to be put under strict government regulation. Four years later, wage levels for guides were fixed at a rate of $2.50 per day as a result of complaints that 'guides sometimes make an arrangement with one party and another comes along and offers them a higher rate of pay and they desert the party they first engaged with and leave them helpless to get about.'[32]

The Northern Ontario Outfitters and Guides Association was formed in 1920. The association's goals included the maintenance of guiding standards, the establishment of uniform rates, and the protection of game. Wage rates were set at six dollars per day for a head guide and five dollars for other staff. Although these charges reflected substantial increases over levels prevailing before the First World War and were no doubt welcomed by the membership, the association can hardly be regarded as having represented the interests of the entire northern population. Indians in particular were to be restricted by the successful implementation of one of the outfitters' early recommendations, to create a game preserve in the region bounded by the Kabinakagami River in the east, the Kenogami in the west, the National Transcontinental Railway in the north, and the height of land to the south. The outfitters' association urged that 'all Indians [be] kept on the outside of its boundaries except those capable of acting as guides, and they be only admitted during the tourist and hunting season, when strict regulations may be maintained.'[33]

A guide's range and usefulness to parties of canoeists was based on a combination of prior knowledge of the terrain and the kind of travel skills that would be of value in new territory. At Lac Seul, George T. Marsh sought directions concerning the Albany River route to James Bay. The post manager, 'the hospitable Pattison,' explained that Fort Albany was a month's hard paddling and perhaps fifty portages from Lac Seul. Pattison persuaded Marsh's party that a guide would be essential if they were to cross over to the Root River, which rises within a short distance of Lake St Joseph, 'as any one not knowing the lake might spend a week hunting through the maze of islands and bays for the mouth of the river.' Marsh employed a resident of Lac Seul, 'Whiteduck by name, which, in picturesque Ojibway, is Wabininishib, to show us the way to Osnaburgh.'[34] Such men were not always available or might be otherwise engaged. Thus, Agnes Laut lamented that 'the time has long since passed when any one man knows the Saskatchewan River from end to end.' She claimed that by the first decade of the twentieth century the available guides knew only sections of the river. In consequence, she covered the first eight hundred miles 'with only one man and the help of the other two big paddles wielded by ourselves.'[35]

Leonidas Hubbard, when preparing for the Labrador expedition on which he hoped to found a reputation, first sought a familiar guide from the Missinaibie district of northern Ontario, where he had previously done some fishing. When this man proved unable to meet Hubbard in New York, he was replaced in the scheme by George Elson, the son of a Cree woman and a Scots trader, whose lack of familiarity with Labrador conditions was not considered a significant deficiency. Elson extended the lives of the members of his party more than once with a fine sense of geography and a keen memory for any landscape through which he had passed.

Through canoeing, recreational paddlers often had opportunities for social contact and a level of exposure to Native life they would never have experienced in the urban environment. However inadequate, the impressions thus formed – or re-formed – were less abstract than understanding derived exclusively from literature and legend. Though distance and distrust might remain characteristic of the relationship between Native guide and canoeist, as in Hanbury's early account, it was not always so. P.G. Downes took comfort from his impression that the indigenous residents of the Barrens 'change so little and are so ageless.' Indeed, he wondered whether 'this is not one of the reasons people go back to the North; the happiness one has found once, in the constancy of everything in the North, can more readily be found again.'[36] Relations of mutual respect sometimes approximating devotion have also been recorded. Mina Hubbard's friendship with George Elson exemplified a deep personal relationship between the urban sojourner in the wilderness and the resident canoeman and guide.[37]

There were also institutional aspects to the relationship between guides and campers. On the occasion of her camp's fiftieth anniversary, Mary S. Edgar, the founder of Camp Glen Bernard, near Sundridge, Ontario, reminded those in attendance that 'every camper who has been here knows that in this place there has always been a deep respect for the traditions, the symbols and the legends of the Indians.' In explaining the origins of Indian themes in Camp Glen Bernard's program, she recounted personal experiences from her youth. Of hearing, at the age of ten, Pauline Johnson read poetry in Sundridge, Edgar said, 'I was fascinated and wished I were related to her.' Later, in 1900, the family was on a fishing trip on Lake Nipissing and got caught in a storm. They were rescued by 'two Indian friends of my father from the Dokis reserve' and taken to Sturgeon Falls. 'We felt we owed our lives to them. We had a debt to pay.'[38]

Often having derived inspiration or encouragement from Ernest Thompson Seton, whose writings launched the League of Seton Indians, or Woodcraft Indians, in 1902, influential figures in the youth movement of the first half of the twentieth century promoted the introduction of Indian themes in the programs of summer camps, with great enthusiasm if not with the degree of personal commitment demonstrated by Mary Edgar.[39] The editors of the *Camps and Camping* volume of Spalding's Athletic Library series included a short chapter on Indian lore in summer camps in which youth leaders were reminded of the opportunities available to 'enrich their program in handicrafts, pageantry and ceremonial, and at the same time to give their work more romance and color.'[40] Decorative designs were recommended, with the thought that images on canoe paddles 'will probably be the first to attract attention.' The camp staff who were responsible for relevant activities were encouraged to emphasize an authentic background, warned against the prevalent tendency to believe 'that an Indian is just an Indian and that all tribes spoke the same language and were exactly alike,' and strongly urged to avoid 'the burlesque type of Indian lore we have had in too many of our camps and schools.' The message was to do it well or not at all, in order to avoid the risk that 'an appreciation of the Indian's finer qualities and the value of his contributions to our civilization' would be lost.[40]

When broader questions about the status and future of Native communities in North American society became subjects of widespread public interest later in the twentieth century, the issue of Indian lore and ceremonials proved to be increasingly problematic for youth camping. Many of those involved reflected on the virtues and limitations of what they had been doing. 'Is There Still a Place for the Indian Council Ring Ceremony?' was the title of a talk given by W.J. Eastaugh at an annual meeting of camp directors in 1972. The question had been stimulated by campers who 'maintained that we were mocking and making fun of the North American Indian and in view of the many indignities already perpetrated upon this undertrod minority ... they could not see any justification for holding such out-dated ceremonies.' Eastaugh, whose experience with Indian lore programs extended back over four decades, expressed the conviction that 'in all those years I cannot recall a single incident in which the Indian was portrayed as anything less than a brave, skillful, naturalist – an artisan, lover of the forest, lake and stream and a heroic figure of stature and nobility.' But he was equally willing to accept that cultural facts had been disregarded in so far as various elements from across the continent had been assembled and somewhat casually combined into an improbable composite: 'We have stolen the tipi from the people of the plains, the grotesque and marvellously hideous masks of the Iroquois, the birch bark crafts of the Hurons and the Rhythmic design of the Haidas and Kootenay Indians of the West Coast.'[41] Measures to restore authenticity to the collage were possibly easier to adopt than measures to respond to another line of questioning, one more likely to have been initiated by Native people themselves.

Linda M. Gerber, a social scientist of aboriginal ancestry, was one of those who had begun to ask about the relationship between camping traditions and contemporary attitudes towards aboriginal communities: 'Does a reenactment of past cultural patterns do justice to present-day Indians, or does it perpetuate stereotypical images of primitiveness that interfere with relations between Indians and non-Indians today?' Gerber was anxious to ensure that the wider participation of Native people in all aspects of contemporary society and their aspirations for cultural development would not be ignored if summer camps continued to incorporate aspects of Native life into their programs. After describing sociological and political changes affecting Native communities, she explained the potential implications for camp directors and outlined the contribution that such individuals were uniquely placed to make:

In a sense camp directors are gatekeepers controlling access into a new area of associational relationships, and as such you can help channel some of the talents and energies of these new Indians. By entering into dialogue with them and listening sincerely to what they have to say, you can accomplish at least two purposes: with respect to your Indian cultural programs at camp, you can tune in to the present state of Indian culture and perhaps get some ideas about what could be added to your existing programs; with respect to native people, you can give them an opportunity to help determine how their culture is presented to non-Indians.[42]

Despite the impressions that P.G. Downes, Eric Morse, and many other northern canoe travellers brought back in the middle decades of the twentieth century, Native people themselves have not totally forsaken the canoe or other traditional watercraft. Yet canoeing now often involves a different set of associations for aboriginal canoe-users: their re-creation of canoe culture sometimes appears more purposeful than that of the non-Native summer paddler.

For Billy Diamond, a respected Cree leader from northern Quebec, the high-tech canoes built by members of his community in cooperation with Japanese investors were intended to symbolize a successful accommodation between modern technology and the traditional cultural priorities of his people, who have travelled on northern inland and coastal waters for centuries.[43] For Bill Reid, the renowned Haida artist from the West Coast, the canoe remains an elemental feature of a Native cultural mythology. Yet he has expressed concern that his work and that of other West Coast artists is not fully appreciated for its cultural origins: 'We feed into the general population these objects which bring satisfaction and enjoyment to the non-native population, and we get money in return individually. But nobody sees beyond the images of the iconography to the people whose ancestors created this kind of thing.'[44] For Alwyn Morris, a Mohawk from Kahnawaké, near Montreal, his joint victory with Hugh Fisher in the men's kayak tandem thousand-metre event at the 1984 Los Angeles Olympics was suitably dedicated to the Native people of North America.

The re-emergence of the canoe in Native political protest and cultural ceremonies also attests to its continuing significance for many communities. To draw public attention to their opposition to the power development plans of Hydro-Québec, and in an effort to publicize the severe environmental damage that would result from river diversion and flooding in their homelands, Cree and Inuit paddlers campaigned across eastern North America and in Europe. New York harbour, the Charles River near Boston, and the Rhine witnessed the hybrid 'odeyak' – part canoe and part kayak – in demonstrations against the Quebec utility's plans for hydro-electric power development on the Great Whale River.[45] Similarly, the canoe is re-emerging as an element of the revival of Native culture on the West Coast, where aboriginal builders and paddlers have recently been active again. Bill Reid built a fifty-foot dugout in connection with Expo '86, and others have followed his lead in helping to restore a nearly lost craft. Such vessels now appear regularly in coastal waters.[46]

These very public and ceremonial tribal journeys, elements in the restoration of communities, have personal counterparts in Native youth programs that function much as some of the canoe trips into the healing pines.[47] The program at Agamatin Wilderness Trails, for example, was designed as a seminar for Native youth, generally from remote northern Ontario communities. Operated by Dryden's Northern Youth Programs office, Agamatin seeks to promote the overall development of its participants – physical, mental, emotional, and spiritual. Although some of those involved, typically ranging in age from the late teens to the early twenties, have had previous outdoor experience, two weeks of canoe travel ordinarily is new for them.

One trip of about two hundred kilometres from Osnaburgh to Sioux Lookout in the summer of 1990 involved five boys and their leaders. The route is arduous enough, but with time along the way for jumping off cliffs and playing aquatic football, there were plenty of opportunities for interaction and discussion. As reported in *Wawatay News*, 'The qualities of trust, endurance, humility, sensitivity to others, patience, love, self-confidence, initiative, service, leadership and self-discipline are built into the life as the team learns to function in the wilderness together.'[48]

This additional example of the canoe trip's contribution to inner journeys invites further reflection on routes and destinations. Does it really matter where you go, as long as you are paddling?

12

Destinations

On first impression, P.G. Downes's autobiographical confession – 'I was not particularly sure where I was going' – hardly seems to provide an adequate foundation for the legendary status enjoyed by this ardent northern traveller of the 1930s. 'Even as I went west on the train,' the Boston schoolteacher disclosed, 'I postponed my final decision until my arrival in Winnipeg, where I might hear something of peculiar interest which would determine my course.' Notwithstanding this uncertainty, Downes clearly intended to reach the Barrens, which were for him the 'one beacon which was unwavering.'[1] Many subsequent would-be adventurers for whom the Barrens' remoteness and the potential for tragedy exercise a peculiar appeal have shared Downes's fascination with the region as a recreational destination. In some respects a model traveller, Downes may have inspired others, but – given the almost casual appearance of his preparations – he was hardly a traveller to emulate. It is not entirely clear, for example, that he would have passed the standards for preparation and precaution later set by Eric Morse for summer travel in the Canadian Barrens.[2]

As a frequent visitor to this challenging northern terrain, Downes was remarkably self-effacing in describing the attraction it held for him. 'I like it there in the land of the little trees, I like the people, I am happy there.' But he acknowledged that 'any reasonable person' might find this explanation 'very inadequate.'[3] It was not the choice of summer pastime that might have puzzled a reasonable person, but the location in which Downes chose to pursue it. Arguably, though, Downes's vague account of his motivation and apparent indifference as to the precise course he would follow are entirely characteristic of a certain species of canoeist, who can be more inclined to explore an area than to complete a route: he undoubtedly enjoyed travel, but he had a particular affinity for place and seemed, by and large, content to be wherever he found himself.

Downes illustrates one long-established tendency among recreational paddlers – to distinguish themselves through their choice of routes and destinations. The lost canoeist's apprehensive query 'Where are we?' may offer insights into the map-reading skills of the inquisitor, but much more is revealed by the prior – and customarily off-season – query 'Where shall we go?' James Edmund Jones cautioned recreational paddlers that it is often 'a great mistake to sacrifice enjoyment to speed.' He warned those who make speed and distance their principal objectives that 'many of the best diversions of a camping party will have to be curtailed or omitted.' Jones counselled wilderness travellers looking for an excuse to put down their loads on the portage trail not to hesitate to idle around a good huckleberry or blueberry patch.[4]

Yet far too frequently, canoeists succumbed to what Stewart Edward White, one of Jones's early twentieth-century contemporaries, described as 'the lust of travel,' an affliction which some considered 'a very real disease.' The lust of travel, White cautioned, 'usually takes you when you have made up your mind that there is no hurry.' A chart or map may trigger the affliction, whose main symptom is 'the feverish delight with which you check off the landmarks of your journey.' A stiff following wind is 'absolutely fatal,' with the consequence that 'good fishing, fine scenery, interesting bays, reputed game, even camps where friends may be visited – all pass swiftly astern.' The lamentable result is that 'the mad joy of putting country behind you' pushes all other interests aside. Victims of the lust for travel were likely to recover only at the end of their journey. But having arrived a week or so early, they 'must then search out new voyages to fill in the time.'[5]

From at least the era of MacGregor's *Thousand Miles in a Rob Roy Canoe*, the impulse to keep score or to tally up one's accomplishments has kept some recreational paddlers on the water whether or not they had anywhere to go. At the close of the 1884 season, J.L. Weller, writing from Lakefield, Ontario, gave notice to his colleagues in the American Canoe Association as follows: 'I have this summer kept a daily account of miles paddled and sailed, and I now have 645 miles to my credit. Most of this, in fact all but about thirty or forty miles, was done in the *Zulu*.' In justification of what some readers might have regarded as a rather modest accomplishment, Weller emphasized that he had 'made no extended trips, or, of course, my score would be much larger.' He explained that all his paddling had been done in off hours on ninety-eight days between 5 May and

22 November.[6] If this explanation successfully appeased one set of observers, others might well have concluded that whatever mileage Weller had accumulated, he had gone precisely nowhere.

The tendency to quantify one's canoeing accomplishments as in 'I have tripped over a thousand miles' may represent more than a bent for scorekeeping. Quantifying is perhaps a surrogate for experience and even for expertise; yet some observers have expressed the suspicion that concentration on distance may indicate an excessive preoccupation with quantity over quality. However appealing it is simply to be in the wilderness, another powerful inspiration – doing the wilderness – has competed effectively. Doing a river, doing *the* big trip, and, especially, getting there first have been irresistible temptations for a surprising number of participants in what so many other devotees have promoted as a carefree, contemplative pastime rather than an arena for fierce competition and personal ambition.

Canoeing 'firsts' may have been easier to contemplate in an earlier age, although whether they were easier to accomplish will remain a matter of some dispute. In the nineteenth century, an element of exploration and discovery, particularly when accompanied by the spirit of competition, heightened the appeal of certain adventures. Thus, in a series of episodes reminiscent of Sir Richard Burton and John Hanning Speke's fabled mid-Victorian rivalry over the source of the Nile, a number of American canoe expeditions set out to identify the true source of the Mississippi, and their participants to be the first paddlers to descend the entire length of that river.

In 1879, a party led by A.H. Siegfried set off in Rushton-built Rob Roys for Lake Itasca, generally believed from the time of Henry Schoolcraft's visit there in 1832 to be the headwaters. Although more or less confirming Schoolcraft's accomplishment, Siegfried carefully defined his own place in the story. 'Beyond any question,' he announced triumphantly, 'our canoes were the first wooden boats that ever traversed those waters.' Shortly thereafter, Willard Glazier, having confused himself, but few professional observers, in the complex waterways around Lake Itasca, announced another true source. Glazier's downstream procession, more or less following Siegfried's route, distinguished itself by paddling the entire distance, rather than sailing as their predecessors had occasionally done. In the immediate aftermath of a controversial publicity battle between the contenders, Minnesota established Itasca State Park. Atwood Manley and Paul Jamieson graciously credit Glazier with being the ultimate source of at least that achievement.[7]

Those less intent on a canoe voyage of discovery might seek their firsts in the form of mammoth, challenging, or innovative journeys over familiar routes. Charles A. Neide and Samuel D. Kendall, for example, journeyed by canoe from Lake George, New York, to Pensacola, Florida, through the fall and winter of 1882–3. In *The Canoe Aurora: From the Adirondacks to the Gulf,* Neide chronicled the route along Lake Champlain, the Hudson River, and the Erie Canal to Buffalo. After a railroad portage to the Allegheny River, Neide and Kendall followed that waterway, the Ohio, and then the Mississippi to the Gulf of Mexico and on to Pensacola, the overall itinerary covering some thirty-three hundred miles.[8]

One of the more recently achieved ambitions has been described as 'the race to raft the Upper Yangtze,' a waterway said to have 'evoked images of liquid thunder, or secret lamaseries clinging to streaked limestone cliffs, or gorges thin as a glacier crevasse, or jade-laced mountains draped by eternal snows.'[9] Chinese authorities, astutely recognizing the attraction that a 'first descent' had for Western whitewater afficionados, and having experience with the sale of rights of 'first ascent' on various mountain peaks, opened the bidding at one million dollars. Eventually the entry fee came down to more affordable levels, and in the mid-1980s the race was on 'to conquer an unconquerable opponent, a race to ride the dragon, to tame the mighty Yangtze.'[10]

Adventure-seekers elsewhere were widely engaged in 'expedition' travel throughout the 1980s. The Niger River, for example, served as the source of a difficult logistical challenge for a joint British and Nigerian Boy Scout adventure. The British contingent, after travelling by plane to Onitsha, Nigeria, on a series of flights from London's Heathrow Airport, through Brussells, en route to Kano and Lagos, declined the first canoe offered:

We were then shown the Motor Canoe that had been earmarked for us. It is about fifty feet long with sides about four feet high. It came with owner, engineer and cook at N30 a day. Although we were supposed to be able to paddle this vessel and only use the engine to reach a suitable village for the night, this was not practicable … If we had used a motorized canoe we would not have been able to set foot in canoeing circles again.

More acceptable arrangements were eventually agreed upon, so that the canoeists were ultimately allowed to record the accomplishment of having operated 'the first canoe to be paddled from Onitsha to Port Harcourt since the Crisis in '69,' a reference to the Nigerian civil war, which had been followed by the introduction of motorized canoes in the 1970s.[11]

Tours of China and the Niger Delta in the 1980s were confirmation of the ubiquity of the canoe and the intrepidity of its crew – two long-exalted features of the pastime.

> You find this fellow wherever you go,
> From the River Jordan to Mexico.
> For he paddles around in his light canoe
> From kingdom come to Kalamazoo[12]

was a well-known claim among early members of the American Canoe Association. The impulse to recreational adventure celebrated here took hold in the minds of more than a few would-be explorers even as the historian Frederick Jackson Turner announced the closing of the American frontier, and Victoria's empire reached its maximum extent with the nineteenth century drawing to a close. The essential objective was to find unfamiliar territory and to set off for a destination not previously reached by European visitors.

One of those inspired and ultimately driven to his death by the prospect of making a discovery was Leonidas Hubbard. Dillon Wallace, who accompanied Hubbard to Labrador in 1903, said of his friend that 'Boone and Crockett were his heroes.' Stimulated by 'tales of their adventures,' Hubbard would sometimes 'steal away to the woods and camp out for two or three days.'[13] His wife, Mina, had much the same understanding of the impulses underlying Hubbard's eagerness for adventure. She described him as passionate about history and geography. Stories about wars, about Indians, and about adventurous journeys inspired him to reflect on the life of the frontier, 'in which the courage, endurance, and high honour of his own pioneer forefathers stood out strong and clear.' Mina found it quite natural that Hubbard's thoughts were always 'reaching towards the out-of-the-way places of the earth where life was still that of the pioneer with the untamed wilderness lying across his path, and on into the wilderness itself.'[14]

After Leonidas Hubbard perished in the interior of Labrador, Dillon Wallace regrouped for a second attempt, and Mina Hubbard separately resumed her husband's work in search of a route across Labrador to the George River and Ungava Bay. Mrs Hubbard took particular satisfaction in the extraordinary accomplishment she was able to claim for herself:

When the day's journey ended I had seen so much that was beautiful, and so varied in its beauty, that I felt confused and bewildered. I had, too, not only seen Seal

Lake, I had seen the Nascaupee River flowing out of it; ... and, best of all there came the realization that I was first in the field, and the honour of exploring the Nascaupee and the George Rivers was to fall to me.[15]

The Gulf of Mexico and Latin America have also had an enduring attraction for northern canoeists. The Starkell expedition of 1980–2 described in *Paddle to the Amazon: The Ultimate 12,000-Mile Canoe Adventure*[16] is undoubtedly the most publicized of recent canoe journeys. Various predecessors, including other Amazonian canoe trips, are less well known. Theodore Roosevelt explored remote reaches of western Brazil in 1913, and in the sixteen-foot vessel *Canadian Friendship* John Nolan and Robert Copeman left Edmonton in the summer of 1928 en route for the Gulf of Mexico.[17] In the same decade, David Hatton of Peterborough and two companions set out to explore the Amazon River; their canoe was specially designed with an inboard motor.

Dana and Ginger Lamb, self-styled 'enchanted vagabonds,' recorded the saga of their '16,000 miles on $4.20,' a three-year trip that began in San Diego in 1933 and took them along the west coast of Mexico and Central America through the Panama Canal to Cristobal, on the Atlantic side. The couple prepared extensively for an encounter with the then largely unfamiliar Baja California – 'hardening our bodies, sleeping on the ground, and eating the coarse unpalatable food – chiefly corn and beans – that we knew we would have to subsist on once we left civilization.' The landscape, if not more nourishing than the local fare, was at least striking:

It is a magnificent and impressive sight. Behind the bold rocky headland of the Cape rise purple peaks, and beyond lie the mysterious mountains of Triunfo, sprawled round the base of a great peak that stands in their midst like a giant's thumb. Nature here has accomplished what man has failed to do – she has gained a foothold. Deep canyons of vivid green gash the mountains' otherwise barren and precipitous slopes.

Having begun the odyssey for personal reasons, the Lambs professed 'no particular belief in its interest or value to any one else.' They returned, however, with firm political views about the civilization they had formerly taken for granted. After living quite comfortably off the land and the sea, they lamented 'the increasing reluctance and inability of large groups to solve their own problems,' and they were disheartened to observe the 'growing distaste for economic, social and political freedom, if it entails personal responsibility.' Too many people, it seemed to the long-absent travellers, naïvely believed 'that a political messiah or an economic formula can do for them the things that all men must do for themselves or perish.'[18]

Canoeists bearing personal witness to the societies to which they returned as strangers, or through which they passed, were remarkably familiar figures in the publishing world of the 1930s. In the same year that the Lambs' saga appeared, William VanTil published the odyssey of his lengthy Danube expedition through Germany, Austria, Czechoslovakia, Hungary, and Yugoslavia in a fold-boat. The rise of Nazism forms a dark backdrop to the canoe journey as any number of passers-by and others met along the route inquire about the prospects of accompanying VanTil out of the increasingly oppressive conditions of the late 1930s. 'Take me. I'll hide in your knapsack,' insisted one desperate acquaintance, his tongue somewhat loosened by an evening in the tavern. Friends drowned out the conversation with singing before spiriting their comrade away, but 'it would be morning before they would know for certain if he had been heard and reported.'[19]

Apart from the various urges to make a discovery, to record a personal accomplishment, and to experience a revelation, the desire to carry out a purpose has exerted more than a little influence on the paddler's agenda. Any number of outings have been oriented towards some goal or mission, to give participants a more plausible justification for their summer pastime than P.G. Downes's somewhat provocative excuse 'I like it there.' F.A. MacDougall was among those who insisted that the canoe trip should have a purpose. 'A hasty scurrying from place to place without time for work, observation or reflection, may perhaps break some record that will soon be broken again, but it is largely wasted mental and physical effort.' Happily for the generation of young paddlers MacDougall was addressing in the 1940s, the burden of guilt for wasting mental and physical effort could readily be alleviated by leaving 'some physical impression on the country.' There were any number of ways to make life easier for those who would follow and thus to give your sojourn in the wilderness a defensible purpose:

You may build a dock, repair a dam, level a few feet of trail, construct a fire place. The land will be better for you having been on it. You made some physical mark on the country. Ever afterwards you will remember that trip by some little improvement you made on your route; photographing or sketching parts of the route, studying the flora and fauna or the rock formation of the country; surveying and mapping parts of the district make the trip of real value.[20]

These instructions to improve the landscape with some practical installation came from no less an authority than the Ontario deputy minister of natural resources, the man ultimately responsible for the administration of parks across the province. Indeed, MacDougall had served for most of the 1930s as superintendent of Algonquin Park.

Other rationales for paddling in interesting places are more likely to be used today. Thus, in the summer of 1988 the Canadian Arctic Expedition's trip along the Kazan River from its origins in the vicinity of the Manitoba border with the Northwest Territories to Baker Lake had a series of accomplishments in mind. The trip was one element of a four-year, around-the-world project scheduled to coincide with the four hundredth anniversary of Sir Walter Raleigh's circumnavigation of the globe. Participants in the Canadian phase ranged in age from seventeen to twenty-four and had been drawn from eleven countries for the undertaking. Their objective was to conduct a multidisciplinary study of the cultural and natural heritage during the course of a five-hundred-kilometre trip along the Kazan River in Canada's eastern Arctic.[21]

Those not fortunate enough to have a practical objective or altruistic purpose for their wanderings have always been able to assimilate the trip and its purpose to an important, if ultimately purely personal, meaning. Well into the course of their formidable undertaking to reach South America by canoe from Winnipeg, Don and Dana Starkell paused to reflect upon the nature of their accomplishment:

The other night, Dana and I had a long conversation, not entirely positive, about all the realities and illusions we've dealt with in getting here. We talked about the sacrifices and benefits and purposes of it all. Lately, however, I'm inclined to think of the trip not so much as having purposes, but of being its own purpose, of having a rich and varied meaning in itself – the journey as the message. I remarked on this to Dana, and he seemed to accept it as valid.[22]

The same thought, simply that 'the journey was the destination,'[23] appears frequently in accounts of the canoeist's motivation, although the sentiment has never been more effectively expressed than in Nick Inman's disarmingly candid analysis of canoeing through life:

Life is like a canoeing trip down a long river (amongst other things) ... Getting into your canoe can be tricky, but once you are in ... there's no stopping, until you reach the end of the river. Being in your canoe can drive you mad at times; you can, of course, get out and walk around the bank for a while – but you soon realise that there is nowhere else to go except down the river.

Half-way down the river you wonder why you didn't bring a map or a guide-book –
then you remember that the river knows where it's going, and you don't need to.[24]

Along many northern rivers the pathways are well worn, the good
camping spots – sometimes few and far between – well scouted out or
known to the guides. And this has been so for a long time.[25] If these
conditions sometimes deterred an earlier generation of exploration-
oriented canoeists, they have enhanced the appeal of certain routes and
destinations for other recreational paddlers.

Like a number of other travellers to York Factory, Manitoba, Kenneth
Campbell and his colleagues journeyed to Norway House by steamer from
the south end of Lake Winnipeg. Campbell, a Winnipeg dentist in his
thirties, was accompanied by Richard W. Craig, Laurie C. Boyd, and
Arthur W. Hogg. At Norway House they hired Solomon Farmer, Johnnie
Robertson, James Fletcher, and Thompson Macdonald to guide the expedition down the Hayes River. Outfitted by courtesy of the Hudson's Bay
Company at Norway House, the canoe party set off on Saturday, 5 August.
The year was 1911, one year after Canada's Governor-General Earl Grey
had covered essentially the same route with a somewhat more elaborate
entourage. The official vice-regal party had consisted of eleven people
accompanied by nineteen guides with twelve canoes.

Campbell and his urban companions saw history in action as they
encountered York boats, still in service freighting over the traditional
water route that linked Winnipeg and the Bay. Corduroy roads and the
occasional tramway eased portages for the canoeists, some of whom might
catch the occasional ride through rapids on the more seaworthy York
boats; the entire party relished a lift as the boats sailed down Oxford Lake.
Campbell recorded: 'Yesterday and today have been days of great experience for us. I have heard of York Boats for years, seen pictures of them,
but these two days have given us the opportunity to get our information
first hand and to learn the habits of the crew.' After a few days at York
Factory spent in re-provisioning and absorbing the atmosphere of what
was once headquarters for the Hudson's Bay Company's Northern Department, Dr Campbell's party returned to Norway House tracking, poling,
and portaging upstream via the Hayes, a difficult seventeen days.[26]

The journeys of many later visitors to York Factory were enriched by
others' having gone before. Over the course of several decades as a
canoeist, Ben Ferrier was a regular northern traveller; he had guided
parties to the Bay seven times prior to an expedition in the mid-1950s that
provided the subject matter for *God's River Country*, an account of north-

ern travel he authored jointly with his wife, Marion, in 1956. The rest of the crew consisted of boys from Chicago and two scientists from the University of Minnesota. In three nineteen-foot Hudson Bay freighters, the twelve-member assemblage travelled for eight weeks, initially by boat. The S.S. *Keenora* transported the party to Warren's Landing, at the north end of Lake Winnipeg, where they boarded the launch *Chickama* and carried on to Norway House. The first phase of the canoe trip itself, a combination of paddle and portage, brought the Ferrier contingent to God's Lake, then down the God's River to York Factory on Hudson Bay. The return journey by way of the Nelson River took the group back to Norway House.[27] Eric Sevareid's view of God's Lake was that 'such sights as this are reserved for those who will suffer to behold them.'[28] For travellers such as Sevareid, the satisfaction to be found was directly attributable to the effort that went into the experience.

Alternative routes to the same destination have been endowed with their own mystique and legitimacy. By choosing one path over another, for example, paddlers have endeavoured to align themselves with a preferred set of forerunners. Thus, a women's trip to York Factory used the middle track via the Bigstone and Fox rivers, joining the Hayes only for the final section to the Bay. 'We chose not to take the Hayes River, easier, more travelled, where the European explorers pushed into the interior in big York boats. Ours is an older Indian route on the Bigstone and Fox, suitable only for small canoes.' The choice of route appears to embody a political preference, distancing these recreational paddlers from the implied wrongdoing of one group and aligning them spiritually with another community. 'The British did this heroic military-style stuff, travelling at top speed to get somewhere else. The Crees lived here, women, men, children, aged people; when they went to York Factory to trade, probably the whole family often went along.'[29]

That canoe routes might have ideological associations has engaged the attention of social commentators. Thus, William C. James of the Department of Theology at Queen's University contemplated the possibility that linear trips might be fundamentally different from canoe journeys over a circular course. Perhaps the linear trip, often assumed to be of the 'let's conquer the river' variety and frequently supported by mechanized transportation at one end or the other, was 'more likely to become an aggressive assault upon the wilderness.' In contrast, James speculated, a circular route 'would be preferred by the environmentalist and the purist as obviously more natural, harmonious, and adaptive.'[30] A brief period of reflection compelled him to abandon the hypothesis, for canoeists are entirely capable of reaching their destinations through serendipitous linearity or in a manner that is aggressively circular.

Islands – Ireland, New Zealand, and Iceland, for example – have been particularly challenging to circumnavigators, who have found few opportunities to enjoy the scenery. Thus, Nigel Foster reported on his tour of the Icelandic coast:

It was about nine and a half weeks before we reached our starting point again at Seydisfjordur, having paddled all the way around Iceland. Our arrival was not the magic moment that we anticipated. Instead it was tinged with sadness. Our reason for being there was gone. Our relaxed timeless existence was over. We could no longer look forward, only backwards to the treasured memories.[31]

Another noteworthy phenomenon in the choice of routes and destinations is the widespread tendency for contemporary paddlers to seek out symbolic predecessors on canoe trips, which can accordingly assume something of the quality of pilgrimages. The destination serves as a shrine, a place to pay homage to major figures from the wilderness pantheon. The authors of a magnificent re-creation of the 1903 and 1905 Hubbard and Wallace journeys through Labrador sought out the campsite near a stream called the Susan where Leonidas Hubbard finally died after his exhausting ordeal. The camp, now the location of a commemorative plaque, lay far removed from human pathways:

There is no road leading to the site of Hubbard's camp – not even the faintest trail. Even now, after more than eighty years, no one hikes here. Around the spot, there is still only the white caribou moss and the scrub pine and the empty swamps. The nearest human dwelling is a trapper's cabin, itself deserted most of the year, some twenty miles distant. The closest settlement remains the outpost that Hubbard had been trying to reach. It is fifty miles away, with only forest and open water intervening.[32]

Similarly, Michael Peake and his associates from the Hide-Away Canoe Club brought back a more tangible trophy from their 1992 trip along another northern route, travelled decades earlier by George M. Douglas, who had left a paddle on a ledge.[33]

A more frequently visited site, again honouring the memory of a wilderness legend, is Beaver Lodge on Ajawaan Lake in Saskatchewan's Prince Albert National Park. Here, for the better part of the 1930s, Archie Belaney lived as Grey Owl, writing many of his best-known stories and personally greeting park visitors who had travelled by canoe to see the beaver Rawhide and Jelly Roll. Some six hundred tourists made the conservation pilgrimage in 1936, to be followed in the decades after Grey Owl's death in 1938 by countless others.[34] In the late twentieth century, canoe enthusiasts recognized Grey Owl as one of the leaders of Canadian environmentalism. As Kenneth Brower explained to the largely American readership of the *Atlantic Monthly*: 'If his deeds had been done at a slightly lower latitude, we all would have heard of him. In the pantheon Grey Owl belongs with Henry David Thoreau, John Muir, Aldo Leopold, and Rachel Carson – or perhaps with Lewis Mumford and Joseph Wood Krutch, on the level just below.'[35]

Other destinations derived their allure from association and promotion. Raymond M. Patterson might have been an improbable figure to direct the attention of the canoeing world to the remote Nahanni, but he was undoubtedly a crucial factor in the later popularity of the river. Patterson was born in England and completed his education there to become a history exhibitioner of St John's College, Oxford. Service with the Royal Field Artillery from 1917–18 and a period spent in captivity were followed by three probationary years at the Bank of England. For reasons that remain somewhat obscure, Patterson was drawn to Canada, where he worked on a dairy farm in the Fraser Valley and in logging camps. He homesteaded in the Peace River country, freighted, hunted, and trapped in the district, and then wandered 'down north' to the South Nahanni River. Some years later, after turning his restless hands to Alberta sheep ranching, Patterson recalled his Nahanni days in *The Dangerous River*, a book which appeared about the time that Eric Morse and elements of his crew were helping to reinvigorate the canoe-tripping tradition.

Patterson claimed he had no qualifications as a whitewater paddler at the time he set off for the Nahanni, recalling simply that 'the art of handling a canoe had been acquired entirely on the Cherwell and the Isis – a very gentle school of rivercraft.' Nevertheless, his passion for the outdoors and his ability to convey the excitement of whitewater laid the foundations for his position as a pioneer and for the cult status of the river, whose legends he brought to a wider audience.[36]

One of the Nahanni's more colourful characters, the prospector Albert Faille, had legendary status conferred upon him by Canada's National Film Board.[37] When the wilderness recreation movement exploded in the late 1960s and early 1970s, the Nahanni emerged as an obvious destination for those seeking a quintessential canoe trip experience. Overcrowding almost threatened the distant Nahanni in the way that too much activity on a river whose attraction was isolation and remoteness was bound to do, and rationing has been introduced to moderate the adverse consequences of excessive popularity.

If it was becoming increasingly difficult to be first anywhere any more, it was often impossible even to be alone. There were, however, more modest ambitions for those recreational paddlers who were prepared to share the pleasures of the outdoors with other like-minded travellers. George Dyson, the baidarka devotee, had a philosophy to reflect the growing need to lower the adventure level a few notches and to accommodate the possibility that other canoeists had been there before you and might very well be there at the time of your arrival:

Long stretches of the coastline from where we lay south to Vancouver Island were deserted now, after the busy days of dugout canoes, when small villages had stood everywhere. The country was waiting to be known again. Most discovery is redis-covery. The best discoveries are personal, anyway, and not the kind commissioned by queens and scientific academies. The idea that Earth's landscapes have been used up in some way was, for me, peculiar.[38]

The notion that the Earth's landscapes had been used up would have been equally peculiar to the thousands of paddlers who took to the rivers and canals of Europe in the earlier decades of the twentieth century. W.S. Holding, a veteran paddler of the decades following 'Rob Roy' MacGregor's outings in Europe, wrote that 'practically every river on the Continent became then the happy roaming-ground of enterprising youths and mature men, who took the fever and tried to do everything that John MacGregor had done. Many tried to go one better.' Holding was among those who remarked that the Canadian canoe had to a considerable degree displaced the Rob Roy–style boat. It 'affords means of giving infinite pleasure to flannel-clad youths and smartly clad maidens on the Thames, at regattas, and on the quiet reaches of many English rivers, and in little land-locked bays where boisterous waves may not be encoun-tered.' Its popularity in England was such, he argued, that there were 'probably more Canadian canoes on the Thames between Oxford and Teddington than on any similar length of water in the world.' The scene he painted featured 'youth in immaculate whites, sleeves up, smoking cigarettes; in the bow, a pink umbrella, and a maiden beautifully dressed beneath it.'

Ranking English rivers for the enjoyment of canoeists, Holding put the Severn in 'premier place' for a hundred-mile stretch from Shrewsbury to

Gloucester, where no serious difficulties would be encountered and where the scenery was of considerable interest. Without explanation the Trent was ranked second, while the Wye, though placed first for scenic grandeur, emerged in third spot as a canoeing river. Other rivers had much appeal, including the 'very interesting' Avon from Rugby to Gloucester, along which route Holding had once endured a five-mile portage by cart when the Earl of Warwick declined to grant permission to paddlers to pass through his parkland.[39]

R.J. Evans was another paddler well versed in the waterways of England. His ranking of the rivers differed from Holding's in that he chose the Avon: 'For beauty of scenery and historic interest it is second only to the Thames, while, as providing a series of pictures of English country life unspoilt by modern innovations, it is the Thames' superior.' On the phenomenon of urban blight, Evans wrote that the twin villages of Goring and Streatley 'occupy what was the most beautiful spot on the Thames, but now, alas, are crowded with the houses of the newly rich; and what was a paradise is now an inferno of money and motor-cars.'[40]

Setting out from Oxford shortly after the Great War, Evans toured sixty-five miles along the Oxford Canal north to Warwick. Along that short section of the vast canal system, there were sixty-three small locks, each capable of being operated by a single individual. As they permitted only one barge at a time to pass through, Evans found them 'wasteful in the extreme, both of time and water.'[41] The route continued along the Avon to Tewkesbury, where the party left the water to travel by train to Crickdale, near the source of the Thames, which they descended to complete the expedition at Windsor.

Algernon Blackwood and a companion spent six weeks on the waterways of Europe travelling from the Black Forest of Germany to the Black Sea, a journey the author described as one of 'four and twenty hundred miles.' For the young British writer, whose success and popularity were still decades ahead of him, departure from the Black Forest allowed him to return to the area of his early education in a school organized by the Moravian Brotherhood. His chosen canoe, if not a Rice Lake original, had similar lines, as the young man, who had recently returned to Europe after spending most of a decade at odd jobs in the United States and Canada, would be able to affirm.[42] Travel along the route from the point of embarkation to Ulm, Germany, proved to be most difficult, since much of the waterway was too shallow for effective paddling. Downstream from Ulm, however, the pair enjoyed easier progress, and the voyage continued without significant interruption through Bavaria, into Austria, and on to

Budapest, Hungary. 'The Germans had been kind in a negative fashion, the Bavarians courteous, the Austrians obliging,' commented Blackwood on his reception by the various communities neighbouring the waterways, 'but the hospitality of the Hungarians was positively aggressive.'[43]

In acknowledging his debt to the National Geographic Society, Melville Chater unequivocally disclaimed any pretence at discovery:

Compared with Arctic voyages, ethnic origins and earth-shakings, what narrative is mine? A mere summer day's tale of placid canals, old-world vistas, and somewhat of the heart of man! Here 'explorer' dwindles to 'gypsy,' and the questship shrinks to that tiny emissary of the National Geographic Magazine (which first chronicled her voyages), the Canadian canoe, named in imitative miniature, 'Nageoma.'[44]

Chater and his wife, Lucine, were displaced from their New York home – where they had been 'hidden away in its purlieu of faded gentility' – by modernity in the form of an apartment building intended to occupy the entire city block in which they lived. Deeming themselves 'victims of that veneration which America entertains for the New,' the Chaters resolved 'to abjure cities forever, to go off and live in a sailboat or a caravan, at any rate, something that couldn't be pulled down to make way for modern improvements.'[45] A canoe met their conditions satisfactorily and accommodated a journey that took them from the historic port of St-Malo to Paris. Having obtained the requisite 'permis de circulation' from French officials, the Chaters prepared to set off from St-Malo on La Rance. They – like so many others – encountered the disbelief of local residents, who thought it absurd to travel 'eight hundred miles by arm' with the alternative of a railway so conveniently at hand. La Rance soon proved itself to be something more than a quiet waterway, as tidal waters surged in and out its length, on occasion leaving the paddlers more or less stranded in mud flats. The first locks on the system proved no less hazardous, but in due course more manageable conditions were encountered and the travelogue began, its particular angle being the 'back doors' to Europe.[46]

Amos Burg, the Oregonian owner of *Song o' the Winds*, had already retraced the Yukon Trail of '98 and Mackenzie's route to the Polar Sea when he embarked on a canal trip across England shortly before the outbreak of the Second World War. Departing from London, the seasoned Burg and a companion called Harry set out on 'a web of freight canals spreading up over England to the rugged Pennines.' A twenty-five-day journey took the pair only from London to Birmingham, but provided them with memorable insights into 'the sturdy life along hedge-hidden canals, the very existence of which is unsuspected by the casual traveler.'

An early departure from the London docks was timed to avoid the rush of traffic, but a day's paddling through and under the industrial district still left the expedition tenting on a small island in the city. Relations with local residents proved less than congenial, as young boys along the bank 'began to shower us with stones and clods.' Once past London, however, progress along the canal network of the Grand Union system through the peaceful countryside was entirely pleasant, and the party concluded the voyage at Birmingham. 'It was a huge thrill,' Burg recalled, 'releasing 63,000 gallons of water at each lock. Between London and Birmingham we used almost ten million gallons just for our little canoe.'[47]

Referring to himself as 'what the French call an invalide, – in English slang, a "crock",' Major R. Raven-Hart explained that he was 'a partially disabled person, but not a sick man.' Certainly, nothing prevented him from appreciating the great distances one could travel through Europe without encountering the inconvenience of a portage: 'For example, there are 500 miles on the Moselle and the Rhine without a single carry, and 1500 miles on the Danube with one only.' The Moselle, one of the more popular rivers of Europe, was used by 'so many canoeists that the railway station at Trier has a special exit for them and the municipality of Berncastel induces them to visit the town by providing a landing stage with free change rooms and guardian, and where one can be sure of jolly companionship all the way.' Raven-Hart also appreciated other less travelled rivers: he said of the Vltava in Czechoslovakia above Prague, 'The river is what we in Europe imagine a Canadian river to be like – steep pine-clad slopes above still black water, varied by mile-long rapids.'[48]

Canoe travellers in Europe, if they were forced to imagine rather than to experience extensive wilderness rivers, nevertheless appeared to enjoy certain advantages. The trains were convenient, and villages and towns along most routes offered provisions, even prepared meals, as well as accommodation, if desired. Such conditions certainly made for greater security in the case of mishap. But were these amenities, in fact, advantages from the perspective of canoeists, who, like P.G. Downes, might want something other than scenery in 'the land of the little trees'?

13

Comfort: Bringing It with You and Finding It There

Idleness, water, and a canoe, accompanied by at least some vague sense of destination, may have been sufficient preconditions for the recreational paddler's launch, but basic outfitting decisions have always been crucial to the overall enjoyment of a canoe holiday. The range of choice might present itself as a set of alternative preferences, which opinion poll veterans are accustomed to rank by assigning numbers between 'one' and 'seven' on a scale. The results of the ranking indicate each canoeist's favoured position on the spectrum between wet and dry, between warm and cold, between full and empty, and between bug-bitten and insect-free. These determinations in turn dictate the specific outfitting and provisioning decisions that help to situate paddlers on an overall comfort and convenience scale. Yet normal preferences – however obvious they might first appear – have never been entirely straightforward for canoeists.

The paddling holiday imposes some distinctive constraints and complicates the application of any comfort index that market surveyors and researchers might devise. Too much convenience produces inconvenience, for anyone proposing to use some particular item of equipment will have to locate it in cumbersome packs, and not necessarily at a convenient moment. Then comes the challenge of storing things away again, possibly without always being able to return the baggage to the ideal degree of water-tightness. And whenever the canoeist lifts or carries equipment at a campsite, in loading canoes, or on the portage trail, he or she will lift and carry every item whether it is used often, once, or not at all.

In the days before lightweight equipment and freeze-dried or dehydrated foodstuffs became readily available to wilderness travellers, canoeists had to assemble their camping kit and supplies with a view to the serviceability of items that were rarely, if ever, designed with canoe camping and portages specifically in mind. Thus, when Canada's Department of the Interior offered the reminder that 'the ideal canoe outfit is light and compact,' it was able to suggest only that 'these features are usually attained by avoiding duplicate articles and non-essentials.'[1] An Outing publication dating from 1912 put the same point somewhat more firmly:

Even though the weight of some of them may be insignificant, the weight of each additional claptrap makes one more thing to look after. There are a thousand and one claptraps, indeed, that outfitters offer, but which do not possess sufficient advantage to pay for the care and labour of transportation, and my advice is, leave them out, one and all.[2]

If the matter of comfort were truly centred on such concerns as weight and convenience, someone might have imagined a formula to reconcile divergent opinion by means of optimal trade-offs. In fact, the situation has proved far more complicated, and the ongoing debate has involved significant philosophical differences. That is, aside from the potential inconvenience of convenience, too much comfort-seeking by canoeists brought them uncomfortably close to the most troublesome dockside inquiry: Why go canoeing at all?

The possibility that too much comfort could undermine the outdoor experience has worried more than a few vacationers over the years. For example, in the early 1900s a group of Chicago authors were dismayed by the level of civilization available at their carefully selected wilderness retreat. They found upon arrival that 'not only had man set foot there before, but he had also built two very modern hotels, and they were disgusted to find that the hotels were lighted with acetylene gas.' Bellboys, push-button room service, regular meals, and, particularly, four o'clock afternoon tea were equally offensive.[3]

Disdain for comfortable surroundings was not universal, for Major Raven-Hart emphasized in his description of the canoe stations of central Europe that these facilities were really inns. They were unrelated to 'the overrated and much more expensive Youth Hostels,' and offered the further attraction 'that one can smoke and drink and go to bed and get up when one pleases.'[4]

Vacationers with the inclination to restrict their reliance on creature comforts have offered both practical and philosophical reasons for this preference. P.G. Downes, who carried little on his adventures in the Barrens, took pains to excuse what some might regard as a 'boastfully small and inadequate' outfit. In the vast northland, where distances are

great, one had to travel fast in order to travel at all. 'To travel fast,' he
explained, 'one must travel light. To travel alone or with Indians one must
travel like an Indian.' Downes was also entirely frank on an underlying
limitation he has shared with a great many holiday paddlers: 'A school-
master's salary does not encourage extravagance.'[5]

Other notable canoe travellers have produced still more elaborate
accounts of their willingness to part with material shelter and mechanical
conveniences:

There is something intensely satisfying about lying in a damp sleeping bag, sipping
hot tea, knowing that it is only simple skills of hand and mind which create such
comfort. In such a primitive environment, where rhythms of sleep and waking take
a natural course, where mere sustenance requires effort, where elimination is an
adventure, it is the connection with all aspects of one's life and capabilities that
builds within the soul an enduring sense of satisfaction and possibility.[6]

Such observations, however, are more readily accepted as the ration-
alizations of the returned voyageur than as positive inducements for
adventuring out in the first place.

Pierre Elliott Trudeau, well before his tenure as prime minister of
Canada, also reflected on the benefits to be found in confining material
equipment to the essentials: 'To remove all the useless material baggage
from a man's heritage is, at the same time, to free his mind from petty
preoccupations, calculations and memories.'[7] This school of thought – at
least its more extreme variants – has certainly had its critics over the years.
More than a century ago the *American Canoeist* cautioned against the self-
deprivation theory of recreational enjoyment: 'There are those who pro-
fess to turn up their nose at "comforts" as antagonistic to true manliness,
and "roughing it," so-called. A canoe trip under the best of circumstances
is "roughing it" and the greater the novice the more wise he be to
surround himself with all the comforts he can conveniently carry in his
small boat.'[8] James Edmund Jones echoed this sentiment with the practical observation that the 'most carefully managed camp is rough enough
without any attempt being made to add to its rugged attractions.'[9] John R.
Rowlands concurred: 'I used to think that going light and roughing it was
the thing to do,' he remarked. 'This is all right if conditions require it,' he
later concluded, 'but I find that the good woodsman is a man who takes
what he needs to live comfortably, making use of what comes to hand
wherever he is.'[10]

In some circumstances – perhaps where portages were not a factor, or where railway lines bordered wilderness shores – canoeists were not even put to the test of distinguishing luxury from necessity. On the Nipigon, it was said, for example, that the need for roughing it would not arise because of the ready availability of help along the portage trails. 'A fishing trip here is in every respect an old man's tranquil outing,' and travellers had no need to economize on luggage: 'Make your kit as elaborate as you please. Anything you consider essential to comfort being so easily transported, you need discard no article that may possibly be serviceable – one is not restricted by pounds or bulk.'[11]

Apart from such situations, the challenge in outfitting and provisioning was to bring enough equipment and supplies to approach an expected level of physical comfort, but not so much as to undermine the sense of moral satisfaction that would be derived from doing without. What the standard of comfort has actually meant for individual canoeists or for canoeists generally has been rather variable. The cuisine and technology of the paddler's vacation have changed significantly over the years, and have always been – as P.G. Downes reminds us – subject to ability and willingness to pay. The ultra-light school of travel championed by the renowned American outdoorsman Nessmuk – a diminutive shoemaker turned woodsman – was never available to more than a few, for paddlers much heavier than Nessmuk's one hundred pounds found that their weight strained the smallest canoes, which were constructed without seats, thwarts, and other structural supports.[12]

Yet as the comments of Pierre Trudeau among others remind us, the spiritual well-being of the modern recreational paddler actually depends on a certain degree of hardship – or at least a sense of hardship. To eliminate the prospect of some physical discomfort would be to deprive the outdoor enthusiast of one of the pastime's distinguishing features. Set apart by voluntary acceptance of a patch of penetrating damp, a spell of cold weather, and other natural occurrences, the wilderness adventurer escapes the shameful perils of decadence and hedonism. Thus are northerners made today.

In 1987, Club Med advertising provoked a passionate outcry with its suggestion that the 'down South' version of vacation comfort should be elevated as a goal, an ideal. The Paris-based international resort chain urged customers to 'try lazing on a warm beach Club Med style' rather than 'splashing in a cold lake' in close proximity to 'the mosquitoes, the hot and cold running mice, the rain,' and the other charms to be found 'up North.' Facing fierce protest, the Club Med ads lasted only a short time, and the long-term fate of a comparable appeal by Outward Bound remains to be seen. In 1992, professionals who were attracted by Outward Bound's philosophy of teaching but were less enthusiastic about self-improvement in the unpredictable conditions of the natural environment could opt for a resort-based course on team-building: 'We'll take you out of your comfort zone without taking away your comforts.'[13]

Without formally embracing deprivation, the average canoeist has customarily put up with what had to be endured, and transformed the experience of discomfort into something positive. In the absence of civilization's comforts and support, the nineteenth-century sportsman would 'quickly ... adapt himself to circumstances, falling back upon those natural mechanical and inventive gifts that Nature has given all men, but which city life causes to become atrophied for want of use.' Moreover, a brief period of doing without increased one's appreciation of those missing conveniences that came to be taken for granted in the context of urban life.[14]

William C. James, an astute late twentieth-century observer, has remarked that the literature of canoeing 'is filled with tales of hardships endured, especially on an initial journey: the first lengthy portage over rough terrain; an upset which soaks all of the gear; a miscalculation resulting in a shortage of provisions or losing one's way; the impossibility of starting a fire to cook supper; the interruption of a journey by winds or rain.' Though hardly to be welcomed, such trials, James explains, 'are significant chiefly as ordeals demanding a re-orientation of the self or of one's values.' Participants, realizing that their business or educational skills are of limited utility in the wilderness, may experience something like humiliation, James observes. 'Thus the perilous journey may lead to a purification of the self, or the dissolution of past images of the self.'[15]

James's predecessors, even at the turn of the century, were entirely familiar with the nature of the challenge. Moreover, some had formulated rules for the contest, and they presented these as ethical principles designed to ensure that the outcome of the encounter with wilderness would bear the hallmarks of legitimacy. Stewart Edward White explained how the ordeal would be judged and the outdoorsman's performance assessed:

To go light is to play the game fairly. The man in the woods matches himself against the forces of nature. In the towns he is warmed and fed and clothed so spontaneously and easily that after a time he perforce begins to doubt himself, to wonder whether his powers are not atrophied from disuse. And so, with his naked soul, he fronts the wilderness. It is a test, a measuring of strength, a proving of his essential pluck and resourcefulness and manhood, an assurance of man's highest potency, the ability to endure and to take care of himself. In just so far as he substitutes the ready-made of civilization for the wit-made of the forest, the pneumatic bed for the balsam boughs, in just so far is he relying on other men and other men's labor to take care of him. To exactly that extent is the test invalidated. He has not proved a courteous antagonist, for he has not stripped to the contest.[16]

A marginal note provided by an early reader of my draft manuscript seems apt: 'rubbish!'

If questing for self-discovery and affirmation of one's potential were expected of the novice canoeist, those already initiated generally subscribe to an entirely different view of the matter. Few experienced canoeists have been known to endorse the need to repeat the ordeals of self-purification. However, a sense of doubt has occasionally complicated a rematch with the outdoors, following a period of absence. Marni Jackson expressed concerns of this nature as she contemplated a return to the water: 'This was my Midlife Canoe Trip, my chance to see whether marriage, motherhood, and staring at orange words on a screen all day had totally trashed me.'[17] Another very experienced canoeist, John Godfrey, MP, has also seen the annual trip as affirming that the temptation to succumb to a life of urban ease has been held at bay for at least one more season:

Every winter we got together for a weekend reunion with our spouses and partners to show slides, tell lies and laugh a lot. I like those reunions. Sometimes I think I like them better than the trips. But without the trips, we'd just be a bunch of aging geezers trading increasingly stale war stories. Only the annual canoe trip proves we haven't given in to a life of comfort.[18]

For those who continue to venture back to the wilds after an initial ordeal and triumph, the operative principle is likely to have been 'by all means, let us learn from our mistakes, but let us not repeat them.' Indeed, with wisdom grounded in experience, veteran paddlers have displayed a singular eagerness to share advice with beginners and their less enlightened fellow-participants. This tendency has been chiefly responsible for the virtually unlimited production of testimonials and how-to-do-it tracts. The advice has ranged over a good many topics, including accommodations, provisions, clothing, and the perils of insects.

In *Campcraft: Modern Practice and Equipment*, Warren H. Miller compared tenting with cottage or cabin life, self-righteously explaining his preference for the former:

The principal function of a tent is to make a real 'woodser' of you. A shack or a log
cabin, located in the heart of the woods, will shelter you from the elements and put
you in reasonable touch with the sights and sounds and smells of the wilderness,
but you are not of it, not in the real heart of the wild life, nor will a year in a cabin
be as beneficial to your health as thirty days in a tent.[19]

Tent dwellers themselves still faced many choices and, as Dillon Wallace
observed, 'personal likes and prejudices have much to do with the form of
tent chosen.' Many styles were offered, in a variety of materials from duck
or drill to balloon silk, also referred to as tanalite. Although commercial
options were much debated, a tent could also be made at home. That the
latter option might be attractive in certain circumstances is suggested by
C.P. Storey. After recounting an unfortunately damp experience on a
canoe trip–honeymoon, he warned others of the 'numerous freak tents'
on the market: 'Some of these tents are made to sell, not to give comfort
and protection to the tired camper who is caught out in a heavy rainstorm.'[20] P.G. Downes's strident criticism of tents was associated with a
costly product whose only impermeable part proved to be the groundcloth,
which, 'refusing to allow the dripping through the roof to run out, kept
me surrounded by almost two inches of water.'[21] Opinion strongly favoured mosquito netting or the less expensive alternative of cheesecloth,
for it was readily admitted that insects were prevalent, bothersome, and
unpleasant.

Albert Bigelow Paine had time to reflect on the reasonably tolerable
limits of inconvenience during the course of his trip through Nova Scotia's
Kejimkujik wilderness in 1908. 'When one has been accustomed to the
comforts of civilised life – the small ones, I mean, for they are the only
ones that count – the beginning of a wild, free life near to nature's heart
begets a series of impressions quite new, and strange – so strange.' Paine
concluded that the 'larger comforts' such as walls, a roof, stairways, and
steam radiators could readily enough be compensated for 'by the sheltering temple of the trees, the blazing campfire and the stairway leading to
the stars.' But other comforts were less easily forsaken: 'When I had
finished our first evening's smoke and the campfire was burning low –
when there was nothing further to do but go to bed, I suddenly realized
that the man who said he would be willing to do without all the rest of a
house if he could keep the bathroom, spoke as one with an inspired

knowledge of human needs.'[22] Another outdoor vacationer later lamenting the cumulative environmental impact of the paddler's 'call of nature' urged that unobtrusive outhouses should be established at strategic locations on the more frequented routes: 'Let's face it, looking at the rapids accelerates anyone's physiological processes.'[23]

Provisions were likewise the subject of understandable interest. The volume of goods and equipment associated with a mid-length trip for a guided party of paddlers could be very considerable. On longer expeditions where it might seem impossible to carry the entire outfit, arrangements could sometimes be made for supply and re-provisioning at intervals.[24] Provisions for the ninety or so paddlers in the Canadian Centennial Voyageur Canoe Pageant in 1967 included 30,000 eggs, two and a half tons of bacon, 10,000 quarts of milk, 60,000 pancakes, a thousand pounds of honey, six tons of steak, two and a half tons of potatoes, 5,000 loaves of bread, and 3,000 pounds of butter.[25] The caloric intake of their non-recreational voyageur predecessors has been estimated. Assuming a daily food ration of three pounds of pemmican or the rough nutritional equivalent in salmon or whitefish, C.E.S. Franks calculated consumption at approximately 7200 calories per day. This was hardly a generous diet, however, for in fifteen hours of paddling and portaging, the voyageurs, weighing perhaps 155 pounds per man on average, would expend 6990 calories.[26]

In some respects the food supplies of the early recreational paddler were similar to those used by the professional woodsman. 'It is surprising how palatable even salt pork may be, after such a morning's exercise in such a locality. Dinner is ready, and the attack commences. There is very little ceremony in the woods, so down we squat on the rocks and grass.' The absence of crockery, table napkins, cruet stands, and other paraphernalia was of no consequence, as 'each man receives a tough shanty biscuit, about an inch thick, topped by a good-sized piece of fried pork, which constitutes his meal.'[27]

Whenever restrictions on the variety or freshness of provisions could be overcome, canoeists welcomed the change. Fresh produce had a special appeal. Thus, in 1883 the Canadian organizers of the American Canoe Association regatta at Stoney Lake earned well-deserved praise for the arrangements they had made on behalf of competitors and other campers. Credited with 'practical ideas of comfort,' the organizers had constructed a well-stocked ice-house for the canoeists' use. They had, moreover, established a store, cooking facilities, and a large mess-tent 'for those who preferred to rely upon the culinary efforts of somebody else, rather than upon their own.' In addition, the Peterborough hosts had made arrangements for daily visits to the canoe camp by a milkman, a baker, a dealer in fresh butter and eggs, and someone from the post office.'[28] Such elaborate arrangements were more consistent with permanent camp facilities than with a short stay, and were therefore very greatly appreciated by competitors and onlookers alike.

Supplementing provisions from the land and waters was one common practice, and, in certain districts, produce might be obtained from settlers, who enjoyed the modest opportunities to dispose of cash crops. Thus, in a detailed account of the rapids, portages, and campsites to be encountered along a route in Quebec's Gatineau district, F.M.S. Jenkins included valuable information on re-supply: 'From the bridge a paddle up stream of about 2 miles will bring you to a small rapid at the side of an island. Land on the flat rocks on the L.H. side and portage from there: excellent camping spots here. The farm on the bank is the famous Edwards Farm where you may procure milk, bread, eggs, etc. of the finest quality.'[29] Other canoeists, in a very persistent practice, might re-supply their outfits from fur trading posts.

When re-provisioning was impossible or where fresh supplies were unavailable, the problem of preserving arose. One member of the Toronto Canoe Club offered this enlightening advice to early canoe cruisers who were concerned about the availability of provisions on longer expeditions:

Get a number of square flat tin cans made like oyster cans, of a handy size to lie under your floor boards. Then cook a turkey, some chickens, a sirloin of beef, etc. Cut the hot meat up into large diceshaped pieces, and put it in the tins hot, then pour melted fat in til the tins are full, and then solder them tight. Get as much meat in as you can before putting in the fat.[30]

Fruit might be put up in much the same way, with the heavy ballast thereby produced available to serve as rations when provisions began to run low. The procedure seemed generally designed to discourage portaging.

Veterans of the trail often shared their views on culinary essentials, personal favourites, or the canoeist's stand-bys. 'Take all the variety you can in the way of dried staples – be sure they are staples – but cut close on your bulky tinned supplies,' cautioned Albert Bigelow Paine. 'It is better to be sure of enough Johnnie-cake and bacon and beans during the last week out than to feast on plum-pudding and California pears the first.'[31]

John R. Rowlands put in a word for a generous ration of rice, 'for rice is a democratic sort of food that mixes just as well with sugar and dried fruits as it does in a stew.' His own particular preference featured hot rice with milk and maple sugar.[32]

Forgotten items are not easily replaced, and the typical camper's willingness to open cans with a tent peg and an axe has been decidedly limited over the years. The increasing availability of published advice on packing, provisioning, campfire cooking, and equipment as the twentieth century progressed suggests that canoeists in significant numbers were organizing their own expeditions. Dr Hubert Brown and his family summered by canoe for much of the late 1920s, provisioning themselves at modest cost with the standard and basic items recommended by many of the old hands. The advent during this era of powdered milk – the soon-to-be ubiquitous KLIM – was much appreciated, although processed and commercially packaged foods played a very modest role in the family menu.[33]

Sustenance and nourishment may have been an underlying objective of the canoe trip diet, but much more was at stake. A significant element of ritual and self-definition worked its way into comparatively simple menus. The list of ingredients of the Nahanni veteran Raymond M. Patterson's western breakfasts reflects his own evidently formidable appetite and intestinal idiosyncrasies: porridge, sheep liver and bacon, bannock, butter, marmalade, and tea, topped off with a bowl of raspberries and cream. In providing details on the porridge, he took pains to emphasize that it was

no invalid dish, nor would it ever figure on the diet sheet of a slimming movie star: porridge as developed by me on the Nahanni consisted of a mixture of rolled oats and whole wheat, and into this was thrown a little salt, a large pat of butter and a handful of seedless raisins. The finished product was served in a large bowl: on top of the porridge a thin slice of cheese was spread, and the dish was topped off with a pouring of dried milk to the consistency of cream, and a liberal sprinkling of brown sugar. It will be easily understood that this porridge lays a good foundation for a good breakfast to follow.[34]

In a challenge that few would care to undertake, Patterson defied anyone 'to better that breakfast menu, or to bring to it a better appetite.'

James Edmund Jones's views on campfire coffee – as on most matters connected with canoe camping – were firm. 'Unlike tea,' he explained, coffee was to be boiled. 'Ten to fifteen minutes suffice. Don't put the coffee in until the water boils. Allow two teaspoonfuls for each person. After the pot is taken off pour condensed cream in, to taste. Then bring it to the boil again.'[35] One can appreciate the attractions of this formula in the context of a canoe trip; it simultaneously increased the level of activity – wood gathering and fire burning – and, by tending to reduce the attractions of the brew and thus presumably lower the rate of consumption, allowed the party to eke out meagre supplies.

The potentially deeper satisfactions of traditional campfire cookery have been spelled out in a more modern account of why canoeists eat what they do. 'Baking bannock on canoe trips is a simple ritualistic expression of a deep basic drive to satisfy hunger,' suggests the trip leader and outdoor educator Bob Henderson of McMaster University in Hamilton. He then elaborates on the other virtues involved. Bannock baking 'is an instinctively warm experience because the canoe tripper is linked to every aspect of the product. One has brought quality ingredients, packed them, carried them and now caringly bakes them over an equally thoughtful fire – soon to eat them. This is an instinctual drive, complete.' For contrast, Henderson directs the reader's attention to another style of dining out – 'popping into a burger place, consuming the food, and you're out the door without any thought. This is an instinctively cold experience that leaves one empty in a qualitative way at least.'[36] Yet campfire cookery is not confined to the simple pleasures of bannock and traditional fare. In the course of recounting the logistical details of his circumnavigation of Britain and Ireland by kayak, Bill Taylor mentions paddling companions who viewed good eating in the context of an expedition as an end in itself, or who regularly exerted themselves for what he refers to as 'a glorified picnic in wild surroundings.' His companions, on occasion, became 'competitively obsessive' in their quest for fine dining on the waters.[37]

The place of alcoholic beverages on a canoe trip is the subject of enduring controversy. The 'no' case was succinctly put in 1903 by James Edmund Jones, about whom it should perhaps be noted at this point that this future Toronto police magistrate was known to friends and colleagues as 'Hymnny Jimmy.' 'The man who desires stimulants while he is living a pure and natural life in the open air ought to be ashamed of himself.'[38] Despite such severe injunctions, and despite the additional burden, liquor was a standard item in the supplies of many summer vacationers.[39]

The tendency was to include alcohol on the provisions list in the light of some practical advantage associated with it. Warington Baden-Powell carried brandy 'to purify the water when bad,' and reported that 'it generally is so.'[40] The medicinal purposes rationale, accepted a few decades ago even by severe critics, accounted for a significant portion of the supply. And more than a few canoe travellers credited spirits with revival. Nathaniel Holmes Bishop in fact thought that spirits might have saved his life.[41] But outside the prohibition era as it operated in various parts of North America, only a small proportion of stimulants can be traced to a doctor's prescription.

Has any wilderness paddler over forty not met someone who knew a canoeist acquainted with a member of the proverbial canoe trip party who came upon some one else's 'stash' too casually deposited alongside the portage trail or lost in the rapids? A contributor to *Athletic Life* magazine known only as Pat recalled meeting a party of four canoeists in the Nipigon district whose supplies included two unopened cases of angostura bitters. These travellers, Pat reported, 'were bemoaning the loss of their whole supply of the "comforter" for which the bitters were intended as a relish, and which had in some unaccountable manner disappeared before they reached the river.' Pat's own party generously shared its liquid provisions with the disheartened paddlers, although he confessed that 'we … twitted them a good deal about the missing jugs, much to their chagrin.'[42]

Yet there is more to the tradition than medical fiction and legend, for the pre- or postprandial libation involved some mix of camaraderie and familiar linkage to civilization. The particular appeal in the woods of something that might ordinarily be taken for granted as one of life's simple pleasures is also part of the tradition: 'Instant coffee with an inch of scotch,' confessed Marni Jackson part way through a wilderness outing, 'now struck me as exquisite, probably worth marketing.'[43] Members of the international diplomatic community were welcome participants on Eric Morse's expeditions for many reasons, including the access they provided to attractively priced or duty-free beverages.[44] And the current competition for the 'dry' beer market is hardly worthy of notice in comparison with the long-neglected matters of dehydrated beer crystals, wine tablets, and portable solar-powered refrigerators.

Tobacco, another questionable indulgence in many contexts, also enjoyed a remarkable level of acceptance among recreational paddlers. An element of tradition crept in, endowing the habit with some measure of legitimacy through its association with the voyageurs and aboriginal pipe-users. P.G. Downes noted astutely that solutions to the limitations of a schoolteacher's salary included a willingness 'to advertise breakfast foods or tobacco.' When he arrived at an isolated trading post which was completely devoid of tobacco, Downes and his companions 'experienced the first real catastrophe of the trip.' Like so many of his wilderness brethren before and since, Downes struggled to cope with 'a loss of comfort that we felt was a real hardship.' The scavenging of pockets and packages was carried out in earnest.[45] 'Rob Roy' MacGregor favoured a cigar.

As he must have been developing a fair understanding of the eventual outcome of his Labrador misadventure, Leonidas Hubbard astonished his companions by reaching for the first pipe he ever smoked, one that had been brought along to trade with Indians encountered on the route. When asked how he liked it, Hubbard is reported to have said, 'Pretty good,' and then vowed, 'If I ever start out again on another expedition of this sort, I am going to learn to smoke; watching you fellows makes me believe it must be great comfort.'[46] Even had he been aware of the health effects of smoking in the late fall of 1903, having exhausted his provisions and facing the onslaught of cold fall weather, Hubbard had more immediate worries in the final days of his life.

The risk that the search for comfort might have unanticipated and undesirable side-effects applied also to the selection of clothing. As one recent and evidently not-fully-satisfied canoeist explained, 'I was wearing a clever orchestration of breathing, wicking, and insulating layers that required us to stop every few minutes while I put something on or peeled it off.'[47] Others have adjusted more readily to the distinctive features of modern camp gear. After Gary and Joanie McGuffin set out in 1983 to cross Canada on a six-thousand-mile honeymoon paddle from Baie Comeau, Quebec, on the St Lawrence to Tuktoyaktuk on the Beaufort Sea, they 'struggled to pull off clammy wetsuits and soaked neoprene boots.' No doubt this disagreeable routine contributed to the enjoyment of what followed: 'Afterward it felt wonderful to pull on warm woolly socks and thick cosy pile jackets.'[48]

The McGuffins may not always have sensed it, but they were the intended beneficiaries of a great many refinements in the design and manufacture of outdoor adventure gear. Their predecessors, especially women, had suffered considerably in garments whose suitability for physical activity was merely coincidental. Leslie Peabody offered advice on the limitations of dysfunctional items:

If a woman wants to feel the glorious stretch of muscles from the top of her head to the tip of her toes she must leave behind her 'the tie that binds', the twelve and a half inch laundered collar, the nineteen-inch waist and the three and a half patent leather shoes – the trammels of conventionality ... The slightest pressure of clothing will spoil the great swing of the paddle and a woman will soon turn round and talk to the man at the other end of the canoe who will be waiting for just this to happen.[49]

The photographic record confirms just how frequently this thoughful warning was disregarded. The alternatives available in the early years had certainly not been designed with the canoeist in mind. Even after it was accepted that 'bifurcated garments' were preferable to skirts, the available choices were limited. 'I prefer riding breeches,' Kathrene Pinkerton remarked. 'Bloomers catch on snags and brush as readily as skirts.'[50]

Other notorious perils of the woods added immensely to the canoeist's sense of undergoing an ordeal. 'The curse of the Canadian wilds in the summer are mosquitoes, black flies and their relations,' lamented one popular account; while a Nova Scotia paddler named the mosquito and sunburn as the 'only two foes ... to be dreaded by the summer camper in this province.'[51] A marked lack of affection for mosquitoes is commonly expressed in the canoe traveller's reminiscences. Anna Jameson, for example, proclaimed the futility of various approaches to relief from mosquitoes she encountered at the entrance to the St Mary's River in the 1830s. And with the benefit of her past international travels and European education, she contemplated the nature of the beast: 'I had suffered from these plagues in Italy; ... but 'tis a jest, believe me, to encountering a forest full of them in these wild regions.' Warnings had failed utterly to convey the extent and severity of the torture she would experience:

Some amiable person, who took an especial interest in our future welfare, in enumerating the torments prepared for hardened sinners, assures us that they will be stung by mosquitoes all made of brass, and as large as black beetles – he was an ignoramus and a bungler; you may credit me, that the brass is quite an unnecessary improvement, and the increase in size equally superfluous. Mosquitoes, as they exist in this upper world, are as pretty and perfect a plague as the most ingenious amateur sinner-tormentor ever devised. Observe, that a mosquito does not sting like a wasp, or a gad-fly; he has a long probiscus like an awl, with which he bores your veins, and pumps the life-blood out of you, leaving venom and fever behind.[52]

Paddlers, most notably along the portage trail, have experienced severe doubts concerning the mosquito's place in the universe. Albert Bigelow Paine was an articulate member of the ranks of those who set themselves to wonder 'what mosquitoes were made for.' He judged the inquiry to be formidable indeed: 'Other people have wondered that before, but you can't overdo the thing. Maybe if we keep on wondering we shall find out. Knowledge begins that way, and it will take a lot of speculation to solve the mosquito mystery.'[53] For his part, Richard Garwood Lewis felt that the annual expeditions of veteran canoeists were made into a 'martyrs' pilgrimage' because 'mosquitoes sting them, black flies and bull dogs bite them, and no-see-ums burn them with a thousand fires.'[54] An Ontario Department of Mines report contained this grim account of mosquito damage from the survivors of a survey and exploration trip in the Abitibi region: 'It is impossible to convey an adequate idea of the suffering which we were obliged to endure from their attacks, and no application of oil or salve to our hands and faces seemed to have any effect in keeping them off.' The same expedition also reported appreciable inconvenience occasioned by the black flies' habit of 'congregating in large numbers in soup, gravy and other articles of diet.'[55]

The prospects for relief appeared limited, yet commentators offered some hope with the suggestion that insect pests 'have practically passed away when August arrives,' or that the insect 'will not, as a rule, attack one while on the water.' Further solace was to be found in the observation that 'after midnight the mosquito seemed to betake himself to repose.'[56] Nathaniel Holmes Bishop found seasonal relief in the 'frosty nights.'[57] Another veteran advised wilderness travellers to camp on high ground, 'where there will be a night breeze to blow off the mosquitoes.'[58] The Department of Mines commentary even ventured the opinion that 'it is altogether probable that as the country becomes cleared and drained and the soil cultivated, they will largely disappear and life will then be as tolerable in this region as in the older parts of the Province.'[59] So much for prophecy.

Eddie, outfitter extraordinaire of the group with whom Albert Bigelow Paine crossed Nova Scotia in the early 1900s, equipped each member of the party with silk head nets of his own invention and manufacture 'to pull on day or night when the insect pests were bad.'[60] Netting rarely proved adequate, and something else was clearly required for daytime activity. Repellants were typically of a do-it-yourself variety. William Hume Blake recommended to readers of In a Fishing Country that a repellant should be pungent and should have enough body that it would not dry off quickly. One possibility was a 20:1 mix of crude petroleum and oil of citronella. 'As the strong odor of citronella becomes exceedingly trying if it is used constantly,' some woodsmen counselled that eucalyptus be carried along as an alternative. Another veteran was cautious in his recommendation of citronella, for he concluded that some 'brands' of mosquito 'seem to prefer it to any other drink.' Blake himself offered this notable concoction: 'An excellent mixture for one who is not pernickety about his complexion is pine tar, three ounces; castor oil, two ounces; penny royal, one ounce; simmered over a slow fire; but there is a choice for all tastes within the general formula.'[61] Dillon Wallace, having been tortured in Labrador, had previously offered his followers the same formula, attributing its origins to Nessmuk and encouraging its adoption with this commendation: 'It is claimed for this mixture that the dead will rise and flee from its compounded odor as they would flee from eternal torment! It certainly should ward off such little creatures as black flies and mosquitoes.' Another Wallace recipe featured oil of tar (three parts), sweet oil (three parts), oil of pennyroyal (one part), and carbolic acid (3 per cent), though he seemed unconvinced that this potion would prove more effective than the custom – which he attributed to the Indians – of rubbing salt pork rind on exposed surfaces.[62] Readers of the Canadian National Railways' manual *Canoe Trips and Nature Photography* were introduced to a mixture of 30 per cent salol, 30 per cent camphor, and 40 per cent heavy petrolatum (jelly), which was said to have no objectionable odour. Whatever the effects of these concoctions on their intended victims, users have not been immune.

Eric Morse's estimate for travellers in the Barrens was that 'allowing for risk of loss, breakage, or leakage, a pocket bottle of repellent lasts about a man-week.'[63] Ninety participants in the Voyageur Canoe Pageant were reportedly supplied with 200,000 ounces of insect repellant for the 3,283-mile trip, which ran from Rocky Mountain House, Alberta, to Montreal.[64] This is equivalent to 60.9 ounces per mile for the expedition overall, or approximately two-thirds of an ounce per paddler per mile.

Relief advice for the camper whose repellant defences had failed or had been neglected also tended to emphasize home-made remedies or improvised solutions. In a comment entitled 'Canoeists and Mosquitoes,' the *American Canoeist* seemed to endorse a suggestion, put forward in Edinburgh's *Medical Journal*, that itching and pain could generally be eliminated by rubbing the affected area with moist soap and allowing the lather to dry on the skin. William Hume Blake offered a remedy handed down by generations of fishermen: 'Sovereign against pain, itching and swelling of all poisoned stings – is acetate of lead, three drachms; carbolic acid, four drachms; tincture of opium, four drachms; rosewater, four ounces.'[65]

In recent years new approaches have come into favour, as opponents of the mosquito and its allies have variously advocated careful selection of clothing colour, the use of electric zapping devices, and, simply, staying very dirty as elements of a successful campaign against the plague. Another approach, less likely to appeal to significant numbers of summer travellers, combines striking originality with ecological correctness.

The January 1991 newsletter of the Teaching Drum Outdoor School in Three Lakes, Wisconsin, listed as a subject of instruction 'Song of the Mosquito.' The course, taught by an instructor named Tamarack, was scheduled to begin at dawn on 18 June and to end at dusk on 19 June, long enough for most, in view of the curriculum. Tamarack, clearly operating at some distance from consensus opinion on the mosquito, advanced an alternative vision of this 'maligned' creature as 'an honored Teacher and respected Guardian of wild places.' Having learned the wisdom of the Mosquito, Tamarack offered to share hard-won insights so that others might also pursue 'the path to knowing and embracing Mosquito.' As explained more fully to potential participants, who were invited to attend during the height of mosquito season for 'one of the most personally challenging – and rewarding' experiences of their lives: 'We'll discover how to walk in peace without the aid of protective clothing or chemicals. We'll learn how to move in the rhythm of the Forest, so we don't stand out as aliens ripe for bloodletting.' Nevertheless, participants were expected to make certain sacrifices in exchange for the enhanced understanding they would take away with them:

We are asked to give in order to receive; for this particular gift, pain is the offering. After ritual preparation, we will strive to walk beyond ourselves into the realm where we are one with the Life-Spirit. There, we will bare ourselves to Mosquito, in order that we might hear her voice. She will likely speak a different verse of her lovesong to each of us, which we will share with each other in order to come to a fuller knowledge of the circle in which she dwells.[66]

However limited the appeal of Tamarack's instructive offering, (and one might be forgiven for suspecting a very limited appeal indeed), the philosophy underlying the program is clearly relevant to the wilderness traveller's dilemma about comfort. You could – with effort – make yourself comfortable and satisfy your wants on the basis of knowledge rather than on the basis of supportive technology. One could 'go light' for a variety of reasons and with a range of consequences. For some, limiting the gear serves to preserve the impression that one is 'roughing it,' with whatever satisfactions flow from physical endurance and survival. Others, from an ascetic perspective, might appreciate a feeling of liberation from material dependence, with all the possibilities this provides for contemplation and self-understanding. In both these senses one is prepared to do without for either the physical or the spiritual satisfaction that the self-imposed deprivation produces. Or, conversely, going light might simply be – as the Tamarack experience reminds us – a function of a supreme confidence that knowledge and understanding of the natural world will allow the traveller to satisfy all wants as they arise. There is no need to do without. In this latter sense, confidence and security are internally derived and not technologically dependent. Those entering the wilderness on its own terms, with an appreciation of how to find or create shelter or how to locate food supplies and medicinal plants as required, had a feeling of autonomy, of control, and of being at home in a way they could not have achieved in the city. Later wilderness travellers appear to have fewer opportunities for such satisfactions than their predecessors, but all those who submit themselves voluntarily to wilderness campsites and portage trails believe the experience is worth something to them. How much?

14

The Price of Adventure

Over the years, the financial burden of lugging a heavy pack across the bog, confirming that last year's bug dope has deteriorated in storage, spending a damp night with spruce roots between your shoulder blades, and perhaps even catching your own dinner has been comparatively modest. That is much as one would expect, and upon reflection, it is much as one would hope to find that experiences of this nature need not be expensive. But the wilderness canoe holiday has never been free; this, too, is no surprise, for the chance to be liberated – albeit temporarily – from routine toil and drudgery and to restore the soul or improve one's character must be worth something. In fact, with a little imagination an adventure in recreational paddling can readily be priced to compete with more luxurious, sedentary, and therefore – as the devotees have always insisted – inherently less worthwhile tourist excursions and resort holidays. However, as wilderness and recreational retreats have become threatened by incessant urban-centred demands for timber, pulpwood, and minerals, many canoeists, though reluctantly, have undertaken the intriguing task of demonstrating to resource planners and economic consultants that the real value of their treasured activity is actually very considerable.

The appearance of canoe company advertisements in widely respected newsmagazines as well as in traditional outdoor journals like *Rod and Gun* confirmed long ago that members of the entrepreneurial community recognized the economic potential of the canoe holiday. The T. Eaton Company, for example, used the well-circulated pages of *Saturday Night* to promote canoe sales, leading off an advertisement for summer equipment with the exhortation, 'Whatever else is lacking, there must be a canoe.'[1] *Saturday Night* was no doubt an attractive location for such promotions, as essays from the early 1920s occasionally drew attention to the unbounded vacation possibilities of northern Ontario and northern Quebec:

Rivers, many of them mighty streams, which for generations have served as highways to adventurers, fur traders and trappers bound to and from Hudson Bay, are almost beyond compute in number, the country being gridironed by them. Wonderfully interesting canoe trips, either extended or limited, are available. Take, for example, the six routes to Moose Factory, all of which find their way into Moose River about 30 miles south of Moose Factory on James Bay.[2]

For general camping use, Eaton's recommended a sixteen-foot, cedar-plank craft 'covered with special grade canvas.' This canoe was 'specially fitted for the rocky lakes and rivers of Muskoka and further north.' At $69.50, the 1922 cost of the vessel showed a considerable advance above prewar price levels. The same was true of the painted basswood model, advertised at $59.50.[3] Department store sales may still have been exceptional, however, as many buyers dealt directly with builders, either purchasing from stock on hand or ordering from the companies' own elaborate catalogues, in which numerous combinations of style, wood, and, if applicable, colour of paint were offered.

North American canoe manufacturers interested in the British market at the turn of the century still had to face the domestic competition, as local English builders of Canadian-style canoes were active in London and along the Thames. In 1893, prices ranged from fifteen to thirty pounds, 'according to the value of the woods used and the elaboration of the upholstery.'[4] A few years later, F.G. Aflalo's eccentric collection of essays *The Cost of Sport* advised that 'the common or English paddling canoe costs some 15s. per foot, and about 1s. per foot more if built of mahogany.' The Canadian model was evidently procurable in basswood for between nine and thirteen pounds. Any buyer who favoured 'fancy woods' could find builders willing to accept as much as twenty-two pounds. Sailing canoes, when built to the specifications of a naval architect, were substantially more expensive.[5]

Vacationers wishing to rent rather than purchase canoes were able to do so readily for most of the first half of the twentieth century in developed resort districts across Canada, and even before that in some locations. The Hudson's Bay Company fur trading post on Bear Island, Lake Temagami, for example, kept a small fleet of canoes available for tourist use from the early 1900s. Canoes were rented out in this era at sixty cents per day or

$3.50 per week. Tents and blankets could also be obtained for a modest daily fee. Company officials predicted that 'there is a continued prospect of a considerable trade being maintained.'[6] In the late 1930s, the provincial Department of Lands and Forests noted 'increasing tourist traffic' returning to the district after the Great Depression. The Temagami post manager Hugh Mackay Ross superintended a fleet of sixty-five rental canoes, most of which were in use by one visitor or another for the entire season, often having been booked during the winter or early spring by eager canoeists who wanted to avoid disappointment.[7]

Outfitters and suppliers represented another sector that catered energetically to the requirements of recreational paddlers and other users of the outdoors. Eaton's first *Summer Catalogue* appeared in 1901, and thereafter the catalogue rapidly became more elaborate. In 1912 Leon L. Bean first offered his 'Maine Hunting Shoe' to customers on a mail order basis, thus launching what became a hugely successful camping and outdoor supply service.[8] Competitors such as Michie's of Toronto used a slightly different promotional approach, involving a combination of advertising and helpful information on vacation opportunities. Michie's regularly published *Tourist Topics*, a pamphlet containing advice for canoeists concerning routes, equipment, and provisions, which Michie's was prepared to supply and deliver. The popularity of Michie's services in the early 1900s was at least partly a consequence of the firm's early interest in provisioning travellers in the northern lakes and rivers: the firm began to give special attention to the 'northern' districts in the 1880s.[9]

In addition to the more obvious commercial dimensions of recreational paddling such as canoe manufacturing and outfitting, ancillary transportation services were vitally interested in the expenditures of the recreational canoeist. In the late nineteenth century, and for many years into the twentieth, railways, including the Canadian Pacific and the Grand Trunk, offered canoeists and sportsmen access to fashionably remote waterways.

At the turn of the century, the railways were enthusiastic promoters of canoe travel. The Temiskaming and Northern Ontario Railway, to take one example, prominently featured canoeing in the cover designs of its colourful brochures as well as in photographs of fishing and camping parties. And, in a series of pamphlets celebrating the recreational pleasure-lands found along its routes, the Grand Trunk Railway urged vacationers to spend time on the water. Of the Kawartha Lakes surrounding the historic Peterborough canoe country, the Grand Trunk said, 'This midland district of Ontario is one broad, continuous network of lakes extending to James Bay, and the voyages to be taken by the enthusiastic lover of the canoe have but one limit – the time at the disposal of the voyager.'[10] To facilitate camping parties, the Canadian Pacific Railway offered shipping arrangements which would no doubt surprise today's railway passengers. A group of five or more outdoorsmen travelling together to CPR resort hotels to hunt or fish could obtain one-month return tickets at reduced rates. Two hundred pounds of baggage and camp equipment, including tents, canoes or skiffs under twenty feet in length, and fifty pounds of captured fish or game, 'will be carried free in certain specific territory for each sportsman.'[11]

The railways did not always accord canoes the gentle treatment their owners might have anticipated, as Pauline Johnson once noted with regret. Upon completion of an eighty-mile train ride, she went to the baggage car to identify her carefully wrapped canoe. 'What should greet my horrified eyes,' she exclaimed, 'but my beautiful canvas-packed darling beneath two commercial traveler's iron bound sample trunks, three stretchers, a box of tins, a crate of blueberries, two valises, a baby carriage, a bunch of lacrosse stocks, four bales of blankets, a basket of house plants and a bicycle.'[12]

The railways' contribution to the widespread awareness of the attractions of the outdoors took other forms. Eager to promote passenger traffic, they continued to advertise and support canoeing holidays throughout the 1920s and 1930s, as they had done before the First World War. Closely tailored to the needs of canoeists, for example, was the lengthy pamphlet *Canoe Trips and Nature Photography*, issued by the Canadian National Railways. This pocket-sized guide made its initial appeal to the independent adventurer with a critical assault on travel packages and routine:

There are types of outdoorsmen and vacation seekers to whom 'ready-made' voyages or 'ready-made' anything savor so much of the timetable and follow-the-leader as to suggest neither sport, recreation, nor any form of personal happiness. Crowds and clatter distress them. 'Organized' recreation leaves them speechless. The very name of sightseeing by bus loads puts their emotions in a jumble. 'Perfect cuisine' and 'dancing pavilion' meet with an audible yawn, and any claim that sport has been so primped and polished as to make it possible to spend a long summer without soiling their laundered ducks brings hardly the reaction of a lifted eyebrow. To many men and women equally – the call of the 'regularized' vacation is not much more than a monotonous repetition of the office and the trolley car if it does not supply some sharp and inspiring contrast, if it fails to draw freely upon the instinct for muscular adventure and for the allurement of strange places.[13]

Canoe Trips and Nature Photography described about thirty routes, combining the 'big stuff requiring five or six weeks or more, with the maximum of novelty and daring' and 'the less exciting canoe trips where every evening ends at a modern hotel and a four-course meal.' The Ontario trips covered the range from travel on the Rideau Canal and Trent Waterway to James Bay trips along the Mattagami, Missinaibi, Abitibi, and Albany rivers. The only Manitoba route mentioned was a 644-mile return trip from The Pas to Fort Nelson or York Factory on Hudson Bay. However, for paddlers who aspired to still longer expeditions, *Canoe Trips* explained the logistics of reaching The Pas from Fort McMurray, Alberta, along a 761-mile route including the Clearwater River and the Churchill. Clearly, in the railway's view, recreational canoeists prepared for serious northern wilderness travel existed in substantial numbers, in both Canada and the United States. They would journey to and from the location of their holiday canoe trip as fare-paying railway passengers.

The business of catering to vacationers, whether 'devotees of the rod and reel' or camping and canoeing parties, evidently merited the attention of public officials as well as of commercial interests. Speaking in 1882 of the forthcoming regatta of the American Canoe Association at Stoney Lake, R.J. Wicksteed asserted that Canada would derive from the event an 'immediately great' benefit, one that would last well beyond the period of the camp itself. He predicted that the hundred or so American canoeists who were expected would return to the United States persuaded of the merits of the Canadian outdoors and 'declaring that the Dominion cannot be equalled as a place for summer resort.'[14] Albert Bigelow Paine urged his Nova Scotia hosts to appreciate that what the province 'most needs is money, and [that] the fisherman and hunter, once through the custom house, become a greater source of revenue than any tax that could be laid on their modest, not to say paltry, baggage.'[15] Governments have long been aware of the potential contribution of leisure to the public accounts, and have made repeated efforts over the years to promote holiday travel, including recreational canoe travel.

The active involvement of the Canadian government in promoting wilderness trips and camping was particularly noteworthy during the interwar years. A series of pamphlets containing recommendations for canoe vacations appeared under the aegis of the Department of the

Interior. *Canoeing in Canada* was directed towards the needs of the non-Canadian canoeist in an effort to introduce the 'unlimited choice' provided by the rich network of river and lake routes that the railways had brought 'within easy access.' The Canadian Shield country's attractions were enthusiastically proclaimed:

This entire region is by nature adapted to the needs of the voyageur who travels by canoe. Large sections are not suitable for agriculture and here nature remains in its primitive condition. One may follow the streams for a long summer outing and never see a village or dwelling, and yet civilization lies so close at hand that return is easily possible. The unevenness of surface presents everchanging and picturesque views of distant heights covered with forest. Waterfalls and rapids, large and small lakes of singular beauty in the forest, islands covered with pine and spruce trees, surprise one by day.

Having lauded the landscape, the pamphlet turned to flatter the potential tourist with the suggestion that 'the modern canoeist is the replica of the historic voyageur and pioneer.' But lest the prospect of a voyageur's existence might constitute more of a deterrent than an attraction for paddlers in the 1920s, the writer was quick to point out the conventional benefits of a summer in the wilds: 'The priceless rewards for all his toil are steady nerves and hardened muscles, self-reliance and resourcefulness, and that self-poise which faces all emergencies.'[16]

In *Camping in Canada*, a promotional brochure prepared for the Natural Resources Intelligence Service of the Department of the Interior, Ernest Voorhis, an early canoeing companion of Archibald Lampman who had long outlived the famous poet, extolled the virtues of the wilderness holiday:

The camper learns to mould himself into conformity with the existing conditions, entering into the harmony of nature, and in the process develops his own individuality. Difficulties, unexpected emergencies and sudden changes will test his power of self-control and stimulate his mental acumen. After facing the forces of nature and discovering the value of a stout heart, one returns to city life a stronger and healthier man.[17]

The Department of the Interior reported that information on canoeing opportunities was 'in great demand,' and in subsequent years the government refined its efforts to provide canoeists with increasingly detailed guidance.[18] By 1930 the National Development Bureau had begun to distribute a series of titles, including *Canoe Routes to Hudson Bay, Canoe Trips in Canada, Canoe Trips in Ontario, Canoe Trips in the Maritime Provinces, Canoe Trips in the Western Provinces*, and *Canoe Trips in Quebec*, the last available in both English and French.

The 1934 edition of *Canoe Trips in Canada* ran to sixty pages, with lists of canoe routes in each of the provinces and the Yukon Territory, where a holiday trip from Fort McPherson via the Rat River and McDougall Pass to the Bell and Porcupine rivers and down these to Fort Yukon was recommended. After the vacationer had selected a specific route or region, detailed descriptions and accompanying charts could be provided by the National Parks of Canada branch of the Department of the Interior. This remarkable federal initiative is further evidence of an official belief in the existence of significant numbers of canoe trippers. Indeed, in the late 1920s, government officials reported that requests for canoe trip information were common, and that 'chain selling' had a significant impact. 'When one party has successfully navigated a chain of Canada's rivers and lakes and experienced the thrill of shooting rapids, many other parties follow.'[19] Nevertheless, the trip recommendations had more the appearance of a service to the public than a purposeful effort to stimulate recreational canoe travel on the basis of its economic contribution to the community.

Beginning in the 1930s, recreation, tourism, and outdoor education were moved, for a variety of reasons, onto the legislative agenda in several jurisdictions. In so far as lack of fitness was occasionally an obstacle to effective training and employment, as well as a factor tending to lower the morale of the public, physical activity programs had a remedial potential. British Columbia's Provincial Recreation Programme, for example, a depression initiative that emerged in 1934 with gymnastics as its core, was intended, in the words of the minister of education and health, 'to preserve our youth from the dangerous effects of enforced idleness, and to build up morale and character that rests upon a good physical basis.'[20] In a few short years, with war on the horizon, the rationale had shifted: 'Physical training is one of the greatest agencies in preventive medicine, and the Pro-Rec scheme, which has proven beneficial to our people in peace-time, will be even more important in wartime. The gymnast of yesterday is the soldier of today.'[21] At the national level, encouragement from international sources such as the health committee of the League of Nations and the example of programs in other countries such as Britain prompted the passage of Canada's National Physical Fitness Act in 1943. According to the National Council on Physical Fitness, which was set up under the legislation, fitness was to be understood as having four dimensions: spiritual, moral, mental, and physical. Accordingly, 'total fitness must originate in the home, the church, the school and the community.'[22]

In the same year that the National Physical Fitness Act was proclaimed, the Canadian Youth Commission came into existence, with the objective of providing postwar youth with a more fulfilling environment than their immediate predecessors had enjoyed. With the publication of the youth commission's report in 1949, recreation, including camping, had yet another social role to play. Democratic societies, having reaffirmed their 'historic belief in the worth of the human personality' had, through their governments, some responsibility to 'provide each person with the widest possible opportunity to develop his capacities.' Yet mindful of the totalitarian menace against which a great struggle had so recently been waged, the Canadian Youth Commission cautioned against 'regimentation' and the risk of 'manipulation' by governments of 'the minds and bodies of young people for their own ends.'[23]

In anticipation of postwar reconstruction and in the hope of a more prosperous peacetime economy, public officials and government leaders began to address the potential of the tourism sector and its requirements. At one postwar planning conference, the chief of the Canadian Government Travel Bureau stressed the need for road improvements to facilitate access to recreational attractions. Ontario's provincial treasurer announced a newly formulated tourism policy, including an advertising campaign and a more comprehensive system of licensing, supervision, and inspection for tourist establishments. As the travel and publicity program got under way, Arthur Walsh, the minister responsible, suggested the desirability of a general promotional theme: 'We are, in a sense, a gigantic department store purveying travel and recreation. Let us get our customer into the store, mentally at least, before we endeavour to sell him shoes or a necktie or a suite of furniture. Once he is "sold" on Canada, then we can all be sure that we will get our share of his trade.'[24]

Despite all the attention given to the rationales for physical activity, the need for standards and infrastructure, and the economic potential of recreation, canoe holidays now largely escaped official notice. Arguably, the paddle and portage section of Arthur Walsh's department store didn't get as much consideration as the necktie counter, and it certainly didn't get the attention lavished on the auto shop, as vehicle production and the recreational use of automobiles expanded dramatically. The Second World War also brought an end to the long-standing efforts of the federal government and of the major railways to promote and facilitate canoe travel as a means of stimulating either their own business or the general public revenues.

George H. Ellis, the assistant director of the Canadian Government Travel Bureau, lamented that his department's many canoeing guidebooks were no longer up to date. The staff of the agency had been depleted during the war, and accurate and detailed information was difficult to come by. The message was confirmed when J.S. McDonald, general tourist agent with the Passenger Traffic Department of the CNR, explained that the railway's booklet *Camp Craft and Woodlore* had last been issued in 1938. The volume had been out of stock for seven or eight years, and it was 'altogether unlikely that we will reprint at any time.'[25] Thus, vigorous efforts by governments and the railways to promote recreational canoe travel through to the late interwar years had not survived the renewal of overseas hostilities. When official attention turned once more to the place of tourism in postwar economic reconstruction, the automobile triumphed as a means of holiday travel. There were no obvious sources of institutional support for paddlers, whose recreational expenditures now appeared minuscule by comparison.

Yet after the Second World War, as modest but notable numbers of recreational canoeists ventured again into the remote sections of Canada, including, increasingly, the northern territories, the availability of canoes and equipment became more problematic. For convenience, and of course to avoid shipping expenses, P.G. Downes, a regular American visitor to the far north, left a canoe in the region.[26] Others contemplating canoe travel faced real difficulty during the short paddling season.

In 1963, Eric Morse, by this time an experienced organizer of northern canoe expeditions, met with the corporate directors of the Hudson's Bay Company and persuaded the company to introduce a canoe rental service in northern and western Canada. The HBC immediately acquired twenty-eight Grumman canoes, and in 1964 it inaugurated its 'U-Paddle Canoe Rental Service.' For a weekly rental charge – initially twenty-five dollars – recreational paddlers could pick up a canoe at one of the HBC's posts and return it to another at the end of the trip. These arrangements encouraged 'experienced canoe-trip fans' to travel along fur trade water-routes in the Canadian northland. Yellowknife, Waterways, Île-à-la Crosse, La Ronge, Norway House, and Winnipeg were originally designated as points of departure.[27]

The popularity of the U-Paddle program among summer voyageurs was immediately evident. The rental fleet eventually was expanded to eighty canoes. The HBC, however, never considered U-Paddle a large operation.

As one company official explained, 'The Bay U-Paddle canoe service is only a small operation formed mainly to accommodate the canoeist interested in the northern wilderness and therefore, our number of canoes is very limited and reservations usually have to be made fully six months ahead of time.'[28]

Canoeists from across Canada, from the United States, and from several European countries took advantage of the U-Paddle plan to arrange extensive northern trips, often availing themselves of the HBC's offer to provide 'general advice on wilderness living.' Some correspondents focused directly on specific informational needs related to the details of a carefully selected trip proposal, while other would-be voyageurs made more open-ended appeals to the Bay's Northern Stores Department for assistance with their holiday-planning. One correspondent, writing from Boulder, Colorado, sought help in preparing for a canoe trip to Hudson Bay. 'At this point all we have is the idea,' he confessed; he was unsure 'of exactly what point would be wise for us to start at or what part of Hudson Bay should be our goal.' The party had no preference one way or another about which province to paddle in, although the canoeists wished the trip 'to start where the roads end.' 'I suppose,' the inquiry continued, 'information on all, including Northwest Territories, would be appropriate, if you have such information.'[29]

Perhaps in response to demands of this kind, which arrived from Europe as well as the United States and Canada, the HBC eventually recommended a series of routes to channel travellers along some of the more familiar and popular waterways: Pickle Lake–Albany, Landsdowne House–Attawapiskat, Yellowknife–Coppermine, Yellowknife–Thelon–Baker Lake. Eric Morse remained an avid supporter and a regular user of the rental service he had inspired, ultimately concluding that he had 'certainly been the principal beneficiary to the tune of somewhere between $2,500–$3,000.'[30] If Morse came out somewhat ahead in his tally with the HBC, this was modest compensation indeed to set against the value of his contribution to recreational paddling.

While he remains best known as a trip leader and organizer, Morse was also a productive writer, a teacher, an adviser to governments, and – up to a point – a very generous consultant who placed his accumulated knowledge and expertise at the service of other would-be voyageurs. As Pamela Morse recalls, people would call in the middle of the night, from around the United States in particular, to say they were planning a canoe trip and to ask for advice and some indication of what they might be getting into. Eric, she explains, would ordinarily say, 'Well, if you send me your maps,

I'll mark on them the things that you have to watch out for, the things that aren't marked on the map.' Demands on the service eventually got out of hand when a group from Sweden, who canoed regularly in northern Canada with Morse's advice, passed on the word to friends, who apparently concluded he was operating an outfitting business. People would write from Sweden to request that canoes be left for them at a designated spot on a certain date and so on. This forced Morse to accept that enough was enough, and he simply forwarded these inquiries to the Swedish embassy.[31]

After almost a decade of operations, the U-Paddle system had clearly contributed to the popularization of the remote northern expedition; the private vacation parties for whom U-Paddle was originally designed were soon followed by increasing numbers of commercial ventures. Thus, Craig Macdonald, now a respected professional naturalist, wrote in the early 1970s on behalf of a group of guides attached to canoe-tripping camps in Ontario and Quebec:

Our director is enthusiastic about extending operations to the above areas, however, the cost of transporting our own canoes in and out of these areas and back to our own region is prohibitive ... Wilderness canoe tripping has become big business especially in Ontario and now many trips are pushing farther north where the Hudson's Bay Company could really be of service. If our organization can demonstrate how these trips are economically feasible at least five other large tripping camps in our area will be quick to follow suit.[32]

Indeed, the far northern trip became a staple offering in the programs of youth camps and of a growing number of commercial outfitters.[33]

By 1984, just before the U-Paddle program was shut down, rental prices for the still-standard seventeen-foot Grumman had reached $125 per week for a minimum of two weeks. The abandonment of the U-Paddle program in 1985, which has been attributed to economic difficulties, may have been brought on by several factors. Fuel and transportation costs increased in the 1970s. Although the program operated on a break-even basis, the administration seems to have involved a good deal of nuisance work relating to minor damage and claims with shipping companies.[34] It is also possible that by the mid-1970s the airlines, the summer camps, and a new generation of private outfitters were in a position to expand their own services to such an extent that they provided effective competition for the HBC. The wilderness canoeing industry now constituted an important economic activity.

Some elements of the industry – children's summer camps, for example – were long-established. Yet many of these institutions were vulnerable to changing economic circumstances. Centennial celebrations, cheap airfares to Europe, the emergence of alternative camps, rising fuel costs and school district levies, and the eventual burden of rehabilitating long-neglected seasonal buildings took their toll in the sixties and seventies. The survival strategies included off-season programs directed at school groups and diversification into adult canoe trips, conference management, and cross-country skiing. But these initiatives were not always successful. Many marginal camps disappeared.

Against this backdrop, a new generation of commercial operations emerged. Young camp veterans who hoped to prolong their love affair with the wilderness for a few seasons, at least, entered the business world. The new outfitters initially sidestepped the issue of physical plant, with all its headaches stemming from remoteness and the fixed year-round costs that made such great demands on summer income. Mountain Equipment Co-op, founded in 1971 by members of the Outdoors Club at the University of British Columbia, ran for several seasons out of a member's basement before launching stores and retail outlets in Vancouver, Calgary, Toronto, and Ottawa.

Wally Schaber's involvement with what eventually became the highly regarded Black Feather and Trailhead operations also began as an attempt on his part to do something he enjoyed for a few years. In 1971, when Camp Ondadawa closed its doors, Schaber and a couple of colleagues launched a modest outfitting venture by leading a commercial trip into Quetico. After several summers of successful operation, the partners formed Black Feather, and attention turned to the possibility of a retail outlet which would generate a year-round income. The Trailhead stores, in Ottawa and in Toronto, were the eventual result.

Although many outfitters claimed to be marginal – operating only slightly above a break-even basis even in a good year – and while the most obvious participants – the camping goods stores, remote outfitters, summer camps – were individually rather modest operations, their cumulative significance was substantial. As Wally Schaber explains, that significance has a financial dimension, but the wilderness industry is also an important ingredient in a broader strategic effort to preserve wild places:

Our industry right now represents about two hundred million dollars in retail sales with probably a thousand retail jobs associated with that. There is probably a hundred million dollars in wholesale manufacturing or distribution and another thousand jobs associated with that. And all the spin-off jobs to do with wilderness preservation – guiding, writing, publishing, researching, movies – probably represents at least the same amount of marketing again. If we continually erode places where these things happen, then that market is going to continually shrink, and I think that for all the tax dollars that are generated out of a half-billion dollar industry, there should be a lot more significant wilderness plan to preserve that industry. We have to do more work statistically to prove that this industry exists, because the other industries – consumer industries like forestry, mining, etc. – are really good at doing this.[35]

The very extensive network of economic activity linked to wilderness and involving outfitting, specialized food processing, equipment manufacturing, travel tours, outdoor photography, publishing, and so on reflects some alteration in underlying social values.

The distinguished American historian Samuel P. Hays argues that increased wilderness activity is part of a profound reorientation of North American values that has taken place since the Second World War, as the quest for a higher standard of living has evolved to encompass a range of environmental concerns linked with quality of life. In *Beauty, Health, and Permanence*, Hays suggests that aesthetic aspirations, the desire for improvements in physical well-being, and a concern for the ecological condition are intertwined aspects of a transformed economy that was gradually coming to recognize environmental fundamentals:

Whereas amenities involved an aesthetic response to the environment, and environmental health concerned a choice between cleaner and dirtier technologies within the built-up environment, ecological matters dealt with imbalances between developed and natural systems that had both current and long-term implications. These questions, therefore, involved ideas about permanence.[36]

The economist Kenneth Boulding has made a similar point somewhat more graphically in his provocative comparison of 'cowboy' and 'spaceman' economies. The cowboy's association with what Boulding describes as 'reckless, exploitative, romantic, and violent behavior' makes him a fit symbol of an economy preoccupied with levels of production and consumption and presuming 'infinite reservoirs' for the extraction of raw materials and the discharge of effluvia. The spaceman, in contrast, having accepted that there are no 'unlimited reservoirs of anything,' would seek to measure economic success in terms of 'the nature, extent, quality, and complexity of the total capital stock, including the state of the human bodies and minds included in the system.'[37] One might well debate the canoeist's proper place on the spectrum linking Boulding's cowboys and spacemen, but if, for the sake of exposition, we put the canoe nearer to the spaceship end, the problem of justifying canoeing within the traditional economic framework may be illustrated.

C.E.S. Franks is one of those who argue that 'canoeing is to boating what cross country is to skiing.' By this he means that it does not involve significant levels of energy and resource consumption, and that its environmental impacts are comparatively modest. In consequence, canoeing is 'not adequately accounted for in measures of economic welfare like the gross national product.' By way of example, Franks explains that

a worker who takes a week off to go canoeing, rather than work overtime to buy a second television set, under our primitive techinques of measurement causes a loss to the GNP regardless of the economic value of his choice to himself or to the world. The value of these types of choices in the use of leisure needs to be rethought to create better measures of economic welfare in modern civilization.[38]

But in the face of seemingly relentless developmental pressures on natural resources, open spaces, and wild rivers, canoeists themselves have become caught up in the moral dilemmas associated with modern land-use planning and allocation as they endeavour to demonstrate the value of a pastime they enjoy.

It is easy enough to assert that the pleasures and benefits of canoeing are priceless. But if you are one of those who have been able to get by for twenty years in the same old canoe, wearing the same old Kodiak boots, and sleeping in a durable down bag you picked up for about seventy-five dollars some years ago – 'thank you very much' – it may appear to the professional analyst of these things that the wilderness can't be worth very much to you. It is not yet entirely fashionable to equate the value of a natural recreational experience with its price, but the point is not far off. Tragically and inexcusably, the value of the North American wilderness is coming to be equated with the willingness of canoeists and other outdoor vacationers to purchase clothing, supplies, equipment, and services. (Less tragically, from my perspective at least, sales of this book may also enter the ledger!)

Members of the Hide-Away Canoe Club demonstrated during the course of an outing from Hudson Bay to Ungava in the summer of 1986 that the trip budget is not entirely under the control of the voyageurs. Careful advance planning allowed the participants to make significant savings on ground transportation and the fly-in to Great Whale on Quebec's Hudson Bay coast. At that point, however, unanticipated complications severely distorted the trip's financial implications, so that the expedition turned out to be worth more to its participants than they had bargained for. The $150 fee for two Inuit guides, whose services had been commissioned well in advance, apparently did not include gasoline charges – ninety gallons at $4.50 per gallon. But ice conditions along the coast and mechanical difficulties prevented the crew from reaching Richmond Gulf, and several crucial paddling days were lost from the perilously short season. Back once again at Great Whale, where the guides requested $150 each, the Hide-Away party reverted to the airways to make up time. A costly Otter with limited canoe-carrying capacity necessitated extra trips. As Michael Peake reported to readers of *Che-Mun*, 'This meant two, virtually empty, flights up to Clearwater in a plane chartered from 120 miles away. The total bill for our 75-minute flight was $3000.' Peake philosophically concluded: 'All of which goes to show anything is possible. And the further north you go the more possible everything gets. Be prepared, be flexible, be rich.'[39]

Canoeists have shown a distinct lack of enthusiasm for one particular form of financial outlay – the licence fee. The rumoured introduction of such a charge has invariably produced outraged protests from members of a constituency who continue to believe their activity falls outside the legitimate range of governmental control. One correspondent found the threat of an annual licence fee on watercraft including canoes and kayaks 'both distasteful and impractical.' David Pelly advanced several arguments against the proposed fee. First, given the historical role of the canoe in the exploration and development of Canada, Pelly argued, a tax on canoes would be an affront to the national heritage. Second, given the status of the canoe as offering one of a very limited number of non-consumptive forms of leisure activity, it would be environmentally regressive to tax the sport. Moreover – and perhaps most fundamentally – Pelly suggested, a licensing regime 'contradicts the very essence of canoeing' and would constitute a violation of the 'sense of celebration of the freedom of the wilderness' that so many canoeists seem to feel.[40]

The importance of the general issue of the value of nature lies in the significance this question has for official attitudes to resource development. An excellent survey of values respecting nature was prepared by Dr Robert Payne for presentation to an environmental assessment panel charged with reviewing proposals for timber management planning in Ontario. As Payne explains, 'values toward nature have not been static in western society.'[41] One stream of thinking promotes the wise management of natural resources, recognizing both the limited extent of forests and waterways, for example, and their limited potential to contribute to economic development. Properly conserved and efficiently managed, natural resources represent an ongoing source of wealth for society. Payne – along with others – views this attitude to the valuation of nature as essentially utilitarian: we value nature to the extent that we can use it for our purposes. 'We' are human beings, and the purposes are very much our own.

Human purposes need not be confined exclusively to the consumption of resources for sale in the marketplace. Indeed, a good deal of thought has been devoted in recent years to the task of extending our understanding of the uses of nature. Today more decision-makers will acknowledge recreational, scientific, aesthetic, and historical values among other utilitarian measures of nature. There is less agreement, though, on the calculus to be applied if a dispute arises about whether to preserve wilderness for public use and enjoyment or to extract its component parts. We have a fair idea of the market value of standing timber: some minor variation on 'volume × unit price' will likely get you into the ballpark. It has proved much more difficult to measure pleasure.

How much is a wild river winding through an old growth forest worth to a canoeist, especially to a canoeist who is disinclined to contribute the cost of a licence to the public coffers? The formulas are of considerable interest, even if their practical utility often leaves more than a little to be desired.[42] One might approach the challenge of valuing natural resources by posing the question as one of compensation for loss. That is, supposing that the environment suffered damage – or even destruction – as a consequence of some wrongful act, what amount of compensation should be paid by the wrongdoers? The efforts of lawyers and economists to address this problem are by no means universally satisfying, but at least the arguments reveal perceptions of the nature of the task. If everyone agrees that compensation should be based on the value or worth of the loss, there are great differences of opinion concerning the relevant factors. For some, the value of natural resources or the environment is equated with utility alone: we have lost value to the extent that we have lost use. Others are more willing to acknowledge additional bases of valuation associated with intrinsic qualities of nature, or non-utilitarian considerations. Those who propose the inclusion of intrinsic values in the calculus might amplify their position in several ways. Even if we don't use resources, we value them because of the option or potential for use which they represent. In addition, we value them on the basis of a desire to pass them on to future generations in the form of a bequest. Intrinsic valuation would also recognize the importance of the mere existence of environmental assets without regard to their actual use by present or future generations. Advocates of intrinsic value would defend their views with the further argument that in each case – option value, bequest value, and existence value – individuals would be willing to pay to maintain these elements of environmental resources. Things get more complicated from here, as the debate moves from consideration of the kinds of values that might be recognized for purposes of compensation to the task of assigning numbers to those values. Methodology is a highly controversial matter.

There are those who advocate a market-based approach to valuation. They suggest that compensation for loss or damage to a resource is simply the difference between its original market value and the commercial value or price after the damage has been done. The market-based approach is defended by its adherents with the claim that markets alone reflect real willingness to pay. In other words, only the actual behaviour of consumers establishes values. They might have some sympathy with the use of surrogate markets to establish environmental values, but that is as far as it goes. For example, the costs of travel and expenses associated with getting to wilderness might represent the value of the wilderness experience. However, it must be noted that even this methodology restricts the value of wilderness to the value of its use. If no one goes there, it can't be worth going to – ever. So it isn't worth preserving as wilderness.

Critics, however, reject the market model, in part because it is just that, a model. Markets for most natural resources don't really exist, they say, and so even if you know what someone might pay for a quantity of lumber, the price tells you nothing at all about the value of the forest. What gets left out includes the intrinsic value of the resource, its service as habitat, and values that we all attach to resources by our enjoyment of them even though we never have to pay. For people with this view, the challenge is to move from assertions about unpriced values to actual quantification. Various alternatives have been advanced.

Could one approximate the value of a damaged natural resource by determining the cost of replacing it or of restoring it to its original condition? It wouldn't take much thought to run up quite a tab, and to the extent that you were successful in restoration, both use values and intrinsic values should be re-established. Another suggested methodology known as the contingent valuation approach involves the use of questionnaire and survey techniques to determine from people what monetary value they would place on non-marketable items such as threatened species, free-running streams, and clear skies. Among the reservations expressed about an approach based on hypothetical transactions, serious controversy has arisen about whether sellers' hypothetical prices are more reliable measures than buyers' willingness to pay, for respondents curiously differ in their valuations, depending on whether they think they are gaining something or giving it up.

These formulas have become a welcome source of ammunition in campaigns to create parks, to safeguard tall pines, and to preserve the sanctity of wild places.[43] They serve that role, of course, but as many have affirmed, something more than price is at stake in the wilderness experience.

15

Consuming Wilderness

Wilderness exploration today is a lot harder than it used to be. This paradox of modernity is simple enough to explain: there is a lot less wilderness than there once was.[1] For recreational canoeists the situation is particularly problematic since members of this group generally assume that a large expanse of uncivilized and largely unmolested terrain is an essential ingredient of a fully respectable holiday. The virtues of this celebrated activity, deriving from the physical exertion required, from the canoe's association with nature, and from the paddler's historical lineage, are important environmental credentials. Yet complicating the matter, muddying the moral waters, so to speak, is the uncertain status of paddlers in relation to the landscape: although conventional wisdom places canoeists in environmentalist ranks as protectors of wilderness, they are also users of wilderness – appreciative users, perhaps, but users nonetheless. Passion for the outdoors occasionally threatens the very places wilderness travellers value so highly. The dilemma – or irony, as it has also been described – has become more acute with the explosion in the numbers of wilderness travellers during the last third of the twentieth century.[2]

The transition from hunting and fishing holidays in a canoe to paddling for pleasure has been gradual and intermittent. Throughout the nineteenth century, canoes transported fishermen and hunters to the secluded places where game and sport fish might be had in abundance. Part of the catch nourished these outdoorsmen – and occasionally women – during the course of their recreational endeavours, while the remainder constituted provisions for later consumption or trophies for display. In this context, reactions to resource depletion were mixed and, from the perspective of the late twentieth century, often tragic. While signs of resource depletion and the obliteration of unique landscapes often stimulated a commitment to conservation, the prospect of those irreversible losses could equally serve as an argument for accelerated consumption. So, as it came to be acknowledged that the 'eastern sportsman, voyager, and explorer' had devastated much of the continent and was turning northward for adventure, observers anticipated the end of the 'forest primeval.' 'In all probability,' railway publicists remarked on the occasion of a royal tour in the early 1900s, 'we of this generation will be the last to relate to our grandchildren the stirring stories of the hunt in the wild forest of Canada.' This was not, however, a call for repentance, rather the reverse:

Therefore it behooves you, O mighty hunter, to go forth and capture your cariboo or moose while you may. The scenes are shifting. Civilization is shoving the wild things further to the north. But you who are lucky enough to live to-day may hurry to these last fastnesses and find here the rarest sport to be had in all North America.[3]

Other contemporary sources provide strong, if less dramatic, evidence of similar perceptions. Canoeing stories from such outdoor magazines as *Rod and Gun, Field and Stream,* and *Forest and Outdoors* were generally oriented towards the trials and successes of the hunter and fisherman. Touring North America before the First World War, Rupert Brooke enjoyed the scenery, but was entirely frank about the future of the landscape:

It awaits the sun, the end for which Heaven made it, the blessing of civilization. Some day it will be sold into large portions, and the timber given to a friend of _____'s and cut down and made into paper, on which shall be printed the praise of prosperity; and the land itself shall be divided into town-lots and sold, and sub-divided and sold again, and boomed and resold, and boosted and distributed to fishy young men who will vend it in distant parts of the country; and then such portions as can never be built upon shall be given in exchange for great sums of money to old ladies in the quieter parts of England.[4]

However, over a period of several generations, North American wilderness paddlers made considerable progress in extricating themselves from the tradition of frontier resource exploitation in which canoe routes originally functioned as a pipeline for beaver skins.

Less disruptive approaches to the paddler's landscape and its natural inhabitants gradually emerged, especially beginning in the late nineteenth century. In February 1882, the inaugural issue of the *American Canoeist* urged paddlers to use the camera in order to support 'the memory of the voyager,'[5] and other writers were soon arguing that 'the canoe and the camera are natural allies,' or predicting that 'photography is such a delightful accompaniment to canoeing that it will probably become a common amusement among our brothers of the paddle.'[6] Certainly, camera use gained in popularity among canoeists, particularly as the technology became more reliable and equipment prices declined. However, from the abundance of triumphal trophy shots in the early years of the twentieth century one may conclude that the camera often supported rather than displaced sport shooting and fishing.

One year before the First World War, *Outing* proclaimed canoe and camera 'an ideal combination,' and soon, among canoeists, the camera emerged as the most accepted means of capturing game.[7] Paddlers were not unwilling to express their preferences. A party of canoeists in the Georgian Bay district, for example, reported an encounter with a deer: 'We had soon a sight worth remembering and it had been more fun shooting that deer with a camera than a rifle, as we had stalked him across the open lake in broad daylight.'[8] A few years later, an extensive review of canoe trip outfitting in *Rod and Gun* devoted far more attention to camera equipment, film packaging, developing, and printing than to fishing and hunting gear.[9]

Several factors may help to explain the dissolution of earlier linkages between hunting and fishing and the canoe. Improved commercial provisioning reduced the vacation paddler's dependence on rod and gun to supplement food supplies. Simultaneously, the proliferation of outboard motors may have reduced the fisherman/hunter's need for the canoe. Women and children were found more frequently in canoeing parties, and perhaps more effective fish and game regulation and enforcement provided a measure of control over off-season activity. Janet Foster, a naturalist, photographer, and historian, has suggested that wildlife conservation came of age in Canada during the second and third decades of the twentieth century, a phenomenon she attributes to the efforts of a dedicated group of public officials, including Gordon Hewitt, Dominion ethnologist, and James B. Harkin, commissioner of Dominion parks.[10] It is also possible that the sensibilities of the recreational paddler were changing and that appreciation of the environment was taking a new form.

A number of prominent writers, Ernest Thompson Seton and Charles G.D. Roberts among them, urged hunters to abandon the rifle for the camera in the years before the First World War. Their efforts were supported by Bonnycastle Dale, whose frequent contributions to *Rod and Gun* and *Westward Ho! Magazine* also emphasized photography as a means of sublimating the destructive, wasteful impulses of the sport hunter into a more conservationist capturing and recording of outdoor experience.[11] The direct effect of such pleading on hunters is impossible to determine, and probably quite modest. However, it is possible to imagine that, in combination with other changes in the canoeist's world, these ideas had some influence.

When recreational canoeing revived in Canada following the cultural gulf created by the First World War, the wilderness and camping tradition rather than canoe sailing and competitive regattas were central. In some respects, the recreational wilderness paddler of the 1920s simply preserved a historical association between canoeists and the landscape, adapted from the Indians and maintained through the exploits of explorers and fur traders, or the last expeditions of surveyors, geologists, prospectors, and nineteenth-century sportsmen. The shifts from birch-bark to wood and to canvas-covered canoes, the transition from railway advertising of canoe vacations to active government promotion of wilderness holidays, and the emergence of an extensive literature on canoe technique may all be regarded as evolutionary changes in the history of a popular summer pastime. Yet these same developments and other transitional events of the interwar years may also be viewed as elements in a more complex and fundamental transformation of recreational canoeists' relationship with their society.

Canoeing acquired an alternative respectability, separate and distinct from the fur trade and exploration story, and for this development club-paddling, the regatta circuit, and other aspects of organized sport canoeing may take some credit. These activities afforded a rationale for canoeing largely unrelated to the frontier legacy. It is also true, of course, that the advent of the airplane and the commercial popularity of the automobile were profoundly relevant. No longer functional or necessary, canoe travel emerged in counterpoint to technological dominance of the landscape as an activity that could be clearly distinguished from modern forms of transportation. A shift in canoeists' priorities in the 1920s may thus be seen as a reflection – at least in part – of this great cultural watershed and transformation.

Despite some overall similarities, the interwar years may be distinguished for the shift suggested by an apparent decline in emphasis on the canoe trip as an activity for fishermen, hunters, and sportsmen, and a greater tendency to regard canoeing as a means of seeing nature, contemplating scenery, and experiencing the landscape. From these 'passive' pleasures of recreational canoeing, which focus on the experience of canoeing for its own sake and the appreciation of landscape in art and photography, it is possible to discern the emergence of an autonomous tradition in recreational paddling. That is, it is now possible to see the popular canoeing holiday as pleasurable and worthwhile in itself, apart from any incidental benefit to be found in character development, physical fitness, and improvement that would aid one in the urban struggle, and apart from the triumph over nature represented by the fisherman's 'string of beauties' or the hunter's trophy. This was what Raoul Clouthier earnestly struggled to explain in 1928 to those whose list of plausible reasons for paddling extended no further than hunting, fishing, and resource exploration.[12]

Canoe campers who had learned to enjoy outdoor travel for its own sake often perceived themselves as defenders of the natural environment. They might report the damage and devastation brought about by forest industry operations, or the adverse impacts of flooding caused by dams and fluctuating water levels in northern lakes and rivers. Thus, no less a figure than Aubrey White, the deputy minister of lands and forests for Ontario, was called to account early in the twentieth century for the condition of Lady Evelyn Lake after a correspondent in *Rod and Gun* sharply criticized the impact of a dam on the scenic beauties of the surrounding countryside.[13]

For much of the past century, canoeists have indeed been active in environmental causes, primarily, though not only, those involving threats to wilderness. The twentieth-century canoe, much less relevant to exploration and exploitation than its predecessor, could be redefined and presented as an ally of the natural world:

Domination is not the mode of the canoe. In its red and green painted canvas, replacing the dust-coloured birch bark, in its playful action on the water, there is a frivolous appearance. For the pleasure of life in the harsh Canadian environment this is not regrettable. And inherently the canoe is and continues to be as functional as a ladle in the moulding action of the Precambrian Shield environment on the forms of life in Canada.[14]

Thus it appeared that at the conclusion of the interwar era, the contemplative pleasures of paddling in harmony with nature were effectively displacing the commercial and institutional foundations of canoe travel derived from the fur trade and voyageur tradition. Recreational paddlers have continued to emphasize this aspect of their activity: many wilderness canoeists regard a commitment to conservation and the environment as axiomatic.

For a generation of canoeists, the nature of wilderness as a refuge, sanctuary, and place of reflection was articulated by Sigurd F. Olson, an ecologist who had studied at the Universities of Wisconsion and Illinois before settling in Ely, Minnesota. In magazine articles and popular books such as *The Singing Wilderness* and *Listening Point*, Olson set out a decidedly post-frontier conception of the rugged landscape of the Quetico-Superior country that he knew so well. *Listening Point*, for example, begins with an extended meditation on how one small strip of land provided connections to the far reaches of geological and human history:

From it I have seen the immensity of space and glimpsed at times the grandeur of creation. There I have sensed the span of uncounted centuries and looked down the path all life has come. I have explored on this rocky bit of shore the great concept that nothing stands alone and everything, no matter how small, is part of a greater whole ...

I believe that what I have known there is one of the oldest satisfactions of man, that when he gazed upon the earth and sky with wonder, when he sensed the first vague glimmerings of meaning in the universe, the world of knowledge and spirit was opened to him ...

Listening Point is dedicated to recapturing this almost forgotten sense of wonder and learning from rocks and trees and all the life that is found there, truths that can encompass all. Through a vein of rose quartz at its tip can be read the geological history of the planet, from an old pine stump the ecological succession of the plant kingdom, from an Indian legend the story of the dreams of all mankind.[15]

Recreational paddlers reading Olson might well imagine themselves as wilderness advocates, respectful of the natural world, and conscious of their place in it. But the independence of recreational paddling from the fur trade tradition of direct resource exploitation was in some respects deceptive. If trophy-seeking hunters and the fisherman were less evident in the ranks of canoeists during the twenties, thirties, and forties, paddlers – even in the midst of summer travel – had by no means disentangled themselves from general social developments.

Manufactured camping gear – 'claptrap' as Dillon Wallace had affirmed – was available ad infinitum. In addition, the outboard, the automobile, and the airplane were increasingly part of the canoeist's equipment and support system, as the railways had been in an earlier era. Even the canoe itself was becoming less and less the work of craftsmen's hands and more obviously the product of an industrial form of manufacture.

The aluminum canoe – a durable but energy-intensive craft – was on the horizon. Some canoeists find the aluminum paddler's commitment to landscape preservation hopelessly contradictory. Rivers are dammed to produce the hydro-electricity required for the production of aluminum, yet the free-flowing natural waterway remains the ideal canoeing environment. In contrast, the birch-bark canoe and to a lesser but still considerable extent its canvas-covered descendant could claim to be 'natural.' 'When it has served its purpose,' explained Bill Mason in reference to the birch-bark craft, 'it returns to the land, part of a never-ending cycle.' By understanding the traditional cycle of natural growth leading to manufacture, use, and eventual return to the land one could fathom why the 'modern canoe is in such trouble.' Its trajectory from manufacture to use to garbage Mason described as a dead end. He urged paddlers to become 'more aware of where we are headed and from whence we came,' adding that 'an appreciation of the canoe and acquisition of the necessary skills to utilize it as a way to journey back to what's left of the natural world is a great way to begin this voyage of discovery.'[16]

This dilemma, which troubled the consciences of many paddlers as the environmental movement emerged to prominence in the 1960s and 1970s, was not the only later recreational canoeing controversy whose roots developed in the interwar period. The expansion of canoeing literature during the 1920s and 1930s certainly broadened access to information and technique, and arguably contributed to the democratization and expansion of canoeing itself. At the same time, however, the basis for conventional standards was laid. Some have found in the development of guidelines and manuals – particularly when these are adopted or endorsed by organized groups in the camping movement, the schools, or government agencies – the unpleasant prospect of regimentation and standardization, or even the eventual possibility of skill-based licensing systems to control access to the wilderness.

Contemporary environmentalists are frequently inclined to portray the forties, fifties, and early sixties as a wasteland, a period of utter disregard for nature. Despite the automobile, consumerism, and massive postwar industrial expansion, the situation is somewhat more complex, and there are certainly indications that problems were being recognized, even if the solutions implemented thoroughly underestimated the intractability of the challenge. Various jurisdictions endeavoured to face up to the problems of long-neglected municipal sewerage systems; health officials contemplated the relationship between environmental pollution and human well-being; and park systems were often substantially expanded.

In the United States, a major milestone was the passage in 1964 of the federal Wilderness Act, providing for congressionally designated areas to be withdrawn from other uses. Significantly, the legislation addressed the question of definition, offering a formulation that has become a benchmark and a rallying cry:

A wilderness, in contrast with those areas where man and his works dominate the landscape, is hereby recognized as an area where the earth and its community of life are untrammeled by man, where man himself is a visitor who does not remain. An area of wilderness is further defined to mean ... an area of undeveloped Federal land retaining its primeval character and influence, without permanent improvements or human habitation, which is protected and managed so as to preserve its natural conditions and which (1) generally appears to have been affected primarily by the forces of nature, with the imprint of man's work substantially unnoticeable; (2) has outstanding opportunities for solitude or a primitive and unconfined type of recreation; (3) ... is of sufficient size as to make practicable its preservation and use in an unimpaired condition; and (4) may also contain ecological, geological, or other features of scientific, educational, scenic, or historic value.

Building on an initial fifteen-million-acre selection, subsequent campaigns resulted in further extensions of designated wilderness lands, including a fifty-million-acre Alaska addition to the National Wilderness Preservation System in 1980.[17]

The wilderness movement has been described as 'the most successful organized citizen effort in the Environmental Era,' a status attributed to the participatory foundations on which it rested: 'The key to the success of wilderness action lay in mobilizing people who knew first hand and enjoyed areas of potential wilderness designation and became committed to political action to protect them.'[18] Wilderness advocates, including significant numbers of canoeists, are rightly credited with a major contribution to the continuing campaign for preservation. And in the middle decades of the twentieth century they vigorously insisted on standards of protection that were significantly more rigid than official policies favouring multiple use had contemplated. Algonquin Park, for example, had been established in 1893 in territory familiar to recreational paddlers through the writing of James Dickson. The park's constituting legislation stated that the area was 'reserved and set apart as a public park and forest reservation, fish and game preserve, health resort and pleasure ground for the benefit, advantage and enjoyment of the people of the Province.' The designation had not, however, curtailed logging, commercial development, road access, and even railway construction; nor had it been intended to do so.

Later visitors to Algonquin Park expressed divergent attitudes to the resulting mix of industrial, recreational, and commercial uses. The Ontario premier Leslie Frost, whose own electoral constituency encompassed sections of the park, sought to honour Dickson for his contribution to the founding of the park. In the introduction to a 1959 reprinting of Dickson's classic 1886 canoe trip account, Frost, who claimed to have visited personally every part of Dickson's route at one time or another, praised the surveyor for the quality of his observations and simultaneously cast official management of the area in a very favourable light: 'His descriptions of the country are amazingly accurate and they can easily be followed to this day. There has been little change. The region is still very much as he saw it. It is still very much as the first white man saw it. Fortunately, it will be kept that way.'[19] The genial Premier, himself an outdoorsman who often paddled in the Lindsay district, was no doubt anxious to promote the virtues of his constituency, but many of his contemporaries would have considered him guilty of wishful thinking.

Within a year or two of Premier Frost's assurances about the state of Algonquin, a suggestion emerged in the context of a pivotal federal-provincial conference called 'Resources for Tomorrow' for the creation of a non-governmental watchdog to monitor park management throughout Canada. The National and Provincial Parks Association of Canada thus came into existence in 1963, to be followed a couple of years later by the creation of the Algonquin Wildlands League, a body which helped to inform naturalists, environmentalists, and members of the outdoor recreational community about crucial wilderness issues and to articulate their concerns in various policy-making forums.[20]

Through the 1960s, individual canoeists also contributed to the general level of awareness about threats to wilderness and waterways. Thus Eric Morse, whose group of voyageurs is better known for the adventurousness of its northern expeditions and an appreciation of fur trade and exploration history than for environmentalism, drew attention to the disappearing legacy. In *Fur Trade Canoe Routes of Canada: Then and Now*, Morse expressed the hope that his study of the geography of the fur trade routes might serve 'indirectly to stimulate interest in visiting and preserving them.' He added the clear warning that 'hydro, industry and settlement obliterate and threaten,' so that the opportunity might be lost to examine sites that had been part of Canada's fur trade history for three centuries.[21] At the same time, in *The Rise and Fall of the Great Lakes* (1966), Bill Mason provided a cinematographic warning about the ecological consequences of continuing disregard for major continental waterways.

Even participants in the 1967 Centennial Voyageur Canoe Pageant were exposed to the massive problem of deteriorating water quality on the once-pristine lakes and rivers of the fur trade. In fact, in order to avoid drinking the unnatural elements through which they paddled on their historic re-enactment, the teams of Centennial voyageurs travelled with bottled water.[22] Organizers of a parallel transcontinental canoe trip for groups of younger campers also recognized the potential significance of the expedition for environmental awareness:

As they travel they will, alas, notice that man has desecrated much of the beauty of the land. It is hoped that the Canadian Camping Association's Centenary Journey will create an awareness of the problems that exist in maintaining such wilderness beauty for this and future generations. Hopefully, their first-hand experience will prompt them to become dedicated guardians of natural wilderness areas for tomorrow.[23]

The United States appeared to respond to some elements of a similar challenge with federal legislation for the protection of rivers endowed with 'outstandingly remarkable scenic, recreational, geologic, fish and wildlife, historic, cultural, or other similar values.' The U.S. Wild and Scenic Rivers Act emerged from an extended campaign to restrain the seemingly unlimited aspirations of dam builders and others dedicated to the management and 'improvement' of waterbasins. One initial rationale for checking developmental initiatives was recreational, but as environmental considerations figured more prominently in the 1960s, they, too, influenced the congressional history. When finally enacted in 1968, the statute provided for the immediate establishment of a National Wild and Scenic Rivers System comprising sections of eight western and midwestern rivers. A further twenty-seven rivers were identified for study and possible future inclusion in the system.[24] The process of extending the system has often been convoluted, yet ten thousand miles of waterway, including all or sections of more than 150 rivers, was subsequently incorporated.[25]

In the late 1960s, planners in Parks Canada proposed a system of wild rivers in order to recognize and protect rivers and river travel as 'an

integral part of the natural and historical heritage of the nation.' Following a survey of seventy-two candidate waterways, Parks Canada selected
about twenty rivers for designation and protection, and by 1974 the
department had formulated a specific proposal for a wild river system.[26]
Similar initiatives sprang up simultaneously in several Canadian provinces. The B.C. Wildlife Federation, for example, campaigned after its
1968 annual convention for wild river protection at the provincial level
and recommended that the Chilko-Chilcotin be first.[27] By this time, Ontario already (as of 1967) had an established wild river classification in the
provincial park system, with sections of the historic Mattawa River and the
remote Winisk flowing into Hudson Bay receiving the first designations.
The provincial wild river system expanded more slowly than had been
anticipated, and its development was soon caught up in controversy surrounding the implementation of an overall approach to land-use planning within the province.[28]

After a decade of contemplation, the wild river concept led federal,
provincial, and territorial ministers to create a task force in 1979. This
body reported two years later, with recommendations for the creation of a
Canadian Heritage Rivers system. The objectives of the reformulated
proposal were somewhat broader and also less environment-oriented than
those of the original wild river enthusiasts. The objectives of the Canadian
Heritage Rivers System were to recognize and manage important rivers so
as to ensure that

the natural heritage which they represent is conserved and interpreted;
the human heritage which they represent is conserved and interpreted;
the opportunities they possess for recreation and heritage appreciation are realized by residents of and visitors to Canada.[29]

The first designations, beginning in 1986, included the French River in
Ontario, the Alsek in the Yukon's Kluane National Park, and the Clearwater
River in Saskatchewan.

Observers anticipated – correctly as it turned out – a variety of obstacles
to the creation of a system of wild rivers across Canada. In particular, the
division of constitutional responsibilities between the federal government
in Ottawa and the provinces as well as the northern territories was a source
of jurisdictional complications. The eternal Canadian question, Who's in
charge here? severely limited the prospects for an independent federal
initiative. The challenge of seeking general support and often specific
consent for a wild rivers program would have implications for administra-

tive structures and management arrangements as well as for the initial creation and implementation phase.[30] Where Native land and treaty claims remained unresolved, aboriginal communities also had an interest in the evolution of the heritage river program, as they did in many parks.

Proponents of wild river protection envisaged consultative mechanisms and other processes to accommodate the potentially divergent interests. But at the same time, there was some awareness of tension between protection and the level of administrative intervention that might be associated with the initiative. As Michael Whittington remarked, '"Management" of a wild river system is a contradiction in terms, and we must strive to protect these watersheds from bureaucratization as much as we should protect them from industrial development.'[31] The canoeist has become something other than passive observer, reporter of environmental atrocities, and champion of wilderness protection. Paddlers do have impacts on the landscape.

One consequence historically involved the opening up of resources for development. Prospectors in the early decades of the twentieth century depended heavily on the canoe for access to remote districts of northern Canada, where the mineral potential remained largely unknown. However, recreational visitors to the wilderness were also seen as potential agents of development. One writer, directing his audience's attention to 'the value of the tourist sportsman as a means of publicity for underdeveloped country' argued that if offered the possibilities of 'legitimate sport,' the visitor in return would 'give to the public the results of his vacation and to the country that offers commercial possibilities, his capital.'[32] In other words, potential investors who became familiar with the timber and mineral resources of hinterland regions during their fishing, hunting, and canoeing vacations could help to advertise and promote those resources and to attract capital for their development. Later in the century, summer camp directors still occasionally linked the canoeing skills they imparted to the continuing process of identifying resource prospects. In retrospect, the canoeist's environmental credentials are somewhat suspect. The canoe continued to appear in resource industry advertising long after its actual usefulness had effectively been undermined by flight and aerial surveillance because the wilderness paddler's personal struggle with the forbidding landscape evokes a far more sympathetic response than would be accorded to exploration crews operating with outboards, skidoos, or ATVs, and supported by airplanes. Accordingly, as late as the mid-fifties the Canadian summer boy – now as agent for the well-developed mineral industry – was still out there alone in the wilderness.

Canoeists have resented the intrusion of mechanization into their sanctuaries. R. Newell Searle, a Minnesota historian, has explained the situation in the context of the Boundary Waters Canoe Area (as the roadless sections of the Superior National Forest were renamed in 1958), although similar accounts might be developed for many other wildernesses. As long as resort traffic and the volume of canoe travel remained light, canoeists generally tolerated minor encounters with stored dinghies, motors, and mechanized portages. With heavier use, however – by about 1960 – many traditional and 'established' activities in the area began to seem incompatible with wilderness, and complaints became more frequent:

Paddlers, who went north for that special solitude, grumbled about the snarling outboard motors on otherwise deserted lakes and considered them symbols of the noisy, automated world from which they thought they had escaped. Very quickly the unfettered freedom of the wilderness, the opportunity to reflect, to move again to the rhythms of the natural world, to view familiar habits from a new perspective were passing away.[33]

Regulatory measures and exclusionary zoning alleviated the impact of mechanization on areas like the Boundary Waters Canoe Area, yet in not too many years canoeists were coming in sufficient numbers that they, too, were at risk of constraining one another's enjoyment.

As the historian of Ontario's provincial parks systems has written, by the early 1960s 'popular canoe routes in both Algonquin and Quetico had become badly refuse strewn, beaten down, and stripped of vegetation,' and parks administrators felt compelled to launch consciousness-raising initiatives such as the 'pack your own litter' project, designed to encourage canoeists to take responsibility for their impact on the outdoors.[34] Even in the far north, traffic volumes were such that Eric Morse now redirected his attention from the impact of dams and industrial use on the voyageur routes to the behaviour of fellow campers:

The northern wilderness can be preserved if its travellers will continue to appreciate the extreme fragility. In an earlier day, boys' and girls' camps were taught to make small runnels around the tents and to cut balsam or cedar boughs for beds; they sometimes cut down trees for 'furniture.' All these practices are now outdated. With today's traffic load, extreme care in garbage disposal and sanitary arrangements is more than ever necessary. A wilderness canoeist treasures the natural environment, and his aim is to leave as visible signs of his passing only his footprints and his fireplace – the latter well doused.[35]

These disheartening consequences were the entirely predictable result of the influx of visitors to the wilderness. The numbers, however, were truly astonishing even to the parks officials who had overseen a significant expansion in the range of available facilities during the late 1950s. The number of campers in Ontario parks rose nearly 1000 per cent in the half decade between 1956 and 1961, increasing from 86,000 at the start of the period to 862,000 at the close. Perhaps even more startling was the increased use of the remote wilderness interiors of Quetico and Algonquin. Visitorship tripled, from 10,000 in 1958 to over 30,000 in 1961.[36] The Grand Canyon, down which no more than an estimated 150 people had travelled before 1950, was soon contending with 20,000 each season.[37] These travellers, according to observers, were in some respects oblivious to the setting:

Transient humans can and do insulate themselves from this barren and lonely place. In a raft full of people, pills, Pepsi and peperoni sausage, beer, batteries, water filters, sleeping bags, tents, tobacco, and tortilla chips, it is as though there is a hospital and restaurant around every bend. In a canoe you are more alone, more open to the Canyon, but if you have raft support, as we did, you can still build these illusory shells of security and comfort in the evening. Until, that is, you have been capsized by a wave, or you have been dragged out of the raft by a hole, or you have seen or heard these things happen.[38]

Wilderness paddlers thus had an impact on one another; moreover, the consequences of recreational canoe travel were becoming a subject of interest to those concerned about the well-being of various other inhabitants of the outdoors. Again, to consider the Boundary Waters Canoe Area as an example, researchers explored the impact of recreational land use on the prospects for the common loon, a species under threat from DDT in many parts of North America. Scientists made their pitch on high ground:

The welfare of the loon should receive special attention in any forest management plan if it is a resident species, because perhaps more than any other species, its presence helps to preserve and enhance the primitive aspect of the area. Its high visibility and haunting mannerisms provide a thrilling experience for thousands who annually travel through our recreational areas. Few, if any, other wildlife species complement the wild northern lake region as does the common loon. And probably no other species so poignantly indicates, by its continued presence, a high level of human stewardship of the wilderness ecosystem.[39]

Researchers noted that slow trolling or the extended use of one location for fishing could keep loons away from their nests, with unfortunate consequences during the incubation period. But the seasonal departure of the anglers and their motors did not necessarily mean that the loons would not be further disturbed. The canoeist's land-use pattern was different, but in its own non-mechanized way presented the loons with a new form of disruption during the later part of the breeding season. Travelling without motors, canoeists more readily crossed portages and were observed to utilize 'all but the most inaccessible lakes and ponds of the study area.'[40] However, they tended to travel quickly across these bodies of water rather than lingering, and were generally – in contrast with the anglers – inclined to keep away from shoreline nesting sites. There had been an 800–900 per cent increase in recreational use of the Boundary Waters Canoe Area in the twenty-five years preceding the study. In their conclusion, the study's authors remarked that 'human use of this wilderness area slightly reduces the nesting and brood rearing success of individual pairs in areas of high human impact but because of undisturbed loon pairs or pairs habituating to human use, the size of the adult breeding population during the 25 years has not declined.'[41]

In the end it has become possible to enjoy 'a wilderness experience you won't have to leave home for' in the form of a thirty-two-minute video on the life of the common loon. After a brief introductory narrative to establish 'the mood for your escape to the northern woods,' VHS owners can experience 'the haunting call of the loons and the lake regions' natural ambience.' In order to ensure the authenticity of the moment, 'the body of the video is accompanied only by the sounds of the environment. No music and no human voice. Just pure nature!'[42] How long can it be before channel surfers will be able to access the digitalized outdoors for a modest monthly fee as cable offers live satellite feeds on the Wilderness Network, or multimedia computer systems introduce the sights, the sounds, and the smells of pine-bordered waterways to our home entertainment centres? 'Click here to savour woodsmoke. Conservation-minded computerized canoeists will prefer the aroma of bottled gas.'

16

The Future of the Voyageur

Over the past century, a remarkable number of canoeists have imagined themselves travelling in the footsteps of the voyageurs, of early European explorers, or of the original human inhabitants of the North American wilderness landscape. A good many others have envisaged encounters with their legendary forebears. 'Could the veil in which the unwritten past is enshrouded be withdrawn,' wrote James Dickson, the surveyor and popularizer of the district that was to become Algonquin Park, 'scenes of valour, scenes of heroism, and scenes of cruelty and blood would be beheld, equal to any told in the histories of the Old World.' Dickson's one-hundred-year-old fantasy continued with the thought that he might 'meet a line of plumed and painted warriors treading noiselessly with moccasined feet' along the portage trail, or 'see them speeding swiftly across the tossing waters or the lakes, or along the silent reaches of the rivers.' Travelling lightly, Dickson's 'red man' lived close to and was supported by his surroundings: 'The forest and water afforded abundance of his frugal food. The naked earth was to him a luxuriant couch, and the foliage of the woods and canopy of heaven an ample covering.'[1]

In a still more reflective vein, another early commentator sensed a historical and spiritual relationship between canoeists of his own generation and the tradition of the voyageurs. 'We may live in imagination and in fact in a life which, save to the devotee of canoe and wild, [has] faded forever into the past,' wrote Walter S. Johnson in 1904. And to convey more vividly the nature of this hidden life, he explained: 'Stealing along dusky banks under old-time elms and maples which have nodded over many a war-party of Braves, over coureurs de bois, zealous Jesuits eager to save souls, or Frenchmen aspiring to the conquest of a continent, we may be not of this present time or circumstance, but voyageurs of an age and time more remote, of an age of boundless aspiration, faith and enterprise.' Johnson himself appeared equally willing to be 'the trapper tracked by malignant foe' or, alternatively, a 'relentless Brave hunting down the enemies of his race.'[2] But Dickson and Johnson are by no means isolated in the wilderness tradition of canoe travellers not only seeking to be outside, but to be outside themselves.

Recent scholarship credits Ernest Thompson Seton with introducing the game of 'playing Indian' through the influence of *Two Little Savages*, which first appeared in the *Ladies Home Journal* in 1903.[3] If Seton created a game, he certainly introduced it to an audience very well primed to receive it, as the imaginary wanderings of James Dickson, Walter Johnson, and others make clear. Whatever its origins, the inspiration to imagine oneself in the place of Native predecessors or European explorers of an uncharted landscape has been persistent.

Ron Perry, a participant in Taylor Statten's early twentieth-century Boys' Work gatherings at Canoe Lake, an educator, and later the author of *The Canoe and You*, received the following confession from a former camper: 'My canoeing experience wasn't very lengthy – and none of it was very arduous or hazardous, but somehow I was never in a canoe that I didn't have a sort of half-baked notion that I was Champlain or Hiawatha or La Verendrye.' Somewhat self-consciously, the writer acknowledged that this was 'a hell of a confession for an adult to make.' Yet it was sufficiently part of his life experience that he needed to account for it clearly: 'Part of my day-dreaming stemmed from an historical sense that I was born with, part came from romantic notions that I imbibed at the knee of a doting grandmother, and part came from you and Blackie – although I suppose neither one of you were aware of what you were doing, or would want to be held guilty of it now.'[4]

If Perry's correspondent felt some sense of anxiety over the revelation of an apparently adolescent experience, validating reasons for these very typical sentiments were at hand. In the autobiographical *Unconventional Voyages*, the distinguished historian Arthur Lower described his professional experience as a combination of an erudite, academic life with the primitive. 'My canoe trips,' he wrote, 'have made the lives and deeds of the original explorers and discoverers infinitely more alive for me than if I had known no more of such matters than one learns out of books.' Lower was insistent about the virtues and empathetic possibilities of experiential learning. 'Only those who have had the experience,' he argued, 'can know what a sense of physical and spiritual excitement comes to one who turns his face away from men towards the unknown. In his small way he is doing what the great explorers have done before him, and his elation recaptures theirs.'[5]

A century after James Dickson's imaginary encounters with his predecessors on remote portage trails, Gary and Joanie McGuffin, preparing for their extended honeymoon expedition, were enthralled by the relationship between historical study and wilderness travel. They 'were astonished to find out how quickly five hours passed in a library' in comparison with the time once spent on tiresome high school and college assignments. 'However,' they subsequently reflected, 'we now had the opportunity to develop the keen interests we shared in Canada's geography, history, people and wild places, for the purpose of experiencing the country in a memorable and meaningful journey.' The McGuffins were accordingly absorbed in the diaries and journals of such figures as Alexander Mackenzie, J.W. Tyrrell, Samuel Hearne, and David Thompson.[6] In anticipation of his paddle to the Amazon, Don Starkell had a still more elaborate vision of a relationship with early European visitors to the Americas:

My reading tells me that the population of Honduras is about 3 million and that Christopher Columbus stopped here on his last voyage in 1502. Cortes came in 1525. Spain ruled the area until 1821. As we paddle the coast, I often do a little time-travelling and can easily imagine myself arriving with those daring explorers of the sixteenth century. In a small way we are fellow travellers.[7]

Not only have there been recreational paddlers' speculations about those who preceded them; any number of systematic and institutional recreations have been staged for ceremonial and commemorative purposes. The Centennial Voyageur Canoe Pageant in 1967 was one of the more elaborate commemorative re-enactments of fur trade canoe travel. As the Centennial Commission, the sponsor of the event, explained, paddlers from each of the provinces and territories, dressed in voyageur costume, would cross Canada by canoe 'as a colourful reminder of early days in Canada when men of courage, vision and stamina were opening up the vast inland areas of trade.'[8] Formally celebrated in the names of the participating canoes were Sir Alexander Mackenzie, Robert Campbell, Simon Fraser, David Thompson, Henry Kelsey, Pierre Radisson, William McGillivray, La Verendrye, Samuel de Champlain, and John Cabot.

Ninety paddlers ranging in age from seventeen to fifty-one travelled thirty-three hundred miles from Rocky Mountain House in Alberta to the site of Expo '67 in Montreal. The route followed the North Saskatchewan River to The Pas, Manitoba, and from there went southward across Lake

Winnipegosis and Lake Manitoba. Then, via the Assiniboine and the Red River, the paddlers entered Lake Winnipeg before proceeding upstream on the Winnipeg River to the Lake of the Woods. After following the Rainy River and other waterways in the territory bordering Ontario and Minnesota, the Canoe Pageant reached Lake Superior. After Superior and Lake Huron the route turned northward up the French River to Lake Nipissing. The long journey finished down the Mattawa, the Ottawa, and the St Lawrence rivers, which brought the ceremonial re-enactment to the Expo '67 site at Montreal.

In preparation for the summer outing, participants were involved in training trips and a winter program of 'road work, weight-lifting, and indoor pool paddling against a wall,' for the organizers – including the retired Canadian army colonel who served as Chief Voyageur for the event – expected the modern voyageurs to demonstrate 'stamina, endurance and courage' as they faced 'difficulties similar to those encountered by their predecessors.'[9]

In much the same fashion as the participants in the Canoe Pageant, younger members of the Canadian Camping Association undertook a coast-to-coast Centenary Canoe Journey. The organizers established three basic objectives for the undertaking:

The first is to map the famous transcontinental water highways used for exploration and commerce during the 17th and 18th centuries. The second is to take the young campers over the actual routes, teaching them along the way the historical importance of the areas they cover. And lastly, when it's all over, to compile a guidebook for Canadians and visitors to Canada, outlining routes that may be taken by outdoorsmen, families, anyone who likes to canoe, camp and study history.[10]

From Savage Harbour, Prince Edward Island, on the Gulf of St Lawrence, paddlers from Emmanuel Bible Camp journeyed to the Hillsborough River. Fellow Islanders continued up the West River before proceeding across the Northumberland Strait – by ferry, it must be admitted – to a rendezvous at Tidnish, Nova Scotia, with representatives of the Nova Scotia Camping Association, who had completed their own leg of the country-wide expedition, and with the campers and staff of a camp for diabetic children at Tidnish. As the log of the Centenary Journey records: 'Greetings were exchanged and a welcome extended. At the evening campfire we related stories of the Centenary Journey and exchanged tokens with the campers and fellow paddlers. We gave many a camper his or her first experience in a canoe.'[11] And so on it went from rendezvous to rendezvous along the St Lawrence, across the Canadian Shield and the prairies to the West Coast, until the last leg was completed at the legislative buildings of British Columbia with the arrival of thirty young canoeists from the Victoria YMCA and Camp Thunderbird.[12]

On the Bank Holiday weekend in August 1979, the John Graves Simcoe Foundation sponsored another canoe pageant. Charles Humber, a teacher at Oakwood Collegiate in Toronto and president of the Simcoe Branch of the United Empire Loyalists, assumed the role of Simcoe for a historical re-enactment of Simcoe's 1793 journey from Toronto to Georgian Bay. The original voyage had been twenty-six days long; the revival was an accelerated expedition of four days' duration, 'authentic,' in the words of the popular broadcaster John Fisher, 'except we won't be giving away barrels of rum as Simcoe did 186 years ago.' Modern-day paddlers set off from Soldier's Bay on the Holland River and travelled northward, with ceremonial stops along the route at Innisfil, Shanty Bay, Barrie, Midhurst, Orillia, Midland, and Penetanguishene, where the re-created Simcoe commemorated past accomplishments or reflected upon progress made during the nearly two centuries since 'his' original visit.[13]

Efforts to sustain interest in canoeing heritage have been formalized in a number of other ways. Outdoor education programs in which the canoe trip is now regularly featured are perhaps the most conspicuous of these undertakings. Such trips take a variety of forms, some involving simply the exercise of retracing earlier journeys, others insisting on a higher level of authenticity and even billing themselves as re-enactments. The use of traditional modes of travel and even of subsistence is an option offering a higher degree of continuity. Bob Henderson of McMaster University speaks of 'honouring the traditions' and of providing access to such 'shrines' as Grey Owl's cabin.

One elaborate re-enactment was conceived around a thirteen-hundred-kilometre expedition from Quebec City in 1648 to supply the Jesuit mission of Ste Marie Among the Hurons on southern Georgian Bay. Sixteen modern-day paddlers, each assuming the character of one of the original participants, prepared themselves through careful study of history and a demanding fitness program. Given their plans to rise early for daily mass at 4 a.m. and to follow with a long paddle in advance of their first meal of corn gruel, the organizers' claim that the trip was 'not a form of recreation' was unlikely to be challenged.[14]

The pattern whereby canoe exploits are romantically re-created has acquired a deeper meaning from those interpreters of Canada's past who have appreciated the influence of the voyageur tradition on the country's collective imagination. Occasionally, past writers even speculated on the cultural significance of the canoeists' sport, whether engaged in strictly for the purpose of wilderness travel and enjoyment or as a means of reaching remote hunting and fishing districts. For essentially geographic reasons, the canoeing vacation was considered 'typically Canadian.' 'No other civilized country has a great northwoods combined with lakes and rivers, where the lover of nature can study her unadorned loveliness in all its grandeur.'[15]

Other commentators took the sentiment somewhat further, explicitly linking the experience of wilderness travel with national feeling in Canada. One such analysis appeared in *Rod and Gun* in 1915:

There is a secret influence at work in the wild places of the North that seems to cast a spell over the men who have once been in them. One can never forget the lakes of such wonderful beauty, the rivers, peaceful or turbulent, and the quiet portage paths, or the mighty forests of real trees. It is really getting to know Canada, to go where these things are. After having made camps along the water routes, one feels a proud sense of ownership of that part of the country, which must develop into a deeper feeling of patriotism in regard to the whole land.[16]

This theme was echoed in Pierre Elliott Trudeau's celebrated essay 'Exhaustion and Fulfilment,' in which the future prime minister wrote, 'I know a man whose school could never teach him patriotism, but who acquired that virtue when he felt in his bones the vastness of his land, and the greatness of those who founded it.'[17] In a similar vein, the Manitoba historian W.L. Morton introduced a volume on the Centenary Journey with reflections on the survival of the canoe as a pleasure craft and carrier of summer paddlers. 'As such,' he wrote, 'it still freights the full Canadian past, moving with the silence of the forest, and the patience of the long reaches of the infinite rivers. As such, it is the one mode of travel which still unites the traveller, the medium by which he travels and the country he travels by.'[18] How many travellers, one might well ask.

Statistics Canada's estimates of the number of canoes in the country have evolved somewhat awkwardly over the years, although the general trends have been clear enough.[19] Canadians were thought to own some 123,000 canoes in 1970, with the total reaching 406,000 in 1980 and 534,000 a decade later. By 1992, an estimated 607,000 households, representing about 6 per cent of the population, owned canoes. Provincial statistics may be somewhat less reliable, owing to the smaller size of the

sample population and the complete absence of reports on some provinces in certain years. However, in the two decades 1971 to 1990 the
official number of canoes in Ontario grew from 66,000 to 208,000, while
the comparable figures for Quebec were 26,000 and 125,000. It is of
interest to note that, on the basis of 1992 figures, canoe ownership is
distributed fairly evenly across Canada. With 4.46 and 4.52 per cent of
households in Saskatchewan and Newfoundland, respectively, reporting
canoe ownership, these provinces were at the low end of the range, but
only slightly less populated by canoes than Quebec, in which 4.71 per cent
of households were reported to own such vessels. Ontario, with 7.43 per
cent of households, and New Brunswick, with 7.42 per cent of households,
were at the other end of the scale. Manitoba, Alberta, and British Columbia all reported that approximately 5.5 per cent of households had a
canoe.

Whether this profile makes for a nation of paddlers is an open question.
On the one hand, it is salutary to set the data on canoe ownership against
other items on the domestic transportation inventory. In 1980, Canadians' 106,000 canoes were held by the occupants of slightly under eight
million households. In the same year, three and a half million of these
households had bicycles, 800,000 had an outboard motor, and more than
550,000 had snowmobiles. The population seemed far more inclined to
pedal than to paddle. On the other hand, enthusiasts argue that many
people do their paddling in someone else's craft, either at school, at
summer camp, or through outfitting programs. Ownership statistics accordingly may fall far short of participation rates, as an industry estimate
of thirty-seven million annual 'recreational canoeing occasions' suggests.[20]

The statistical picture is in need of additional refinement, although it is
some consolation to compare existing data with the pathetic insights that
emerged from the U.S. National Recreation Survey, conducted several
decades ago under the auspices of the Outdoor Recreation Resources
Review Commission.[21] The authors of this study found a canoeing participation rate of 0.12 occasions per person twelve years of age and over, but
were unable – on account of data limitations – to present an analysis of the
demographic characteristics of canoeists. They were confident in one
conclusion, however: 'Canoeing is chiefly a summer activity.' Insights of
this depth perhaps simply confirm a national preoccupation with satellites
and space travel during the study era.

The existence of an imaginary tradition of wilderness history centred
on the canoe and of interpretations attaching broader cultural significance to recreational paddling raises a number of questions. One won-

ders, for example, whether the pattern is distinctive, whether any real significance should be attached to it at all, and what the future prospects of the voyageur may be.

Canadian canoeists were sometimes differentiated from their American counterparts precisely on the basis of a historical association with the landscape. Wilderness travel had been recognized – by Canadians and by visitors – as a distinguishing feature of canoeing in Canada, whereas competition, canoe sailing, and closed-canoe paddling dominated in parts of the United States and Britain. British and early American recreational canoeing is usually regarded as an outgrowth of the enthusiasm aroused by 'Rob Roy' MacGregor's celebrated travels and considered to have been strongly influenced by design developments in sailing canoes and the competitive environment of canoe clubs. These influences were not absent in Canada, but they were combined with a proportionately stronger wilderness tradition. The combination helped to set Canadian canoeing apart from its British and American counterparts, and helped to sustain its growth into the twentieth century despite the apparent decline in interest in the United States and England. As a result, it is possible to speak of a continuing canoeing tradition which links Indians, fur traders, geological survey crews, prospectors, forest rangers, artists like Tom Thomson and the Group of Seven, and the early vacationers discussed here.

Judith Niemi, a frequent American visitor to Canadian waterways, made plain the differences between canoeing in her country and in Canada, in a presentation to the Wilderness Canoe Association in Toronto: 'Here people like to talk about history and ideas and not just how to waterproof things.'[22] Her characterization of American paddlers ignores many exceptions. J. Arnold Bolz is an example of the American as historian with a interest in the past and the cultural dimensions of the wilderness as part of the experience. Bolz began his own journal of a 1957 canoe trip with a historical survey of the writings of such predecessors as Peter Pond, Sir Alexander Mackenzie, and the Reverend George Grant. 'Through their worn pages,' he reflected, 'the modern voyageur may penetrate the north country and partake of the freedom, pleasures, adventures, mishaps, and dangers of its early travelers.' Paddling the same waterways produced 'a feeling of intimacy with the past' and would foster 'a greater appreciation of the wilderness area and its heritage.'[23] Any number of examples could be found of modern American canoe trips the purpose of which was at least in part the re-creation of historic journeys. 'Our goal was a double one: to reach the Arctic – and get back again – under our own power, by canoe; and to follow as closely as we could the route taken by Alexander

Mackenzie down the river that bears his name when he made his voyage of discovery, also by canoe, in 1789.'[24] Henry Rushton's biographers noted that more than a century ago recreational paddlers were to some degree inspired by predecessors: 'The brave little craft in which fur traders had roved the continent sparked once again the adventurous spirit. The frontier was rapidly being closed, but with the canoe Americans could still push into remaining primitive areas and recover something of the pioneering past.'[25]

There is even some irony in Eric Morse's explanation that the Minnesota Historical Society's sign on the Grand Portage out of the Lake Superior watershed was an element of the inspiration that led him and his colleagues to retrace the voyageur routes. At the end of the 1954 summer's paddling at Fort Frances, the party made its decision: 'This pattern now became a theme for our canoe trips in the fifties and sixties, retracing historic Canadian rivers – historic in the sense of having been used in the fur trade or by early explorers.'[26]

The frequently repeated suggestion that Canadian canoeists have developed a deeper appreciation of their distinctive heritage has not gone unchallenged. A correspondent from Ann Arbor, Michigan, wrote *Paddler* magazine 'to demonstrate how useless nationalism is to our exploration of the central concerns of canoeists,' and in particular 'to challenge the notion that nationality defines our canoeing experience.' The writer argued that the essence of canoeing was to be found in a series of elements which he listed as 'the environmental, spiritual, historical, social and personal dimensions of canoeing.' His ultimate explanation for the claim that a nationalistic frame of reference was without relevance to the canoeing experience rested on the assertion that 'national boundaries neither define nor confine any of these values.'[27]

One might well ask whether any of these claims should be taken seriously at all. Indeed there is a strong temptation to dismiss claims about the continuity of the tradition as romantic misconceptions impossible to sustain on a proper understanding of historical change. Arthur Lower observed in his autobiography, 'There have always been in Canada great numbers of young men who, either by their way of life as lumbermen, fishermen, bushmen, and so on, or because of the summer water tradition which is so strong amongst us, have been competent in all the skills of the small craft, in canoes and rowboats, dinghies, sloops, tugs and launches.'[28] Yet even in Lower's time commentators expressed the view that a vast gulf had developed between the real tradition of the outdoors and pleasure paddling. One reviewer of Ron Perry's instructional classic

The Canoe and You, describing it as 'a book to save lives,' provided evidence of canoeing's linkages to the past but lamented their deterioration:

Old fire rangers and prospectors, reading here of regattas and that a candidate for a certificate in canoemanship must prove that he has paddled 100 miles, will be sadly reminded that, in our generation, canoeing has become a mere recreation and is no longer regarded seriously as a means of transportation. Yet though the days of the voyageur have at last ended, the Indian has left as a heritage the only rival to the sail-boat in beauty and sensitive performance.[29]

In the same vein, Sidney N. Cooper, reviewing *The Canoe and You* in the June 1949 issue of *Beaver,* remarked:

It is plain … that the author regards canoe paddling as a sport – as indeed it is to the great majority of its participants. Those who used the canoe for many years and over many thousands of miles in the course of their daily work, before the advent of the outboard motor (as this reviewer did), may be inclined to take issue with him on certain points.

Cooper proceeded to do so.[30]

These sentiments about lost modes of travel have not been confined to canoeing by any means. Paul Fussell, a literary critic and a provocative observer of countless common and uncommon subjects, traces in *Abroad* the transition in forms of the journey. 'Before tourism,' he writes, 'there was travel, and before travel there was exploration.' The explorer, the traveller, and the tourist each make journeys, 'but the explorer seeks the undiscovered, the traveler that which has been discovered by the mind working in history, the tourist that which has been discovered by entrepreneurship and prepared for him by the arts of mass publicity.'[31] Several decades ahead of Fussell, Arthur Doughty and Gustave Lanctot had provided a comparable assessment in their introduction to Cheadle's *Journal of a Trip across Canada, 1862–1863,* which recorded the mid-nineteenth century expedition of Walter Butler Cheadle and Lord Milton. 'It is to be remarked that in the title of the book, the tourist trip of the authors is raised to the dignity of an exploration.'[32]

Well short of cyberspace it is not difficult to identify artificial environments created for the purpose of providing water-based entertainment. Competitive slalom canoeing is reponsible for some of the more challenging creations of this tradition, with the Olympic slalom course at Augsburg, south of Munich, constituting a prime example: 'The slalom course had been specially built for the 1972 Olympics and was a unique man-made rough water course of vast, smooth concrete rocks with an abundance of severe falls and rapids, all controlled by giant sluices.'[33] Those with only a limited amount of time to spare might take advantage of a half hour trip at Old Fort William, where one can 'discover the life of the voyageurs ... by helping to paddle a 36 foot canoe.' Canada's Wonderland offers a popular commercial variant of the experience: 'You ... park your fannies inside yellow inner tubes and embark on a leisurely 12-minute float along a gently winding fake river inside Wonderland. A few minutes along, just as you're dozing ... your slumber ends when you're blasted with cold water that emits from a giant fake Fred Flintstone.'[34]

As the Water Show program from the Earl's Court Exhibition grounds in London more than a hundred years ago reveals, the attempt to provide whitewater experiences in convenient settings has been made for a very long time:

Shooting 'chutes' at the Water Show at Earl's Court Exhibition will certainly be enjoyed by canoe men. Those who have done real rapid shooting and full-water dam-jumping in small canoes will probably say the excitement obtainable at Earl's Court falls short of the canoe work, and of course, also, one is but a passenger at the Earl's Court Shoot; none the less there is an exciting slide, followed by three tremendous jumps across the water and a shower of spray. The water motion is very like that enjoyed in ... racing on rough salt water, where the little yacht takes to jumping, in effect if not in reality, from sea to sea when going fast to windward; but in the seaworld this sport lasts for a couple of miles or more, while in the Exhibition shoot it is only about 50 yards. But the lumpy, briny ocean ... cannot be brought to the midst of London.[35]

Despite these indignities to nature in which canoeing has figured as an accomplice, wilderness paddlers have generally appreciated the distinctive virtues of the natural and historical heritage and have often worked to preserve its integrity. As they approached Chats Falls on the Ottawa River, Gary and Joanie McGuffin recognized from the dam the inescapable twentieth-century character of their journey. Nonetheless, with no one else in sight at the entry to the portage, they could readily imagine an arrival at the same point two hundred years earlier.

An unmistakable trail had been etched in the ancient bedrock by hundreds of thousands of load-bearing footsteps. Through eyes that squinted against the salty sweat trickling from overheated brows, we envisaged ahead of us on that trail ghostly images of short, stocky voyageurs hunched and straining beneath bulky loads. Slowly and steadily we completed the portage, then forged against the icy spring-fed current.[36]

Eric Morse, in the course of his historical investigation into the fur trade routes of the voyageurs, had been intrigued a few years earlier by some of the same landmarks that prompted the McGuffins' musings. In studying the portage at the Chaudière on the Ottawa River – a few miles downstream from Chats Falls – he recorded the efforts of a predecessor to protect the site: 'I found then that Mr Chief Justice Latchford of the Ontario Supreme Court had discovered the old portage in the early 1920s and had realized its historic and national significance. He had made representations for its preservation and marking, but then it had been forgotten.'[37]

Well before Morse and his associates undertook to perpetuate the voyageur tradition on the water, others had assumed the task of preserving the material culture of canoeing. Judge F.W. Howay, a member of the Historic Sites and Monuments Board, shared his fascination with the watercraft of the voyageur in the article 'Building the Big Canoes,' in which he recorded the results of his research on the construction process. The references he assembled from the journals of such early North American travellers as Nicolas Denys, Alexander Henry, Nicolas Garry, and Lieutenant Robert Hood were his attempt to overcome the impression 'that canoes grew like grass, indigenous to the soil, so scanty are references to their construction.'[38]

To the extent that Howay's inquiries constituted a challenge to his mid-twentieth-century contemporaries to undertake construction, that challenge was accepted by David A. Gillies, an Ottawa Valley lumberman and amateur historian who could observe the river from his home at 'The Grove' in Arnprior and knew the history of the river well. In 1955, Gillies suggested to National Museum officials in Ottawa that a replica of the fur trade canoes should be in the collection, and he then identified Matt Bernard from the Golden Lake Indian Reserve as the man most suited to oversee construction of the thirty-six-foot-long Montreal canoe that was eventually presented to the museum.[39] In 1961, George Frederick Clarke called for the preservation of 'every birch bark canoe that has escaped the ravages of the years,' and reported that in the preceding forty years only one had been built on the St John River, formerly a centre of construction and use.[40] Others, including the camp director Kirk Wipper, who founded a canoe museum in the 1970s, also endeavoured to sustain interest in the disappearing skills of master bark canoe builders.[41]

These isolated and recurring initiatives demonstrated a continuing interest in traditional watercraft, but the most enduring contribution to the preservation of material canoe culture was made by a dedicated and eccentric character, originally from Ohio, whose painstaking work over a period of more than half a century sustained a vulnerable legacy. Frederick Hill, the director of the Mariners Museum in Newport News, Virginia, and his wife, Nola, were among those professionally interested during the 1930s in the artefactual heritage of Canadian canoeing. While visiting Montreal as field representatives of the museum to scout out possible acquisitions, they identified an important collection. As the Hills' memoir of their collecting efforts explains, 'In one museum of prominence we saw a group of Indian bark canoe models. They were stacked carelessly on top of each other, covered with a heavy accumulation of dust and apparently given little attention.' Recognizing the potential importance of the models and the 'infinitely painstaking work' of the builder, they made inquiries which led them eventually to the home of Edwin Tappan Adney in Woodstock, New Brunswick.

The Ohio-born Adney, a sometime journalist and artist, had developed a passionate interest in bark canoe construction and design as a young man. After serving in the Canadian army during the First World War, he settled in his new homeland in Montreal, Quebec. Here he pursued the career of artist and illustrator, supplementing his resources with occasional work as an adviser on North American Indian affairs to governments and museums alike. Through travel, correspondence, and model-building he engaged in a lifelong study of Native watercraft, eventually to become a victim of his extraordinarily wide but undisciplined talents: the Hills' inventory of elements in Adney's career refers to him as 'artist, architect, historian, lecturer, former officer in the Canadian Army, writer, model-maker, once an honorary consultant on Indian affairs for McGill University, student of heraldry, photographer, nurseryman, bookbinder, anthropologist, musician.' Financial misfortune and the illness of his wife led Adney back to her family home in Woodstock.

The beautifully crafted model canoes which the Hills had unearthed were in fact serving as collateral for a small and long overdue loan. Adney welcomed the Hills' interest in his past work and in his continuing passion for aboriginal watercraft. In due course he accepted an offer from the Mariners Museum to pay off the loan, purchase the Montreal collection along with other more recent models, and have him join the museum's staff for the purpose of preparing a manuscript on the basis of his extensive research on bark canoes. The arrangement brought some 125 canoe models to Virginia, prompting the Hills to reflect subsequently, 'It was not without some misgivings that the Museum paid off the loan of $1,000.00, and took a very fine collection from the country where it rightfully belonged.'[42]

The Hills' interest in Adney's work and a genuine concern for his welfare persisted for many years. But actual progress on the manuscript was intermittent at best, and Adney's work remained incomplete at the time of his death in 1950.[43] The task of organizing Adney's records and preparing a manuscript fell to Howard I. Chapelle. Having completed a text for the Mariners Museum, Chapelle accepted an appointment as curator of transportation at the Smithsonian Institution in Washington, D.C. The Smithsonian eventually published the classic reference work *The Bark Canoes and Skin Boats of North America,* which contained the results of Adney's inquiries along with Chapelle's own original work on Eskimo skin boats and kayaks.[44]

The material culture of the voyageurs and their aboriginal forerunners exerts a continuing fascination, for the watercraft themselves combine function and elegance in ways that constantly invite reflection on the relationships between various human societies and between human society and the environment. Even Mordecai Richler's less than reverent description of a late twentieth-century Montreal restaurant suggests the challenge of reconciling natural origins with the possibilities of civilization: 'Sheldon had invited them to a restaurant in one of the new hotels, a restaurant oppressively elegant, where the waiters came dressed like eighteenth-century voyageurs. Snowshoes and muskets and stretched beaver skins were mounted on the walls.'[45] Entering such a restaurant, the modern diner might face a choice of cultural allegiances perhaps as varied as the menu. Although some guests would instinctively admire the entrepreneurial inventiveness behind the ambience, many would no doubt give at least a moment's sympathetic attention to the beaver. Still others might wonder if the snowshoes appear through cultural appropriation or technology transfer, and whether in either case royalties are due. How many of those looking forward to a good meal would immediately put themselves in the moccasins of the attendant voyageurs with the delights of pemmican awaiting them at the end of an eighteen-hour day is another matter entirely. Yet speaking of Canadians, William C. James has argued that 'we are never more nostalgic, never more atavistic, than when we get into a canoe.'[46]

James is also the source of another assessment, that 'modern accounts of canoe trips are almost unanimous in their testimony that the major change experienced by the canoeist is an inner one, the exploration of the wilderness becoming a voyage into the interior of the self.'[47] And this, surely, is a route most recreational voyageurs travel on their initial or later journeys.

Recreational paddlers frequently observe that their avocation has influenced their outlook on a much wider range of subjects. The experience of landscape provided by canoeing has offered insights to enrich personal development or to increase understanding of the social past of aboriginal peoples, lumbermen, and explorers. More recently, perhaps, the search for an ever more elusive wilderness offers a vision of the environmental future. Thus experiences, images, and symbolic impressions remain intertwined in the lives of countless thousands of summer paddlers whose personal sense of the best place to begin an odyssey is about sixteen feet long.

Conclusion

'Cowboys are much more important than canoes,' asserted a prominent Vancouver-based journalist in condemning federal financial support for a canoe museum in Prime Minister Jean Chrétien's Shawinigan constituency. Robert Mason Lee may just have been having a bad day, but the evidentiary base of his conclusion merits repeating: 'People do not walk around wearing canoe hats, canoe boots or canoe buckles. They don't listen to canoe music or read *Even Canoe Girls Get the Blues*. On the other hand, cowboys do not drive down the highway with a horse strapped to the roof, which would be terribly dangerous; canoe boys do. Canadians can make love in a canoe, but ... this is not considered romantic outside Shawinigan.' Paddlers willing to defend their pastime this far into the critique were then forced to confront the matter of symbolism. The canoe, Lee argued, was 'the original instrument of centralist oppression; the cowboy the original subversive.' Canoes, he continued, were the first objects of cultural appropriation, 'but when native people adopted back, what did they choose? Cowboy hats, country music and pickup trucks.'[1]

The relative merits of cowboys and canoeists are doubtless worth a moment's consideration, and might be debated on a number of planes. There are significant numbers of canoeists and canoe enthusiasts in all parts of Canada, including the west, particularly if you are willing to fit kayaks, dugouts, and dragon boats into your vision of a canoe, or to add rafters to the community of paddlers. A still more generous view would include the civil engineering students who participate in an annual Concrete Canoe Competition after building their own boats.

Within Canada, there are regional traditions among paddlers, as geography plays its role. The appeal of the canoe, however, seems more broadly based to me than Robert Mason Lee allows. I tend to think that

Jacques and Cousteau could use a little more water in their quest for a cold 'Blue' on the prairies, but they are otherwise quite at home with big sky and a canoe over their heads. As the continuing episodes of their televised quest reveal, it is yet to be determined whether Canoe Boys Get the Blues. That uncertainty has more to do, I suspect, with the regulation of advertising for alcoholic beverages than with limitations in the appeal and suitability of the canoe as a modern cultural icon.

Nor does one really need to disparage the cowboy to promote the canoeist; the canoeist and the cowboy share some common passions. Grey Owl saw his old-time canoemen – the rivermen and voyageurs – as 'gay caballeros of the White Water who whooped and laughed and shouted their way down or up unmapped rivers,'[2] while modern rock dodgers are frequently inclined to describe their gatherings as rodeos. Even Holling C. Holling, the creator of the *Paddle to the Sea* story that inspired the imagination of Bill Mason and countless others, was the author of *The Book of Cowboys*, in which he advanced for the benefit of his youthful audience insights into 'where the cowboy gets on and off, and if so, why.' Anyone who saw 'wild horses racing with the speed of the wind, sometimes bucking riders off their backs'[3] might understand some of the experiences that paddlers and riders share.

But what virtue would there be in reconciling the canoeist and the cowboy if neither has any real importance in the broader scheme of things? Confidently described in 1908 as Canada's foremost aquatic sport, and the seasonal activity of generations of young Canadians, canoeing did not make the final cut when Canadian legislators conferred official recognition on two national sports – ice hockey and lacrosse.[4]

Perhaps there is consolation in the thought that paddling is not a sport at all, but something a good deal more important than that. The expansion of organized canoeing across North America in the final decades of the nineteenth century certainly stimulated the foundations for important dimensions of paddling. Club-centred activities and the competitive aspects of their programs contributed to a period of innovation in design and manufacturing during which the traditional Native craft temporarily seemed irrelevant to British and American sporting enthusiasts and even in some Canadian centres. But although competition became the defining element of the canoe club program, the traditions of cruising, canoe camping, and tripping were never entirely displaced. Nor, ultimately, did elaborate technical innovations associated with clubs and competition have more than a passing influence on the basic nature and design of the traditional watercraft. Indeed, the proliferation of novel gadgetry ultimately provided only the backdrop or counterpoint against which the broader and more enduring tradition could be more clearly defined.

A good deal of canoeing still has the features of sport, and these remain a vital attraction for many participants. But what I have often decribed as a pastime and recreational activity approaches a way of life for many others. It is, at least, a form of experience about which paddlers reminisce with fondness and to which they look forward with great anticipation. Canoeing has made some, such as Ralph Connor, fit, and has helped others to grow, perhaps simultaneously nurturing both leaders and team players. For Lois Wilson, canoeing northern waters became virtually synonymous with summer, a period of renewal and refreshment in a setting where proximity to nature fostered spiritual insights and offered valued moments for personal reflection.

My aspirations for *Idleness, Water, and a Canoe* have been largely bounded by the hope that off-season paddlers will find enjoyment in reading about the modern recreational paddler's evolution and in contemplating the impressions of fellow participants in a pleasurable (generally) pastime. If you got this far in the text, I have to be more than satisfied, and I will presume you found the narrative more illuminating than the Presidential commission on outdoor activity, which concluded that there was not enough empirical data about canoeing for any certainty other than that most recreational canoeing was a summertime phenomenon. Surely not even those devoted to crossing the St Lawrence ice floes by canoe at break-up imagined otherwise.

Can anything be confidently asserted about paddling for pleasure, an activity that is more likely taken for granted by participants (however numerous) than treated as a subject worthy of penetrating analysis? Speaking for myself, I'm going back to the water, but perhaps these pages have raised a number of intriguing – possibly even important – themes and questions for future fireside contemplation.

Notes

Chapter 1: Popular Images and Personal Experiences

1 For a survey of the artistic development of Tom Thomson and the Group of Seven, see Dennis Reid, *A Concise History of Canadian Painting*, 2d ed. (Toronto: Oxford University Press, 1988) chap. 10.

2 J. Russell Harper, *Painting in Canada: A History*, 2d ed. (Toronto: University of Toronto Press, 1977) 273

3 Blodwen Davies, *A Study of Tom Thomson: The Story of a Man Who Looked for Beauty and Truth in the Wilderness* (Toronto: Ryerson, 1937) 51

4 Harold Town and David Silcox, *Tom Thomson: The Silence and the Storm* (Toronto: McClelland and Stewart, 1977) 197

5 A.Y. Jackson, *A Painter's Country: The Autobiography of A.Y. Jackson* (Toronto and Vancouver: Clarke, Irwin, 1958)

6 Donald B. Smith, *From the Land of Shadows: The Making of Grey Owl* (Saskatoon: Western Producer Prairie Books, 1990)

7 Grey Owl, *Tales of an Empty Cabin* (Toronto: Macmillan, 1936) 172

8 Grey Owl, *Men of the Last Frontier* (Toronto: Macmillan, 1936)

9 Ramsay Cook, 'Landscape Painting and National Sentiment in Canada,' in *The Maple Leaf Forever* (Toronto, 1977) 158–79

10 Catherine Harris, 'The Economy: Paddling Our Own Canoe,' *Financial Post*, 23 November 1985

11 Frank Edwards, Interview, 10 August 1996

12 British Museum Library, 'Paddle Your Own Canoe,' Irish Ballad, ca 1840

13 *Times*, 17 March 1864, quoted in A.W.B. Simpson, 'Legal Liability for Bursting Reservoirs: The Historical Context of Rylands v. Fletcher,' *Journal of Legal Studies* 228

14 *Globe and Mail*, 25 April 1987

15 Keith Spicer, Chairman's Foreword, *Citizens' Forum on Canada's Future: Report to the People and Government of Canada* (Minister of Supply and Services Canada, 1991) 9–10

16 Ontario, Ministry of Natural Resources, 'Ontario Proclaims Alexander Mackenzie Voyageur Route,' news release, 18 July 1992

17 Ben Portis, Letter to the Editor, *Globe and Mail*, 4 April 1992

18 Ovide Mercredi and Mary Ellen Turpel, *In the Rapids: Navigating the Future of First Nations* (Toronto: Viking, 1993) 9

19 Canada, House of Commons, *Indian Self-Government in Canada: Report of the Special House of Commons Committee on Indian Self-Government*, Keith Penner, Chair (October 1983) cover

20 Robert Bringhurst, *The Black Canoe: Bill Reid and the Spirit of Haida Gwaii* (Vancouver and Toronto: Douglas and McIntyre, 1991) 13

21 Andrew Cohen, 'Corporate Climbers Head Outdoors: Executives Scale New Ladder on Outward Bound Escape,' *Financial Post*, 20 July 1987

22 Canadian Outward Bound Wilderness School, 'Outward Bound,' promotional brochure (n.d.)

23 James Fleming, 'Roughing It in the Bush,' *Report on Business Magazine*, September 1987, 49

24 Mark Smith, 'Out of the Office into the Woods,' Outward Bound advertising supplement, *Financial Post*, 13 March 1989

25 Cohen, 'Corporate Climbers,' 12

26 Pierre Berton, attributed by Dick Brown, 'It Was a Very Good Year,' *Canadian Magazine*, 22 December 1973, 3

27 'Sex Lives of Canadians,' *Maclean's*, 5 January 1987, 66

28 Quoted in Kenneth G. Roberts and Philip Shackleton, *The Canoe: A History of the Craft from Panama to the Arctic* (Toronto: Macmillan, 1983) 232

29 With proper funding and the support of empirically minded co-inquirers, the author would be prepared to develop and administer a questionnaire for national distribution. In the absence of such a comprehensive review, however, informed readers are invited to submit reminiscences to the publisher. Photographs are neither requested nor encouraged.

30 Margaret Atwood, 'Wilderness Tips,' in *Wilderness Tips* (Toronto: McClelland and Stewart, 1991) 199

31 Michael Ondaatje, *In the Skin of a Lion* (Markham, Ont.: Penguin, 1988) 186

32 Mark Schreiber, *Princes in Exile* (General, 1990) 149–50

33 Sandra Gwyn, *The Private Capital: Ambition and Love in the Age of Laurier* (Toronto: McClelland and Stewart, 1984)

34 Amaryllis's account, published in *Saturday Night*, is quoted in Gwyn, *Private Capital*, 306–7.

35 Gwyn, *Private Capital,* 308–9
36 Ibid., 438. Scott and Lampman were hardly novice paddlers, the latter having spent the formative period of his youth, from the ages of seven to thirteen, as a resident of Gore's Landing on Rice Lake, one of the leading canoeing centres of the day.
37 See Pierre Berton, *Hollywood's Canada* (Toronto: McClelland and Stewart, 1975) for discussion of the several versions of the film made between 1928 and 1954.

Chapter 2: A Useful Vessel

1 Michael Payne, 'The Sports, Games, Recreations, and Pastimes of the Fur Traders: Leisure at York Factory,' in Morris Mott, ed., *Sports in Canada: Historical Readings* (Toronto: Copp Clark Pitman, 1989) 57
2 Keewaydin, 'The Trout of the Menjamagossippi, Ontario, Canada,' *Rod and Gun* 6:11 (April 1905) 606
3 Bergathora, 'A Woman's Outing on the Nepigon,' *Outing* 30 (September 1897) 584
4 *The Canadian Sportsman and Naturalist* 2:1 (January 1882) 99–100
5 Robert Barnwell Roosevelt, *Superior Fishing; or, The Striped Bass, Trout, and Black Bass of the Northern States* (St Paul: Minnesota Historical Society, 1985) 19, quoted in Colleen J. Sheehy, 'American Angling: The Rise of Urbanism and the Romance of the Rod and Reel,' in Kathryn Grover, ed., *Hard at Play: Leisure in America, 1840–1940* (Rochester, N.Y.: Strong Museum, 1992) 84
6 W.H. Blake, *Brown Waters* (Montreal: Reprint Society of Canada, 1948) 10–11
7 For a fascinating account of Walton's *Compleat Angler* as a book of consolation for deprived Royalists and Anglicans in the midst of seventeenth-century turmoil and upheaval, see Jonquil Bevan, *Izaak Walton's 'The Compleat Angler': The Art of Recreation* (Brighton: Harvester, 1988). 'Anglers are presented,' Bevan remarks, 'not as mere possessors of a certain skill, but as peaceable, quiet, meek-spirited men, who give their first fruits to the poor; indeed, angling seems more a kind of moral vocation than a sport,' 27.
8 John Hersey, *Blues* (New York: Vintage, 988) 9
9 Sidney C. Kendall, *Among the Laurentians: A Camping Story* (Toronto: William Briggs, 1885) 45–51
10 Thomas P. Bresnan, 'The Delights of Temagami: An Ideal Fishing Ground,' *Rod and Gun* 7:12 (May 1906) 1327
11 J. Henry Rushton, 'Single vs. Double Blades,' *American Canoeist* 1:6 (July 1882) 94
12 Susanna Moodie, *Roughing It in the Bush* (1834), 154–5

13 John MacGregor, *Our Brothers and Cousins: A Summer Tour in Canada and the United States* (London, 1859), 6–7

14 Arthur P. Silver, 'A Birch-Bark Canoe Trip,' in *Farm-Cottage, Camp, and Canoe in Maritime Canada* (London: Routledge; Toronto: Musson, 1907) 238

15 Richard H. Little, 'Chicago Authors in Temagami,' *Rod and Gun* 9:7 (December 1907) 634

16 E.E. Millard, *Days on the Nepigon* (New York: Foster and Reynolds, 1917) 17

17 Archives of Ontario [AO], Reginald Drayton Papers, 'Canadian Note Book'

18 Perry D. Frazer, *Canoe Cruising and Camping* (New York: Forest and Stream, 1897) 79–80

19 Town and Silcox, *Tom Thomson: The Silence and the Storm*, 59

20 Christopher Hassall, *Rupert Brooke: A Biography* (London: Faber and Faber, 1964) 409

21 Rupert Brooke, *Letters from America* (Toronto: McClelland, Goodchild, and Stewart, 1916) 120

22 Sheehy, 'American Angling,' 86

23 Kelly Evans, 'Fish and Game Preservation in Ontario,' in Association of Ontario Land Surveyors, *Annual Report, 1910*, 151

24 F.G. Aflalo, *A Fisherman's Summer in Canada* (London, 1911) 78

25 A.E. Elias, *Canoeing in Canada* (Ottawa, 1925)

26 Elias, *Canoeing in Canada*

27 Stewart Edward White, *The Forest* (Toronto, 1904) 244

28 Canadian National Railways, *Canoe Trips and Nature Photography* (1928) 3–5

29 Silver, 'A Birch-Bark Canoe Trip,' 117–18

30 Dillon Wallace, *The Lure of the Labrador Wild* (New York, 1905) 52; James West Davidson and John Rugge, *Great Heart: The History of a Labrador Adventure* (New York: Penguin, 1989)

31 *Globe and Mail*, 16 August 1988

32 Eric Sevareid, *Canoeing with the Cree* (St Paul: Minnesota Historical Society, 1968; originally pub. 1935) 35

33 Sevareid, *Canoeing with the Cree*, 30

34 Ibid., 31

35 Robert Louis Stevenson, *The Travels and Essays of Robert Louis Stevenson: An Inland Voyage; Travels with a Donkey; Edinburgh* (New York: Scribner's, 1903) 27–8. For a brief account of the canoe trip and a less than flattering report on literary reaction to the book, see Frank McLynn, *Robert Louis Stevenson: A Biography* (London: Hutchinson, 1993) 103–7.

36 *The Field*, 4 May 1895, 626; 1 June 1895, 796; and 15 June 1895, 883

37 Nigel Nicolson, 'Paddling My Own Canoe,' *The Spectator*, 16 October 1993

38 See the joint document 'Angling and Canoeing Statement of Intent' from the British Canoe Union and the National Anglers Council.

39 Raoul Clouthier, *From Maniwaki to Angliers by Way of Barrière and Grand Lake Victoria Posts: Being the Account of a 300-Mile Canoe Trip along the Upper Ottawa River, through the Forests of Hull, Pontiac, and Temiskaming Counties in the Province of Quebec* (Montreal, 1928) 39–40

Chapter 3: The Healing Pines

 1 James Dickson, *Camping in the Muskoka Region* (Ontario, Department of Lands and Forests, 1959; originally pub. 1886) 164

 2 Ella Walton, 'A Woman's Views on Camping Out,' *Rod and Gun* 1:4 (September 1899) 72

 3 Edwin Hodder, *John MacGregor ('Rob Roy')* (London: Hodder, 1894) 284

 4 Canadian Northern Railway, *Sparrow Lake and Severn River* (April 1914)

 5 J.H.H.D., 'Canoeing,' *Dominion Illustrated* 1:26 (29 December 1888) 414

 6 Jane Eblen Keller, *Adirondack Wilderness: A Story of Man and Nature* (Syracuse: Syracuse University Press, 1980) 128

 7 J.C.G., 'Camping in Canada,' *Rod and Gun* 1:2 (June 1899) 9

 8 Kendall, *Among the Laurentians*, 11

 9 Charles Gordon (Ralph Connor), *Postscript to Adventure: The Autobiography of Ralph Connor* (Toronto: McClelland and Stewart, 1975) 53

10 W.J. Keith, *Literary Images of Ontario* (Toronto: University of Toronto Press, 1992) 29, 32

11 'The Men with the Hearts of Boys,' *Outdoor Canada* 4:8 (1908) 67

12 Julian Durham (Wanderer), 'The Rest Cure in a Canoe,' *Rod and Gun* 12:5, (October 1910)

13 Stevenson, *The Travels: An Inland Voyage*, 112–13

14 Frank Graham, *The Adirondack Park: A Political History* (New York: Knopf, 1978) 29

15 Atwood Manley and Paul F. Jamieson, *Rushton and His Times in American Canoeing* (Syracuse: Adirondack Museum and Syracuse University Press, 1968) 9–10

16 Keller, *Adirondack Wilderness*, 134–7

17 *Canadian Summer Resort Guide*, 7th ed. (1900) 53

18 AO, Records of the Attorney General, RG 4–32 (1915) no. 341

19 Ontario, Department of Lands and Forests, *Summer Homes for Tourists, Campers, and Sportsmen* (1927) 27–9

20 Ontario, Lands and Forests, *Summer Homes*, 40

21 Temiskaming and Northern Ontario Railway, *Solid Vestibule Trains to the Sportsman's Paradise* (n.d.) 8

22 John Boyle O'Reilly, *Athletics and Manly Sport* (Boston: Pilot, 1890), quoted in Walter M. Teller, ed., *On the River: A Variety of Canoe and Small Boat Voyages* (New Brunswick, N.J.: Rutgers University Press, 1976) 149

23 Canadian National Railways, *Camp Craft and Woodlore* (n.d.) Foreword

24 Eric W. Morse, *Freshwater Saga: Memoirs of a Lifetime of Wilderness Canoeing in Canada* (Toronto: University of Toronto Press, 1987) 45

25 Denis Coolican, Interview, 18 June 1991

26 Jack Hambleton, *Fisherman's Paradise* (Toronto, London, New York: Longman's, Green, 1946) 21

27 Don Starkell, *Paddle to the Amazon: The Ultimate 12,000-Mile Canoe Adventure*, ed. Charles Wilkins (Toronto: McClelland and Stewart, 1988) 16, 19

28 Douglas LePan, 'Canoe-Trip,' in *Weathering It: Complete Poems, 1948–1987* (Toronto: McClelland and Stewart, 1987) 75

29 L.O. Armstrong, 'Boredom and One of Its Antidotes,' *Rod and Gun* 6:5 (October 1904) 212

30 Trent University Archives [TUA], Ebbs Papers, Bernadette Ferry, 'A Descriptive Study of the Beneficial Aspects of a Month Long Camp for Children with Cystic Fibrosis,' manuscript (1974) 5, 6, 14, 15, 23

31 Canadian Outward Bound Wilderness School, 'Course Schedule, 1990'

32 Sue Sherrod, 'Celebration,' in Judith Niemi and Barbara Wieser, eds, *Rivers Running Free: Stories of Adventurous Women* (Minneapolis: Bergamot, 1987) 246, 248

33 Allan Bayne and Paul Nelham, Interview, 9 September 1994

34 Michael Arthur and Stacy Ackroyd-Stolarz, *A Resource Manual on Canoeing for Disabled People* (Hyde Park: Canadian Recreational Canoe Association, n.d.) 1

35 Geoff Smedley, *A Guide to Canoeing with Disabled Persons*, 2d ed. (British Canoe Union, 1989)

36 John Harris, 'The Summer of Their Content,' *Financial Post Moneywise Magazine*, April 1988, 53

37 Herb Hamilton, 'Camp Outlook: A Summer Success Story,' *Queen's Alumni Review*, July–August 1989, 48

38 William C. James, 'Canoeing and Gender Roles,' in James Raffan and Bert Horwood, eds, *Canexus: The Canoe in Canadian Culture* (Toronto: Betelgeuse, 1988) 37

39 A list of participating agencies and supporters may be found in the *Boundless Adventures Annual Report, 1993–1994.*

40 Steven Gottlieb, Interview, 21 February 1995

41 Jim Risk, Interview, 25 April 1991

42 For a statement of the background and objectives of the Women of Courage program, see Ruth Goldman, 'Canadian Outward Bound Wilderness School and the "Women of Courage" Program,' in Bernadine Dodge and Bruce W. Hodgins, eds, *Using Wilderness: Essays on the Evolution of Youth Camping in Ontario* (Peterborough: Frost Centre for Canadian Heritage and Development Studies, 1992) 60–8.

43 Philip Blackford, Interview, 24 February 1995

44 G.R. Cardwell, 'Wilderness and Adventure Programmes: An Alternative for Troubled Youth,' Paper presented at the Annual Meeting of the Society of Camp Directors of Ontario, Toronto, 28 April 1977, 7–8

Chapter 4: God's Country

1   Arthur O. Wheeler, 'Canada's Mountain Heritage,' Address delivered before the Canadian Club of Toronto, 20 December 1909, quoted in George Altmeyer, 'Three Ideas of Nature in Canada, 1893–1914,' *Journal of Canadian Studies* 11:3 (August 1976) 31

2   Bill Mason, *Path of the Paddle: An Illustrated Guide to the Art of Canoeing* (Toronto: Van Nostrand Reinhold, 1980) 2. For a biography of Mason, see James Raffan, *Fire in the Bones: Bill Mason and the Canadian Canoeing Tradition* (Toronto: HarperCollins, 1996).

3   For background information on the evolution of the Inter-Varsity Christian Fellowship movement, see John G. Stackhouse, Jr, *Canadian Evangelicalism in the Twentieth Century* (Toronto: University of Toronto Press, 1993) chap. 5.

4   Mason's films and awards are detailed in 'Bill Mason: His Camera: The Land and Its Creatures,' a National Film Board brochure printed in 1979. Nominations from the Academy of Motion Picture Arts and Sciences were for *Blake*, a short film about Mason's friend Blake James, and *Paddle to the Sea*.

5   *Waterwalker* (National Film Board and Imago, 1984)

6   Mason, *Path of the Paddle*, 3

7   Pamela Morse, Interview, 18 August 1991

8   Raffan, *Fire in the Bones*, 286

9   Altmeyer, 'Three Ideas of Nature,' 31

10 Kendall, *Among the Laurentians*, 9

11 Brooke, *Letters from America*, 117–18

12 Kendall, *Among the Laurentians*, 10

13 Silver, 'A Birch-Bark Canoe Trip,' 229

14 Tiphys, *Practical Canoeing: A Treatise on the Management and Handling of Canoes* (London: Norie and Wilson, 1883) 77–8

15 John MacGregor, *The Rob Roy on the Jordan, Nile, Red Sea, and Gennesareth, etc.:*

A Canoe Cruise in Palestine and Egypt, and the Waters of Damascus (London: John Murray, 1870) 115

16 MacGregor, *The Rob Roy*, 213, 315
17 National Maritime Museum Library, Greenwich, MacGregor Papers
18 Greater London Record Office, MacGregor Papers
19 Leslie Peabody, 'The Canoe and the Woman,' *Outing* 38 (August 1901) 534
20 Isobel Knowles, 'Two Girls in a Canoe,' *Cosmopolitan Magazine* 39 (1905) 650
21 Eric Sevareid, *Canoeing with the Cree*, 148
22 Florence Page Jaques, *Canoe Country* (St Paul: University of Minnesota Press, 1938) 66
23 Jonathan Bordo, 'Tom Thompson and the Jack Pine,' Paper delivered to the Frost Centre, Trent University, Fall 1990, quoted in Dodge and Hodgins, eds, *Using Wilderness* (see chap. 3, n42) 122
24 James Raffan, 'Frontier, Homeland, and Sacred Place: A Collaborative Investigation into Cross-Cultural Perceptions of Place in the Thelon Game Sanctuary, Northwest Territories,' Ph.D. Thesis, Queen's University (1992) 350–1.
25 Lynn White, Jr, 'The Historical Roots of Our Ecologic Crisis' *Science* 155 (1967) 1203–7
26 TUA, Canadian Camping Association Papers, 'Klahowya Tillicum: Temagami 1923'
27 Ontario, Lands and Forests, *Summer Homes*, 24, 17
28 C.A.M. Edwards, *Taylor Statten: A Biography* (Toronto: Ryerson, 1960) 58
29 Bruce W. Hodgins, 'The Written Word on Canoeing and Canoe Tripping before 1960,' in Bruce W. Hodgins and Margaret Hobbs, eds, *Nastawgan: The Canadian North by Canoe and Snowshoe* (Toronto: Betelgeuse, 1985) 145
30 See Richard Allen, *The Social Gospel: Religion and Social Reform in Canada, 1914–1928* (Toronto: University of Toronto Press, 1971).
31 David MacLeod, 'A Live Vaccine: The YMCA and Male Adolescence in the United States and Canada, 1870–1920,' *Social History* 11 (1978) 20
32 Edwards, *Taylor Statten*, 68, 70–3
33 Gerald Killan, *Protected Places: A History of Ontario's Provincial Parks System* (Toronto: Dundurn, 1993) 5–16
34 Henry Burton Sharman, *Records of the Life of Jesus Christ* (New Haven: Yale, 1917)
35 Lois Wilson, Letter to the author, 13 February 1995
36 I am grateful to Rev. John Freeman of Winnipeg, who worked at Camp Minnesing as a young student, for a copy of the 1942 promotional literature.
37 National Archives of Canada [NAC], Sharman Papers, including an undated article from *The Canadian Student*

38 MacLeod, 'A Live Vaccine,' 18

39 Dorothy Sangster, 'Should You Send Your Child to Camp?' *Maclean's*, May 1958, 56

40 Pierre Elliott Trudeau, 'Exhaustion and Fulfilment: The Ascetic in a Canoe,' in Borden Spears, ed., *Wilderness Canada* (Toronto and Vancouver: Clarke, Irwin, 1970) 4. Trudeau's essay originally appeared in *Jeunesse étudiante catholique*, November 1944.

41 Barbara Slater, ed., *On the Shores: Manitoba Pioneer Camp 50th Anniversary* (1992) 12

42 Gordon Stewart, Interview, 15 April 1993

43 Lois Wilson, Interview, 19 September 1991. For further information on Dr Wilson's early life and family canoeing experiences, see her autobiography, *Turning the World Upside Down: A Memoir* (Toronto: Doubleday, 1989).

Chapter 5: The Canadian Summer Boy

1 W.S. Johnson, 'By Canoe,' *Canadian Magazine* 23 (June 1904) 125

2 R.E. Pinkerton, *The Canoe: Its Selection, Care, and Use* (New York: Macmillan, 1914) 161–2

3 TUA, Ontario Camping Association Papers, 'Camp Temagami, 1905'

4 'The Men with the Hearts of Boys,' 67

5 Hodgins, 'The Written Word on Canoeing,' 142

6 Fred A. Talbot, 'Back to the Woods,' *World's Work* 18 (1911) 443

7 'What Shall a Boy Do with His Vacation?' *Chicago Inter-Ocean*, 22 September 1907

8 Talbot, 'Back to the Woods,' 443

9 F.F. Appleton, 'Campcraft,' in R.G. MacBeth, ed., *The Trail Makers Boy's Annual*, vol. 1 (1920) 123

10 Tanneguy de Wogan, *Voyages du canot en papier, le 'Qui-vive'* (Paris, 1887) 2

11 Kristopher Churchill, 'Learning about Manhood: Gender Ideals and "Manly Camping,"' in Dodge and Hodgins, eds, *Using Wilderness* (see chap. 3, n42) 26; see also David I. Macleod, *Building Character in the American Boy: The Boy Scouts, YMCA, and Their Forerunners, 1873–1920* (Wisconsin: University of Wisconsin Press, 1983).

12 Churchill, 'Learning about Manhood,' 5

13 Ibid., 11

14 Henry Chadwick, *Sports and Pastimes of American Boys* (1884) 162

15 William C. James, 'The Canoe Trip as Religious Quest,' *Studies in Religion/Sciences religieuses* 10:2 (1981) 151, and 'The Quest Pattern and the Canoe Trip,' in Hodgins and Hobbs, eds, *Nastawgan* (see chap. 4, n29) 9

16 Sevareid, *Not So Wild a Dream* (New York, 1946) 16, 19, quoted in Sevareid, *Canoeing with the Cree*, x

17 Sevareid, *Canoeing with the Cree*, 200–1

18 Budge Wilson, 'The Canoe Trip,' in Kathleen Tudor and Renee Davis, eds, *Islands in the Harbour: A Collection of Stories by Writers from Nova Scotia's South Shore* (Lockeport, N.S.: Roseway, 1990)

19 Ontario, Ministry of Tourism and Recreation, 'The Inside Story: Incredible Ontario,' advertisement (n.d.)

20 Michael Valpy, 'Breeze from Canada Touches Sudan,' *Globe and Mail*, 4 October 1986; Peter Dalglish, Interview, 11 December 1995

21 Roderick A. Macdonald, 'Of Canoes and Constitutions,' in Raffan and Horwood, eds, *Canexus* (see chap. 3, n38) 161, 166, 167

22 Marni Jackson, 'In Man's Country,' *Outside*, February 1990, 67

23 Mike Jones, *Canoeing down Everest* (London, Sydney, Auckland, Toronto: Hodder and Stoughton, 1979) 165

24 Hedley S. Dimock and Charles E. Hendry, *Camping and Character: A Camp Experiment in Character Education* (New York: Association Press, 1929) 18

25 NAC, Department of National Health and Welfare, RG 29 vol. 801, file 537

26 Hedley S. Dimock, *Administration of the Modern Camp* (New York: Association Press, 1950) 22, 24, 27

27 NAC, Department of National Health and Welfare, RG 29 vol. 801, file 537, 'Canadian Camping – Day Camps, March, 1968'

28 NAC, Department of National Health and Welfare, RG 29 vol. 801, file 537, 'Canadian Camping Outdoor Education Report, March 1968'

29 Although the brief attributes this passage to Bruce Hutchison in *The Unknown Country*, I have been unable to locate it there.

30 A.R.M. Lower, *Unconventional Voyages* (Toronto: Ryerson, 1953) 13

31 Caroline Byrne, '900 Ranger Jobs Offer Outdoor Experience,' *Globe and Mail*, 27 March 1989

32 Roy MacGregor, 'Summer Camp Choice Crucial for Eighties Power Parents,' *Ottawa Citizen*, 16 April 1988

33 Harris, 'The Summer of Their Content,' 45–6

34 Paul Rush, '"Executive Escape" That Turned into Test,' *Financial Post*, 27 November 1989

Chapter 6: Women and Wilderness

1 Moodie, *Roughing It in the Bush*, 155

2 Anna Jameson, *Winter Studies and Summer Rambles in Canada*, vol. 8 (London, 1838) 288–9, quoted in Jean Murray Cole, 'Kawartha Lakes Regattas,' in Hodgins and Hobbs, eds, *Nawstagan* (see chap. 4, n29) 203

3 E. Pauline Johnson, 'Striking Camp,' *Saturday Night*, 29 August 1891, 7

4 Johnson, 'Striking Camp,' 7

5 E. Pauline Johnson, 'Canoe and Canvas: The ACA Meets in Canadian Waters,' *Saturday Night*, 2 September 1893, 6

6 Johnson, 'Striking Camp,' 6

7 Johnson, 'Canoe and Canvas,' 6

8 Meg Stanley, 'The Not So Lazy Days of Summer: The Ontario Camping Association and Accreditation, 1933–1980,' in Dodge and Hodgins, eds, *Using Wilderness* (see chap. 3, n42) 32

9 Leila G. Mitchell McKee, 'Nature's Medicine: The Physical Education and Outdoor Recreation Programmes of Toronto's Voluntary Youth Organizations, 1880–1930,' in Bruce Kidd, ed., *Proceedings of the 5th Canadian Symposium on the History of Sport and Physical Education*, mimeograph (Toronto, 1982) 133

10 Peabody, 'The Canoe and the Woman,' 534

11 Kathrene Pinkerton, 'Paddling Her Own Canoe,' *Outing* 64 (May 1914) 223

12 Mildred Low, 'Earthworms,' *Canadian Magazine* 61 (July 1923) 242–5

13 Wendy Mitchinson, 'Medical Perceptions of Healthy Women: The Case of Late Nineteenth Century Canada,' *Canadian Woman Studies* 8 (Winter 1987) 42

14 Helen Lenskyj, 'Common Sense and Physiology: North American Medical Views on Women and Sport, 1890–1930,' *Canadian Journal of the History of Sport* 21 (May 1990) 49

15 For a recent collection of historical and contemporary narratives on women canoeists, see Judith Niemi and Barbara Wieser, eds, *Rivers Running Free* (see chap. 3, n32).

16 Knowles, 'Two Girls in a Canoe,' 647–50

17 Walton, 'A Woman's Views on Camping Out,' 72

18 Pinkerton, 'Paddling Her Own Canoe,' 221

19 Jeannette Marks, *Vacation Camping for Girls* (New York and London: Appleton, 1913) 193–4

20 Mrs Knox, 'A Lady's Canoe Trip,' *Rod and Gun* 6:4 (October 1904) 230–2

21 Bergathora, 'A Woman's Outing on the Nepigon,' 583

22 Walton, 'A Woman's Views on Camping Out,' 73

23 Mina Hubbard, *A Woman's Way through Unknown Labrador* (St John's: Breakwater, 1981; originally pub. 1908)

24 Anna Kalland, 'It Can't Be Done,' *Outing* 81 (March 1923) 267–72

25 Bergathora, 'A Woman's Outing on the Nepigon,' 583

26 Pinkerton, 'Paddling Her Own Canoe,' 220

27 Ruth Terborg, 'Timagami for Women,' *Appalachia*, June 1936, 8–9

28 TUA, Perry Papers, Kay McMillan to C.B. Storr, 21 December 1948

29 Walton, 'A Woman's Views on Camping Out,' 73

30 TUA, Windy Pine Papers
31 Quoted, without attribution, in James, 'Canoeing and Gender Roles,' 41
32 Margaret Atwood, 'Death by Landscape,' *Harper's Magazine*, August 1990, 50
33 Meg Stanley, 'More Than Just a Spare Rib, But Not Quite a Whole Canoe: Some Aspects of Women's Canoe Tripping Experiences, 1900–1940,' in Dodge and Hodgins, eds, *Using Wilderness* (see chap. 3, n42) 52, 59
34 Women in the Wilderness, 1992 trip schedule and application form
35 Goldman, 'Canadian Outward Bound Wilderness School and the "Women of Courage" Program,' 65
36 'Women Startle Firecrew,' *Winnipeg Free Press*, 25 July 1989
37 Kathleen Brewer, *How to Shit in the Woods: An Environmentally Friendly Approach to a Lost Art* (Berkeley: Ten Speed, 1989); Horace Kephart, *Camping: A Handbook for Vacation Campers and for Travellers in the Wilderness* (New York: Macmillan, 1927)
38 Gwyneth Hoyle, 'Women of Determination: Northern Journeys by Women before 1940,' in Hodgins and Hobbs, eds, *Nastawgan* (see chap. 4, n29) 117–40
39 Robert Stacey, 'Frances Anne Hopkins and the Canoe-Eye-View,' in Janet E. Clark and Robert Stacey, *Frances Anne Hopkins, 1838–1919: Canadian Scenery* (Thunder Bay: Thunder Bay Art Gallery, 1990) 45
40 Janet E. Clark, 'Frances Anne Hopkins (1838–1919): Canadian Scenery,' in Clark and Stacey, *Frances Anne Hopkins* (see n39) 21
41 Kristopher Churchill, 'Character Building and Gender Socialization in Early Private Youth Camps in Ontario,' M.A. thesis, University of Guelph (1991), contains a chapter entitled 'Lady Campers, Not Mannish Women.'

Chapter 7: Rock Dodging and Other Perils

1 Algernon Blackwood, 'Down the Danube in a Canadian Canoe,' *Living Age* 231 (14 and December 1901) 682
2 *Manitoba Colonist*, 3 December 1888, 322
3 Albert Bigelow Paine, *The Tent Dwellers* (Halifax: Nimbus, 1985; originally pub. 1908) 132
4 Matheron, *L'Enchantement des Rapides* (Paris 1944)
5 Hubbard, *A Woman's Way through Unknown Labrador*, 38–9, 185–6
6 Smith, *From the Land of Shadows*
7 Grey Owl, *Tales of an Empty Cabin*, 207
8 James Dickey, *Deliverance* (New York: Dell, 1971) 14
9 Robert E. Pinkerton, *White Water: A Novel* (Chicago, 1925) 19

10 Harold Horwood, *White Eskimo* (Toronto: Doubleday, 1972) 222–3

11 Anna Jameson, quoted in Hoyle, 'Women of Determination,' 120

12 *Camping in Canada* (1939) 3

13 'Real Sport for the Angler,' *Saturday Night*, 16 August 1924, 12

14 Gary and Joanie McGuffin, *Where Rivers Run* (Toronto: Stoddart, 1988) 73

15 Denis Coolican, Interview, 18 June 1991

16 L.W. Bingay, 'Running the Rapids with an Amateur,' *Rod and Gun* 10:6 (November 1908) 516

17 This information was provided by the Royal Life Saving Society.

18 Ronald H. Perry, *The Canoe and You* (Toronto and Vancouver: Dent, 1948) 7, 14

19 Ronald H. Perry, *Canoe Trip Camping* (Toronto and Vancouver: Dent, 1953) 19

20 Waldemar Van Brunt Claussen, *Canoeing* (New York: Boy Scouts of America, 1931) 27–8

21 Lloyd Delaney, 'Balsam Lake Remembered,' *Kanawa Magazine*, Summer 1992, 37

22 AO, Records of the Attorney General, 'Investigation of Balsam Lake Drowning'

23 AO, Records of the Attorney General, 'Investigation of Balsam Lake Drowning,' A.L. Cochrane to E. Bayly, Deputy Attorney General, 25 August 1926

24 James Edmund Jones, *Camping and Canoeing: What to Take, How to Travel, How to Cook, Where to Go* (Toronto, 1903) 7

25 Jackson, *A Painter's Country*, 84

26 Morse, *Freshwater Saga*, 20

27 Howe Martyn, 'The Canadian Canoe,' *Queen's Quarterly* 47 (Spring 1940) 153. I am grateful to Paul Banfield, Archivist, Queen's University, for biographical information on Martyn.

28 A.R.M. Lower, *My First Seventy-five Years* (Toronto: Macmillan, 1967) 61–86

29 Omond Solandt, Interview, 19 September 1991

30 Richard Garwood Lewis, *Small Watercraft: How to Select, Handle, and Care for All Kinds of Small Watercraft* (Toronto: Fullerton, 1931) 27

31 Perry, *The Canoe and You*, 16

32 Lewis, *Small Watercraft*, 25

33 Richard Garwood Lewis, 'Riding the White Water,' *Forest and Outdoors*, August 1929, 466

34 John C. Hurd, 'Twenty Years of White-Water Canoeing,' *Appalachia* 26 (June 1947) 364

35 N.A. Powell, 'The Most Beautiful Canoe Trip in the World,' *Rod and Gun* 10:5 (October 1908) 415

36 John MacGregor, *A Thousand Miles in the Rob Roy Canoe on Twenty Rivers and Lakes of Europe,* 300
37 *The Field,* 21 May 1892, 742
38 Elton Jessup, *The Boy's Book of Canoeing* (New York, 1926) 110
39 Lewis, *Small Watercraft,* 26
40 Lewis, 'Riding the White Water,' 466
41 Warren H. Miller, *Camping Out* (New York, 1918), 88
42 Martin K. Bovey, 'On Becoming a Backpaddler,' *Appalachia* 21 (December 1936) 183
43 Calvin Rutstrum, *The New Way of the Wilderness,* quoted in C.E.S. Franks, 'White Water Canoeing: An Aspect of Canadian Socio-Economic History,' *Queen's Quarterly* 82 (Summer 1975) 184 n8
44 William Bliss, *Canoeing: The Art and Practice of Canoeing on English Rivers, Navigations, and Canals* (London: Methuen, 1934) 41–2
45 John W. Worthington, 'Quick-Water Canoeing,' *Appalachia* (June 1929) 268
46 Worthington's *Appalachia* essay was reproduced in John C. Phillips and Thomas D. Talbot, *Quick Water and Smooth: A Canoeist's Guide to New England Rivers* (1935).
47 William G. Luscombe and Louis J. Bird, *Canoeing,* 2d ed. (London, 1948) 33–4, explain: 'In America, where canoeing is really a national sport, the technique consists in running the smooth portion of the stream as fast as the canoeist wishes. The moment he approaches heavy water he definitely backwaters so as to check the headlong plunge of the canoe and give the bow ample time to rise easily and steadily to the crest of the wave, then slide down into the trough slowly, and rise again to the second wave and so on. Over there many of the fast streams are so dotted with exposed rocks that a straight course through them is impossible, and the technique of holding back, therefore, not only enables the canoeist to come through dry, but also allows him to draw the canoe sideways, either to starboard or port, as often as may be necessary to dodge the rocks which may be in the course.'
48 Mason, *Path of the Paddle,* 59
49 Ibid., 60
50 Carey French, 'Risk Takers Most on the Move, New Travel Industry Poll Shows,' *Globe and Mail,* 27 May 1989
51 Stasia Evasuk, 'Challenging the Human Spirit' and 'Group Provides Special Adventures,' *Toronto Star,* 18 August 1989
52 Glenda Hanna, *Outdoor Pursuits Programming: Legal Liability and Risk Management* (Edmonton: University of Alberta Press, 1991) 105
53 Jones, *Canoeing down Everest,* 165–6
54 Ibid., 43

55 'Dartmouth College Group Led by A.B. Moffatt Plans Trip over Canadian NW
     Territories Route Last Explored in 1893,' *New York Times*, 15 May 1955; '5
     Reach Baker Lake,' *New York Times*, 25 September 1955; A. Moffatt, 'The
     Barren Grounds,' *Sports Illustrated*, 9 March 1959, 68–76, and 16 March 1959,
     80–8; George J. Grinnell, 'Art Moffatt's Wilderness Way to Enlightenment,'
     Canoe, July 1988, 18–21, 56
56 Graham Fraser, 'Blair Fraser, 1909–1968,' in John Fraser and Graham Fraser,
     eds, *Blair Fraser Reports: Selections, 1944–1968* (Toronto: Macmillan, 1969) xx

Chapter 8: Getting Organized

1 C. Fred Johnston, 'Canoe Sport in Canada: Anglo-American Hybrid?' in
    Raffan and Horwood, eds, *Canexus* (see chap. 3, n38) 59
2 John MacTaggart, *Three Years in Canada*, vol. 1 (London: Henry Calhoun,
    1829) 308, quoted in Peter Lindsay, 'The Pioneer Years Prior to Confedera-
    tion,' in Nancy Howell and Maxwell L. Howell, *History of Sport in Canada*
    (Champaign, Ill.: Stipes, 1985) 53
3 Roberts and Shackleton, *The Canoe: A History*, 223
4 *My Canadian Journal, 1872–8* (London: John Murray, 1891) 256–7, quoted in
    Nancy and Maxwell L. Howell, *Sports and Games in Canadian Life: 1700 to the
    Present* (Toronto: Macmillan, 1969) 124
5 Hugh Gray, *Letters from Canada Written during a Residence There in the Years 1806,
    1807, 1808* (London: Longman, Hurst, et al., 1809) 257–8
6 Robert D. Day, 'The British Garrison at Halifax: Its Contribution to the
    Development of Sport in the Community,' in Mott, ed., *Sports in Canada* (see
    chap. 2, n1) 30
7 A.J. Young, *Beyond Heroes: A Sport History of Nova Scotia*, vol. 2 (Hantsport, N.S.:
    Lancelot, 1988) 116
8 Johnston, 'Canoe Sport,' 63; Young, *Beyond Heroes*, 126
9 Johnston, 'Canoe Sport,' 64; Rice Lake Regatta, Program, 12 September 1849
    (author's collection); Cole, 'Kawartha Lakes Regattas,' 203
10 Johnston, 'Canoe Sport,' 63–4
11 Leonidas Hubbard, 'Paddling Your Own Canoe,' *Outing* 44 (August 1904)
    524–5
12 *American Canoeist* 1:1 (February 1882) 1
13 S. F. Wise, 'Sport and Class Values in Old Ontario and Quebec,' in W.H.
    Heick, ed., *His Own Man: Essays in Honour of Arthur Reginald Marsden Lower*
    (Montreal: McGill-Queen's University Press, 1974) 101
14 Editorial, *American Canoeist* 1:1 (February 1882) 9
15 *American Canoeist* 1:5 (June 1882) 72

16 *The Field*, 6 July 1895, 8
17 Hodder, *John MacGregor 'Rob Roy,'* 284–5; O.J. Cock, *A Short History of Canoeing in Britain* (British Canoe Union, 1974) 5
18 Cock, *A Short History of Canoeing in Britain*, 5; Gerald F. Stephenson, *John Stephenson and the Famous 'Peterborough' Canoe* (Peterborough: Peterborough Historical Society, 1987) 7; John Murray Gibbon, *The Romance of the Canadian Canoe* (Toronto: Ryerson, 1951) 120
19 John Arlott, ed., *The Oxford Companion to Sports and Games* (London, New York, Toronto: Oxford University Press, 1975) 164
20 Warington Baden-Powell, *Canoe Travelling: Log of a Cruise on the Baltic and Practical Hints in Building and Fitting Canoes* (London, 1871)
21 J.D. Hayward, *Canoeing with Sail and Paddle* (London, 1893) 141; F.G. Aflalo, *The Cost of Sport* (London: John Murray, 1899) 202–3
22 *The Field*, 27 February 1892, 279
23 Hayward, *Canoeing with Sail and Paddle*, 2
24 Ibid., 3–4
25 *The Field*, 19 January 1895, 83; 11 February 1899, 173
26 Stevenson, *The Travels: An Inland Voyage*, 16, 18
27 Roberts and Shackleton, *The Canoe: A History*, 241
28 Cole, 'Kawartha Lakes Regattas,' 225
29 *American Canoeist* 3:3 (April 1884) 46
30 *American Canoeist* 1:3 (April 1882) 46
31 *American Canoeist* 3:3 (April 1884) 46
32 *American Canoeist* 2:3 (April 1883) 42; 3:3 (April 1884) 46
33 *American Canoeist* 1:8 (September 1882) 127; Charles Ledyard Norton, 'The Canoe Convention on Lake George,' *Rose Belford's Canadian Monthly* 6 (1881) 426
34 *American Canoeist* 2:2 (March 1883) 28
35 W.L. Alden, 'The Canoe Service,' *American Canoeist* 2:2 (March 1883) 18
36 *American Canoeist* 2:8 (September 1883) 112
37 *American Canoeist* 2:4 (May 1883) 59
38 *American Canoeist* 2:6 (July 1883) 88
39 *American Canoeist* 3:1 (February 1884) 7
40 *American Canoeist* 3:4 (May 1884) 60
41 Manley and Jamieson, *Rushton*
42 Ibid., 61
43 Ibid., 100
44 *The Field*, 26 August 1893, 325
45 'Club Life in Toronto,' *Saturday Night*, 18 April 1903, 7
46 NAC, Ottawa Canoe Club House Company Records

47 Larry Turner, *Recreational Boating in the Rideau Waterway, 1890–1930*, vol. 1 (Parks Canada, 1986) 59

48 NAC, Henry Harper Papers, W.W. Moore to Harper, 26 June 1900

49 Turner, *Recreational Boating*, 59

50 Ibid., 233

51 Ibid., 59, 235

52 Marcus Van Steen, *Pauline Johnson: Her Life and Work* (Toronto: Hodder and Stoughton, 1965); Gibbon, *The Romance of the Canadian Canoe*, 139–42; E. Pauline Johnson, *Flint and Feather: The Complete Poems* (Toronto: Musson, 1913)

53 E. Pauline Johnson, 'With Paddle and Peterboro,' *Saturday Night*, 28 June 1890, 6

54 Johnson, 'Princes of the Paddle,' *Saturday Night*, 9 September 1893, 6

55 Johnson, 'Striking Camp,' 7

56 NAC, J.E.G. Curran Papers, Orillia Canoe Club, Annual Regatta, 7 August 1905

57 *The Field*, 4 March 1899, 309

58 See the *Globe and Mail*, 8 July 1915, for discussion of the planned women's war canoe race involving competitors from Island Aquatic, Balmy Beach, and Parkdale at the Canadian Canoe Association western division regatta.

59 Hubbard, 'Paddling Your Own Canoe,' 532

60 *The Red Ring: The Official Organ of the Toronto Canoe Club* 3:9 (1 August 1924) 3

61 Provincial Archives of Manitoba [PAM], Winnipeg Canoe Club Records, Canadian Canoe Association, 14th Annual Report. For additional information on the growth of the organization over the years, see C. Fred Johnston, *Book of Champions of the Canadian Canoe Association, 1900–1984* (Ottawa: Canadian Canoe Association, 1988).

62 *The Field*, 23 June 1900, 904

63 For a list of member clubs in the Canadian Canoe Association from 1900 to 1984, see Johnston, *Book of Champions*, 8–10.

64 PAM, Winnipeg Canoe Club Records

65 'The Toronto Canoe Club,' *Athletic Life* 3:6 (June 1896) 244

66 PAM, Winnipeg Canoe Club Records, 'Paddling, 1911–1929,' 262, 276

67 Ibid., 253

68 PAM, Winnipeg Canoe Club Records, 'Aquatic, June 1931–Sept 1936,' 120, with a clipping from the *Winnipeg Free Press* for 21 August 1936

69 Edward W. Waud, 'A Notable Canadian Canoe Race,' *Rod and Gun* 16:5 (October 1914) 451

70 NAC, Borden Papers, C.E. Mortueux to Borden, 17 September 1919. Despite the Prime Minister's insistence that long-distance racing was distinctively

Canadian, similar contests were under way in other parts of the world. See, for example, Cock, *A Short History of Canoeing in Britain*, 23–5.

71 PAM, Winnipeg Canoe Club Records, 'Paddling, 1911–1929,' 200
72 Claude Lessard and Jean-Paul Massicotte, 'Histoire du canotage en Mauricie,' *Revue d'ethnologie du Québec* 4 (1976) 99–114
73 W.G. Cleevely, 'Olympic Report from 1961 Annual Meeting,' in *Canadian Paddling Yearbook, 1960–61*
74 *Canadian Paddler*, 1963

Chapter 9: What Kinda Boat Ya Got?

1 Peabody, 'The Canoe and the Woman,' 533
2 Ron Perry, *The Canoe and You*, iii
3 C.L. Norton, 'September on the Bay,' *American Canoeist* 3:10 (October 1884) 151, repr. from *Hour*
4 *Visit to Oxford* (1818), cited by the *OED* under 'Canoe'
5 Hodder, *John MacGregor ('Rob Roy')*, 291–2
6 Ibid., 294–5
7 Ibid., 291
8 Robert F. Berkhofer, Jr, *The White Man's Indian: Images of the American Indian from Columbus to the Present* (New York: Knopf, 1978)
9 Hodder, *John MacGregor ('Rob Roy')*, 277
10 MacGregor, *Our Brothers and Cousins*, 39
11 Ibid., 23
12 W.H. De Puy, *The People's Cyclopedia of Universal Knowledge*, 4th ed. (New York, 1883)
13 Perhaps the sharpest rejection of linkage between aboriginal watercraft and recreational canoes came from *Forest and Stream* in 1874. In reply to a correspondent who had inquired about bark vessels, the magazine stated: 'We are reluctant to inform our anxious inquirer that the birchbark canoe is not named or known in the category of civilized craft which our modern canoemen paddle and sail ... It is the peculiar toy and vehicle of the aboriginal redskin and although it is light and buoyant and full of poetry and well adapted to his requirements, the palefaces are conceited enough to believe that they can manufacture something better in all respects.' Quoted in Jerry Stelmok and Rollin Thurlow, *The Wood and Canvas Canoe: A Complete Guide to Its History, Construction, Restoration, and Maintenance* (Gardiner, Maine: Harpswell, 1987) 17
14 C. Stansfeld-Hicks, *Yachts, Boats, and Canoes* (London, 1887) 180–1, 178
15 'Ancient Canoe,' *The Field*, 10 September 1898, 453

16 Roberts and Shackleton, *The Canoe: A History*, 2

17 *American Canoeist* 1:1 (February 1882) 1

18 *American Canoeist* 2:1 (February 1883) 9

19 Hayward, *Canoeing with Sail and Paddle*, 7

20 W.P. Stephens, *Canoe and Boat Building: A Complete Manual for Amateurs* (New York: Forest and Stream, 1885) 7–8. For descriptions of the principal models in existence at the time, see Stephens, 137–66.

21 *The Field*, 5 November 1892, 710

22 'The Canadian Canoe,' *Forest and Stream*, 29 December 1887, 456

23 *American Canoeist* 3:9 (September 1884) 141

24 Chadwick, *Sports and Pastimes of American Boys*, 160

25 'Canvas and Wood Canoes,' *Outing* 74 (June 1919) 168; see also Dillon Wallace, 'The American Canoe,' *Outing* 56 (July 1910) 417

26 John Boyle O'Reilly, *Ethics of Boxing and Manly Sport* (Boston: Ticknor, 1888) 244

27 C. Bowyer Vaux, *Canoe Handling: The Canoe: History, Uses, Limitations and Varieties, Practical Management and Care, and Relative Facts* (New York: Forest and Stream, 1888) 10

28 *Rowe v. Granite Bridge Corp.*, 38 Mass. (21 Pick.) 344 (1838)

29 Wallace, 'The American Canoe,' 406

30 Millard, *Days on the Nepigon*, 38–9

31 Robert E. Pinkerton, 'The Canoe – Half Stolen,' *Outing* 62 (May 1913) 162

Chapter 10: The Craft and the Craftsman

1 St Croix, 'Peterboro vs. Birchbark,' *Rod and Gun* 2:10 (March 1910) 490

2 Pinkerton, *The Canoe*, 20

3 Millard, *Days on the Nepigon*, 38–40

4 Edwin Tappan Adney, 'The Passing of the North Canoe,' *Outing* 41 (October 1902) 3–11

5 Wallace Kirkland, 'The Making of a Birch Bark Canoe,' *Forest and Outdoors*, July 1931, 352; Armand Tremblay, 'How the Birch Bark Canoe Is Made,' *Forest and Outdoors*, October 1936, 296

6 Silver, 'A Birch-Bark Canoe Trip,' 238

7 Robert E. Ritzenthaler, 'The Building of a Chippewa Indian Birch-Bark Canoe,' *Bulletin of the Public Museum of the City of Milwaukee* (November 1950) 96

8 Tremblay, 'How the Birch Bark Canoe Is Made,' 296

9 Tappan Adney, 'The Building of a Birch Canoe,' *Outing* 36 (May 1900) 185

10 *American Canoeist* 2:2 (March 1883) 15

11 'The Canadian Canoe,' 456
12 Samuel Strickland, *Twenty-seven Years in Canada West* (Edmonton: Hurtig 1970)
13 Gray, *Letters from Canada*, 258–9
14 On the origin of dugouts in Ontario, see E.S. Rogers, 'The Dugout Canoe in Ontario,' *American Antiquity* 30 (1965) 454–9
15 Donald Cameron, 'The Peterborough Canoe,' Paper read at the Peterborough Historical Society, 18 March 1975
16 Stephenson, *John Stephenson*
17 Robert Tyson, 'Modern Canoeing,' *Rose Belford's Canadian Monthly* 6 (1881) 537–8
18 *American Canoeist* 1:4 (May 1882) 59. The Ontario Canoe Company's work, including the cedar rib model, is described in detail in *American Canoeist* 3:6 (July 1884) 81.
19 *American Canoeist* 1:6 (July 1882) 89
20 *American Canoeist* 2:4 (May 1883) 60
21 *American Canoeist* 2:12 (January 1884) 182
22 Stephenson, *John Stephenson*, 12
23 C.L. Norton and John Habberton, *Canoeing in Kanuckia, or Haps and Mishaps Afloat and Ashore* (New York: Putnam, 1878) 249–50; Stelmok and Thurlow, *The Wood and Canvas Canoe*, 24–5
24 'Origin of Some Canoes,' *American Canoeist* 2:10 (November 1883) 143
25 See Stelmok and Thurlow, *The Wood and Canvas Canoe*, esp. 17–24
26 Wallace, 'The American Canoe,' 404; Stelmok and Thurlow, *The Wood and Canvas Canoe*, 3
27 James Bonfitto, 'The Golden Times,' *Canoe*, August–September 1980, 18
28 Stelmok and Thurlow, *The Wood and Canvas Canoe*, 24–5. The June 1882 issue of *American Canoeist* (1:5) thought it worthwhile to refer to the existence of 'at least one canvas canoe' in Lowell, Massachusetts, and also refers to new racing canoes with removable canvas decks from Racine, Wisconsin. In *Canoe and Boat Building*, 111, W.P. Stephens provided details on construction alternatives, but offered no speculation on origins, other than to suggest that the idea of covering a frame with a skin was as old as the coracle.
29 Wallace, 'The American Canoe,' 406
30 Manley and Jamieson, *Rushton*, 148
31 Richard Garwood Lewis, 'Advice on Canadian Canoes,' *Forest and Outdoors*, May 1927, 251
32 C.F. Paul of the *Montreal Star*, in a letter to *Rod and Gun*, June 1906, 45
33 *Rod and Gun*, July 1906, 156
34 On the early development of home-made sponsons, see *Rowing, Sculling, and*

Canoeing (London: Ward and Lock, 1882) 45–6: 'Take a strip of linen drill, duck, or very strong calico, about twelve or fourteen inches wide, and the length of the gunwale; sew the edges close together, thus forming a bag; fill this with cork shavings, sew the ends up, and give two or three coats of good oil paint (white). Then lash one on each side of the Canoe, neatly on the outside, just below the gunwale and above the water line. The weight added to the boat is trifling; but it serves to turn her into a lifeboat not easy to capsize; for, as soon as the cork rubber comes down to the water, you may sit on the gunwale, if you care to, with perfect safety, and carry on sail almost as long as you like. To all who indulge in the capital recreation of Canoeing we advise this method of providing safety from a ducking, if not drowning, particularly as the expense is so trifling.'

35 Archives of New Brunswick [ANB], Chestnut Canoe Company Papers; Roger MacGregor, 'Retrospective on the Chestnut Canoe,' in Roger MacGregor, ed., *Chestnut Canoe: 1950* (Lansdowne, Ont.: Plumsweep, 1994)

36 ANB, Chestnut Canoe Company Papers, Minutes of the Directors' Meeting, 16 July 1923

37 Francis H. Love, 'Peterborough ... Canoe Capital of the World,' *Forest and Outdoors*, September 1949, 22

38 *Rod and Gun*, June 1928, 65

39 *Forest and Stream*, 24 September 1891, 196–7

40 'You Can Build the Aluminum Canoe,' *Popular Mechanics* 66 (August 1936) 274

41 John R. Rowlands, *Cache Lake Country: Life in the Canadian North Woods* (London: Adam and Charles Black, 1948) 23

42 *Appalachia*, 25 December 1945, 541

43 Douglas M. Brown, 'Canoeing,' *Appalachia*, June 1946, 117

44 Kim Pressnail, 'The Essence of Omer,' *Paddler* 3:2 (Fall 1988) 6–9

45 John Coleman, Letter, *Canoe*, May 1993

46 See also George Pontin, 'How to Make a Sectional Canoe,' in A.L. Haydon, ed., *Canoes, Dinghies, and Sailing Punts with Numerous Diagrams and Illustrations* (London: Boys Own Paper, 1923) 125–32

47 Canadian Patent #13721, 21 February 1898

48 Luscombe and Bird, *Canoeing* 30

49 Roberts and Shackleton, among others, credit C.M. Douglas with the invention. *The Field*, 9 September 1876, 334, contained an item, 'Portable Canvas Canoe,' in which a reader asked for information on 'a canvas canoe, 10 ft. long, with 30 in. beam, constructed in separate parts, so that it can be packed in a case 30 in. long, 12 in. broad, and $4\frac{1}{2}$ in. deep, the whole not weighing more than 18 lb.'

50 Lewis, 'Advice on Canadian Canoes,' 252
51 Ozark Ripley, 'The Evolution of Outboard Motoring,' *Forest and Outdoors*, April 1928, 224–6
52 See *American Canoeist* 2:10 (November 1883) 151.
53 The Buyer's Guide section of *Paddler* 15:6 (December 1995) 85 provides a valuable description of contemporary construction materials and processes: 'Fiber-reinforced plastic includes fiberglass, exotic fabrics such as Kevlar and Spectra, and foam-corded FRP. The material is either hand-laid in layers of fabric and wet out by hand, or the laminate "stack" is wet out and vacuum bagged to produce a hull. Royalex is a proprietary material consisting of an ABS foam core sandwiched between sheets of ABS plastic, and covered with a vinyl "skin" on both sides. The material is then thermoformed into a hull. Rotomolded polyethylene and foam, a process often called "triple dump" molding, is done by dumping polyethylene powder into a heated mold that's rotated and rocked. After the powder is melted and distributed, a foaming agent is added to the next dump of powdered resin, to create a lighter core of what might best be called expanded polyethylene. A third dump of resin forms a thin protective skin over the foam.'
54 Stelmok and Thurlow, *The Wood and Canvas Canoe*, Introduction
55 Kenneth Brower, *The Starship and the Canoe* (New York: Harper and Row, 1978); George Dyson, *Baidarka* (Seattle: Alaska Northwest, 1986), and 'Form and Function of the Baidarka: The Framework of Design,' in E.Y. Arima et al., eds, *Contributions to Kayak Studies* (Hull: Canadian Museum of Civilization, 1991) 261
56 John McPhee, *The Survival of the Bark Canoe* (New York: Farrar, Straus, Giroux; Toronto: McGraw-Hill Ryerson, 1975); Stelmok and Thurlow, *The Wood and Canvas Canoe*, 4–16

Chapter 11: Native Impressions

1 David Gidmark, *Birchbark Canoe: The Story of an Apprenticeship with the Indians* (Burnstown, Ont.: General Store, 1989) 55. See also Gidmark, *The Algonquin Birchbark Canoe* (Aylesbury: Shire, 1988).
2 Brower, *The Starship and the Canoe*, 50
3 Dyson, 'Form and Function of the Baidarka,' 262
4 Silver, *Farm-Cottage, Camp, and Canoe in Maritime Canada*, 173
5 Wallace, 'The American Canoe,' 404
6 Bill Holm and George Irving Quimby, *Edward S. Curtis in the Land of the War Canoes: A Pioneer Cinematographer in the Pacific Northwest* (Seattle and London: University of Washington Press, 1980) 55

7 Richard Barsam, *The Vision of Robert Flaherty: The Artist as Myth and Filmmaker* (Bloomington and Indianapolis: Indiana University Press, 1951); Arthur Calder-Marshall, *The Innocent Eye: The Life of Robert Flaherty* (London: Allen, 1963); Paul Rotha, *Robert J. Flaherty: A Biography*, ed. Jay Ruby (Philadelphia: University of Pennsylvania Press, 1983). Kayak models collected by Flaherty during his northern travels now form part of the ethnology collection at the Royal Ontario Museum.

8 Millard, *Days on the Nepigon*, 39–40

9 J. King Gordon, 'Birkencraig: 1907–1983,' manuscript, 44, and Interview, 14 April 1987

10 Pinkerton, 'The Canoe – Half Stolen,' 159

11 Rowlands, *Cache Lake Country*, 15

12 P.G. Downes, *Sleeping Island: The Story of One Man's Travels in the Great Barren Lands of the Canadian North* (Saskatoon: Western Producer Prairie Books, 1988; originally pub. 1943) 10

13 Kamil Pecher, *Lonely Voyage: By Kayak to Adventure and Discovery* (Saskatoon: Western Producer Prairie Books, 1978) 161

14 Berkhofer, *The White Man's Indian*, 68

15 Sevareid, *Canoeing with the Cree*, 87

16 Downes, *Sleeping Island*, 38–9

17 See Cloutier, *From Maniwaki to Angliers*. This is another example of the kind of encounter Downes had with Indians who didn't understand why you would choose to paddle if you could use an outboard motor.

18 TUA, Perry Papers, YMCA to Carter Storr, 21 December 48

19 TUA, Perry Papers, E.F. Mills to Carter Storr, 10 December 1948

20 Morse, *Freshwater Saga*, 21

21 Tony Sloan, *Black Flies and White Water* (Toronto: McClelland and Stewart, 1977) 11

22 Twyla Wright, '40, and at Sea,' in Niemi and Wieser, eds, *Rivers Running Free* (see chap. 3, n32) 78

23 David T. Hanbury, *Sport and Travel in the Northland of Canada* (London: Edward Arnold, 1904) 20

24 Hanbury, *Sport and Travel*, 33, 41

25 Agnes C. Laut, 'Fifteen Hundred Miles down the Saskatchewan,' *Scribner's Magazine* 45 (April 1909) 464

26 'The Sportsman Tourist,' *Forest and Stream*, 2 April 1904, 266

27 Albert Bigelow Paine, *The Tent Dwellers*, 66

28 Jaques, *Canoe Country*, 15

29 Patricia Jasen, 'Native People and the Tourist Industry in Nineteenth-Century Ontario,' *Journal of Canadian Studies* 28:4 (Winter 1993–4) 21

30 K. Baedeker, *The Dominion of Canada* (New York: Scribner's, 1907) 237

31 Jasen, 'Native People,' 18

32 AO, Woods and Forests Branch Report, Book 3, 248, 'Memorandum: Re Remuneration to the Paid Guides in Temagami Forest Reserve'

33 'Ontario Guides Will Organize,' *Rod and Gun* 22:1 (June 1920) 15–17; 'Northern Ontario Guides and Outfitters Association,' *Rod and Gun* 22:4 (October 1920) 602–4

34 George T. Marsh, 'The Albany Trail to James Bay,' *Scribner's Magazine* 51 (April 1912) 436–7

35 Laut, 'Fifteen Hundred Miles down the Saskatchewan,' 460

36 Downes, *Sleeping Island*, 29–30

37 See Davidson and Rugge, *Great Heart*.

38 TUA, 'Our Indebtedness to Our Indian Friends,' Talk given in the Glen Bernard Camp chapel, Sunday, 15 August 1971, as part of the fiftieth anniversary ceremonies, 1

39 On Seton and the League, see John Henry Wadland, *Ernest Thompson Seton: Man in Nature in the Progressive Era, 1880–1915* (New York: Arno, 1978) chap. 4.

40 Julian Harris Salomon, 'Indian Lore in Summer Camps,' in Eugene H. Lehman and Ralph Hill, eds, *Camps and Camping*, Spalding's Athletic Library (New York: American Sports, 1929) 69

41 TUA, Society of Camp Directors Papers, W.J. Eastaugh, 'Is There Still a Place for the Indian Council Ring Ceremony?' Address to the Society of Camp Directors, 12 April 1972, 1, 2

42 TUA, Society of Camp Directors Papers, Linda M. Gerber, 'Indian Culture in Camp Programs: Its Relevance to the Native People of Today,' Address to the Society of Camp Directors, 12 April 1972, 1, 9

43 Roy MacGregor, *Chief: The Fearless Vision of Billy Diamond* (Markham, Ont.: Penguin, 1990)

44 Bill Reid, quoted in Karen Duffek, *Bill Reid: Beyond the Essential Form* (Vancouver: University of British Columbia Press in association with the UBC Museum of Anthropology, 1986) 26

45 André Picard, 'Native Enterprises Building Foundation for Arctic Nation,' *Globe and Mail*, 14 April 1990; Eric Siblin, 'New York Legislators Renew Vow to Block Hydro-Quebec Deal,' *Globe and Mail*, 10 August 1991; 'Hydro-Quebec Assails Crees Plan,' *Globe and Mail*, 13 February 1992; 'Crees Plan Campaign against Great Whale,' *Globe and Mail*, 15 April 1993; Michael Posluns, *Voices from the Odeyak* (Toronto: NC Press, 1993)

46 Stephen Godfrey, 'Bank to Paddle Historic Canoe,' *Globe and Mail*, 2 August 1885; Deborah Wilson, 'Feast Does Justice to the Judge,' *Globe and Mail*, 30 November 1990; David Neel, *The Great Canoes: Reviving a Northwest Coast*

Tradition (Seattle: University of Washington Press; Vancouver and Toronto: Douglas and McIntyre, 1995)

47 See chap. 3, 'The Healing Pines,' above.

48 *Wawatay News*, 17 August 1990

Chapter 12: Destinations

1 Downes, *Sleeping Island*, 3, 10

2 Eric W. Morse, 'Summer Travel in the Canadian Barrens,' *Canadian Geographical Journal*, May 1967

3 Downes, *Sleeping Island*, 5

4 Jones, *Camping and Canoeing*, 70–1

5 White, *The Forest*, 62

6 J.L. Weller, Letter to *American Canoeist* 3:12 (December 1884) 191

7 Manley and Jamieson, *Rushton*, 36–43

8 Ibid., 80–1

9 Richard Bangs and Christian Kallen, *Riding the Dragon's Back: The Race to Raft the Upper Yangtze* (New York: Dell, 1989) xiv

10 Bangs and Kallen, *Riding the Dragon's Back*, 4

11 Brian Sheen, *1st St. Austell Scout and Nigerian Boy Scout Canoe Expedition to the Niger Delta, 1981* (n.p., n.d.) 13, 48

12 Orinoco, 'The Canoeist,' *American Canoeist* 2:4 (May 1883) 53

13 Wallace, *The Lure of the Labrador Wild*, 15

14 Hubbard, *A Woman's Way through Unknown Labrador*, 7

15 Ibid., 75–6

16 Starkell, *Paddle to the Amazon*. The *New York Times*, 16 November 1956, reported that three German paddlers completed a fifteen-thousand-mile trip to the Olympic Games at Melbourne, Australia.

17 PAM, Winnipeg Canoe Club Records, 'Paddling, 1911–1929,' 277

18 Dana Lamb, *Enchanted Vagabonds* (London and New York: Harper, 1938) 4, 72, 414

19 William VanTil, *The Danube Flows through Fascism: Nine Hundred Miles in a Fold-Boat* (New York and London: Scribner's, 1938) 108–9

20 TUA, Canadian Camping Association Papers, F.A. MacDougall, 'Camping Trips,' May 1940

21 David F. Pelly and Christopher C. Hanks, eds, *The Kazan: Journey into an Emerging Land* (Yellowknife: Outcrop, 1991)

22 Starkell, *Paddle to the Amazon*, 162

23 Brower, *The Starship and the Canoe*, 187

24 Nick Inman, *Canoeing through Life* (Forres, Scotland: Findhorn, 1985)

25 For a description of many northern routes and an inventory of recreational

paddlers, see Bruce W. Hodgins and Gwyneth Hoyle, *Canoeing North into the Unknown: A Record of River Travel, 1874–1974* (Toronto: Natural Heritage / Natural History, 1994).

26 Kenneth C. Campbell, 'By Canoe to York Factory, Summer, 1911,' *Beaver* 72:4 (August–September 1992) 19–35

27 Marion and Ben Ferrier, *God's River Country* (Englewood Cliffs, N.J.: Prentice-Hall, 1956)

28 Sevareid, *Canoeing with the Cree*, 145

29 Judith Niemi, 'Mucky Waters: A Hudson Bay Journal,' in Niemi and Wieser, eds, *Rivers Running Free* (see chap. 3, n32) 126

30 James, 'The Quest Pattern and the Canoe Trip,' 19

31 Nigel Foster, 'Shorebound – On Iceland,' in Terry Storry, Marcus Baillie, and Nigel Foster, eds, *Raging Rivers, Stormy Seas* (Yeovil, Somerset: Oxford Illustrated Press, 1989) 25

32 Davidson and Rugge, *Great Heart*, 3

33 George M. Douglas, *Lands Forlorn: A Story of an Expedition to Samuel Hearne's Coppermine River* (New York: Putnam's, 1914)

34 Bill Waiser, *Saskatchewan's Playground: A History of Prince Albert National Park* (Saskatoon: Fifth House, 1989) 75–85

35 Kenneth Brower, 'Grey Owl,' *Atlantic Monthly*, January 1990, quoted in Smith, *From the Land of Shadows*, 295 n20

36 Raymond M. Patterson, *The Dangerous River* (London: Allen and Unwin, 1954) 14. *Far Pastures* (Sydney, B.C.: Gray's, 1963) contains a chapter on Patterson's explorations of the Bow River.

37 In the film *Nahanni* (National Film Board, 1962)

38 Brower, *The Starship and the Canoe*, 174

39 W.S. Holding, 'The Canadian Canoe on English Rivers,' *World's Work* 8 (1906) 199, 200, 203

40 R.J. Evans, 'Through the Heart of England in a Canadian Canoe,' *National Geographic Magazine*, May 1922, 473, 493

41 Evans, 'Through the Heart of England in a Canadian Canoe,' 473

42 For biographical information on Blackwood, including his canoe travels in the Rainy River gold fields and along the shores of the Muskoka district, see John Robert Colombo, *Blackwood's Books: A Bibliography Devoted to Algernon Blackwood* (Toronto: Hounslow, 1981).

43 Algernon Blackwood, 'Down the Danube in a Canadian Canoe,' 677–85, 754

44 Melville Chater, *Two Canoe Gypsies: Their Eight-Hundred-Mile Canal Voyage through Belgium, Brittany, Touraine, Gascony, and Languedoc: Being an Account of Backwoods Life on a Bargeman's Holiday* (New York: Brewer, Warren, and Putnam, 1932)

45 Chater, *Two Canoe Gypsies*, 4
46 Melville Chater, 'Through the Back Doors of France: A Seven Weeks' Voyage in a Canadian Canoe from St. Malo, and through the Chateau Country, to Paris,' *National Geographic Magazine*, July 1923, 1–51
47 Amos Burg, 'Britain Just before the Storm: A Canadian Canoe Threads Old English Waterways Athrob with the Midlands' Industrial Life,' *National Geographic Magazine*, August 1940, 194
48 R. Raven-Hart 'Odyssey of a Sixty-Per-Center,' *Atlantic Monthly*, April 1934, 440, 443, 448, 447

Chapter 13: Comfort

1 Canada, Department of the Interior, *Canoe Trips in Canada* (1934) 59
2 Dillon Wallace, *Packing and Portaging* (New York: Outing, 1912) 20
3 Little, 'Chicago Authors in Temagami,' 634
4 Raven-Hart, 'Odyssey of a Sixty-Per-Center,' 446
5 Downes, *Sleeping Island*, 6
6 James Raffan, 'Probing Canoe Trips for Persistent Meaning,' in Raffan and Horwood, eds, *Canexus* (see chap. 3, n38) 176–7
7 Trudeau, 'Exhaustion and Fulfilment,' 4. For an extreme version of an experiment in self-deprivation, see André-François Bourbeau, *Surviethon: Au gré de la nature* (Les Editions JCL, 1988)
8 *American Canoeist* 1:8 (September 1882) 117
9 Jones, *Camping and Canoeing*, 8
10 Rowlands, *Cache Lake Country*, 171
11 Millard, *Days on the Nepigon*, 98
12 Stephenson, *John Stephenson*, 13
13 Outward Bound, Advertisement, *Business Traveller*, October 1992, 44
14 W.R. Wadsworth, 'With Rifle and Rod in the Moose Lands of Northern Ontario,' *Canadian Magazine* 13 (1899) 262
15 James, 'The Quest Pattern and the Canoe Trip,' 13
16 White, *The Forest*, 5
17 Jackson, 'In Man's Country,' 66
18 John Godfrey, 'Eight Men Out,' *Destinations*, June 1993, 35
19 Warren H. Miller, *Campcraft: Modern Practice and Equipment* (New York: Scribner's, 1915) 26
20 C.P. Storey, 'Outfitting for the Long Canoe Trip,' *Rod and Gun* 28:10 (March 1927) 595–7, 629–32
21 Downes, *Sleeping Island*, 96

22 Paine, *The Tent Dwellers*, 45
23 John S. Crysdale, Letter to the editor, *Globe and Mail*, 12 December 1987
24 Ferrier, *God's River Country*, Appendix
25 'Centennial Canoe Pageant,' *Beaver*, Summer 1967, 27
26 C.E.S. Franks, *The Canoe and White Water: From Essential to Sport* (Toronto: University of Toronto Press, 1977) 142; see also Ronald S. Lappage, 'The Physical Feats of the Voyageur,' *Canadian Journal of the History of Sport*, May 1984, 30
27 Kendall, *Among the Laurentians*, 47
28 *American Canoeist* 2:8 (September 1883) 114
29 NAC, F.M.S. Jenkins Papers, 'Notes Relating to a Canoe Trip'
30 *American Canoeist* 1:3 (April 1882) 41
31 Paine, *The Tent Dwellers*, 164
32 Rowlands, *Cache Lake Country*, 175
33 Bruce W. Hodgins, 'The Lure of the Temagami-based Canoe Trip,' in Hodgins and Hobbs, eds, *Nastawgan* (see chap. 4, n29) 198–9
34 Patterson, *The Dangerous River*, 68
35 Jones, *Camping and Canoeing*, 77
36 Bob Henderson, 'Reflections of a Bannock Baker,' in Raffan and Horwood, eds, *Canexus* (see chap. 3, n38) 87
37 Bill Taylor, *Commitment and Open Crossings* (London: Diadem, 1990) 22
38 Jones, *Camping and Canoeing*, 42
39 Hodgins, 'The Written Word on Canoeing,' 143
40 Baden-Powell, *Canoe Travelling*, 168
41 Nathaniel Holmes Bishop, 'Voyage of the Paper Canoe,' in Teller, ed., *On the River: A Variety of Canoe and Small Boat Voyages*, 39
42 Pat, 'With the Flies on the Nepigon,' *Athletic Life* 1:3 (March 1895) 97
43 Jackson, 'In Man's Country,' 67
44 Omond Solandt, Interview, 19 September 1991
45 Downes, *Sleeping Island*, 6, 210, 222
46 Wallace, *The Lure of the Labrador Wild*, 124–5
47 Jackson, 'In Man's Country,' 67
48 McGuffin, *Where Rivers Run*, 14
49 Peabody, 'The Canoe and the Woman,' 533
50 Pinkerton, 'Paddling Her Own Canoe,' 221
51 'Canoeing in Canada,' in *Canada Today, 1913* (London and Toronto, 1913) 71
52 Anna Jameson, *Winter Studies and Summer Rambles in Canada* (Toronto: McClelland and Stewart, 1965) 126–7
53 Paine, *The Tent Dwellers*, 71

54 Richard Garwood Lewis, 'Paddle Your Own Canoe,' *Forest and Outdoors*, June 1930, 43

55 Ontario, Department of Mines, *Annual Report, 1903*, 127–8

56 Martyn, 'The Canadian Canoe,' 156

57 Bishop, 'Voyage of the Paper Canoe,' 36

58 Martyn, 'The Canadian Canoe,' 36

59 Ontario, Department of Mines, *Annual Report, 1903*, 127–8

60 Paine, *The Tent Dwellers*, 23

61 William Hume Blake, *In a Fishing Country* (Toronto: Macmillan, 1922) 247

62 Wallace, *Packaging and Portaging*, 26–7

63 Morse, 'Summer Travel in the Canadian Barrens,' 19

64 'Centennial Canoe Pageant,' 28

65 Blake, *In a Fishing Country*, 247

66 Quoted in *Harper's Magazine*, September 1991, 35

Chapter 14: The Price of Adventure

1 T. Eaton Company, Advertisement, *Saturday Night*, 27 May 1922, 36

 2 'The "New North" – A Sportsmans' Paradise,' *Saturday Night*, 15 July 1922, 12

 3 T. Eaton Company, Advertisement, *Saturday Night*, 27 May 1922, 36

 4 Hayward, *Canoeing with Sail and Paddle*, 23

 5 Aflalo, *The Cost of Sport*, 185–200

 6 PAM, Hudson's Bay Company [HBC] Archives, A.12./FT MIsc./291 A.12/L Misc.6. For details on the economic position of the HBC's Temagami post to 1920, see PAM, HBC Archives, A 74/9–A74/28

 7 PAM, HBC Archives, Temagami Post Journal, B488 a/2, 16 August 1938; Hugh Mackay Ross, *The Apprentice's Tale* (Winnipeg, 1986) 158; letter of Ross to the author, 1 December 1986

 8 Bill Riviere with the staff of L.L. Bean, *The L.L. Bean Guide to the Outdoors* (New York: Random House, 1981)

 9 Metro Toronto Reference Library, Baldwin Room, Michie Papers, *Michie's Tourist Topics: A Manual of Information for Those Who Purpose Spending Their Holidays among the Beautiful Lakes and Rivers of Ontario* (1905)

10 Grand Trunk Railway, *Kawartha Lakes*, 7th ed. (1903) 5

11 Canadian Pacific Railway, *Summer Tours via Canadian Pacific Railway*, no. 4, West (1900) 10

12 Johnson, 'Striking Camp,' 7

13 Canadian National Railways, *Canoe Trips and Nature Photography*, 3

14 R.J. Wicksteed, letter, *Ottawa Citizen*, 4 December 1882, quoted in *American Canoeist* 1:12 (January 1883) 183

15 Paine, *The Tent Dwellers*, 19
16 Elias, *Canoeing in Canada* (Ottawa, 1925)
17 E. Voorhis, *Camping in Canada* (Ottawa: Natural Resources Intelligence Service, Department of the Interior, 1928)
18 *Canada*, 29 December 1928, 391
19 Ibid.
20 Hon. Dr G.M. Weir, British Columbia minister of education and health, quoted in A.P. Woollacott, 'Gymnastic Movements May Sweep All Canada,' *Saturday Night*, 26 August 1939, 20
21 I. Eisenhardt, 'Recreation and Physical Recreation,' British Columbia Department of Education Annual Report of Public Schools, 69:H90, 1939–40, quoted in James L. Gear, 'Factors Influencing the Development of Government Sponsored Physical Fitness Programmes in Canada from 1850 to 1972,' *Canadian Journal of the History of Sport* 4 (December 1973) 17
22 I. Eisenhardt, 'Canada's National Physical Fitness Programme,' *Ontario Library Review and Canadian Periodical Index* 29 (August 1945) 300, quoted in Gear, 'Factors Influencing the Development of Government Sponsored Physical Fitness Programmes,' 19
23 Canadian Youth Commission (Sidney Smith, Chair), *Youth and Recreation: New Plans for New Times* (Toronto: Ryerson, 1949), quoted in Stanley, 'The Not So Lazy Days of Summer,' 34–6
24 Dominion-Provincial Tourist Conference, *Report of Proceedings* (Ottawa, 1947) 5–9
25 TUA, Perry Papers, 'Correspondence and Book Reviews, *The Canoe and You*,' Ellis to Perry, 10 February 1949; McDonald to Perry, 18 February 1949
26 Downes, *Sleeping Island*, 13
27 Morse, *Freshwater Saga*, 32; U-Paddle, Advertisement, *Beaver*, Summer 1964
28 PAM, HBC Archives, E.A. Brucey to Nick Nickels, 3 August 1972
29 PAM, HBC Archives, Douglas Swope to HBC Northern Stores Department, 1972
30 PAM, HBC Archives, Morse to Brucey, 25 August 1972
31 Pamela Morse, Interview, 14 August 1991
32 PAM, HBC Archives, Craig Macdonald to HBC Northern Stores Department, 22 September 1972
33 Hodgins and Hoyle, *Canoeing North into the Unknown*
34 Peter C. Newman, *Merchant Princes* (Toronto: Viking, 1991) 248 n
35 Wally Schaber, Interview, 10 February 1995. For an overview of other dimensions of the economic benefits associated with wilderness and protected spaces, see Monte Hummel, 'Business, Economics, and the Wise-Use

Movement,' in Hummel, ed., *Protecting Canada's Endangered Spaces: An Owner's Manual* (Toronto: Key Porter, 1995) 27–33.

36 Samuel P. Hays, *Beauty, Health, and Permanence: Environmental Politics in the United States* (Cambridge: Cambridge University Press, 1987) 26–7

37 Kenneth Boulding, 'The Economics of the Coming Spaceship Earth,' in Henry Jarrett, ed., *Environmental Quality in a Growing Economy* (Baltimore: Johns Hopkins University Press for Resources for the Future, Inc.) 9

38 Franks, 'White Water Canoeing,' 188

39 Michael Peake, *Che-Mun*, August 1986, 2

40 David Pelly, 'Open Letter to Transport Canada,' *Che-Mun*, Summer 1991, 2

41 Robert Payne, 'The Forest and the Trees: Non-Timber Values and Forest Management in Ontario,' Witness statement no. 4, filed on behalf of Forests for Tomorrow, in the matter of a hearing before the Environmental Assessment Board regarding a class environmental assessment for timber management on crown lands in Ontario

42 For the following summary, I have relied heavily on an excellent condensation of some legal/economic literature prepared for the Ontario Law Reform Commission and published in Ontario Law Reform Commission, *Report on Damages for Environmental Harm* (Toronto, 1990).

43 Monte Hummel, ed., *Endangered Spaces: The Future for Canada's Wilderness* (Toronto: Key Porter, 1989), and *Protecting Canada's Endangered Spaces*

Chapter 15: Consuming Wilderness

1 Marcel Hamelin, *Nordicité canadienne* (Montreal: Hurtubise HMH, 1975)

2 Bruce W. Hodgins, 'Canoe Irony: Symbol and Harbinger,' in Raffan and Horwood, eds., *Canexus* (see chap. 3, n38) 45; Jamie Benidickson, 'Idleness, Water, and a Canoe: Canadian Recreational Paddling between the Wars,' in Hodgins and Hobbs, eds, *Nastawgan* (see chap. 4, n29) 178–9

3 Grand Trunk Railway, *Tour of His Royal Highness, Prince Arthur of Connaught, through the Province of Ontario and Quebec, Canada* (April 1906)

4 Brooke, *Letters from America*, 118–19

5 Clarence E. Woodman, 'Canoe-Photography,' *American Canoeist* 1:1 (February 1882) 6–7

6 C.H.F. 'Photography,' *American Canoeist* 2:2 (March 1883) 17–18; Vesper, 'Photography Again,' *American Canoeist* 2:3 (April 1883) 40. See also Thomas Sedgwick Steele, *Canoe and Camera: Two Hundred Miles through the Maine Forests* (Boston: Estes and Lauriat, 1882).

7 'Canoeing As the Film Remembered It,' *Outing* 62 (August 1913) 577

8 L.C.T. Beveridge, 'Blazing a New Canoe Trail,' *Forest and Outdoors*, November 1923, 700

9 Storey, 'Outfitting for the Long Canoe Trip,' 595–7, 629–32

10 Janet Foster, *Working for Wildlife: The Beginning of Preservation in Canada* (Toronto: University of Toronto Press, 1978)

11 Altmeyer, 'Three Ideas of Nature in Canada,' 30

12 See chap. 2, 'A Useful Vessel: A Trout, a Moose, and a Canoe,' above.

13 'Concerning Lady Evelyn Lake,' *Rod and Gun* 13:8 (January 1912) 1000

14 Martyn, 'The Canadian Canoe,' 159

15 Sigurd F. Olson, *Listening Point* (New York: Knopf, 1958) 3–4

16 Mason, *Path of the Paddle*, 3

17 Hays, *Beauty, Health, and Permanence*, 118–21

18 Ibid., 120

19 Leslie Frost, Foreword to James Dickson, *Camping in the Muskoka Region*, 7

20 Killan, *Protected Places*, 159, 170–80

21 Eric W. Morse, *Fur Trade Canoe Routes of Canada: Then and Now* (Ottawa: Queen's Printer, 1969) 1

22 'Centennial Canoe Pageant,' 27

23 TUA, Perry Papers, brochure

24 A. Dan Tarlock and Roger Tippy, 'The Wild and Scenic Rivers Act of 1968,' *Cornell Law Review* 55 (1970) 707. The rivers initially in the system were the Rogue River in Oregon; the Middle Fork of the Salmon River in Idaho; the Clearwater River in Montana; the Rio Grande in New Mexico; the Wolf and the St Croix rivers in Wisconsin; the Eleven Point River in Missouri; and the Feather River in Iowa.

25 Sally K. Fairfax, Barbara T. Andrews, and Andrew P. Buchsbaum, 'Federalism and the Wild and Scenic Rivers Act: Now You See It, Now You Don't,' *Washington Law Review* 59 (1984) 417

26 Michael Whittington, 'A Canadian Wild River System: Legal and Administrative Considerations,' manuscript (1978), author's collection

27 B.C. Wildlife Federation, *Wild Rivers: A Proposal for Wild, Scenic, and Recreation Rivers in British Columbia* (n.d.)

28 Killan, *Protected Places*, 271–2

29 *The Canadian Heritage Rivers System: Objectives, Principles, and Procedures* (Ottawa: Minister of Supply and Services, 1984) 3

30 Whittington, 'A Canadian Wild River System'

31 Ibid., 22

32 W.T. Robson, 'The Value of the Tourist Sportsman as a Means of Publicity for Undeveloped Country,' *Rod and Gun* 12:11 (April 1911) 1466–7

33 R. Newell Searle, *Saving Quetico-Superior: A Land Set Apart* (St Paul: Minnesota Historical Society, 1977) 218

34 Killan, *Protected Places*, 151

35 Eric W. Morse, *Maps and Wilderness Canoeing* (Ottawa: Surveys and Mapping Branch, Energy, Mines, and Resources, 1976)

36 Killan, *Protected Places*, 105

37 Terry Storry, 'The Grand Canyon of the Colorado River,' in Storry, Baillie, and Foster, eds, *Raging Rivers* (see chap. 12, n31) 77

38 Storry, 'The Grand Canyon,' 78

39 James R. Titus and Larry W. VanDruff, 'Response of the Common Loon to Recreational Pressure in the Boundary Waters Canoe Area, Northeastern Minnesota,' Wildlife Monographs, no. 79 (October 1981) 54

40 Titus and VanDruff, 'Response of the Common Loon,' 29

41 Ibid., 55

42 The Nature Loft, Advertisement, *Globe and Mail*, 31 October 1989

Chapter 16: The Future of the Voyageur

1 Dickson, *Camping in the Muskoka Region*, 105

2 Johnson, 'By Canoe,' 125–6

3 'Two Little Savages' appeared in seven parts, beginning with the January 1903 edition of *Ladies Home Journal*, and was published in book form later the same year by Doubleday.

4 TUA, Perry Papers, Correspondence and Book Reviews, *The Canoe and You*, including excerpts from a letter to Perry from Pickering College, Newmarket, Ont., signed 'Barney'

5 Lower, *Unconventional Voyages*, viii, 24

6 McGuffin, *Where Rivers Run*, 2

7 Starkell, *Paddle to the Amazon*, 132

8 Canada, Secretary of State, Centennial Commission, *Centennial Guide Book for Teachers* (1967) 14

9 'Centennial Canoe Pageant,' 26–9

10 TUA, Perry Papers, 'Press Release,' 82-016/4 Folder 3

11 Sandra Gillis and Bruce W. Hodgins, eds, 'Canada's Centenary Journey: In the Steps of the Voyageurs,' mimeograph (1971) 19, author's collection

12 Gillis and Hodgins, eds, 'Canada's Centenary Journey'

13 AO, John Fisher Papers, Subject File on the Simcoe Canoe Pageant

14 Mark Bourrie, 'Arduous Canoe Trip to Echo 1648 Saga,' *Globe and Mail*, 4 January 1982

15 *North Bay Times*, 26 July 1906
16 W.R. Bocking, 'A Canoe Trip,' *Rod and Gun* 17:6 (November 1915) 580
17 Trudeau, 'Exhaustion and Fulfilment,' 5
18 W.L. Morton, 'North West by Canoe,' in Gillis and Hodgins, eds, 'Canada's Centenary Journey,' 5
19 Statistics Canada data are drawn primarily from Catalogue 64-202, a series begun in 1947 and modified slightly over the years.
20 A recreational canoeing occasion is considered to involve being in a canoe for at least thirty minutes. I am grateful to Joseph Agnew, the executive director of the Canadian Recreational Canoeing Association, for this information.
21 National Recreation Survey, ORRRC Study Report no. 19 (Washington, D.C., 1962) 23
22 Judith Niemi, 'George River Perspectives,' Wilderness Canoe Association Symposium, Toronto, January 1992
23 J. Arnold Bolz, *Portage into the Past: By Canoe along the Minnesota-Ontario Boundary Waters* (St Paul: University of Minnesota Press, 1960) 10–11
24 Robert Douglas Mead, *Ultimate North: Canoeing Mackenzie's Great River* (New York: Doubleday, 1976) 17
25 Manley and Jamieson, *Rushton*, 44
26 Morse, *Freshwater Saga*, 15–16; see also Eric W. Morse, 'Canoe Routes of the Voyageurs: The Geography and Logistics of the Canadian Fur Trade,' pamphlet repr. from *Canadian Geographic*, May, July, August 1961
27 Brian Ewart, Letter, *Paddler*, Summer 1989, 5
28 Lower, *Unconventional Voyages*, 79
29 The comments are from an unidentifed clipping in the Perry Papers, TUA.
30 TUA, Perry Papers, Correspondence and Book Reviews, *The Canoe and You*
31 Paul Fussell, *Abroad: British Literary Traveling between the Wars* (Oxford: Oxford University Press, 1980) 38–9
32 A.G. Doughty and Gustave Lanctot, Introduction to Walter Butler Cheadle, *Cheadle's Journal of a Trip across Canada, 1862–1863* (Ottawa: Graphic, 1931) 9–10
33 Jones, *Canoeing down Everest*, 40
34 Jim Cormier, 'Cooling Off with a Splash,' *Toronto Life*, August 1992, 12
35 *The Field*, 17 June 1893, 910
36 McGuffin, *Where Rivers Run*, 52
37 Morse, *Freshwater Saga*, 69. For Latchford's notes on canoes used in the fur trade, see NAC, Latchford Papers, MG 27 II F7 vol. 15, file 67.
38 F.W. Howay, 'Building the Big Canoes,' *Beaver*, December 1939, 38

39 Ontario, Department of Lands and Forests, 'The Birch Bark Canoe' (1961);
    'Last of the Great Canoes,' *Weekend Magazine* 7:47 (23 November 1957) 18–21
40 George Frederick Clarke, 'The Birch-Bark Canoe: Its Influence on Canadian
    History,' *Collections of the New Brunswick Historical Society* 16 (1961) 58
41 Percy Rowe, 'A Museum with 600 Canoes, Dugouts and Kayaks,' *Canadian
    Geographic*, August–September 1980, 46–51. The Kanawa International
    Collection is now part of the holdings of the Canadian Canoe Museum in
    Peterborough, Ontario. Brenda Lee-Whiting, 'Daniel Sarazin Still Makes
    Birchbark Canoes,' *Canadian Geographic*, April 1966
42 Mariners Museum, Newport News, Va. [MM], Frederick F. and Nola Hill,
    'The Museum Pieces,' manuscript, 24
43 MM, Hill, 'The Museum Pieces,' 20–30
44 Edwin Tappan Adney and Howard I. Chapelle, *The Bark Canoes and Skin Boats
    of North America* (Washington, D.C.: Smithsonian Institution, 1964)
45 Mordecai Richler, *Joshua Then and Now* (Toronto: McClelland and Stewart,
    1980), 147
46 James, 'The Quest Pattern and the Canoe Trip,' 21
47 Ibid., 15

Conclusion

 1 Robert Mason Lee, 'Why Does Ottawa Consider a Canoe More Canadian
    Than a Cowboy? Eh?' *Globe and Mail*, 6 August 1994
 2 Grey Owl, 'The Rivermen,' in *Tales of an Empty Cabin*, 171
 3 Holling C. Holling, *The Book of Cowboys* (New York: Platt and Munk, 1936)
    dedication, Foreword
 4 The National Sports of Canada Act, SC 1994 c 16

Index